Scott Stark, Marc Fleury, and
The JBoss Group

JBoss Administration and Development

201 West 103rd Street, Indianapolis, Indiana 46290

JBoss Administration and Development

International Standard Book Number: 0-672-32347-8

Library of Congress Catalog Card Number: 2001095485

Printed in the United States of America

First Printing: March, 2002

05 04 03 02   4 3 2 1

Trademarks

Warning and Disclaimer

Executive Editor
Michael Stephens

Development Editor
Christy A. Franklin

Managing Editor
Matt Purcell

Project Editor
George Nedeff

Copy Editor
S. A. Hobbs

Indexer
Erika Millen

Proofreader
Melissa Lynch

Technical Editor
Piroz Mosheni

Team Coordinator
Pamalee Nelson

Interior Designer
Gary Adair

Cover Designer
Gary Adair

Contents at a Glance

Table of Contents

Appendixes

About the Authors

Scott Stark, Ph.D., was born in Washington State in 1964. He started out as a chemical engineer, graduated with a B.S. from the University of Washington, and later received a Ph.D. from the University of Delaware. While in Delaware it became apparent to him that computers and programming were to be his passion, and so he made the study of applying massively parallel computers to difficult chemical engineering problems the subject of his Ph.D. research. It has been all about distributed programming ever since. Scott currently serves as the Chief Technology Officer of the JBoss Group, LLC.

Marc Fleury, Ph.D., was born in Paris in 1968. Marc started in Sales at Sun Microsystems France. A graduate of the Ecole Polytechnique, France's top engineering school, and an ex-Lieutenant in the paratroopers, he has a master in Theoretical Physics from the ENS ULM and a Ph.D. in Physics for work he did as a visiting scientist at MIT (X-Ray Lasers). Marc currently serves as the President of the JBoss Group, LLC, an elite services company based out of Atlanta, GA.

JBoss Group LLC is a service company dedicated to support, training, and consulting around the free JBoss platform. Based in Atlanta, GA, this LLC regroups core JBoss programmers around the world.

JBoss is an Open Source, standards-compliant, J2EE application server implemented in 100% Pure Java. The JBoss/Server and complement of products are delivered under a public license. With 50,000+ downloads per month, JBoss is arguably the most downloaded J2EE based server in the industry.

Dedication

I dedicate this book to my parents who continue to love and support me even though I work at providing free software and have not yet demonstrated that I will one day surpass the empire of Bill Gates. - Scott Stark

Acknowledgments

We would like to thank Vladimir Blagojevic for his help on Chapter 2, "JBoss Server Architecture Overview," as well as the proofreading of several chapters. Ole Husgaard, who leads the JBossTX development, also provided a great deal of help with Chapter 6, "JBossTX." I would also like to thank the JBoss users who have contributed work to the early JBoss documentation effort. Key people from this group include Andreas Schaefer, Simone Bordet, David Jencks, Kevin Boone, Sebastien Alborini, Vincent Harcq, Aaron Mulder, Tom Coleman, Peter Antman, Tobias Frech, and Vladimir Blagojevic.

Tell Us What You Think!

As the reader of this book, *you* are our most important critic and commentator. We value your opinion and want to know what we're doing right, what we could do better, what areas you'd like to see us publish in, and any other words of wisdom you're willing to pass our way.

As an Executive Editor for Sams Publishing, I welcome your comments. You can fax, e-mail, or write me directly to let me know what you did or didn't like about this book—as well as what we can do to make our books stronger.

Please note that I cannot help you with technical problems related to the topic of this book, and that due to the high volume of mail I receive, I might not be able to reply to every message.

When you write, please be sure to include this book's title and author as well as your name and phone or fax number. I will carefully review your comments and share them with the author and editors who worked on the book.

Fax: 317-581-4770

E-mail: feedback@samspublishing.com

Mail: Michael Stephens
            Executive Editor
            Sams Publishing
            201 West 103rd Street
            Indianapolis, IN 46290 USA

Introduction

About This Book

This book is for the JBoss content developer and administrator. The topics covered are those necessary to install, configure, and use version 2.4.x of the JBoss Open Source application server.

About Open Source

"The basic idea behind open source is very simple: When programmers can read, redistribute, and modify the source code for a piece of software, the software evolves. People improve it, people adapt it, people fix bugs; this can happen at a speed that, if one is used to the slow pace of conventional software development, seems astonishing.

We in the open source community have learned that this rapid evolutionary process produces better software than the traditional closed model, in which only a very few programmers can see the source and everybody else must blindly use an opaque block of bits.

Open Source Initiative exists to make this case to the commercial world.

Open source software is an idea whose time has finally come. For twenty years it has been building momentum in the technical cultures that built the Internet and the World Wide Web. Now it's breaking out into the commercial world, and that's changing all the rules. Are you ready?"

About J2EE

The Java 2 Platform, Enterprise Edition (J2EE), defines the standard for developing multitier enterprise applications. J2EE simplifies enterprise applications by basing them on standardized, modular components, by providing a complete set of services to those components, and by handling many details of application behavior automatically, without complex programming. The J2EE platform encompasses a number of technologies.

J2EE: A Standard Web Operating System with Industry Momentum

Sun Microsystems, IBM, and a host of industry participants have deemed J2EE a standard as defined through the Java Community Process (JCP, http://www.jcp.org). Today, there are about 30 J2EE application server vendors. The most popular charges more than $50,000 for a medium-sized installation.

The goal of the J2EE standards is to simplify the enterprise development process as well as improve portability of components between vendor J2EE implementations. Enterprise developers can draw on J2EE to speed up their application development. Instead of writing database code by hand, or pooling management, they can leverage Enterprise Java Beans (EJBs) to automatically manage data. Instead of manually dealing with transactions, system developers can use J2EE's built-in capabilities to run transactions in an automated fashion. Instead of creating all business code from scratch, consultants can assemble components to build their application in a "Lego" fashion.

J2EE APIs

J2EE is a set of standards that, when used together, provide an excellent Web application development and deployment platform. J2EE includes standards for middleware (EJB and JMS), database connectivity (JDBC), transactions (JTA/JTS), presentation (servlets and Java Server Pages), and directory services (JNDI). A summary of the range of APIs/technologies included in J2EE is given in Table I.1.

TABLE I.1   The J2EE APIs and Their Descriptions

API Name	Description (JavaSoft URL)
EJBs	Enterprise JavaBeans (http://java.sun.com/products/ejb)
CORBA	Common Object Request Broker Architecture (http://java.sun.com/j2ee/corba)
Servlets	Java Servlets (http://java.sun.com/products/servlet)
JNDI	Java Naming and Directory Interface (http://java.sun.com/products/jndi)
JDBC	Database Connectivity (http://java.sun.com/products/jdbc)
XML	Extensible Markup Language (http://java.sun.com/xml)
JMS	Java Message Service (http://java.sun.com/products/jms)
JTA/JTS	Transactions (http://java.sun.com/j2ee/transactions.html)

TABLE I.1　Continued

API Name	Description (JavaSoft URL)
Connector	Enterprise Information Systems Connector (http://java.sun.com/j2ee/connector)
JSP	Java Server Pages (http://java.sun.com/products/jsp)

For additional information on the technologies of the J2EE platform, see the URLs referenced in Table I.1, or see the JavaSoft J2EE home page at http://java.sun.com/j2ee.

Why Open Source for J2EE?

As a Web operating system, J2EE is infrastructure. As such, we believe it is a natural fit for the collaborative, Open Source mode of development facilitated by the Internet. Our group, composed of volunteers from around the world, chooses to open the server and container development. Our belief is that there should be an Open Source J2EE server environment that makes J2EE available to anyone.

The extreme size and complexity of this sort of operating system is yet another compelling reason for it to exist in Open Source. Even Microsoft has had difficulties stabilizing Windows 2000. We at JBoss believe that Open Source technology is a credible, efficient and cost-effective way to scale the development of these large systems.

Who Uses J2EE Technology?

As seen from Table I.1, the range of middleware functionality covered by the J2EE platform is quite extensive. These technologies can be used as a single comprehensive platform, individually as an enabling technology, or even as a single component. This leads to the question of how the technologies of the J2EE platform are used, and by whom. The following list provides some example of who is making use of J2EE.

- **Independent software vendors**—Two years ago, many independent software vendors (ISVs) developing Enterprise applications took the Java route. ISVs develop in-house proprietary infrastructure software because of the lack of a defined, open standard. This development is time-consuming, expensive, and complex. Today, most ISVs outsource that infrastructure development to a J2EE server vendor to be able to focus more on business logic. Choosing an open source server makes sense from a pricing standpoint because the application price won't reflect the infrastructure cost. It also makes sense from a technological standpoint because you have access to the code, which makes for a tighter integration with applications. According to our statistics, about 20% of people who download JBoss do so with the objective of embedding it in their applications.

- **IT departments and startups**—A recent study showed that Java/J2EE, which claims 60 percent of IT development, is already the dominant platform for Enterprise Web Software. Most people use our container as a stand-alone Web application server. In many instances, we have been chosen over more pricey competitors for both development and production. We sport features such as hot deploy, runtime-generated stub, and skeleton objects (distributed invocation enablers) that can't be found in most commercial tools...no matter how much you are willing to pay!

- **ISP/ASP, the next wave of Enterprise Software Hosting**—Most ISP providers already offer Web Hosting for static Web pages. For more enterprise level hosting, you need a J2EE platform. Going beyond simple logic and cgi-bin, JBoss was designed for Application Service Provider (ASP) settings. You can deploy its applications on a set of hosted machines, and have a Web-based Java Management Extension (JMX) console to manage the remote servers. Our integration with Java Server Page (JSP) engines makes JBoss the candidate of choice for ISP usage. While most J2EE vendors do not focus on this market, JBoss is well suited for it in two ways. First, the code is modular so you can administer various configurations to fit every client's specific needs. Second, there is no license fee per CPU, so you can grow a J2EE server farm at little cost.

- **Module and third-party developers**—Behind JBoss' Open Source success is a highly modular design, which allows us to scale development and integrate code. From the ground up, JBoss is built around the concept of modules and plug-ins. We use the JMX specification to configure and administer the different plug-ins. We integrate various modules, from Tomcat to cocobase, to offer a state-of-the-art J2EE container. By integrating in JBoss, developers gain access to the dominant application development market and increase the deployment potential for their technology.

About JBoss

JBoss, one of the leading java Open Source groups, integrates and develops these services for a full J2EE-based implementation. JBoss provides JBossServer, the basic EJB container, and Java Management Extension (JMX) infrastructure. It also provides JBossMQ, for JMS messaging, JBossTX, for JTA/JTS transactions, JBossCMP for CMP persistence, JBossSX for JAAS based security, and JBossCX for JCA connectivity. Support for web components, such as servlets and JSP pages, is provided by an abstract integration layer. Implementations of the integration service are provided for third party servlet engines like Tomcat and Jetty. JBoss enables you to mix and match these components through JMX by replacing any component you want with a JMX compliant implementation for the same APIs. JBoss doesn't even impose the JBoss components. Now **that** is modularity.

JBoss: A Full J2EE Implementation with JMX

Our goal is to provide the full Open Source J2EE stack. We have met our goal, and the reason for our success lies on JMX. JMX, or Java Management Extension, is the best weapon we have found for integration of software. It provides a common spine that allows one to integrate modules, containers, and plug-ins. Figure I.1 illustrates how JMX is used as a bus through which the components of the JBoss architecture interact.

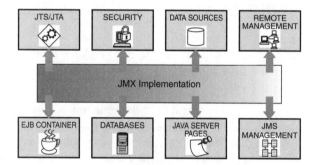

FIGURE I.1   The JBoss JMX integration bus and the standard JBossXX components.

While we provide JBoss implementations for many of these services, you are free to include your favorite implementation in the JMX enabled base, therefore dropping your own transaction or persistence service in JBoss, all dynamically.

JBoss Architecture Overview

This section provides an overview of the components that ship with the standard JBoss 2.4 distribution. The various named elements in Figure I.1 correspond to JBoss components as follows. The JMX bus, EJB container, and remote management elements are the domain of the JBossServer component while the JMS element corresponds to the JBossMQ component. The JTS/JTA element corresponds to the JBossTX component, and the Databases element represents persistent store of objects as managed by the JBossCMP component. The Security element responsibilities are the domain of the JBossSX component. The Data Sources element includes an example of a managed resource, and integration of resource is the domain of the JBossCX component. The Java Server Pages element corresponds to servlets as well as JSP Web components. Support for Web components is handled by JBoss Web server integration services.

JBossServer

In addition to the fact that JBoss/Server is an EJB 1.1-compliant application server, there are some innovative features that make our server a pleasure to use. Specifically, two features make application deployment extremely easy to perform, saving developers much time and effort. JBoss/Server takes the grunt work out of EJB application development.

First, there's dynamically, runtime-generated stub and skeleton classes. In many commercial EJB servers, the generation of these classes must be performed in an additional step prior to deployment (such as using an `ebjc` tool). It goes without saying that this extra step requires additional developer overhead, adding significant time to each change-compile-deploy cycle. By generating stub and skeleton classes on the fly, JBoss/Server takes at least several seconds, and perhaps minutes, off of each deployment. As an added benefit, the method used by JBoss/Server to accomplish this time- and effort saving feature also conserves memory and other server resources because only a single server object supports every deployed Enterprise JavaBeans component.

A second time- and effort saving feature is automatic hot deploy and redeploy. Some of the top commercial EJB servers require you to bounce the server to be able to successfully deploy your application changes. However, JBoss/Server allows you to deploy new applications and redeploy existing applications without stopping and restarting the server. In fact, the feature is as easy as copying your newly built EJB JAR file to the server deployment directory where JBoss/Server picks up the new file, automatically undeploys the old JAR (if any), and deploys the new JAR within seconds. This feature definitely provides the benefit of slicing minutes off of each change-compile-deploy cycle.

JBossMQ

JBossMQ (originally spyderMQ) was released in April 2000 as the first free implementation of the Java Messaging Service (JMS) specification. Based on the 1.0.2 JMS specification, JBossMQ is a clean room, pure java implementation.

It is not uncommon for the Web to fail, for nodes to fail, and for communications in general to fail. Therefore, distributed applications cannot always depend on a synchronous messaging model to reliably deliver notifications. That's why, in addition to synchronous messaging, JMS also provides an asynchronous messaging model that implements the Publish/Subscribe design pattern. A Publish/Subscribe model is critical for successful collaboration between the various participants of a distributed, e-business application. We believe JMS, through our JBossMQ component, plays a central role in the J2EE-based Web operating system provided by the JBoss.

Every aspect of the JMS 1.0.2 spec has been implemented, including

- Both point-to-point and publish-subscribe style messaging

- Durable subscribers

- JMS Application Server Facilities

- The ability to participate in global units of work coordinated by a transaction manager

JBossMQ supports several different kinds of message transport/invocation layers that include

- **RMI**—RMI-based invocation layer.

- **OIL**—Optimized Invocation Layer. This layer uses custom TCP/IP sockets to obtain good network performance and small memory footprint.

- **UIL**—For client applications that cannot accept network connections originating from the server.

JBossTX

JBossTX is a transaction monitor with JTA/JTS support. The Java Transaction Service (JTS) specifies the implementation of a Transaction Manager, which supports the Java Transaction API (JTA) 1.0 specification at the high level and implements the Java mapping of the OMG Object Transaction Service (OTS) 1.1 specification at the low level.

JTA allows you to demarcate transactions in a manner that is independent of the transaction manager implementation. JBossTX implements the transaction manager with the Java Transaction Service (JTS), but your code doesn't call the JTS methods directly. Instead, it invokes the JTA methods, which then call the lower level JTS routines.

JBossTX offers the following services:

- Provides applications and application servers the capability to control the scope and duration of a transaction

- Allows multiple application components to perform work that is part of a single, atomic transaction

- Provides the capability to associate global transactions with work performed by transactional resources

- Coordinates the completion of global transactions across multiple resource managers

- Supports transaction synchronization

JBossCMP

During development of JBoss/Server version 1.0 (then known as EJBoss), we put together an object-to-relational (O-R) mapping tool. Enter JAWS, the acronym for Just Another Web Storage, which is an API for mapping Enterprise JavaBeans objects to relational database persistent stores. JAWS has since been renamed JBossCMP and the project has since taken on a life of its own. That's because we are not only maintaining and enhancing the original code base that defined a simple, yet proprietary O-R mapping tool. We are also extending the product to support the popular third-party O-R mapping tools being employed by some JBoss/Server users.

The Minerva JDBC connection pooling module has been added to the codebase. This module complements JBossCMP by adding a pluggable connection pooling mechanism.

O-R mapping technology grew out of the differences between how object-oriented languages represent objects in memory and how relational databases store data on disk. Objects in the Java language might contain only primitive data types, such as int, double, and very simple aggregate objects such as String, making it easy to express the object's layout on disk. In the case of storing such a simple object in a flat disk file, you would just write each primitive data type variable and each String object in their string form sequentially into the flat file. As you can imagine, reading such objects back from disk into a memory-based object would be just as easy. However, what about storing more complex objects such as those that contain other objects that contain yet other objects? And what about storing both simple and complex objects into relational databases?

Of course, the more complex the object that must be stored, the more intelligent the O-R mapping tool must be. An O-R mapping tool must understand how to traverse the complex object's memory graph and figure out how to store it to and read it from the persistent store. To add to the complexity, the graph of a single object might contain multiple objects that each reference a single, unique object, and it could also contain objects that recursively reference themselves or the original object. In these cases, the O-R mapping tool would have to avoid persisting the same object multiple times, perhaps even ending up in an endless loop because of the self-referencing composition! On the other hand, all complex Java objects finally boil down to variables of primitive data types and those of class String. Therefore, while it can be quite challenging to persist very complex objects, it is not impossible. There is definitely light at the end of the tunnel.

The JBossCMP features include

- CMP 1.1 implementation
- JDBC 1.0, 2.0 compatible

- Table creation at deploy time

- Flexible configurable datatypes

- Differential metadata

- Multiple DataSources support

- Full java object support

- Collections supported

- EJB-references supported

- Low admin overhead in automated mode

- Advanced table mapping

- Complex finders support

- Pre-defined mappings to 17 JDBC databases, including Oracle, SQLServer, DB2, Sybase, PointBase, Cloudscape, HypersoncicSQL, PostgreSQL, mySQL, and more

JBossSX

JBossSX is a security service integration layer that supports both non-JAAS and JAAS based security implementations.

J2EE provides for a limited role based declarative security model, but does not specify how roles are obtained from the operation environment. This is an implementation detail left to the application server. JBossSX provides the standard J2EE security implementation layer and a great deal more. In our product security, you will find features that you won't find anywhere else—no matter how much you are willing to pay.

The key features of JBossSX are as follows:

- Secure authentication of users via JAAS login modules

- Extensible authentication of users via JAAS login modules

- Support for custom per method authentication of users via integration with the EJB container method interceptor

- Support for JAAS Subject based authorization of users

- Flexible mapping from legacy security systems to JAAS Subject based permissions

JBossCX

JBossCX is the JBoss-specific part of a JCA implementation; it takes care of handling resource adapter deployment, interfacing to the JBoss transaction and security services, and making services available through JNDI. Essentially, it's plumbing.

The J2EE Connector Architecture (JCA) specifies how J2EE application components can access connection-based resources. The JCA will be a required part of J2EE 1.3.

The key features of JBossCX are as follows:

- Support for resource adapters that support local transactions, XA transactions, and for those that don't support transactions at all.

- Flexible resource principal mapping architecture. Currently the only principal mapping scheme implemented is to a single resource principal per connection factory.

- Support for basic password credentials.

- Resource adapters can be automatically deployed by placing the resource adaptor archive (RAR) into the JBoss deployment directory, just like other J2EE components.

Web Servers

The 2.4.x version of JBoss includes two services for Web containers—a Tomcat 3.2.4 service, and a Jetty 3.x service. Using one of these Web services requires non-trivial modification of the JBoss configuration as well as the servlet engine. Because of this, we provide pre-configured bundles of JBoss/Tomcat and JBoss/Jetty that provide a complete J2EE compatible solution.

What this Book Covers

The primary focus of this book is the presentation of the standard JBoss components, from the perspective of both configuration and architecture. As a user of a standard JBoss distribution you will gain an understanding of how to configure the standard components. In addition, the final chapter presents a detailed discussion of building and deploying an enterprise application to help you master the details of packaging and deploying applications with JBoss.

As a JBoss developer, you will acquire a thorough understanding of the architecture and integration of the standard components to enable you to extend or replace the standard components for your infrastructure needs. You will also learn how to obtain the JBoss source code, along with how to build and debug the JBoss server.

ile:
[mkdir] Created dir: /tmp/2.4.4/
[javac] Compiling 154 source fil
install:
[copy] Copyin
[copy] Copyin

1

p/2
p/2

Installing and Building the JBoss Server

JBoss is the highly popular, free J2EE compatible application server that has become the most widely used Open Source application server. The highly flexible and easy to use server architecture has made JBoss the ideal choice for users just starting out with J2EE, as well as senior architects looking for a customizable middleware platform. The server is available as a binary distribution with or without a bundled servlet container. The source code for each binary distribution is also available from the server source repository located at http://www.SourceForge.net. The source code availability allows you to debug the server, learn its inner workings, and create customized versions for your personal use.

This chapter presents a step-by-step tutorial on how to install and configure JBoss 2.4.x. You will learn how to use the binaries provided on the accompanying CD, and how to obtain updated binaries from the JBoss Web site. You will also learn the installation of the binary, how to test the installation, and review the installation directory structure as well as understand the key configuration files that an administrator may want to use to customize the JBoss installation. You will also learn how to obtain the source code for the 2.4.4 release from the SourceForge CVS repository, and how to build the server.

Getting the Binary

The book comes with a CD containing the 2.4.4 distribution of JBoss. You can obtain the core JBoss server binary archive from the dist/JBoss-2.4.4.zip path on the CD. The Tomcat and Jetty bundles are dist/JBoss-2.4.4_Tomcat-3.2.4.zip and dist/JBoss-2.4.4_Jetty-3.1.RC8-1.zip, respectively.

PREREQUISITES

Before installing and running the server, you should check that your JDK 1.3+ installation is working. The simplest way to do this is to execute the java - version command to ensure that the java executable is in your path, and that you're using at least version 1.3. For example, running this command on a Linux system with the Sun 1.3.1 JDK produces the following:

```
/tmp 1206>java -version
java version "1.3.1"
Java(TM) 2 Runtime Environment, Standard Edition (build 1.3.1-b24)
Java HotSpot(TM) Client VM (build 1.3.1-b24, mixed mode)
```

NOTE

If you want to find a more recent 2.4.x release, check the binaries page on the JBoss site at http://www.jboss.org/binary.jsp. The latest version will be displayed there. All versions including beta releases as well as legacy binaries are available from the SourceForge JBoss project files page at http://sourceforge.net/projects/jboss.

It does not matter where you install JBoss. Note, however, that installation of JBoss into a directory that has a name containing spaces causes problems in some situations with Sun based VMs. This is due to bugs with file URLs not correctly escaping the spaces in the resulting URL. There is no requirement for root access to run JBoss on Unix/Linux systems because none of the default ports are below the 0-1023 privileged port range.

Installing the Binary Package

Once you have the binary archive you want to install, use the JDK jar tool to uncompress it to the place where you want JBoss installed. The extraction process will create a JBoss-2.4.4 directory. We'll look at the contents of this directory next.

NOTE

The unzip command found on many Unix/Linux systems does not work correctly. This is because of incorrect/inadequate file attributes stored in the zip archive produced by the Ant zip task. If you do extract the archive using the unzip command, the directories fail to have the executable bit set and are unusable until this is done.

Directory Structure

Installation of the JBoss distribution creates a JBoss-2.4.4 directory that contains server start scripts, jars, configuration files and working directories. You do need to know your way around the distribution layout to locate jars for compilation, updating configurations, deploying your code, etc. Figure 1.1 shows the installation directory of the JBoss server.

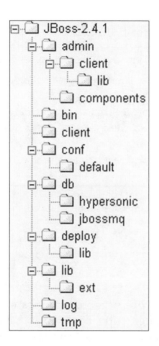

FIGURE 1.1   The directory structure of the JBoss distribution installation.

Throughout the book we will refer to this directory as the JBOSS_DIST directory. The purposes of the various directories are discussed in Table 1.1.

TABLE 1.1   The JBoss Server Installation Directories and Descriptions

Directory	Description
bin	All the entry point jars and start scripts included with the JBoss distribution are located in this directory.
client	Jars required for clients are found in the client directory. A typical client requires `jboss-client.jar`, `jbosssx-client.jar`, `jaas.jar`, `jnp-client.jar`, and `jboss-j2ee.jar`. If your client is not running JDK 1.3, it will require `jndi.jar` as well. If you use JBossMQ JMS provider, you will also need `jbossmq-client.jar`.
conf	The JBoss configuration set(s) is located here. By default there is only one configuration set—default. Adding more than one configuration set is permitted. If you run JBoss bundled with a Web container (Tomcat or Jetty), a special configuration set is used (tomcat or jetty). The key configuration files contained in the default configuration set will be discussed in more detail in the following section, "Configuration Files."

TABLE 1.1   Continued

Directory	Description
lib	This directory contains jars used by JBoss that must be on the system classpath due to class loading issues. Classes in these jars are either loaded by code that does not use the thread context class loader, or fail to load code/resources using the thread context class loader.
lib/ext	This is the main jar directory. Any jar in this directory is loaded by the main JBoss classloader.
db	This is the directory that contains hypersonic and instantdb databases related files (configuration files, indexing tables, and so on) as well as JBossMQ—JMS provider message queue files.
deploy	This is JBoss's deployment directory. Drop your jars here and they will be deployed automatically.
log	JBoss log files are located in this directory. File logging is turned on by default.
tmp	This is a working directory used by JBoss during deployment of content found in the deploy directory.

Configuration Files

The conf directory contains one or more configuration file sets. The default JBoss configuration file set is located in the conf/default directory. JBoss allows the possibility of more than one configuration set so that a server can easily be run using alternate configurations. Creating a new configuration file set typically starts with copying the default file set into a new directory name and then modifying the configuration files as desired. The contents of the default configuration file set are shown in Figure 1.2.

auth.conf

The auth.conf file is a JAAS login module configuration file as supported by the default javax.security.auth.login.Configuration implementation. It contains sample server side authentication configurations that are applicable when using JAAS based security. See Chapter 8, "JBossSX—The JBoss Security Extension Framework," for additional details on the JBoss security framework.

jboss.conf

Configuration file jboss.conf typically contains only those core service MBeans necessary to achieve the initial "bootstrap" of JBoss. These services include the classpath extension inclusion mechanism, logging, configuration service, and service control.

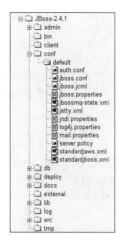

FIGURE 1.2   A view of the JBoss server default configuration set.

The jboss.conf file is loaded by an instance of the javax.management.loading.MLet class, and uses standard MLET syntax for JMX MBeans (Chapter 2, "JBoss Server Architecture Overview," will discuss the details of the syntax). Any standard JMX MBean could be placed in the jboss.conf file as long as it does not depend on JBoss service Mbeans, such as naming. MBeans that do depend on JBoss service MBeans need to be configured in the jboss.jcml file so that startup dependencies can be controlled.

jboss.jcml

The jboss.jcml file lists all JMX MBeans (services) that are going to be included in a running instance of JBoss. Contrary to the JMX MLET file syntax, this file contains well-formed XML.

The need for deviation from MLET syntax is justified because MLET doesn't allow named parameters, but only TYPE-VALUE pairs. Having only TYPE-VALUE pairs leads to mismatching MBean parameter problems.

The jboss.jcml file is loaded by the org.jboss.configuration.Configuration Service MBean. This service acts much like the standard JMX MLet class in that it loads and configures MBeans. The dependencies between MBeans are managed by the org.jboss.util.ServiceControl MBean. The order of registration determines the order of initialization and startup. The ordering is based on the order in which MBeans are specified in the jboss.jcml file. For more details about creating an MBean with dependencies on other Mbeans, see Chapter 2.

jboss.properties

jboss.properties is a standard Java Properties format file that is loaded into the System properties on startup of the JBoss server. System properties that are not required to be available prior to invocation of the JBoss server main method can be specified here. This file currently contains no properties, and it will be removed in the next release.

jbossmq-state.xml

The jbossmq-state.xml is the JBossMQ configuration file that specifies the user to password mappings file, and the user to durable subscription. For additional details on its syntax, see Chapter 4, "JBossMQ—The JBoss Messaging Service."

jndi.properties

The jndi.properties file specifies the JNDI InitialContext properties that are used within the JBoss server whenever an InitialContext is created using the no-arg constructor.

log4j.properties

The log4j.properties file configures the Apache log4j framework category priorities and appenders used by the JBoss server code.

mail.properties

JBoss provides javax.mail.Sesssion mail resources for use with the JavaMail APIs. This file specifies mail provider properties, such as where to find SMTP servers, POP servers, and other mail related configuration information.

NOTE

You are allowed to have multiple mail configurations by using multiple mail.properties files. All you have to do is to specify additional MailService mbeans with different configuration file attributes in your jboss.jcml file. See the MailService discussion in Chapter 2 for additional details.

---

server.policy

The server.policy is a default Java2 security policy file that allows all permissions. Running with a security manager is an advanced topic covered in Chapter 8.

standardjaws.xml

The standardjaws.xml represents a default configuration file for JBossCMP engine. It contains the JNDI name of a default DataSource, per database JDBC-to-SQL mappings, default CMP entity beans settings, and so on. See Chapter 5, "JBossCMP—The JBoss Container Managed Persistence Layer," for additional details.

standardjboss.xml

The standardjboss.xml file provides the default container configurations. Use of this file is an advanced topic covered in Chapter 9, "Advanced JBoss Configuration Using jboss.xml."

Testing the Installation

Once you have installed the JBoss distribution, it is wise to perform a simple startup test to validate that there are no major problems with your Java VM/operating system combination. To test your installation, move to the JBoss-2.4.4/bin directory and execute the run.bat or run.sh script as appropriate for your operating system. Your output should be similar to that shown below and contain no error or exception messages:

```
[starksm@banshee bin]$ ./run.sh
JBOSS_CLASSPATH=:run.jar:../lib/crimson.jar
jboss.home = /tmp/JBoss-2.4.4
Using JAAS LoginConfig: file:/tmp/JBoss-2.4.4-beta/conf/default/auth.conf
JBoss release: JBoss-2.4.4 CVSTag=JBoss_2_4_4
JBoss version: 2.4.4.2001-11-28 12:18:17 PST
Using configuration "default"
[INFO,root] Started Log4jService, config=file:/tmp/JBoss-
2.4.4/conf/default/log4j.properties
[INFO,Info] Java version: 1.3.1_01,Sun Microsystems Inc.
[INFO,Info] Java VM: Java HotSpot(TM) Server VM 1.3.1_01,Sun Microsystems Inc.
[INFO,Info] System: Linux 2.4.7-10,i386
[INFO,Shutdown] Shutdown hook added
[INFO,ServiceControl] Initializing 46 MBeans
. . .
[INFO,ServiceControl] Started 46 services
[INFO,Default] JBoss-2.4.4 Started in 0m:9s.116
```

If your output is similar to this (accounting for installation directory differences), you should now be ready to use JBoss. To shut down the server, simply issue a Ctrl-C sequence in the console in which JBoss was started.

Building the Server from Source Code

Source code is available for every JBoss module, and you can build any version of JBoss from source by downloading the appropriate version of the code from SourceForge. You can build the 2.4.4 release of the core server and the various JBossXX modules discussed in this book, as well as the Tomcat service, but you first need to access the SourceForge CVS using the cvs program.

Accessing the JBoss CVS Repositories at SourceForge

The JBoss source is hosted at SourceForge, a great Open Source community service provided by VA Linux Systems.

With nearly 30,000 Open Source projects and over 300,000 registered users, SourceForge.net is the largest Open Source hosting service available. Many of the top Open Source projects have moved their development to the SourceForge.net site. The services offered by SourceForge include hosting of project CVS repositories and a Web interface for project management that includes bug tracking, release management, mailing lists, and more. Best of all, these services are free to all Open Source developers. For additional details, and to browse the plethora of projects, see the SourceForge home page at http://sourceforge.net/.

Understanding CVS

CVS (Concurrent Versions System) is an Open Source version control system that is used pervasively throughout the Open Source community. CVS is a Source Control or Revision Control tool designed to keep track of source changes made by groups of developers who are working on the same files. CVS enables developers to stay in sync with each other as each individual chooses.

Anonymous CVS Access

The JBoss project's SourceForge CVS repository can be accessed through anonymous (pserver) CVS with the following instruction set. The module you want to check out must be specified as the *modulename*. When prompted for a password for *anonymous*, simply press the Enter key. The general syntax of the command line version of CVS for anonymous access to the JBoss repositories is:

```
cvs -d:pserver:anonymous@cvs.jboss.sourceforge.net:/cvsroot/jboss login
```

```
cvs -z3 -d:pserver:anonymous@cvs.jboss.sourceforge.net:/cvsroot/jboss co➥ module-
name
```

The first command logs into JBoss CVS repository as an anonymous user. This command only needs to be performed once for each machine on which you use CVS because the login information will be saved in your HOME/.cvspass file or equivalent for your system. The second command checks out a copy of the *modulename* source code into the directory from which you run the cvs command. To avoid having to type the long cvs command line each time, you can set up a CVSROOT environment variable with the value pserver:anonymous@cvs.jboss.sourceforge.net: /cvsroot/jboss and then use the following abbreviated versions of the previous commands:

```
cvs login
cvs -z3 co modulename
```

Obtaining a CVS Client

The command line version of the CVS program is freely available for nearly every platform, and is included by default on most Linux and Unix distributions. A good port of CVS as well as numerous other Unix programs for Win32 platforms are available from Cygwin at http://sources.redhat.com/cygwin/. The syntax of the command line version of CVS will be examined because this is common across all platforms.

NOTE

For complete documentation on CVS, check out the CVS home page at http://www.cvshome.org/.

Understanding the JBoss CVS Modules

There are a large number of JBoss-related CVS modules. Not all modules are relevant to the 2.4.x version of JBoss—some are obsolete, and others are for future versions of JBoss. This book covers those listed in Table 1.2.

TABLE 1.2 JBoss CVS Module Names and Information

CVS Modulename	Description
jboss	The main JBossServer + JBossTX code module
jnp	The JBossNS code module
jbossmq	The JBossMQ code module
jbosscx	The JBossCX code module
jbosspool	The JBossCX pooling code module
jbosssx	The JBossSX code module
contrib/tomcat	The JBoss/Tomcat-3.2.x integration module
contrib/catalina	The JBoss/Tomcat-4.x integration module
jboss-j2ee	The J2EE interface API code
jbosstest	The JBoss unit test suite code

The CVS Modulename column gives the `modulename` value to use in the previous CVS syntax example. At one time, each CVS module was a standalone module that could be built independent of any other. This was perceived as useful early on, because it allowed developers of the modules to work independently. However, the independence was achieved by copying snapshots of compiled code from the jboss module and any other module that was required for building. These code snapshots tended to get out of date, and when it came time to build a complete release, there were integration problems due to inconsistencies between the independent builds. Today, all CVS modules depend on the jboss CVS module for the code they need to build. Therefore, for example, to update and build the jbosssx CVS module, you must check out both the jboss and jbosssx CVS modules. Likewise, to completely rebuild a JBoss distribution from all of the CVS module code, you must check out all CVS modules and build the dependent modules against the jboss module. This process has been automated using a master Ant build script. The build process is covered in the next section, "Building the JBoss-2.4.4 Distribution Using the CVS Source Code."

Building the JBoss-2.4.4 Distribution Using the CVS Source Code

This section will guide you through the task of building a JBoss distribution from the CVS source code. To start, create a directory into which you will download the CVS modules. This directory is referred to as the CVS_WD directory, which stands for CVS working directory. The examples in this book check out code into a `/tmp/2.4.4` directory on a Linux system. Next, obtain the `build.xml` Ant script for the 2.4.4 version of the jboss module. To check out the correct version of the `build.xml` script into your directory, perform the `cvs co` command and then pass in the version tag of the code you want to access. To access the 2.4.4 version of JBoss, use the tag `JBoss_2_4_4` as follows:

```
[starksm@banshee starksm]$ cd /tmp/2.4.4/
[starksm@banshee 2.4.4]$ cvs co -r Branch_2_4 jboss/build.xml
U jboss/build.xml
```

The resulting `jboss/build.xml` file is an Ant script that automates the checkout of the required CVS modules, and the build commands required to build a JBoss distribution. To execute the build script, you must have Ant version 1.4.1 installed. This is included on the accompanying CD, and a tutorial on installing and using Ant can be found in Chapter 11, "Using JBoss." To build the JBoss 2.4.4 distribution, copy the `jboss/build.xml` file to your CVS_WD and then execute the ant command with no arguments, as shown in Listing 1.1. Note that the output of the build process has been truncated in Listing 1.1 to show only the key events, and #n annotations have been added at the start of the key event lines so they can be referenced for discussion.

LISTING 1.1   The JBoss 2.4.x Branch Build Process

```
[starksm@banshee 2.4.4]$ cp jboss/build.xml .
[starksm@banshee 2.4.4]$ ant

Buildfile: build.xml

cvs-co:

#1 do-cvs:
    [echo] Checking out JBossServer
    [echo] Checking out JBossNS
    [echo] Checking out JBossSX
    [echo] Checking out JBossMQ
    [echo] Checking out JBossCX
    [echo] Checking out JBossPool
    [echo] Checking out JBossJ2EE
    [echo] Checking out Tomcat
    [echo] Checking out Catalina

build:

#2 build-jboss:
    [echo] +++ Building JBossServer(module=jboss) for compilation

compile:
    [mkdir] Created dir: /tmp/2.4.4/jboss/build/classes
    [javac] Compiling 406 source files to /tmp/2.4.4/jboss/build/classes
...
main:
    [mkdir] Created dir: /tmp/2.4.4/jboss/dist
    [mkdir] Created dir: /tmp/2.4.4/jboss/dist/bin
    [mkdir] Created dir: /tmp/2.4.4/jboss/dist/lib/ext
    [mkdir] Created dir: /tmp/2.4.4/jboss/dist/db
    [mkdir] Created dir: /tmp/2.4.4/jboss/dist/db/hypersonic
    [mkdir] Created dir: /tmp/2.4.4/jboss/dist/deploy
    [mkdir] Created dir: /tmp/2.4.4/jboss/dist/deploy/lib
    [mkdir] Created dir: /tmp/2.4.4/jboss/dist/log
    [mkdir] Created dir: /tmp/2.4.4/jboss/dist/db/jbossmq
    [mkdir] Created dir: /tmp/2.4.4/jboss/dist/conf
    [mkdir] Created dir: /tmp/2.4.4/jboss/dist/client
    [mkdir] Created dir: /tmp/2.4.4/jboss/dist/tmp
    [mkdir] Created dir: /tmp/2.4.4/jboss/dist/admin/client/lib
```

LISTING 1.1   Continued

```
    [mkdir] Created dir: /tmp/2.4.4/jboss/dist/admin/components
     [copy] Copying 1 file to /tmp/2.4.4/jboss/dist/deploy
     [copy] Copying 1 file to /tmp/2.4.4/jboss/dist/db/hypersonic
     [copy] Copying 1 file to /tmp/2.4.4/jboss/dist/db/jbossmq
     [copy] Copying 1 file to /tmp/2.4.4/jboss/dist/lib
     [copy] Copying 1 file to /tmp/2.4.4/jboss/dist/log
     [copy] Copying 1 file to /tmp/2.4.4/jboss/dist/db
     [copy] Copying 1 file to /tmp/2.4.4/jboss/dist/tmp
     [copy] Copying 15 files to /tmp/2.4.4/jboss/dist/conf
     [copy] Copying 4 files to /tmp/2.4.4/jboss/dist/bin
     [copy] Copying 5 files to /tmp/2.4.4/jboss/dist/lib
     [copy] Copying 24 files to /tmp/2.4.4/jboss/dist/lib/ext
     [copy] Copying 1 file to /tmp/2.4.4/jboss/dist/bin
     [copy] Copying 1 file to /tmp/2.4.4/jboss/dist/lib/ext
     [copy] Copying 4 files to /tmp/2.4.4/jboss/dist/client
     [copy] Copying 13 files to /tmp/2.4.4/jboss/dist/client
     [copy] Copying 1 file to /tmp/2.4.4/jboss/dist/client
     [copy] Copying 1 file to /tmp/2.4.4/jboss/dist/admin
     [copy] Copying 4 files to /tmp/2.4.4/jboss/dist/admin/client
     [copy] Copying 5 files to /tmp/2.4.4/jboss/dist/admin/client/lib
     [copy] Copying 1 file to /tmp/2.4.4/jboss/dist/deploy/lib
     [copy] Copying 1 file to /tmp/2.4.4/jboss/dist/deploy/lib

#3 build-jbossj2ee:
     [echo] +++ Building JBoss-J2EE(module=jboss-j2ee)


...
compile:
    [mkdir] Created dir: /tmp/2.4.4/jboss-j2ee/build/classes
    [javac] Compiling 154 source files to /tmp/2.4.4/jboss-j2ee/build/classes
...
src-install:
     [copy] Copying 1 file to /tmp/2.4.4/jboss/src/client
     [copy] Copying 1 file to /tmp/2.4.4/jboss/src/lib
     [copy] Copying 1 file to /tmp/2.4.4/jboss/src/lib

#4 build-jbossns:
     [echo] +++ Building JBossNS(module=jnp)


...
compile:
```

LISTING 1.1   Continued

```
    [mkdir] Created dir: /tmp/2.4.4/jnp/build/classes
    [javac] Compiling 12 source files to /tmp/2.4.4/jnp/build/classes
...
src-install:
    [copy] Copying 1 file to /tmp/2.4.4/jboss/src/client
    [copy] Copying 1 file to /tmp/2.4.4/jboss/src/lib

#5 build-jbosssx:
    [echo] +++ Building JBossSX(module=jbosssx)

...
compile:
    [javac] Compiling 11 source files to /tmp/2.4.4/jbosssx/build/classes
    [javac] Compiling 64 source files to /tmp/2.4.4/jbosssx/build/classes
...
src-install:
    [copy] Copying 1 file to /tmp/2.4.4/jboss/src/client
    [copy] Copying 1 file to /tmp/2.4.4/jboss/src/lib
    [copy] Copying 1 file to /tmp/2.4.4/jboss/src/lib

#6 build-jbosscx:
    [echo] +++ Building JBossCX(module=jbosscx)

...
compile:
    [javac] Compiling 17 source files to /tmp/2.4.4/jbosscx/build/classes
...
src-install:
    [copy] Copying 1 file to /tmp/2.4.4/jboss/src/lib
    [echo] +++ Building JBossCX(module=jbosspool)
...
compile:
    [mkdir] Created dir: /tmp/2.4.4/jbosspool/build/classes
    [javac] Compiling 53 source files to /tmp/2.4.4/jbosspool/build/classes
...
src-install:
    [copy] Copying 1 file to /tmp/2.4.4/jboss/src/lib
    [copy] Copying 1 file to /tmp/2.4.4/jboss/src/etc/deploy

#7 build-jbossmq:
    [echo] +++ Building JBossMQ(module=jbossmq)
```

LISTING 1.1   Continued

```
...
compile:
    [mkdir] Created dir: /tmp/2.4.4/jbossmq/build/classes
    [javac] Compiling 147 source files to /tmp/2.4.4/jbossmq/build/classes
...
src-install:
    [copy] Copying 1 file to /tmp/2.4.4/jboss/src/client
    [copy] Copying 1 file to /tmp/2.4.4/jboss/src/lib

#8 build-jbossdist:
    [echo] +++ Rebuilding JBossServer(module=jboss)

...
main:
    [copy] Copying 2 files to /tmp/2.4.4/jboss/dist/lib
    [copy] Copying 6 files to /tmp/2.4.4/jboss/dist/lib/ext
    [copy] Copying 1 file to /tmp/2.4.4/jboss/dist/bin
    [copy] Copying 1 file to /tmp/2.4.4/jboss/dist/lib/ext
    [copy] Copying 3 files to /tmp/2.4.4/jboss/dist/client
    [copy] Copying 4 files to /tmp/2.4.4/jboss/dist/client
    [copy] Copying 4 files to /tmp/2.4.4/jboss/dist/admin/client/lib
    [copy] Copying 1 file to /tmp/2.4.4/jboss/dist/deploy/lib

dist:

...

#9 dist-zip:
    [mkdir] Created dir: /tmp/2.4.4/jboss/zip/JBoss-2.4.4
    [copy] Copying 90 files to /tmp/2.4.4/jboss/zip/JBoss-2.4.4
    [copy] Copied 1 empty directory to /tmp/2.4.4/jboss/zip/JBoss-2.4.4
    [zip] Building zip: /tmp/2.4.4/jboss/JBoss-2.4.4.zip

#10 tomcat3x-dist:

#11 tomcat4x-dist:

BUILD SUCCESSFUL

Total time: 2 minutes 40 seconds
```

The key events are as follows:

1. The do-cvs task performs a check out of all the required JBoss source code from the SourceForge CVS repository using the anonymous login. The echo messages indicate the source code modules that are retrieved.

2. The build-jboss task performs a compilation of the JBossServer code, and creates an initial distribution directory structure. This build must be performed first because the other JBossXX components require a JBoss distribution for their compilation.

3. The build-jbossj2ee task creates the jboss-j2ee.jar that contains the standard J2EE interfaces required by classes that use any of the J2EE interfaces. The src-install task that follows installs the jars from the build-jbossj2ee task into the jboss CVS module source tree. This is the common pattern that all modules dependent on the jboss module use. They compile against the core jboss module classes and then place their component jars into jboss module source trees.

4. The build-jbossns task creates the `jnpserver.jar` and `jnp-client.jar` files for the JBossNS component. These jars are placed into the jboss module source tree by the src-install step.

5. The build-jbosssx task creates the `jbosssx.jar`, `jbosssx-client.jar` and `jboss-jaas.jar` files for the JBossSX component. These jars are placed into the jboss module source tree by the src-install step.

6. The build-jbosscx task creates the `jbosscx.jar`, `jbosspool.jar`, and `jbosspool-jdbc.rar` files for the JBossCX component. The JBossCX component spans two CVS modules due to the historic fact that two different developers contributed distinct elements. The JBossCX jars are placed into the jboss module source tree by the src-install step.

7. The build-jbossmq task creates the `jbossmq.jar` and `jbossmq-client.jar` files for the JBossMQ component. The JBossMQ jars are placed into the jboss module source tree by the src-install step.

8. The second run of the build-jbossdist task copies the updated JBossXX component jars that have been updated in the jboss module source tree into the distribution tree.

9. The dist-zip task creates a zip archive of the distribution tree that was produced by step 8. This is the archive that is uploaded to SourceForge for distribution.

10. The tomcat3x-dist task creates a JBoss/Tomcat-3.2.x bundle that contains a custom integration service for the Tomcat-3.2.x series of servlet containers. This task did not produce a bundle in this execution because a jakarta-tomcat-3.2.x

binary distribution was not available. You will go through the task of building the JBoss-2.4.4/Tomcat-3.2.4 bundle in the next section.

11. The tomcat4x-dist task creates a JBoss/Tomcat-4.x bundle that contains a custom integration service for the Tomcat-4.x series of servlet containers. This task did not produce a bundle in this execution because a jakarta-tomcat-4.x binary distribution was not available. The procedure for creating a JBoss/Tomcat-4.x bundle is similar to the JBoss-2.4.4/Tomcat-3.2.4 bundle procedure you will see in the next section.

The ultimate goal of this build process is the jboss/JBoss-2.4.4.zip archive that represents the complete JBoss 2.4.4 distribution. Distributions that bundled the 3.2.x and 4.x series of Tomcat servlet containers would have also resulted had you placed the appropriate Tomcat distribution into your CVS_WD directory. You will be lead through the extra step required to create the 2.4.4/Tomcat-3.2.4 bundle in the following section.

Building the JBoss-2.4.4/Tomcat-3.2.4 Integrated Bundle Using the CVS Source Code

The JBoss-2.4.4 distribution you built in the previous section does not contain a servlet container. A common requirement for a JBoss installation is to have a servlet container to enable handling of Web content, such as HTML pages, JSP pages, and servlets. In this section you create a JBoss-2.4.4/Tomcat-3.2.4 distribution bundle using the build.xml script from the preceding section. The only thing that prevented the build of the JBoss-2.4.4/Tomcat-3.2.4 distribution bundle during the previous build process was the fact that a Tomcat-3.2.4 distribution was not available during the build. To enable the build of this distribution, you need to place the jakarta-tomcat-3.2.4 binary distribution directory into your CVS_WD. The Jakarta-tomcat-3.2.4 binary can be obtained from the book CD, or the Apache site here http://jakarta.apache.org/builds/jakarta-tomcat/release/v3.2.4/bin/jakarta-tomcat-3.2.4.zip. You can then rerun the build.xml script to build the JBoss/Tomcat distribution bundle. Listing 1.2 demonstrates the build of the distribution using the build.xml Ant script. Only the tail portion of the output that begins with the tomcat3x-dist event line is shown in the following listing.

LISTING 1.2   The Build of the JBoss/Tomcat Distribution

```
[starksm@banshee 2.4.4]$ ant
Buildfile: build.xml
...
tomcat3x-dist:
     [echo] +++ Building JBoss/Tomcat bundle(module=contrib/tomcat)
```

LISTING 1.2   Continued

```
Overriding previous definition of reference to tomcat.path

...

bundle:
 [mkdir] Created dir:/tmp/2.4.4/contrib/tomcat/bundle/JBoss-2.4.4_Tomcat-3.2.4
  [copy] Copying 371 files to .../tomcat/bundle/JBoss-2.4.4_Tomcat-3.2.4/tomcat
  [copy] Copying 90 files to ...ib/tomcat/bundle/JBoss-2.4.4_Tomcat-3.2.4/jboss
  [copy] Copied 1 empty directory to ...t/bundle/JBoss-2.4.4_Tomcat-3.2.4/jboss
  [copy] Copying 14 files to ...ndle/JBoss-2.4.4_Tomcat-3.2.4/jboss/conf/tomcat
  [copy] Copying 1 file to ...cat/bundle/JBoss-2.4.4_Tomcat-3.2.4/jboss/lib/ext
 [patch] patching file ...Boss-2.4.4_Tomcat-3.2.4/jboss/conf/tomcat/jboss.conf
 [patch] Hunk #1 succeeded at 37 (offset -3 lines).
 [patch] patching file ...Boss-2.4.4_Tomcat-3.2.4/jboss/conf/tomcat/jboss.jcml
 [patch] patching file ...ndle/JBoss-2.4.4_Tomcat-3.2.4/tomcat/conf/server.xml
  [copy] Copying 1 file to ...mcat/bundle/JBoss-2.4.4_Tomcat-3.2.4/jboss/deploy

BUILD SUCCESSFUL

Total time: 14 seconds
```

The build output has been truncated to show only the final bundle task, which creates the JBoss/Tomcat bundle. The file paths in the listing have been truncated to fit in the listing size constraints, but all have the same `/tmp/2.4.4/contrib/tomcat/bundle/JBoss-2.4.4_Tomcat-3.2.4` prefix path. This is the bundle distribution directory that contains the JBoss/Tomcat bundle. This directory need simply be zipped up into an archive, and it is equivalent to the archive available from the SourceForge download page.

Debugging the JBoss Server

Now that you can obtain the source code for the JBoss server and its associated modules, it would be nice to be able to debug the server using the downloaded source. The easiest way to do this is to use a debugger that supports remote debugging. This way you don't need to set up your debugger classpath to be the equivalent of that set up by the JBoss start scripts. To do this you need to enable remote debugging by adding additional Java Virtual Machine (JVM) options to configure the Java Platform Debugger Architecture (JPDA). This is JVM specific, so you'll need to know the JPDA options for the Sun 1.3.1 JVM. If these options don't work for you, check your JVM documentation for its JPDA setup.

For Win32 platforms, modify the JBoss server run.bat script to include the following changes shown in bold:

```
@echo off
@if not "%ECHO%" == ""  echo %ECHO%
@if "%OS%" == "Windows_NT"  setlocal

set JBOSS_CLASSPATH=%JBOSS_CLASSPATH%;run.jar

REM Add all login modules for JAAS-based security
REM and all libraries that are used by them here
set JBOSS_CLASSPATH=%JBOSS_CLASSPATH%

REM Add the XML parser jars and set the JAXP factory names
REM Crimson parser JAXP setup(default)
set JBOSS_CLASSPATH=%JBOSS_CLASSPATH%;../lib/crimson.jar
set JAXP=-Djavax.xml.parsers.DocumentBuilderFactory=org.apache.crimson.jaxp.Docu
mentBuilderFactoryImpl
set JAXP=%JAXP% -Djavax.xml.parsers.SAXParserFactory=org.apache.crimson.jaxp.SAX
ParserFactoryImpl

REM Enable JPDA debugger
set DBG=-classic -Xdebug -Xnoagent
set DBG=%DBG% -Xrunjdwp:transport=dt_socket,server=y,address=12345,suspend=y

echo JBOSS_CLASSPATH=%JBOSS_CLASSPATH%
java %DBG% %JAXP% -classpath "%JBOSS_CLASSPATH%" org.jboss.Main %1 %2 %3
```

The equivalent changes for the run.sh script for Unix/Linux platforms is:

```
#!/bin/sh

# Minimal jar file to get JBoss started.

JBOSS_CLASSPATH=$JBOSS_CLASSPATH:run.jar

# Add all login modules for JAAS-based security
# and all libraries that are used by them here
JBOSS_CLASSPATH=$JBOSS_CLASSPATH

# Check for SUN(tm) JVM w/ HotSpot support
#
HOTSPOT=`java -version 2>&1 | grep HotSpot`"x"
```

```
if [ "$HOTSPOT" != "x" ]; then
        HOTSPOT="-server"
else
        HOTSPOT=""
fi

# Add the XML parser jars and set the JAXP factory names
# Crimson parser JAXP setup(default)
JBOSS_CLASSPATH=$JBOSS_CLASSPATH:../lib/crimson.jar
JAXP=-Djavax.xml.parsers.DocumentBuilderFactory=org.apache.crimson.jaxp.Document
BuilderFactoryImpl
JAXP="$JAXP -Djavax.xml.parsers.SAXParserFactory=org.apache.crimson.jaxp.SAXPaser-
FactoryImpl"

# Enable JPDA debugger
DBG="-classic -Xdebug -Xnoagent"
DBG="$DBG -Xrunjdwp:transport=dt_socket,server=y,address=12345,suspend=y"
HOTSPOT=""

echo JBOSS_CLASSPATH=$JBOSS_CLASSPATH
java $DBG $HOTSPOT $JAXP -classpath $JBOSS_CLASSPATH org.jboss.Main $@
```

In both scripts you are building a script variable named DBG that contains the JVM options that enable debugging via the JPDA protocol. The various options in the DBG variable include the following:

- -Classic, which disables HotSpot and greatly improves the startup time of the VM

- -Xdebug, which enables the JPDA debugging

- -Xnoagent, which is required to disable the old sun.tools.debug agent that is not used with JPDA

- -Xrunjdwp:transport=dt_socket,server=y,
  ➥address=12345,suspend=y, which loads the JPDA reference implementation of JDWP using TCP sockets as the transport, listens for a debugger connection on port 12345 on any local interface, and suspends the VM until a debugger attaches and resumes the VM

When you start JBoss using either of these scripts, the JVM creates a listening port at 12345 and waits for a JPDA client to attach on this port. The JBoss server will not actually start until the debugger client attaches and resumes the JVM.

There are many tools that support debugging using JPDA. Nearly all major Java IDEs do; there are also a few stand-alone JPDA clients as well. An Open Source debugging client is JSwat (`http://bluemarsh.com/java/jswat/`). An inexpensive commercial offering is BugSeeker2 (`http://www.karmira.com`). For whatever debugging client you choose, the setup procedure is basically the same.

- Set up the sourcepaths for the debugging session. This should include the parent directory of any source tree that contains a Java package structure with classes you want to debug.

- Set up the remote debugging options. This entails selecting the socket transport option and then entering the host and port where the JBoss server VM is listening for connections.

Summary

This chapter covered how to obtain, install, and navigate the JBoss binary distribution. You learned how to obtain the source code for any version of JBoss from the CVS repository at SourceForge. You also learned how to build a distribution from the source using the Ant `build.xml` script included in the jboss CVS module. With these skills, you can obtain, build, run, and debug any version of JBoss that you use.

Now you are ready to begin learning the details of the various JBoss components highlighted in the introduction. The starting point will be the JBossServer component, which is the heart of the JBoss architecture.

```
ile:
[mkdir] Created dir: /tmp/2.4.4/
[javac] Compiling 154 source file
install:
[copy] Copyin
[copy] Copyin
```

2

JBoss Server Architecture Overview

Modularly developed from the ground up, the JBoss server and container are completely implemented using component-based plug-ins. The modularization effort is supported by the use of JMX, the Java Management Extension API. Using JMX, industry-standard interfaces help manage both JBoss/Server components and the applications deployed on it. Ease of use is still the number one priority, and the JBossServer version 2.x architecture sets a new standard for modular, plug-in design as well as ease of server and application management. This high degree of modularity benefits the application developer in several ways. The already tight code can be further trimmed down in support of applications that must have a small footprint. For example, if EJB passivation is unnecessary in your application, simply take the feature out of the server. If you later decide to deploy the same application under an Application Service Provider (ASP) model, simply enable the server's passivation feature for that Web-based deployment. Another example is the freedom you have to drop your favorite object to relational database (O-R) mapping tool, such as TOPLink, directly into the container.

This chapter introduces you to JMX and its role as the JBoss server component bus. You also learn about the JBoss MBean service notion that adds life-cycle operations to the basic JMX management component. You are then given a thorough introduction to the EJB container architecture and its extensible plug-in design.

JMX

The success of the full Open Source J2EE stack lies with the use of JMX (Java Management Extension). JMX is the best tool for integration of software. It provides a common spine that allows the user to integrate modules, containers, and plug-ins.

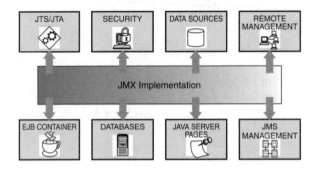

FIGURE 2.1   The JBoss JMX integration bus, and the standard JBoss components.

Figure 2.1 shows the role of JMX as an integration spine or bus into which components plug. Components are declared as MBean services that are then loaded into JBoss. The components may subsequently be administered using JMX.

An Introduction to JMX

Before looking at how JBoss uses JMX as its component bus, it would help to get a basic overview what JMX is by touching on some of its key aspects.

> **NOTE**
>
> JMX components are defined by the Java Management Extensions Instrumentation and Agent Specification, v1.0, which is available from the JSR003 Web page at `http://jcp.org/aboutJava/communityprocess/final/jsr003/index.html`.
>
> The material in this JMX overview section is derived from JMX instrumentation specification, with a focus on the aspects most used by JBoss. A more comprehensive discussion of JMX and its application can be found in JMX: Managing J2EE with Java Management Extensions written by Juha Lindfors (Sams, 0672322889, 2002).

JMX is about providing a standard for managing and monitoring all varieties of software and hardware components from Java. Further, JMX aims to provide integration with the large number of existing management standards. Figure 2.2 shows examples of components found in a JMX environment, and illustrates the relationship between them as well as how they relate to the three levels of the JMX model. The three levels are:

- Instrumentation—The resources to manage

- Agents—The controllers of the instrumentation level objects

- Distributed services—The mechanism by which administration applications interact with agents and their managed objects

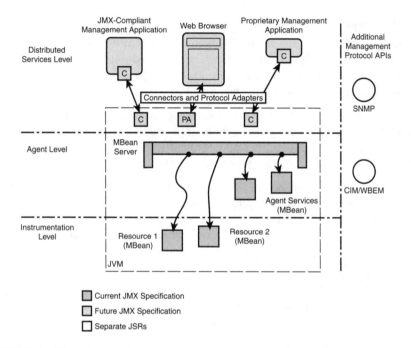

FIGURE 2.2 The relationship between the components of the JMX architecture.

Instrumentation Level

The instrumentation level defines the requirements for implementing JMX manageable resources. A JMX manageable resource can be virtually anything, including applications, service components, devices, and so on. The manageable resource exposes a Java object or wrapper that describes its manageable features, which makes the resource instrumented so that it can be managed by JMX-compliant applications.

The user provides the instrumentation of a given resource using one or more managed beans, or MBeans. There are four varieties of MBean implementations:

standard, dynamic, model, and open. The differences between the various MBean types is discussed in "Managed Beans or MBeans" later in this chapter.

The instrumentation level also specifies a notification mechanism. The purpose of the notification mechanism is to allow MBeans to communicate changes with their environment. This is similar to the JavaBean property change notification mechanism, and can be used for attribute change notifications, state change notifications, and so on.

Agent Level

The agent level defines the requirements for implementing agents. Agents are responsible for controlling and exposing the managed resources that are registered with the agent. By default, management agents are located on the same hosts as their resources. This collocation is not a requirement.

The agent requirements make use of the instrumentation level to define a standard MBeanServer management agent, supporting services, and a communications connector. JBoss provides an html adaptor via the Sun JMX reference implementation as well as a JBoss implementation of an RMI adaptor.

The JMX agent can be located in the hardware that hosts the JMX manageable resources when a Java Virtual Machine (JVM) is available. This is currently how the JBoss server uses the MBeanServer. A JMX agent does not need to know which resources it will serve. JMX manageable resources may use any JMX agent that offers the services it requires.

Managers interact with an agent's MBeans through a protocol adaptor or connector, as described in the "Distributed Services" section later in this chapter. The agent does not need to know anything about the connectors or management applications that interact with the agent and its MBeans.

> **NOTE**
>
> The Sun reference implementation of the JMX agent is a set of Java classes that provide an implementation of an MBeanServer and all of the supporting agent services, and is available on the JavaSoft Web site at
> `http://java.sun.com/products/JavaManagement/download.html`.
>
> IBM also provides an implementation of the JMX specification that is available from their alphaWorks Web site at `http://www.alphaworks.ibm.com/tech/TMX4j`.

JMX agents run on the Java 2 Platform Standard Edition. The goal of the JMX specification is to allow agents to run on platforms like PersonalJava and EmbeddedJava, once these are compatible with the Java 2 platform.

Distributed Services Level

The JMX specification notes that a complete definition of the distributed services level is beyond the scope of the initial version of the JMX specification. This was indicated in Figure 2.2 by the component boxes with the horizontal lines. The general purpose of this level is to define the interfaces required for implementing JMX management applications or managers. The following points highlight the intended functionality of the distributed services level as discussed in the current JMX specification.

- Provides an interface for management applications to interact transparently with an agent and its JMX manageable resources through a connector

- Exposes a management view of a JMX agent and its MBeans by mapping their semantic meaning into the constructs of a data-rich protocol (for example HTML or SNMP)

- Distributes management information from high-level management platforms to numerous JMX agents

- Consolidates management information coming from numerous JMX agents into logical views that are relevant to the end user's business operations

- Provides security

It is intended that the distributed services level components will allow for cooperative management of networks of agents and their resources. These components can be expanded to provide a complete management application.

JMX Component Overview

This section offers an overview of the instrumentation and agent level components. The instrumentation level components include the following:

- MBeans (standard, dynamic, open, and model MBeans)
- Notification model elements
- MBean metadata classes

The agent level components include:

- MBean server
- Agent services

Managed Beans or MBeans

An MBean is a Java object that implements one of the standard MBean interfaces and follows the associated design patterns. The MBean for a resource exposes all necessary information and operations that a management application needs to control the resource.

The scope of the management interface of an MBean includes the following:

- Attributes values that may be accessed by name

- Operations or functions that may be invoked

- Notifications or events that may be emitted

- The constructors for the MBean's Java class

JMX defines four types of MBeans to support different instrumentation needs:

- Standard MBeans—These use a simple JavaBean style naming convention and a statically defined management interface. This is currently the most common type of MBean used by JBoss.

- Dynamic MBeans—These must implement the `javax.management.DynamicMBean` interface, and they expose their management interface at runtime when the component is instantiated for the greatest flexibility. JBoss makes use of Dynamic MBeans in circumstances where the components to be managed are not known until runtime.

- Open MBeans—These are an extension of dynamic MBeans. Open MBeans rely on basic data types for universal manageability and which are self-describing for user-friendliness. As of the 1.0 JMX specification these are incompletely defined. JBoss currently does not use Open MBeans.

- Model MBeans—These are also an extension of dynamic MBeans. Model MBeans must implement the `javax.management.modelmbean.ModelMBean` interface. Model MBeans simplify the instrumentation of resources by providing default behavior. JBoss currently does not use Model MBeans.

Notification Model

JMX Notifications are an extension of the Java event model. Both the `MBeanServer` and MBeans can send notifications to provide information. The JMX specification defines the `javax.management` package `Notification` event object, `NotificationBroadcaster` event sender, and `NotificationListener` event receiver interfaces. The specification also defines the `MBeanServer` operations that allow for the registration of notification listeners.

MBean Metadata Classes

There is a collection of metadata classes that describe the management interface of an MBean. Users can obtain a common metadata view of any of the four MBean types by querying the MBeanServer with which the MBeans are registered. The metadata classes cover an MBean's attributes, operations, notifications, and constructors. For each of these, the metadata includes a name, a description, and its particular characteristics. For example, one characteristic of an attribute is whether it is readable, writable, or both. The metadata for an operation contains the signature of its parameter and return types.

The different types of MBeans extend the metadata classes to be able to provide additional information as required. This common inheritance makes the standard information available regardless of the type of MBean. A management application that knows how to access the extended information of a particular type of MBean is able to do so.

MBean Server

A key component of the agent level is the managed bean server. Its functionality is exposed through an instance of the `javax.management.MBeanServer`. An `MBeanServer` is a registry for MBeans that makes the MBean management interface available for use by management application. The MBean never directly exposes the MBean object itself; rather, its management interface is exposed through metadata and operations available in the MBeanServer interface. This provides a loose coupling between management applications and the MBeans they manage.

MBeans can be instantiated and registered with the `MBeanServer` by the following:

- Another MBean
- The agent itself
- A remote management application

When you register an MBean, it must be given unique object name. The object name then becomes the unique handle by which management applications identify the object on which to perform management operations. The operations available on MBeans through the MBeanServer include the following:

- Discovering the management interface of MBeans
- Reading and writing attribute values
- Invoking operations defined by MBeans
- Registering for notifications events
- Querying MBeans based on their object name or their attribute values

Protocol adaptors and connectors are required to access the MBeanServer from outside the agent's JVM. Each adaptor provides a view via its protocol of all MBeans registered in the MBeanServer the adaptor connects to. An example adaptor is an HTML adaptor that allows for the display MBeans using a Web browser. As was indicated in Figure 2.2, there are no protocol adaptors defined by the current JMX specification. Later versions of the specification will address the need for remote access protocols.

A connector is an interface used by management applications to provide a common API for accessing the MBeanServer in a manner that is independent of the underlying communication protocol. Each connector type provides the same remote interface over a different protocol. This allows a remote management application to connect to an agent transparently through the network, regardless of the protocol. The specification of the remote management interface will be addressed in a future version of the JMX specification.

Adaptors and connectors make all MBean server operations available to a remote management application. For an agent to be manageable from outside of its JVM, it must include at least one protocol adaptor or connector. JBoss currently includes the HTML adaptor from the Sun JMX reference implementation and a custom JBoss RMI adaptor.

Agent Services

The JMX agent services are objects that support standard operations on the MBeans registered in the MBean server. The inclusion of supporting management services helps you build more powerful management solutions. Agent services are often themselves MBeans, which allow the agent and their functionality to be controlled through the MBean server. The JMX specification defines the following agent services:

- A Dynamic class loading MLet (management applet) service—This allows for the retrieval and instantiation of new classes and native libraries from an arbitrary network location.

- Monitor services—These observe an MBean attribute's numerical or string value, and can notify other objects of several types of changes in the target.

- Timer services—These provide a scheduling mechanism based on a one-time alarm-clock notification or on a repeated, periodic notification.

- The relation service—This service defines associations between MBeans and enforces consistency on the relationships.

Any JMX-compliant implementation will provide all of these agent services. JBoss only directly makes use of the dynamic class loading M-Let service.

The Dynamic Loading M-Let Service This section introduces the capabilities and configuration syntax of the JMX dynamic loading service. The M-Let service provides the capability to retrieve and instantiate MBeans from a remote location specified by a URL.

The M-Let service allows you to instantiate and register in the MBean server one or more MBeans located among a listing of URLs. The MBeans to be loaded are specified in a text based configuration file that uses an XML-like syntax with each MBean specified using an MLET tag. When an M-Let configuration file is loaded, all classes specified in MLET tags are downloaded, and an instance of each MBean specified in the file is created and registered.

The MLet Configuration File The M-Let service can load a text file known as an MLET configuration file. The M-Let file may contain any number of MLET tags, each for instantiating a different MBean in a JMX agent. The MLET tag has the following syntax shown in Listing 2.1:

LISTING 2.1   MLET configuration file syntax

```
<MLET
  CODE = class | OBJECT = serfile
  ARCHIVE = "archivelist"
  [CODEBASE = codebaseURL]
  [NAME = MBeanName]
  [VERSION = version]
 >
  [arglist]
</MLET>
```

The attributes of the MLET tag are:

- CODE = class—This attribute specifies the fully qualified class name of the MBean to create. The class file of the MBean must be contained in one of the JAR files specified by the ARCHIVE attribute. Either the CODE or the OBJECT attribute must be present.

- OBJECT = serfile—This attribute specifies the .ser file that contains a serialized representation of the MBean to create. This file must be contained in one of the JAR files specified by the ARCHIVE attribute. If the JAR file contains a directory hierarchy, this attribute must specify the path of the file within this hierarchy, otherwise a match will not be found.

- ARCHIVE = archiveList—This mandatory attribute specifies one or more JAR files containing MBeans or other resources used by the MBean to be obtained. One of the JAR files must contain the file specified by the `CODE` or `OBJECT` attribute. If archivelist contains more than one file:

- Each file must be separated by a comma (,).

- The entire list must be enclosed in double quote marks (*""*).

All JAR files in the archive list must be stored in the directory specified by the code base URL, or in the same directory as the MLet file, because this is the default code base when none is given.

- `CODEBASE` = codebaseURL—This optional attribute specifies the code base URL of the MBean to create. It identifies the directory that contains the JAR files specified by the `ARCHIVE` attribute. This attribute is used when the JAR files are not in the same directory as the m-let configuration file. If this attribute is not specified, the base URL of the m-let file is taken as the code base URL.

- `NAME` = MbeanName—This optional attribute specifies the string format of an object name to be assigned to the MBean instance when the MLet service registers it in the MBean server.

- `VERSION` = version—This optional attribute specifies the version number of the MBean and associated JAR files to be obtained. This version number can be used to specify whether or not the JAR files need to be loaded from the server to update those already loaded by the m-let service. The version must be a series of non-negative decimal integers each separated by a dot (.), for example 3.0, 2.4.4.

- arglist—The optional contents of the MLET tag specify a list of one or more arguments to pass to the constructor of the MBean to be instantiated. The MLet service will look for a constructor with a signature that matches the order and types of the arguments specified in the arglist. Instantiating objects with a constructor other than the default constructor is limited to constructor arguments for which there is a string representation. Each item in the arglist corresponds to an argument in the constructor. Use the following syntax to specify the argList:
  `<ARG TYPE=argumentType VALUE=argumentValue>` where:

  - argumentType is the fully qualified class name of the argument (for example `java.lang.Integer`)

  - argumentValue is the string representation of the value of the argument

The classes that make up the m-let service are found in the `javax.management.loading` package. The `MLet` class is a standard MBean that implements the `MLetMBean` interface. The `MLet` class also extends java.net.URLClassLoader, meaning that MLet is class loader. Its primary operation is:

```
java.util.Set getMBeansFromURL(java.lang.String url)
    throws javax.management.ServiceNotFoundException
```

This loads an MLET configuration file that defines the MBeans to be added to the MBeanServer. The location of the file is specified by the url argument. The MBeans specified in the MLET file will be instantiated and registered by the MBean server. The Set returned contains one entry per MLET tag, and the type of entry specifies either the javax.management.ObjectInstance for the created MBean, or a java.lang.Throwable object for any error that prevented the MBean from being created. The JBoss server utilizes the getMBeansFromURL method during server startup to load the bootstrap JBoss MBean services. The complete JavaDoc for the MLet class API can be found in the reference implementation.

JBoss and JMX

When JBoss starts up, one of the first steps performed is to create an MBean server instance (javax.management.MBeanServer). The JMX MBean server in the Jboss architecture plays the role of a microkernel aggregator component. All other manageable MBean components are plugged into JBoss by registering with the MBean server. The kernel in that sense is only an aggregator and not a source of actual functionality. The functionality is provided by MBeans, and in fact all major JBoss components are manageable MBeans interconnected through the MBean server.

The step following the creation of the MBean server is the creation of an MLet instance (javax.management.loading.MLet). These two steps are shown in the following code segment, Listing 2.2.

LISTING 2.2   The setup of the MBeanServer and MLet on JBoss startup

```
// Create MBeanServer
MBeanServer server = MBeanServerFactory.createMBeanServer();
// Add configuration directory to MLet classpath
URL confDir = File("../conf/"+confName);
URL confURL = confDir.toURL();
URL[] urls = {confDirectory};
// Create MLet
MLet mlet = new MLet(urls);
ObjectName domain = server.getDefaultDomain();
ObjectName mletName = new ObjectName(domain, "service", "MLet");
server.registerMBean(mlet, mletName);
// Set MLet as classloader for this app
Thread.currentThread().setContextClassLoader(mlet);
```

The JBoss server's initial state consists of a JMX MBean server, and an MLet class loader whose classpath contains only the configuration file set directory that was specified on the command line.

JBoss now loads its configured components by first using the JMX MLet to load a bootstrap MLET configuration file called jboss.conf. This invokes a JBoss specific configuration service MBean that loads MBeans from a custom configuration file called jboss.jcml. Finally, this initializes all MBeans services defined in the jboss.jcml file. This sequence of steps is performed by the code fragment given in Listing 2.3.

LISTING 2.3   Using JMX to load the JBoss configured components

```
// Load bootstrap configuration
URL mletConf = mlet.getResource("jboss.conf");
Set beans = (Set) mlet.getMBeansFromURL(mletConf);
// Load JBoss configuration
ObjectName cfgName = new ObjectName(":service=Configuration");
Object[] args = {};
String[] sig = {};
server.invoke(cfgName, "loadConfiguration", args, sig);
// Init and Start MBeans
ObjectName scName = new ObjectName(":service=ServiceControl");
server.invoke(scName, "init", args, sig);
server.invoke(scName, "start", args, sig);
```

There are two reasons for splitting the JBoss components loading into a bootstrap and final step. First, the MLET configuration file syntax is rather cryptic and so editing it is prone to errors. Second, there is no notion of MBean service dependency specification in the MLET configuration file. Dependency means that one MBean service needs other MBean services to function correctly. Because of these issues, a JBoss specific MBean XML configuration file named jboss.jcml was created as well as an MBean(org.jboss.configuration.ConfigurationService) to read it. The DTD for the jboss.jcml file is given in Figure 2.3.

The jboss.jcml file allows for more readable configuration entries since each attribute of an mbean element is named as illustrated by the following jboss.jcml fragment in Listing 2.4:

LISTING 2.4   A sample jboss.jcml MBean declaration

```
<mbean code="org.jboss.jdbc.HypersonicDatabase"
  name="DefaultDomain:service=Hypersonic">
  <attribute name="Port">1476</attribute>
```

LISTING 2.4   Continued

```
<attribute name="Silent">true</attribute>
<attribute name="Database">default</attribute>
<attribute name="Trace">false</attribute>
</mbean>
```

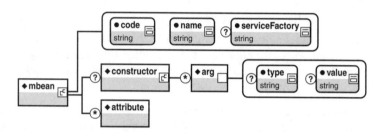

FIGURE 2.3   The DTD structure for the `jboss.jcml` configuration file.

The corresponding MLET tag is as shown in Listing 2.5:

LISTING 2.5   The corresponding MLET tag for Listing 2.4

```
<MLET CODE=" org.jboss.jdbc.HypersonicDatabase"
  NAME="DefaultDomain:service=Hypersonic">
<ARG TYPE="java.lang.Integer" VALUE="1476">
<ARG TYPE="java.lang.Boolean" VALUE="true">
<ARG TYPE="java.lang.String" VALUE="default">
<ARG TYPE="java.lang.Boolean" VALUE="false">
</MLET>
```

The `jboss.jcml` version is easier to read and maintain because you don't have to know the order of the corresponding MBean constructor arguments. The other feature of the `ConfigurationService` MBean is that the order of the mbean element declarations in the `jboss.jcml` file defines the MBean dependencies. As each mbean element is read by the `ConfigurationService`, it is registered with a JBoss life cycle MBean service (`org.jboss.util.ServiceControl`). The order in which MBeans are registered with the `ServiceControl` MBean defines the order in which the services are initialized and started. This is also the reverse of the order in which services are stopped on shutdown of the JBoss server. Thus, if you need add a new MBean declaration to the `jboss.jcml` file, and the MBean needs the JNDI naming service MBean, you would add the MBean declaration anywhere after the naming service MBean declaration.

The JBoss server starts out as nothing more than a container for the JMX MBean server. It then loads its personality based on the `jboss.conf` and `jboss.jcml` MBean configuration files from the named configuration set passed to the server on the command line. Because MBeans therefore define the functionality of a JBoss server instance, it is important to understand how the core JBoss MBeans are written, and how you should integrate your existing services into JBoss using MBeans.

Writing JBoss MBean Services

As you have seen, JBoss relies on JMX to load in the MBean services that make up a given server instance's personality. All of the bundled functionality provided with the standard JBoss distribution is based on MBeans. The best way to add services to the JBoss server is to write your own JMX MBeans.

There are two classes of MBeans: those that are independent of JBoss services, and those that are dependent on JBoss services. MBeans that are independent of JBoss services are the trivial case. They can be written per the JMX specification and added to a JBoss server by adding their MLET tag to the `jboss.conf` file, or equivalently adding an MBean tag anywhere to the `jboss.jcml` file. Writing an MBean that relies on a JBoss service such as naming requires you to follow the JBoss service pattern. The JBoss MBean service pattern consists of a set of life cycle operations that provide state change notifications. The notifications inform an MBean service when it can initialize, start, stop, and destroy itself. The management of the MBean service life cycle is the responsibility of two JBoss MBean services—`ConfigurationService` and `ServiceControl`.

The `ConfigurationService` MBean

JBoss manages the configuration of its MBean services via a custom MBean that loads an XML variation of the standard MLet configuration file. This custom MBean is implemented in the `org.jboss.configuration.ConfigurationService` class. The `ConfigurationService` MBean is loaded when JBoss starts up by the JMX MLet and loads the `jboss.conf` file. This is because the `ConfigurationService` MBean is declared in the `jboss.conf` file that ships with any JBoss distribution. The `ConfigurationService` MBean is a bootstrap service that has no dependencies on other JBoss provided MBeans. After the `jboss.conf` file is loaded to create the bootstrap MBeans, the `jboss.jcml` configuration is loaded by invoking `loadConfiguration` method on the `ConfigurationService` MBean. The `loadConfiguration` method performs the following steps:

1. Load the jboss.jcml file as a resource using the current Thread context ClassLoader.

2. Parse the jboss.jcml file and instantiate all MBeans that the file contains.

3. Apply the attribute settings from the jboss.jcml file to each MBean.

4. Register each MBean with the JBoss `ServiceControl` MBean so that the `ServiceControl` MBean will manage MBean service's life cycle. If the MBean does not implement the `org.jboss.util.Service` interface, the MBean is wrapped in a proxy implementation of the `Service` interface that delegates any of the methods of the Service interface to the matching MBean methods.

The Service Life Cycle Interface

The JMX specification does not define any type of life cycle or dependency management aspect for MBeans. The JBoss `ConfigurationService` and `ServiceControl` MBeans do introduce this notion. A JBoss MBean is an extension of the JMX MBean in that an MBean is expected to decouple creation from the life cycle of its service duties. This is necessary to implement any type of dependency management. For example, if you are writing an MBean that needs a JNDI naming service to be able to function, your MBean needs to be told when its dependencies are satisfied. This ranges from difficult to impossible to do if the only life cycle event is the MBean constructor. Therefore, JBoss introduces a service life cycle interface that describes the events a service can use to manage its behavior. Listing 2.6 shows the `org.jboss.util.Service` interface:

LISTING 2.6   The `org.jboss.util.Service` interface

```
package org.jboss.util;
public interface Service
{
    public void init() throws Exception;
    public void start() throws Exception;
    public void stop();
    public void destroy();
}
```

The `ServiceControl` MBean invokes the methods of the `Service` interface at the appropriate times of the service life cycle.

NOTE

There is a J2EE management specification request (JSR 77, http://jcp.org/jsr/detail/77.jsp) that introduces a state management notion that includes a start/stop life cycle notion. When this standard is finalized, JBoss will likely move to a JSR 77 based service life cycle implementation.

The `ServiceControl` **MBean**

JBoss manages dependencies between MBeans via the
`org.jboss.util.ServiceControl` custom MBean. The `ServiceControl` MBean is
another bootstrap MBean loaded by the JMX `MLet` from the `jboss.conf` file on
startup of the JBoss server. The `ServiceControl` MBean is a simple MBean that
contains an ordered collection of Service interface implementations. After the
ConfigurationService loads an MBean from the jboss.jcml configuration file, it populates the MBean with the MBean's configured attributes, and then the MBean is registered with the `ServiceControl` MBean by invoking the `register` method on
`ServiceControl` with the MBean or its Service proxy as the argument. The order in
which services are registered with the `ServiceControl` MBean defines the dependency ordering between the services. That is to say, the order in which services are
registered with the `ServiceControl` MBean defines the order in which the services
are initialized and started.

The `ServiceControl` MBean has four key methods: init, start, stop, and destroy.
These methods correspond to the `Service` interface life cycle methods.

The `init` **Method**   The JBoss server main entry point calls the `ServiceControl` `init`
method after the `jboss.jcml` configuration has been loaded. At the point the
`ServiceControl` init method is called, the `ConfigurationService` MBean has registered all MBeans defined in the `jboss.jcml` file with the `ServiceControl` MBean.
The init method makes a copy of current list of `Service` instances and then proceeds
to invoke the `init` method on each instance.

The order of initialization is the order of registration, which is the same as the ordering of MBean element entries in the `jboss.jcml` file. When a service's init method
is called, all services that were registered ahead of it have also had their `init` method
invoked. This gives an MBean an opportunity to check that required MBeans or
resources exist. The service typically cannot utilize other MBean services at this
point, as most JBoss MBean services do not become fully functional until they have
been started via their `start` method. Because of this, service implementations often
do not implement `init` in favor of just the `start` method because that is the first
point at which the service can be fully functional.

The `start` **Method**   The JBoss server main entry point calls the `ServiceControl`
start method after the `init` method has returned. The `start` method makes a copy
of current list of `Service` instances and then proceeds to invoke the `start` method
on each instance. When a service's `start` method is called, all services that were
registered ahead of it have also had their `start` method invoked. Receipt of a `start`
method invocation signals a service to become fully operational since all services
upon which the service depends have been initialized and started if possible.

The `stop` **Method**   The `stop` method is invoked by the by the JBoss server shutdown process, which is managed by the `org.jboss.util.Shutdown` MBean. The

stop method makes a copy of the current list of service instances and then invokes the stop method on each service in reverse order from that of the init and start methods. Thus, services that were last to start are the first to be stopped.

The destroy Method   The destroy method is invoked by the by the JBoss server shutdown process after the stop method. The destroy method makes a copy of the current list of service instances and then invokes the destroy method on each service in reverse order from that of the init and start methods. Service implementations often do not implement destroy in favor of simply implementing the stop method, or neither stop nor destroy if the service has no state or resources that need cleanup.

Writing JBoss MBean Services

Writing a custom MBean service that integrates into the JBoss server requires the use of the org.jboss.util.Service interface pattern if the custom service is dependent on other JBoss services. When a custom MBean depends on other MBean services you cannot perform any JBoss service dependent initialization in any of the javax.management.MBeanRegistration interface methods. Instead, you must do this in the Service interface init or start methods. You can do this by using any one of the following approaches:

- Add any of the Service methods that you want called on your MBean to your MBean interface. This allows your MBean implementation to avoid dependencies on JBoss specific interfaces.

- Have your MBean interface extend the org.jboss.util.Service interface.

- Have your MBean interface extend the org.jboss.util.ServiceMBean interface. This is a sub interface of org.jboss.util.Service that adds String getName(), int getState(), and String getStateString() methods.

The approach you choose depends if you want to be associated with JBoss specific code. If you don't, you would use the first approach. If you don't mind dependencies on JBoss classes, the simplest approach is to have your MBean interface extend from org.jboss.util.ServiceMBean and your MBean implementation class extend from the abstract org.jboss.util.ServiceMBeanSupport class. This class implements the org.jboss.util.ServiceMBean interface except for the String getName() method. ServiceMBeanSupport provides implementations of the init, start, stop, and destroy methods that integrate logging and JBoss service state management. Each method delegates any subclass specific work to initService, startService, stopService, and destroyService methods respectively. When subclassing ServiceMBeanSupport, you would override one or more of the initService, startService, stopService, and destroyService methods in addition to getName as required.

A Simple Custom MBean Example

This section develops a simple MBean that binds a `HashMap` into the JBoss JNDI namespace at a location determined by its `JndiName` attribute to demonstrate what is required to create a custom MBean. Because the MBean uses JNDI, it depends on the JBoss naming service MBean and must use the JBoss MBean service pattern to be notified when the naming service is available.

The MBean you develop is called `JNDIMap`. Version one of the `JNDIMapMBean` interface and `JNDIMap` implementation class, which is based on the service interface method pattern, is given in Listing 2.7. This version of the interface makes use of the first approach in that it incorporates the `Service` interface methods needed to start up correctly, but does not do so by using a JBoss-specific interface. The interface includes the `Service start` method, which will be informed when all required services have been started, and the `stop` method, which will clean up the service.

LISTING 2.7   `JNDIMapMBean` interface and implementation based on the service interface method pattern

```
// The JNDIMap MBean interface
import javax.naming.NamingException;

public interface JNDIMapMBean
{
  public String getJndiName();
  public void setJndiName(String jndiName) throws NamingException;
  public void start() throws Exception;
  public void stop() throws Exception;
}
// The JNDIMap MBean implementation
import java.io.InputStream;
import java.util.HashMap;
import javax.naming.CompositeName;
import javax.naming.Context;
import javax.naming.InitialContext;
import javax.naming.Name;
import javax.naming.NamingException;
import org.jboss.naming.NonSerializableFactory;

public class JNDIMap implements JNDIMapMBean
{
  private String jndiName;
  private HashMap contextMap = new HashMap();
  private boolean started;
```

LISTING 2.7   Continued

```java
public String getJndiName()
{
   return jndiName;
}
public void setJndiName(String jndiName) throws NamingException
{
  String oldName = this.jndiName;
  this.jndiName = jndiName;
  if( started )
  {
    unbind(oldName);
    try
    {
      rebind();
    }
    catch(Exception e)
    {
      NamingException ne = new
        NamingException("Failed to update jndiName");
      ne.setRootCause(e);
      throw ne;
    }
  }
}
public void start() throws Exception
{
  started = true;
  rebind();
}

public void stop()
{
  started = false;
  unbind(jndiName);
}

private static Context createContext(Context rootCtx, Name name)
  throws NamingException
{
  Context subctx = rootCtx;
```

LISTING 2.7   Continued

```java
for(int n = 0; n < name.size(); n ++)
{
  String atom = name.get(n);
  try
  {
    Object obj = subctx.lookup(atom);
    subctx = (Context) obj;
  }
  catch(NamingException e)
  {        // No binding exists, create a subcontext
    subctx = subctx.createSubcontext(atom);
  }
}

return subctx;
}

private void rebind() throws NamingException
{
  InitialContext rootCtx = new InitialContext();
  // Get the parent context into which we are to bind
  Name fullName = rootCtx.getNameParser("").parse(jndiName);
  System.out.println("fullName="+fullName);
  Name parentName = fullName;
  if( fullName.size() > 1 )
    parentName = fullName.getPrefix(fullName.size()-1);
  else
    parentName = new CompositeName();
  Context parentCtx = createContext(rootCtx, parentName);
  Name atomName = fullName.getSuffix(fullName.size()-1);
  String atom = atomName.get(0);
  NonSerializableFactory.rebind(parentCtx, atom, contextMap);
}
private void unbind(String jndiName)
{
  try
  {
    Context rootCtx = (Context) new InitialContext();
    rootCtx.unbind(jndiName);
    NonSerializableFactory.unbind(jndiName);
  }
```

LISTING 2.7   Continued

```
    catch(NamingException e)
    {
      e.printStackTrace();
    }
  }
}
```

Version two of the JNDIMapMBean interface and JNDIMap implementation class, which is based on the ServiceMBean interface and ServiceMBeanSupport class, is given in Listing 2.8. In this version, the implementation class extends the ServiceMBeanSupport class and overrides the startService method and the stopService method. JNDIMapMBean also implements the abstract getName to return a descriptive name for the MBean. The JNDIMapMBean interface extends the org.jboss.util.ServiceMBean interface and only declares the setter and getter methods for the JndiName attribute because it inherits the Service life cycle methods from ServiceMBean. This is the third approach mentioned earlier in this chapter, in "Writing JBoss MBean Services". The implementation differences between Listing 2.7 and 2.8 are highlighted in bold in Listing 2.8.

LISTING 2.8   JNDIMap MBean interface and implementation based on the ServiceMBean interface and ServiceMBeanSupport class

```
// The JNDIMap MBean interface
import javax.naming.NamingException;

public interface JNDIMapMBean extends org.jboss.util.ServiceMBean
{
  public String getJndiName();
  public void setJndiName(String jndiName) throws NamingException;
}

// The JNDIMap MBean implementation
import java.io.InputStream;
import java.util.HashMap;
import javax.naming.CompositeName;
import javax.naming.Context;
import javax.naming.InitialContext;
import javax.naming.Name;
import javax.naming.NamingException;
import org.jboss.naming.NonSerializableFactory;
```

LISTING 2.8   Continued

```
public class JNDIMap extends org.jboss.util.ServiceMBeanSupport
  implements JNDIMapMBean
{
  private String jndiName;
  private HashMap contextMap = new HashMap();

  public String getJndiName()
  {
    return jndiName;
  }
  public void setJndiName(String jndiName) throws NamingException
  {
    String oldName = this.jndiName;
    this.jndiName = jndiName;
    if( super.getState() == STARTED )
    {
      unbind(oldName);
      try
      {
        rebind();
      }
      catch(Exception e)
      {
        NamingException ne = new
          NamingException("Failed to update jndiName");
        ne.setRootCause(e);
        throw ne;
      }
    }
  }

  public String getName()
  {
    return "JNDIMap(" + jndiName + ")";
  }

  public void startService() throws Exception
  {
    rebind();
  }
  public void stopService()
```

LISTING 2.8 Continued

```
{
  unbind(jndiName);
}
private static Context createContext(Context rootCtx, Name name)
  throws NamingException
{
  Context subctx = rootCtx;
  for(int n = 0; n < name.size(); n ++)
  {
    String atom = name.get(n);
    try
    {
      Object obj = subctx.lookup(atom);
      subctx = (Context) obj;
    }
    catch(NamingException e)
    {        // No binding exists, create a subcontext
      subctx = subctx.createSubcontext(atom);
    }
  }

  return subctx;
}
private void rebind() throws NamingException
{
  InitialContext rootCtx = new InitialContext();
  // Get the parent context into which we are to bind
  Name fullName = rootCtx.getNameParser("").parse(jndiName);
  log.debug("fullName="+fullName);
  Name parentName = fullName;
  if( fullName.size() > 1 )
    parentName = fullName.getPrefix(fullName.size()-1);
  else
    parentName = new CompositeName();
  Context parentCtx = createContext(rootCtx, parentName);
  Name atomName = fullName.getSuffix(fullName.size()-1);
  String atom = atomName.get(0);
  NonSerializableFactory.rebind(parentCtx, atom, contextMap);
}
private void unbind(String jndiName)
```

LISTING 2.8   Continued

```
{
  try
  {
    Context rootCtx = (Context) new InitialContext();
    rootCtx.unbind(jndiName);
    NonSerializableFactory.unbind(jndiName);
  }
  catch(NamingException e)
  {
    log.error("Failed to unbind map", e);
  }
}
}
```

A sample `jboss.jcml` MBean entry for either implementation of the `JNDIMap` MBean is given in Listing 2.9 along with a sample client usage code fragment. The `JNDIMap` MBean binds a `HashMap` object under the `"inmemory/maps/MapTest"` JNDI name and the client code fragment demonstrates retrieving the `HashMap` object from the `"inmemory/maps/MapTest"` location.

LISTING 2.9   A sample `jboss.jcml` entry for the `JNDIMap` MBean and a client usage code fragment

```
<!--   The jboss.jcml file -- >
<server>
...
  <!--   The JNDI Naming service -- >
  <mbean code="org.jboss.naming.NamingService"
    name="DefaultDomain:service=Naming">
    <attribute name="Port">1099</attribute>
  </mbean>

  <!--   Add the JNDIMap entry after the NamingService because the
    NamingService must be running for the JNDIMap
    bean to start.
  -- >
  <mbean code="JNDIMap"
      name="DefaultDomain:service=JNDIMap,jndiName=inmemory/maps/MapTest">
    <attribute name="JndiName">inmemory/maps/MapTest</attribute>
  </mbean>
```

LISTING 2.9   Continued

```
...
</server>

// Sample lookup code
InitialContext ctx = new InitialContext();
HashMap map = (HashMap) ctx.lookup("inmemory/maps/MapTest");
```

The Core JBoss MBeans

This section on JBoss and JMX concludes with an overview of the JBoss bootstrap MBeans defined in the jboss.conf file. The JBoss service MBeans defined in the jboss.jcml file as shipped in the standard JBoss 2.4.1 distribution will also be examined.

The Bootstrap MBeans, jboss.conf

Listing 2.10 shows the default jboss.conf configuration file shipped with the standard JBoss server distribution, and shows only those entries that are not commented out.

LISTING 2.10   The default jboss.conf bootstrap configuration file from the standard JBoss distribution

```
<!--    JBoss JMX Bootstrap Configuration               -- >

<!--   The log4j based logging service based on the conf
    log4j.properties file -- >
<MLET CODE = "org.jboss.logging.Log4jService"
    ARCHIVE="jboss.jar,log4j.jar" CODEBASE="../../lib/ext/">
</MLET>

<!--   The log dir needs to be in the classpath to allow
    location of log.properties -- >
<MLET CODE="org.jboss.util.ClassPathExtension" ARCHIVE="jboss.jar"
    CODEBASE="../../lib/ext/">
   <ARG TYPE="java.lang.String" VALUE="../../log/">
</MLET>
<!--   Place the lib/ext directory in the classpath -- >
<MLET CODE="org.jboss.util.ClassPathExtension" ARCHIVE="jboss.jar"
    CODEBASE="../../lib/ext/">
   <ARG TYPE="java.lang.String" VALUE="./">
```

LISTING 2.10   Continued

```
</MLET>

<MLET CODE = "org.jboss.util.Info" ARCHIVE="jboss.jar"
    CODEBASE="../../lib/ext/">
</MLET>

<MLET CODE="org.jboss.util.ClassPathExtension" ARCHIVE="jboss.jar"
    CODEBASE="../../lib/ext/">
  <ARG TYPE="java.lang.String" VALUE="../../tmp/">
</MLET>

<MLET CODE="org.jboss.util.ClassPathExtension" ARCHIVE="jboss.jar"
    CODEBASE="../../lib/ext/">
  <ARG TYPE="java.lang.String" VALUE="../../db/">
</MLET>

<MLET CODE = "org.jboss.configuration.ConfigurationService"
    ARCHIVE="jboss.jar,../xml.jar" CODEBASE="../../lib/ext/">
</MLET>

<MLET CODE = "org.jboss.util.Shutdown" ARCHIVE="jboss.jar"
    CODEBASE="../../lib/ext/">
</MLET>

<MLET CODE = "org.jboss.util.ServiceControl" ARCHIVE="jboss.jar"
    CODEBASE="../../lib/ext/">
</MLET>
```

Notice that all MLET tags use the same CODEBASE attribute of `"../../lib/ext"`. The CODEBASE is relative to the configuration file set directory. The reason for this is that the URL passed to the MLet constructed by the JBoss startup code corresponds to the configuration file set directory, thus the configuration directory is in the MLet classpath and can be used as the starting point for relative paths.

Recall from Figure 1.1, the installation directory structure diagram, that a configuration file set would be a directory like JBOSS_DIST/conf/default, and therefore, the CODEBASE refers to the JBOSS_DISS/lib/ext directory. This is the directory that contains all of the server jars that did not need to be on the system classpath. Similarly, all MLET tags include the jboss.jar in their ARCHIVE attribute. This is because all of the JBoss server MBean services are located in the jboss.jar archive.

WARNING

Although the MLET tags in the jboss.conf file look like XML elements, they are not. Because of this, you cannot comment out entries by surrounding them in the XML begin and end comment elements <!-- -->. Rather, a commented out element has this pseudo XML comment form:

```
<!--   A commented MLET
--    MLET CODE = "..." ARCHIVE="..." CODEBASE="...">
--    ARG TYPE="..." VALUE="...">
--    /MLET>
--  >
```

Each line within the XML comment elements must begin with "--" (double dashes).

org.jboss.logging.Log4jService   The Log4jService MBean configures the Apache log4j system. JBoss uses the log4j framework as its internal logging API. The Log4jService can be used without any arguments passed to its constructor, in which case the service looks for a log4j.properties file as a resource using the Thread context ClassLoader. A second constructor allows for a single String parameter that specifies the path to the log4j configuration file. The file may be either a Java Properties file, or an XML file ending with a .xml suffix. The Log4jService will choose either the org.apache.log4j.xml.DOMConfigurator or the org.apache.log4j.PropertyConfigurator parser, depending on whether the configuration file is an XML document. The ARCHIVE attribute of the MLET tag specifies the log4j.jar archive in addition to the common jboss.jar. This is necessary because the Log4jService has explicit references to log4j classes and so the log4j.jar must be included in the list of jars the MLet uses to completely load the service.

org.jboss.util.ClassPathExtension   The ClassPathExtension MBean provides the capability to augment the classpath of the MLet that was constructed by the JBoss server startup code. The ClassPathExtension service takes a single argument that specifies the URL that should be added to the MLet classpath. If the URL is a file URL or a file path that ends in a '/' character and resolves to a directory, all jars found in the directory are added to the MLet classpath. If the file path is a relative path, it is resolved with respect to JBOSS_DIST/lib/ext directory.
Note that three different directories are added to the MLet classpath using relative paths. These resolve to the following directories:

- "./" resolves to JBOSS_DIST/lib/ext

- "../../tmp/" resolves to JBOSS_DIST/tmp

- "../../db/" resolves to JBOSS_DIST/db

The JBOSS_DIST/lib/ext directory reference places all the jars in the directory into the MLet classpath. This directory contains the JBoss server jars and third-party support jars. You will typically also place your common jars into lib/ext as well to make them available to MBeans and J2EE components.

The JBOSS_DIST/tmp and JBOSS_DIST/db directories are added to the MLet classpath to allow services that need to know the tmp and db directory locations to search for the directories as classpath resources.

`org.jboss.util.Info`   The Info MBean is a simple service the displays key information from the java.lang.System properties, such as VM vendor, VM version, OS name, and OS version as INFO priority log4j messages. It also dumps out the entire system Properties map as DEBUG priority log4j messages. Note that because this MBean used log4j messages, it technically depends on the Log4jService. Although JMX has not documented a dependency mechanism, MBeans are created in the order declared in the jboss.conf file for the Sun and IBM JMX implementations.

`org.jboss.configuration.ConfigurationService`   The `ConfigurationService` MBean is the JBoss MBean service loader that we have talked about in some detail. Typically, no constructor arguments are required to configure this service. In particular note that the location of the `jboss.jcml` file is not specified. This file is located by the service as a resource on the classpath.

`org.jboss.util.Shutdown`   The `Shutdown` service allows you to shut down the JBoss server in one of two ways. The first is through a shutdown operation that may be invoked directly or through the JMX server. The second is by virtue of the fact that the `Shutdown` service hooks into the `java.lang.Runtime ShutdownHook` so that you can use Ctrl-C or send the equivalent OS signal to cause the server to shut down cleanly during a `System.exit()`. The integration with the `ShutdownHook` mechanism is a JDK 1.3+ specific feature.

`org.jboss.util.ServiceControl`   The `ServiceControl` MBean is the service life cycle manager that was discussed earlier in this chapter in conjunction with the `ConfigurationService`. This service has no configurable attributes.

The Standard MBean Services, `jboss.jcml`
Listing 2.11 shows the default `jboss.jcml` configuration file shipped with the standard JBoss server distribution. The listing shows only those entries that are most commonly used.

LISTING 2.11   The default `jboss.jcml` services configuration file from the standard JBoss distribution

```
<?xml version="1.0" encoding="UTF-8"?>
<!-- This is where you can add and configure your MBeans
```

LISTING 2.11   Continued

```
  ATTENTION: The order of the listing here is the same order as
    the MBeans are loaded. Therefore, if a MBean depends on another
    MBean to be loaded and started, it has to be listed after all
    the MBeans it depends on.
-- >

<server>
  <!-- ================================================================ -- >
  <!-- Classloading                                                     -- >
  <!-- ================================================================ -- >
  <mbean code="org.jboss.web.WebService"
      name="DefaultDomain:service=Webserver">
    <attribute name="Port">8083</attribute>
  </mbean>


  <!-- ================================================================ -- >
  <!-- JNDI                                                             -- >
  <!-- ================================================================ -- >
  <mbean code="org.jboss.naming.NamingService"
      name="DefaultDomain:service=Naming">
    <attribute name="Port">1099</attribute>
  </mbean>
  <mbean code="org.jboss.naming.JNDIView"
      name="DefaultDomain:service=JNDIView" />



  <!-- ================================================================ -- >
  <!-- Transactions                                                     -- >
  <!-- ================================================================ -- >
  <mbean code="org.jboss.tm.TransactionManagerService"
      name="DefaultDomain:service=TransactionManager">
    <attribute name="TransactionTimeout">300</attribute>

    <!-- Use this attribute if you need to use a specific Xid
         implementation
    <attribute name="XidClassName">oracle.jdbc.xa.OracleXid</attribute>
    -- >
  </mbean>

  <mbean code="org.jboss.tm.usertx.server.ClientUserTransactionService"
```

LISTING 2.11   Continued

```
name="DefaultDomain:service=ClientUserTransaction">
  </mbean>


  <!-- ====================================================================== -- >
  <!-- Security                                                            -- >
  <!-- ====================================================================== -- >

  <!-- JAAS security manager and realm mapping -- >
  <mbean code="org.jboss.security.plugins.JaasSecurityManagerService"
      name="Security:name=JaasSecurityManager">
    <attribute name="SecurityManagerClassName">
      org.jboss.security.plugins.JaasSecurityManager
     </attribute>
  </mbean>

  <!-- ====================================================================== -- >
  <!-- JDBC                                                                -- >
  <!-- ====================================================================== -- >

  <mbean code="org.jboss.jdbc.JdbcProvider"
       name="DefaultDomain:service=JdbcProvider">
    <attribute name="Drivers">org.hsql.jdbcDriver</attribute>
  </mbean>

  <mbean code="org.jboss.jdbc.HypersonicDatabase"
      name="DefaultDomain:service=Hypersonic">
    <attribute name="Port">1476</attribute>
    <attribute name="Silent">true</attribute>
    <attribute name="Database">default</attribute>
    <attribute name="Trace">false</attribute>
  </mbean>

  <mbean code="org.jboss.jdbc.XADataSourceLoader"
      name="DefaultDomain:service=XADataSource,name=DefaultDS">
    <attribute name="PoolName">DefaultDS</attribute>
    <attribute name="DataSourceClass">
      org.jboss.pool.jdbc.xa.wrapper.XADataSourceImpl
    </attribute>
    <attribute name="Properties"></attribute>
    <attribute name="URL">jdbc:HypersonicSQL:hsql://localhost:1476</attribute>
```

LISTING 2.11 Continued

```
  <attribute name="GCMinIdleTime">1200000</attribute>
  <attribute name="JDBCUser">sa</attribute>
  <attribute name="MaxSize">10</attribute>
  <attribute name="Password" />
  <attribute name="GCEnabled">false</attribute>
  <attribute name="InvalidateOnError">false</attribute>
  <attribute name="TimestampUsed">false</attribute>
  <attribute name="Blocking">true</attribute>
  <attribute name="GCInterval">120000</attribute>
  <attribute name="IdleTimeout">1800000</attribute>
  <attribute name="IdleTimeoutEnabled">false</attribute>
  <attribute name="LoggingEnabled">false</attribute>
  <attribute name="MaxIdleTimeoutPercent">1.0</attribute>
  <attribute name="MinSize">0</attribute>
</mbean>


<!-- ===================================================================== -- >
<!--   J2EE deployment                                                      -- >
<!-- ===================================================================== -- >

<mbean code="org.jboss.ejb.ContainerFactory"
    name=":service=ContainerFactory">
  <attribute name="VerifyDeployments">true</attribute>
  <attribute name="ValidateDTDs">false</attribute>
  <attribute name="MetricsEnabled">false</attribute>
  <attribute name="VerifierVerbose">true</attribute>
  <attribute name="BeanCacheJMSMonitoringEnabled">false</attribute>
</mbean>



<!-- ===================================================================== -- >
<!--   JBossMQ                                                              -- >
<!-- ===================================================================== -- >
<mbean code="org.jboss.mq.server.JBossMQService"
    name="JBossMQ:service=Server"/>

<!--   The StateManager is used to keep JMS persisitent state data. -- >
<!--   For example: what durable subscriptions are active. -- >
<mbean code="org.jboss.mq.server.StateManager"
    name="JBossMQ:service=StateManager">
  <attribute name="StateFile">jbossmq-state.xml</attribute>
</mbean>
```

LISTING 2.11   Continued

```xml
<!--   The PersistenceManager is used to store messages to disk. -- >
<mbean code="org.jboss.mq.pm.rollinglogged.PersistenceManager"
    name="JBossMQ:service=PersistenceManager">
  <attribute name="DataDirectory">../../db/jbossmq/</attribute>
</mbean>


<!--   InvocationLayers are the different transport methods that can be used
   to access the server -- >
<mbean code="org.jboss.mq.il.jvm.JVMServerILService"
    name="JBossMQ:service=InvocationLayer,type=JVM">
  <attribute name="ConnectionFactoryJNDIRef">java:/ConnectionFactory
  </attribute>
  <attribute name="XAConnectionFactoryJNDIRef">java:/XAConnectionFactory
  </attribute>
</mbean>


<mbean code="org.jboss.mq.il.rmi.RMIServerILService"
    name="JBossMQ:service=InvocationLayer,type=RMI">
  <attribute name="ConnectionFactoryJNDIRef">RMIConnectionFactory
  </attribute>
  <attribute name="XAConnectionFactoryJNDIRef">RMIXAConnectionFactory
  </attribute>
</mbean>


<mbean code="org.jboss.mq.il.oil.OILServerILService"
    name="JBossMQ:service=InvocationLayer,type=OIL">
  <attribute name="ConnectionFactoryJNDIRef">ConnectionFactory
  </attribute>
  <attribute name="XAConnectionFactoryJNDIRef">XAConnectionFactory
  </attribute>
</mbean>


<mbean code="org.jboss.mq.il.uil.UILServerILService"
    name="JBossMQ:service=InvocationLayer,type=UIL">
  <attribute name="ConnectionFactoryJNDIRef">UILConnectionFactory
  </attribute>
  <attribute name="XAConnectionFactoryJNDIRef">UILXAConnectionFactory
  </attribute>
</mbean>
```

LISTING 2.11   Continued

```
<!--    The following three lines create three topics named testTopic,
  example, and bob --  >
<mbean code="org.jboss.mq.server.TopicManager"
  name="JBossMQ:service=Topic,name=testTopic"/>
<mbean code="org.jboss.mq.server.TopicManager"
  name="JBossMQ:service=Topic,name=example"/>
<mbean code="org.jboss.mq.server.TopicManager"
  name="JBossMQ:service=Topic,name=bob"/>


<!--    The following nine lines create nine topics named testQueue,
    controlQueue, A, B, C, D, E, F, and ex --  >

<mbean code="org.jboss.mq.server.QueueManager"
  name="JBossMQ:service=Queue,name=testQueue"/>
<mbean code="org.jboss.mq.server.QueueManager"
  name="JBossMQ:service=Queue,name=controlQueue"/>
<mbean code="org.jboss.mq.server.QueueManager"
  name="JBossMQ:service=Queue,name=A"/>
<mbean code="org.jboss.mq.server.QueueManager"
  name="JBossMQ:service=Queue,name=B"/>
<mbean code="org.jboss.mq.server.QueueManager"
  name="JBossMQ:service=Queue,name=C"/>
<mbean code="org.jboss.mq.server.QueueManager"
  name="JBossMQ:service=Queue,name=D"/>
<mbean code="org.jboss.mq.server.QueueManager"
  name="JBossMQ:service=Queue,name=E"/>
<mbean code="org.jboss.mq.server.QueueManager"
  name="JBossMQ:service=Queue,name=F"/>
<mbean code="org.jboss.mq.server.QueueManager"
  name="JBossMQ:service=Queue,name=ex"/>


<!--    Used for backwards compatibility with JBossMQ versions
    before 1.0.0 --  >
<mbean code="org.jboss.naming.NamingAlias" name="DefaultDomain:service=Namin-
gAlias,fromName=QueueConnectionFactory">
    <attribute name="ToName">ConnectionFactory</attribute>
    <attribute name="FromName">QueueConnectionFactory</attribute>
  </mbean>
<mbean code="org.jboss.naming.NamingAlias" name="DefaultDomain:service=Namin-
gAlias,fromName=TopicConnectionFactory">
    <attribute name="ToName">ConnectionFactory</attribute>
```

LISTING 2.11   Continued

```
    <attribute name="FromName">TopicConnectionFactory</attribute>
</mbean>


<!--   For Message Driven Beans --  >
<mbean code="org.jboss.jms.jndi.JMSProviderLoader"
    name=":service=JMSProviderLoader,name=JBossMQProvider">
  <attribute name="ProviderName">DefaultJMSProvider</attribute>
  <attribute name="ProviderAdapterClass">org.jboss.jms.jndi.JBossMQProvider
  </attribute>
  <attribute name="QueueFactoryRef">java:/XAConnectionFactory</attribute>
  <attribute name="TopicFactoryRef">java:/XAConnectionFactory</attribute>
</mbean>
<mbean code="org.jboss.jms.asf.ServerSessionPoolLoader"
    name=":service=ServerSessionPoolMBean,name=StdJMSPool">
  <attribute name="PoolName">StdJMSPool</attribute>
  <attribute name="PoolFactoryClass">
    org.jboss.jms.asf.StdServerSessionPoolFactory
  </attribute>
</mbean>


<!--   Make sure you change EmbeddedTomcat to Jetty if you are using Jetty --  >
<mbean code="org.jboss.deployment.J2eeDeployer"
    name="J2EE:service=J2eeDeployer">
  <attribute name="DeployerName">Default</attribute>
  <attribute name="JarDeployerName">:service=ContainerFactory</attribute>
  <attribute name="WarDeployerName">:service=EmbeddedTomcat</attribute>
</mbean>


<!--   ===================================================================== --  >
<!--   JBossCX setup, for J2EE connector architecture support          --  >
<!--   ===================================================================== --  >


<mbean code="org.jboss.resource.RARDeployer" name="JCA:service=RARDeployer">
</mbean>


<!--   Minerva no transaction connection manager factory.

    Use this for resource adapters that don't support
    transactions. --  >
<mbean code="org.jboss.resource.ConnectionManagerFactoryLoader"
```

LISTING 2.11   Continued

```
        name="JCA:service=ConnectionManagerFactoryLoader,➥name=MinervaNoTransCM-
Factory">
    <attribute name="FactoryName">MinervaNoTransCMFactory</attribute>
    <attribute name="FactoryClass">
      org.jboss.pool.connector.jboss.MinervaNoTransCMFactory
    </attribute>
    <attribute name="Properties"></attribute>
  </mbean>

  <!--   Minerva local transaction connection manager factory.
         Use this for resource adapters that support "local"
       transactions. --  >
  <mbean code="org.jboss.resource.ConnectionManagerFactoryLoader"
         name="JCA:service=ConnectionManagerFactoryLoader,➥name=MinervaSharedLo-
calCMFactory">
    <attribute name="FactoryName">MinervaSharedLocalCMFactory</attribute>
    <attribute name="FactoryClass">
      org.jboss.pool.connector.jboss.MinervaSharedLocalCMFactory
    </attribute>
    <attribute name="Properties"></attribute>
  </mbean>

  <!--   Minerva XA transaction connection manager factory

       Use this for resource adapters that support "xa"
       transactions. --  >
  <mbean code="org.jboss.resource.ConnectionManagerFactoryLoader"
         name="JCA:service=ConnectionManagerFactoryLoader,➥name=MinervaXACMFac-
tory">
    <attribute name="FactoryName">MinervaXACMFactory</attribute>
    <attribute name="FactoryClass">
      org.jboss.pool.connector.jboss.MinervaXACMFactory
    </attribute>
    <attribute name="Properties"></attribute>
  </mbean>

  <!--   Connection factory for the Minerva JDBC resource adapter. This
       points at the same database as DefaultDS. --  >
  <mbean code="org.jboss.resource.ConnectionFactoryLoader"
         name="JCA:service=ConnectionFactoryLoader,name=MinervaDS">
    <attribute name="FactoryName">MinervaDS</attribute>
```

LISTING 2.11   Continued

```
<attribute name="RARDeployerName">JCA:service=RARDeployer</attribute>
<attribute name="ResourceAdapterName">
  Minerva JDBC LocalTransaction ResourceAdapter
</attribute>
<attribute name="Properties">
  ConnectionURL=jdbc:HypersonicSQL:hsql://localhost:1476
</attribute>

<attribute name="ConnectionManagerFactoryName">
  MinervaSharedLocalCMFactory
</attribute>
<!--   See the documentation for the specific connection manager
      implementation you are using for the properties you can set --  >
<attribute name="ConnectionManagerProperties">
  # Pool type - uncomment to force, otherwise it is the default
  #PoolConfiguration=per-factory

  # Connection pooling properties - see
  # org.jboss.pool.PoolParameters
  MinSize=0
  MaxSize=10
  Blocking=true
  GCEnabled=false
  IdleTimeoutEnabled=false
  InvalidateOnError=false
  TrackLastUsed=false
  GCIntervalMillis=120000
  GCMinIdleMillis=1200000
  IdleTimeoutMillis=1800000
  MaxIdleTimeoutPercent=1.0
</attribute>

<!--   Principal mapping configuration --  >
<attribute name="PrincipalMappingClass">
  org.jboss.resource.security.ManyToOnePrincipalMapping
</attribute>
<attribute name="PrincipalMappingProperties">
  userName=sa
  password=
</attribute>
</mbean>
```

LISTING 2.11 Continued

```
<!--   JMS XA Resource adapter, use this to get transacted JMS in beans -- >
<mbean code="org.jboss.resource.ConnectionFactoryLoader"
       name="JCA:service=ConnectionFactoryLoader,name=JmsXA">
  <attribute name="FactoryName">JmsXA</attribute>
  <attribute name="RARDeployerName">JCA:service=RARDeployer</attribute>
  <attribute name="ResourceAdapterName">JMS Adapter</attribute>
  <attribute name="ConnectionManagerFactoryName">MinervaXACMFactory
  </attribute>
  <!--   See the documentation for the specific connection manager
       implementation you are using for the properties you can set -- >
  <attribute name="ConnectionManagerProperties">
    # Pool type - uncomment to force, otherwise it is the default
    #PoolConfiguration=per-factory

    # Connection pooling properties - see
    # org.jboss.pool.PoolParameters
    MinSize=0
    MaxSize=10
    Blocking=true
    GCEnabled=false
    IdleTimeoutEnabled=false
    InvalidateOnError=false
    TrackLastUsed=false
    GCIntervalMillis=120000
    GCMinIdleMillis=1200000
    IdleTimeoutMillis=1800000
    MaxIdleTimeoutPercent=1.0
  </attribute>

  <!--   Principal mapping configuration -- >
  <attribute name="PrincipalMappingClass">
    org.jboss.resource.security.ManyToOnePrincipalMapping
  </attribute>
  <attribute name="PrincipalMappingProperties">
  </attribute>
</mbean>


<!-- ===================================================================== -- >
<!--   Auto deployment                                                     -- >
<!-- ===================================================================== -- >
```

LISTING 2.11   Continued

```xml
<mbean code="org.jboss.ejb.AutoDeployer" name="EJB:service=AutoDeployer">
  <attribute name="Deployers">
    J2EE:service=J2eeDeployer;
    JCA:service=RARDeployer
  </attribute>
  <attribute name="URLs">../deploy,../deploy/lib</attribute>
</mbean>


<!-- ================================================================= -- >
<!-- JMX adaptors                                                      -- >
<!-- ================================================================= -- >

<mbean code="org.jboss.jmx.server.JMXAdaptorService"
  name="Adaptor:name=RMI" />


<mbean code="org.jboss.jmx.server.RMIConnectorService"
  name="Connector:name=RMI" />


<mbean code="com.sun.jdmk.comm.HtmlAdaptorServer" name="Adaptor:name=html">
  <attribute name="MaxActiveClientCount">10</attribute>
  <attribute name="Parser" />
  <attribute name="Port">8082</attribute>
</mbean>


<!-- ================================================================= -- >
<!-- Mail Connection Factory                                           -- >
<!-- ================================================================= -- >
<mbean code="org.jboss.mail.MailService" name=":service=Mail">
  <attribute name="JNDIName">Mail</attribute>
  <attribute name="ConfigurationFile">mail.properties</attribute>
  <attribute name="User">user_id</attribute>
  <attribute name="Password">password</attribute>
</mbean>


<!-- ================================================================= -- >
<!-- Scheduler Service                                                 -- >
<!-- ================================================================= -- >
<!-- Uncomment this to enable Scheduling - -->
<mbean code="org.jboss.util.Scheduler" name=":service=Scheduler">
  <constructor>
```

LISTING 2.11   Continued

```
      <arg type="java.lang.String" value=":server=Scheduler"/>
      <arg type="java.lang.String"
        value="org.jboss.util.Scheduler$SchedulableExample"/>
      <arg type="java.lang.String" value="Schedulabe Test,12345"/>
      <arg type="java.lang.String" value="java.lang.String,int"/>
      <arg type="long" value="0"/>
      <arg type="long" value="10000"/>
      <arg type="long" value="-1"/>
    </constructor>
  </mbean>
  <!- - -- >

  <!-- =================================================================== -- >
  <!--   Add your custom MBeans here                                       -- >
  <!-- =================================================================== -- >

</server>
```

As you can see from Listing 2.11, there are a large number of configured MBean services that ship in the standard JBoss distribution.

org.jboss.web.WebService   The WebService MBean provides dynamic class loading for RMI access to the server EJBs. The configurable attributes for the WebService are as follows:

- Port—The WebService listening port number. A port of 0 will use any available port.

- Host—Set the name of the public interface to use for the host portion of the RMI codebase URL.

- BindAddress—The specific address the WebService listens on. This can be used on a multi-homed host for a java.net.ServerSocket that will only accept connect requests to one of its addresses.

- Backlog—The maximum queue length for incoming connection indications (a request to connect) is set to the backlog parameter. If a connection indication arrives when the queue is full, the connection is refused.

- DownloadServerClasses—A flag indicating if the server should attempt to download classes from thread context class loader when a request arrives that does not have a class loader key prefix.

org.jboss.ejb.ContainerFactory   The ContainerFactory MBean is used to deploy EJB applications. It can be given a URL to an EJB-jar or an EJB-JAR XML file, which will be used to instantiate containers and make them available for use by remote clients.

The configurable attributes of the ContainerFactory include the following:

• VerifyDeployments—This flag enables the verification of EJB jar components in accordance with the EJB specifications. Because the EJB specification leaves a number of implementation details as patterns that the bean developer must perform, it is easy to construct an incorrect deployment. The VerifyDeployments flag tells the ContainerFactory to validate that the beans in the EJB deployment do correctly conform to the expected patterns. The deployment will fail if any bean fails the verification.

• VerifierVerbose—This flag turns on additional output from the verification step. Enabling this flag is useful if an EJB deployment fails verification, and you can't tell what the problem is from the non-verbose output.

• ValidateDTDs—This flag enables the validation of EJB deployment descriptors against their DTDs. The container factory parses the standard ejb-jar.xml and JBoss specific jboss.xml deployment descriptors located in the META-INF directory of the EJB jar deployment. When ValidateDTDs is true, the XML parser will validate the deployment descriptor document against the document's DTD.

• MetricsEnabled—This is an experimental flag that enables rudimentary metrics for EJB invocations.

• BeanCacheJMSMonitoringEnabled—This is an experimental flag that enables the viewing of collected metrics as JMS messages.

org.jboss.deployment.J2eeDeployer   The J2eeDeployer MBean service allows the deployment of single EJB jars, Web application archives (WARs), and enterprise application archives (EARs). For wars to be deployed, there must be a servlet container, such as Tomcat, embedded in JBoss.

The configurable attributes of the J2eeDeployer service are as follows:

• DeployerName—A name that is appended to the base "J2eeDeployer" service name to create a unique name for the JMX service attribute used in the javax.management.ObjectName.

• JarDeployerName—The JMX ObjectName string for the EJB jar deployer service. The default value is ":service=ContainerFactory".

• WarDeployerName—The JMX ObjectName string for the WAR jar deployer service. The default value is ":service= EmbeddedTomcat". You would change the default value if using a servlet container other than Tomcat.

`org.jboss.jmx.server.RMIConnectorService`   The `RMIConnectorService` MBean service binds an implementation of the `org.jboss.jmx.interfaces.RMIConnector` into JNDI under the name `"jmx:<hostname>:rmi:"` where `<hostname>` is the server hostname. The `RMIConnector` interface is an RMI interface that exposes a number of the `javax.management.MBeanServer` interface methods to allow remote clients access to the `MBeanServer` associated with the JBoss JMX bus. There are no configurable attributes for the `RMIConnectorService`.

`com.sun.jdmk.comm.HtmlAdaptorServer`   The `HtmlAdaptorServer` MBean acts as an HTML server that allows an HTML browser to manage all MBeans in the agent. The HTML protocol adaptor provides the following main HTML pages for managing MBeans in an agent:

- Agent View—Provides a list of object names of all the MBeans registered in the agent

- Agent Administration—Registers and unregisters MBeans in the agent

- MBean View—Reads and writes MBean attributes and performs operations on MBeans in the agent

The configurable attributes of the `HtmlAdaptorServer` service include the following:

- MaxActiveClientCount—The maximum number of concurrent requests the server will accept

- Port—The HTTP port on which the adaptor listens for clients

`org.jboss.mail.MailService`   The `MailService` MBean provides JavaMail support. The `MailService` binds a javax.mail.Session in JNDI under the java:/ to allow mail to be sent through the `Session` object.

The configurable attributes of the `MailService` service include the following:

- User—The user id used to connect to a mail server.

- Password—The password used to connect to a mail server.

- ConfigurationFile—The file name of the configuration mail file used by JavaMail to send mail. This file normally resides in the configuration directory of JBoss, and contains name-value pairs (such as `"mail.transport.protocol = smtp"`) as specified in the JavaMail API documentation.

- JNDIName—The JNDI subcontext name under the java:/ context into which javax.mail.Session objects are bound. The default is "Mail".

`org.jboss.util.Scheduler`   This `Scheduler` MBean service defines the manageable interface for a scheduler that allows you to request an `org.jboss.util.Schedulable` implementation be run periodically by the service.

The configurable attributes of the `Scheduler` service include the following:

- SchedulableClass—The fully qualified class name of the `org.jboss.util.Schedulable` implementation to use with the Scheduler.

- SchedulableArguments—The comma separated list of arguments for the Schedulable class. This list must have as many elements as the Schedulable Argument Type list; otherwise, the start of the Scheduler will fail. Currently only basic data types, string, and classes with a constructor with a string as only argument are supported.

- SchedulableArgumentTypes—The comma separated list of argument types for the Schedulable class. This will be used to find the right constructor, and to create the right instances with which to call the constructor. This list must have as many elements as the Schedulable Arguments list; otherwise, the start of the Scheduler will fail. Currently only basic data types, string, and classes with a constructor with a string as only argument are supported.

- SchedulePeriod—The time between two scheduled calls (after the initial call) in milliseconds. This value must be greater than 0.

- InitialRepetitions—The number of periods for which the instance will be scheduled. Set to -1 for unlimited repetitions.

The EJB Container Architecture

The JBoss 2.4 EJB container architecture is a third-generation design that emphasizes a modular plug-in approach. All key aspects of the EJB container may be replaced by custom versions of a plug-in by a developer. This approach allows for fine-tuned customization of the EJB container behavior to optimally suit your needs.

To understand how the EJB container works, you focus on the components encountered along the path an EJB method invocation travels. You are introduced to the architecture from the perspective of understanding how an EJB call is passed to JBoss through the network layer, and then dispatched to the EJB container.

EJBObject **and** EJBHome

As is discussed in many EJB references, a `javax.ejb.EJBObject` is an object that represents a client's view of the Enterprise Java Bean. It is the responsibility of the container provider to generate the `javax.ejb.EJBHome` and `EJBObject` for an EJB implementation. A client never references an EJB bean instance directly, but rather references the `EJBHome`, which implements the bean home interface, and the `EJBObject`, which implements the bean remote interface.

Virtual EJBObject—The Big Picture

EJBObject is more of an abstract idea than a physical implementation. Clients are given a remote handle to EJBObjects, but how is the EJBObject physically implemented on the server side? The answer is that it is not implemented at all!

In JBoss there is only one physical object that serves all logical EJBObjects referenced by clients. That physical object is the container. For each type of EJB there is one container object that plays the role of EJBObject by wrapping all instances of a particular EJB type.

JBoss' approach is superior to creating an explicit server-side EJBObject in many aspects, and simplifies the container architecture significantly. Clients, however, never notice this. They have an object (dynamic proxy) that looks and feels like a real server EJBObject, but this is merely an illusion. Behind the scenes there is only one instance of a container handling all method invocations for a given class of EJB. The result is full EJBObject conformity.

Dynamic Proxies and EJBObject

A dynamic proxy is an object that implements a list of interfaces specified at runtime when the object is created. A proxy interface is an interface that is implemented by a proxy class. Each proxy class instance has an associated invocation handler object, which implements the java.lang.reflect.InvocationHandler interface.

The EJBObject and EJHome object are created as dynamic proxies using the java.lang.reflect.Proxy.newProxyInstance method, whose signature is as follows:

```
public static Object newProxyInstance(java.lang.ClassLoader loader,
                            java.lang.Class[] interfaces,
                            java.lang.reflect.InvocationHandler h)
                  throws IllegalArgumentException
```

The parameters are as follows:

- **loader**—The class loader in which to define the proxy class. JBoss passes in the ClassLoader of the home or remote interface class depending on whether an EJBHome or EJBObject is being proxied.

- **interfaces**—The list of interfaces for the proxy class to implement. For the EJBHome proxy, the interface list includes the home interface of the bean as well as the javax.ejb.Handle. For the EJBObject proxy, the interface list includes the remote interface of the bean.

- **h**—The invocation handler to which method invocations are dispatched. For the EJBHome proxy, the handler is a org.jboss.ejb.plugins.jrmp.interfaces.HomeProxy object. For the EJBObject proxy, one of the EntityProxy,

StatefulSessionProxy, or StatelessSessionProxy objects from the
org.jboss.ejb.plugins.jrmp.interfaces package is used depending on the
type of the EJB.

Because the java.lang.reflect.Proxy class is serializible, it can be sent to the
remote client across the network. The EJBHome proxy is bound into JNDI under the
name the chosen for the EJBHome by the deployment descriptor. When a client
looks up the EJBHome from JNDI, they are unserializing the proxy instance. Because
the proxy implements the bean's home interface, it can be cast and used as the
home interface.

EJB Proxy Types

Depending on the type of the EJB on the server, there are four proxy classes:
EntityProxy, HomeProxy, StatelessSessionProxy and StatefulSessionProxy. Recall
that these classes are not the proxy objects that implement bean home and remote
interfaces. These are implementations of the java.lang.reflect.InvocationHandler
interface. They are referred to as proxies as well because they serve as proxies for the
server EJB container that manages the bean instance with which the client interfaces
are associated. All four of the proxy class' subclass the
org.jboss.ejb.plugins.jrmp.interfaces.GenericProxy class. The GenericProxy
class contains an RMI reference to a
org.jboss.ejb.plugins.rmp.interfaces.ContainerRemote interface implementation
from the JBoss server. The implementer of ContainerRemote in the JBoss server is the
JRMPContainerInvoker.

From Client to Server

When a client invokes a home or remote method interface on the proxy object they
obtained from the JBoss server, the proxy forwards the call to the
InvocationHandler, which, as you have seen, is an object of type EntityProxy,
HomeProxy, StatelessSessionProxy or StatefulSessionProxy. An attempt is first
made to handle the method on the client side. This is possible for methods like
toString, equals, hashCode, getEJBMetaData, and so on. When the method invocation is for a method that is implemented by the server-side EJB, the call is forwarded
to the server using the ContainerRemote RMI reference.

Summarize the components involved in delivery of a client request to the server by
tracing a remote call of some business method B of an entity bean. Figure 2.4
provides a high level view of the components involved. First, the method call goes to
the proxy that implements the entity bean remote interface. It is then dispatched by
the proxy to its invocation handler, which in this case is an EntityProxy. The
EntityProxy converts the call into a RemoteMethodInvocation object and then places
it into a MarshalledObject. Using the RMI ContainerRemote interface stub of the

`JRMPContainerInvoker`, the remote call is sent to the server's `JRMPContainerInvoker` object where it is unpacked from `MarshalledObject`, and handed off to the container.

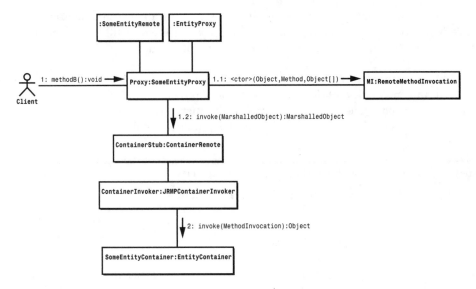

FIGURE 2.4   The JBoss components involved in delivering an EJB method invocation to the EJB container.

Design Advantages

This design of client objects gives maximum flexibility in the following sense: All calls that can be handled by the clients are handled locally, preventing the roundtrip across the wire and saving the container from unnecessary calls. Calls coming from clients inside of the server JVM can be optimized by calling the server container invoker directly, and thus avoiding an RMI call and its associated overhead. Finally, only calls that absolutely must leave the local VM are passed across the wire using RMI.

`ContainerInvoker`—**The Container Transport Handler**

Certainly one of the most important parts of a distributed system is its remote procedure call (RPC) interface, as well as techniques used in passing that RPC call between different parts of the system. The component that plays the role of the container entry point in JBoss is the `ContainerInvoker` interface. The role of the `ContainerInvoker` is to isolate the transport protocol used to deliver method invocations, and return the reply from the actual dispatch of the method to the EJB implementation. Thus, a given `ContainerInvoker` implementation is associated with a specific RPC transport. The separation of the client access protocol from the EJB container implementation allows for inclusion of multiple access protocols without changing the EJB container. JBoss can easily add support for RMI/IIOP, SOAP, and any other required transport scheme by simply associating a new `ContainerInvoker` implementation with a container configuration. Look at the RMI/JRMP version of the `ContainerInvoker` to get a better understanding of its duties.

The `JRMPContainerInvoker`

The RMI implementation of the `ContainerInvoker` provides an RMI version of the `org.jboss.ejb.Container` invoke and invokeHome methods in the `ContainerRemote` interface. Listing 2.12 provides the `ContainerRemote` interface method signatures.

LISTING 2.12   The `org.jboss.ejb.plugins.jrmp.interfaces.ContainerRemote` interface implemented by the `JRMPContainerInvoker` class

```
public interface ContainerRemote extends java.rmi.Remote
{
    /**
     * Invoke the remote home instance.
     *
     * @param mi  The marshalled object representing the method to
     *                 invoke.
     * @return Return value of method invocation.
     *
     * @throws Exception On failure to invoke method.
     */
    MarshalledObject invokeHome(MarshalledObject mi)
        throws Exception;

    /**
     * Invoke a remote object instance.
     *
     * @param mi  The marshalled object representing the method to
     *                 invoke.
     * @return  Return value of method invocation.
     *
     * @throws Exception    Failed to invoke method.
     */
    MarshalledObject invoke(MarshalledObject mi)
        throws Exception;
```

LISTING 2.12   Continued

```
/**
 * Invoke the local home instance.
 *
 * @param m          The method to invoke.
 * @param args       The arguments to the method.
 * @param tx         The transaction to use for the invocation.
 * @param idendity   The principal to use for the invocation.
 * @param credential The credentials to use for the invocation.
 * @return           Return value of method invocation.
 *
 * @throws Exception    Failed to invoke method.
 */
Object invokeHome(Method m, Object[] args, Transaction tx,
                  Principal identity, Object credential)
    throws Exception;

/**
 * Invoke a local object instance.
 *
 * @param id         The identity of the object to invoke.
 * @param m          The method to invoke.
 * @param args       The arguments to the method.
 * @param tx         The transaction to use for the invocation.
 * @param idendity   The principal to use for the invocation.
 * @param credential The credentials to use for the invocation.
 * @return           Return value of method invocation.
 *
 * @throws Exception    Failed to invoke method.
 */
Object invoke(Object id, Method m, Object[] args, Transaction tx,
              Principal identity, Object credential)
    throws Exception;
}
```

When a JBoss EJB container that is configured to use RMI/JRMP as its transport protocol is initialized, it starts its JRMPContainerInvoker object. This results in the EJB home proxy being bound into JNDI. The home proxy contains a reference to the ContainerRemote interface of the container's JRMPContainerInvoker. The JRMPContainerInvoker also exports itself to the RMI subsystem so that it can begin to accept RMI requests.

`ContainerRemote` **Interface—Two Forms of Invoke Methods**

The RMI interface of the JRMPContainerInvoker is the `ContainerRemote` interface. It has two methods—invoke and invokeHome—each of which has two flavors:

```
public MarshalledObject invoke(MarshalledObject mi) throws Exception;
public MarshalledObject invokeHome(MarshalledObject mi) throws Exception;
```

and

```
public Object invoke(Object id, Method m, Object[] args,
   Transaction tx, Principal identity, Object credential ) throws Exception;
Object invokeHome(Method m, Object[] args, Transaction tx,
   Principal identity, Object credential) throws Exception;
```

The first flavor accepts only one parameter—an RMI `MarshalledObject`, while the second flavor accepts a method reflection style of parameters. The different signatures exist to allow the `JRMPContainerInvoker` to accept both remote and local client calls. This allows a caller in the same VM as the EJB container the choice of a standard call by reference method invocation as an optimization over the RMI call-by-value semantics. Note that because the EJB specification requires that the semantics of an EJB method invocation follow the RMI call-by-value semantics, if an in-VM caller wants to preserve these semantics it would use the form that accepted and returned the `MarshalledObject`. The optimization choice is a non-EJB 1.1 specification option that offered performance over specification conformance. However, the EJB 2.0 local interfaces notion adds the option of call-by-reference semantics. Thus, a caller using the EJB 2.0 local-interfaces semantics would make use of the optimized method invocation.

Handling the Method Invocations

Remote calls are delivered to the `JRMPContainerInvoker` object in the RMI subsystem. The contents of the method invocation are unpacked from `MarshalledObject` and then passed to the invokeHome or invoke methods. A `MarshalledObject` contains a byte stream with the serialized representation of an object. As was discussed earlier in this chapter, the serialized object is `RemoteMethodInvocation` generated by the client-side `GenericProxy` subclass. The `RemoteMethodInvocation` instance contains all the attributes of the original EJB method invocation, along with any security and transaction contexts. The `RemoteMethodInvocation` is deserialized from the `MarshalledObject`, converted to an `org.jboss.ejb.MethodInvocation`, and handed off to the container.

Local calls coming from clients in the same VM, such as an EJB to EJB method call, are directly handed off to the container unless the container is configured to adhere to RMI call-by-value semantics. This bypasses the network layer, as well as any object marshalling of the call that RMI calls have to go through.

Other `ContainerInvoker` **Duties**

Before forwarding a call to the container, the `ContainerInvoker` is responsible for establishing the thread context `ClassLoader` to that of the container, as well as propagating any transaction and security context information.

Another important role played by the `ContainerInvoker` is that it provides implementation of the `EJBObject` and `EJBHome` parts of the container that are appropriate for the `ContainerInvoker` protocol transport. As mentioned earlier in this chapter, the `JRMPContainerInvoker` creates `EJBObject` and `EJBHome` in the form of dynamic proxies. The `EJBHome` is created during the initialization phase of the container. `EJBObjects` are created as they are needed. For example, an `EntityBean` finder may result in a set of primary keys whose `EJBObjects` must be returned to the client. The `ContainerInvoker` is then responsible for creating `EJBObject` instances that can be used by the client in accord with the `ContainerInvoker` RPC protocol.

The EJB Container

An EJB container is the component that manages a particular class of EJB. In JBoss there is one instance of the `org.jboss.ejb.Container` created for each unique class of EJB that is deployed. The actual object that is instantiated is a subclass of `Container` and the creation of the container instance is managed by a `ContainerFactory` MBean.

`ContainerFactory` **MBean**

The `org.jboss.ejb.ContainerFactory` MBean is responsible for the creation of EJB containers. Given an EJB-jar that is ready for deployment, the `ContainerFactory` will create and initialize the necessary EJB containers, one for each type of EJB. The key methods of the `org.jboss.ejb.ContainerFactoryMBean` interface are given in Listing 2.13.

LISTING 2.13   The `org.jboss.ejb.ContainerFactoryMBean` interface

```
public interface ContainerFactoryMBean
    extends org.jboss.util.ServiceMBean
{
  /** Returns the applications deployed by the container factory
   */
  public java.util.Iterator getDeployedApplications();
  /**
```

LISTING 2.13   Continued

```
 *        Deploy an application
 *
 * @param   url URL to the directory with the given EJBs
         to be deployed
   * @param   appId Id of the application this EJBs belongs
   *             to use for management
 * @exception   MalformedURLException
 * @exception   DeploymentException
 */
public void deploy(String url, String appId )
   throws MalformedURLException, DeploymentException;

/** Deploy an application
   *
   * @param   appUrl Url to the application itself
   * @param   jarUrls Array of URLs to the JAR files containing
   *          the EJBs
   * @param   appId Id of the application this EJBs belongs to
   *             used for management
 * @exception   MalformedURLException
 * @exception   DeploymentException
 */
public void deploy( String appUurl, String[] jarUrls, String appId )
   throws MalformedURLException, DeploymentException;

   /** Undeploy an application
   *
   * @param   url
   * @exception   MalformedURLException
   * @exception   DeploymentException
   */
public void undeploy(String url)
   throws MalformedURLException, DeploymentException;

/** Enable/disable bean verification upon deployment.
  *
 * @param  verify  true to enable the verifier; false to disable
 */
public void setVerifyDeployments(boolean verify);
```

LISTING 2.13   Continued

```
/** Returns the state of the verifier (enabled/disabled)
 *
 * @return   true if verifier is enabled; false otherwise
 */
public boolean getVerifyDeployments();


/** Enable/disable bean verifier verbose mode.
 *
 * @param     verbose true to enable verbose mode; false to disable
 */
public void setVerifierVerbose(boolean verbose);
/** Returns the state of the verifier (verbose/non-verbose mode).
 *
 * @return   true if the verbose mode is enabled; false otherwise
 */
public boolean getVerifierVerbose();


/** Enables/disables the metrics interceptor for containers.
 *
 * @param enable   true to enable; false to disable
 */
public void setMetricsEnabled(boolean enable);
/** Checks if this container factory initializes the
 *   metrics interceptor.
 *
 * @return   true if metrics are enabled; false otherwise
 */
public boolean isMetricsEnabled();


   /** Is the aplication with this url deployed
    *
    * @param    url
    * @exception   MalformedURLException
    */
public boolean isDeployed(String url)
   throws MalformedURLException;


/** Enable/disable the JMS monitoring of the bean cache.
 */
```

LISTING 2.13   Continued

```
public void setBeanCacheJMSMonitoringEnabled(boolean enable);

/** Get the flag indicating that ejb-jar.dtd, jboss.dtd &
  jboss-web.dtd conforming documents should be validated
  against the DTD.
  */
public boolean getValidateDTDs();
/** Set the flag indicating that ejb-jar.dtd, jboss.dtd &
  jboss-web.dtd conforming documents should be validated
  against the DTD.
  */
public void setValidateDTDs(boolean validate);
}
```

The factory contains two central methods: `deploy` and `undeploy`. The deploy method takes a URL, which either points to an EJB-jar, or to a directory whose structure is the same as a valid EJB-jar (which is convenient for development purposes). Once a deployment has been made, it can be undeployed by calling `undeploy` on the same URL. A call to `deploy` with an already deployed URL will cause an `undeploy`, followed by deployment of the URL, such as a re-deploy. JBoss has support for full re-deployment of both implementation and interface classes, and will reload any changed classes. This will allow you to develop and update EJBs without ever stopping a running server.

Container Configuration Information   JBoss externalizes most, if not all, of the setup of the EJB containers through an XML file that conforms to the jboss_2_4 DTD.

The section of the jboss_2_4 DTD that relates to container configuration information is shown in Figure 2.5.

The `container-configurations` element and its subelements specify container configuration settings for a type of container as given by the `container-name` element. Each configuration specifies information such as container invoker type, the container interceptor makeup, instance caches/pools and their sizes, persistence manager, security, and so on. Because this is a large amount of information that requires a detailed understanding of the JBoss container architecture, JBoss ships with a standard configuration for the four types of EJBs. This configuration file is called `standardjboss.xml` and it is located in the configuration file set directories of any JBoss distribution. Listing 2.14 gives a sample of the content of `standardjboss.xml` configuration.

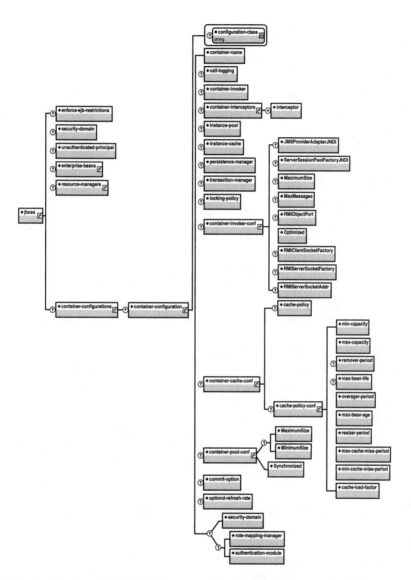

FIGURE 2.5   The jboss_2_4 DTD elements related to container configuration.

LISTING 2.14   The most common container-configuration elements in the default distribution standardjboss.xml file

```
<?xml version = "1.0" encoding = "UTF-8"?>
<!DOCTYPE jboss PUBLIC
       "-//JBoss//DTD JBOSS 2.4//EN"
       "http://www.jboss.org/j2ee/dtd/jboss_2_4.dtd">
<jboss>
 <enforce-ejb-restrictions>false</enforce-ejb-restrictions>
 <container-configurations>
  <container-configuration>
   <container-name>Standard CMP EntityBean</container-name>
   <call-logging>false</call-logging>
   <container-invoker>org.jboss.ejb.plugins.jrmp.server.JRMPContainerInvoker</con-
tainer-invoker>
   <container-interceptors>
    <interceptor>org.jboss.ejb.plugins.LogInterceptor</interceptor>
    <interceptor>org.jboss.ejb.plugins.SecurityInterceptor</interceptor>
    <interceptor>org.jboss.ejb.plugins.TxInterceptorCMT</interceptor>
    <interceptor metricsEnabled = "true">org.jboss.ejb.plugins.MetricsIntercep-
tor</interceptor>
    <interceptor>org.jboss.ejb.plugins.EntityLockInterceptor</interceptor>
    <interceptor>org.jboss.ejb.plugins.EntityInstanceInterceptor</interceptor>
    <interceptor>org.jboss.ejb.plugins.EntitySynchronizationInterceptor</intercep-
tor>
   </container-interceptors>
   <instance-pool>org.jboss.ejb.plugins.EntityInstancePool</instance-pool>
   <instance-cache>org.jboss.ejb.plugins.EntityInstanceCache</instance-cache>
   <persistence-manager>org.jboss.ejb.plugins.jaws.JAWSPersistenceManager</persis-
tence-manager>
   <transaction-manager>org.jboss.tm.TxManager</transaction-manager>
   <locking-policy>org.jboss.ejb.plugins.lock.QueuedPessimisticEJBLock</locking-
policy>
   <container-invoker-conf>
    <RMIObjectPort>4444</RMIObjectPort>
    <Optimized>True</Optimized>
   </container-invoker-conf>
   <container-cache-conf>
    <cache-policy>org.jboss.ejb.plugins.LRUEnterpriseContextCachePolicy</cache-pol-
icy>
    <cache-policy-conf>
     <min-capacity>50</min-capacity>
     <max-capacity>1000</max-capacity>
```

LISTING 2.14 Continued

```
      <overager-period>300</overager-period>
      <max-bean-age>600</max-bean-age>
      <resizer-period>400</resizer-period>
      <max-cache-miss-period>60</max-cache-miss-period>
      <min-cache-miss-period>1</min-cache-miss-period>
      <cache-load-factor>0.75</cache-load-factor>
     </cache-policy-conf>
    </container-cache-conf>
    <container-pool-conf>
     <MaximumSize>100</MaximumSize>
     <MinimumSize>10</MinimumSize>
    </container-pool-conf>
    <commit-option>A</commit-option>
   </container-configuration>
  </container-configurations>
</jboss>
```

Verifying EJB Deployments   Another role that the ContainerFactory performs is
the verification of EJB deployments. An option shown in the description of the
ContainerFactoryMBean was a flag to validate EJB deployments. When this option is
set to true, any bean in an EJB deployment unit is checked for EJB specification
compliance. This entails validating that the EJB deployment unit contains the
required home and remote interfaces and that the objects appearing in these interfaces are of the proper types. This is a useful behavior that is enabled by default
because there are a number of steps that an EJB developer and deployer must
perform correctly to construct a proper EJB jar. It's easy to make a mistake. The verification stage attempts to catch any errors and fail the deployment with an error that
indicates what needs to be corrected.

NOTE

Probably the most problematic aspect of writing EJBs concerns a disconnection between the
bean implementation and its remote and home interfaces, as well as its deployment descriptor configuration. It is easy to have these separate elements get out of synch. One tool that
helps eliminate this problem is XDoclet, an extension of the standard JavaDoc Doclet engine.
It works off of custom JavaDoc tags in the EJB bean implementation class and creates the
remote and home interfaces as well as the deployment descriptors. See the XDoclet home
page at http://sourceforge.net/projects/xdoclet for additional details.

Deploying EJBs into Containers   The most important roles performed by the
ContainerFactory is the creation of an EJB container and the deployment of the EJB

into the container. The deployment phase consists of iterating over EJBs in an EJB jar, and extracting the bean classes and their metadata as described by the ejb-jar.xml and jboss.xml deployment descriptors. For each EJB in the EJB jar, the following steps are performed:

1. Create subclass of orb.jboss.ejb.Container depending on the type of the EJB, Stateless, Stateful, BMP Entity, CMP Entity, or MessageDriven. The container is assigned a unique ClassLoader from which it can load classes and resources. The uniqueness of the ClassLoader is also used to isolate the standard "java:comp" JNDI namespace from other J2EE components.

2. Set all container configurable attributes from a merge of the jboss.xml and standardjboss.xml descriptors.

3. Create and add the container interceptors as configured for the container.

4. Associate the container with an application object. This application object represents a J2EE enterprise application, and may contain multiple EJBs and Web contexts.

If all EJBs are successfully deployed, the application is started which in turn starts all containers and makes the EJBs available to clients. If any EJB fails to deploy, a deployment exception is thrown and the deployment module is failed.

Inside the EJB org.jboss.ejb.Container **Class**
The JBoss EJB container uses a framework pattern that allows you to change implementations of various aspects of the container behavior. The container itself does not perform any significant work, other than connecting the various behavioral components together. Implementations of the behavioral components are referred to as plug-ins, because you can plug in a new implementation by changing a container configuration. Examples of plug-in behavior you may want to change include persistence management, object pooling, object caching, and container invokers. There are four subclasses of the org.jboss.ejb.Container class, each one implementing a particular bean type:

- org.jboss.ejb.EntityContainer handles javax.ejb.EntityBean types

- org.jboss.ejb.StatelessSessionContainer handles Stateless javax.ejb.SessionBean types

- org.jboss.ejb.StatefulSessionContainer handles Stateful javax.ejb.SessionBean types

- org.jboss.ejb.MessageDrivenContainer handles javax.ejb.MessageDrivenBean types

Container Plug-in Framework   The interfaces that make up the container plug-in points include the following:

- org.jboss.ejb.ContainerPlugin

- org.jboss.ejb.ContainerInvoker

- org.jboss.ejb.Interceptor

- org.jboss.ejb.InstancePool

- org.jboss.ejb.InstanceCache

- org.jboss.ejb.EntityPersistanceManager

- org.jboss.ejb.EntityPersistanceStore

- org.jboss.ejb.StatefulSessionPersistenceManager

The container's main responsibility is to manage its plug-ins. This means ensuring that the plug-ins have all the information they need to implement their functionality.

org.jboss.ejb.ContainerPlugin   The ContainerPlugin interface is the parent interface of all container plug-in interfaces. It provides a callback that allows a container to provide each of its plug-ins a pointer to the container the plug-in is working on behalf of. The ContainerPlugin interface is given in Listing 2.15.

LISTING 2.15   The org.jboss.ejb.ContainerPlugin interface

```
public interface ContainerPlugin extends org.jboss.util.Service
{
    /** This callback is set by the container so the plug-in
     * can access its container
     *
     * @param con  the container that owns the plug-in
     */
    public void setContainer(Container con);
}
```

org.jboss.ejb.Interceptor   The Interceptor interface enables you to build a chain of method interceptors through which each EJB method invocation must pass. The Interceptor interface is given in Listing 2.16.

LISTING 2.16   The org.jboss.ejb.Interceptor interface

```
public interface Interceptor extends ContainerPlugin
{
    public void setNext(Interceptor interceptor);
```

LISTING 2.16   Continued

```
    public Interceptor getNext();
    public Object invokeHome(MethodInvocation mi) throws Exception;
    public Object invoke(MethodInvocation mi) throws Exception;
}
```

All interceptors defined in the container configuration are created and added to the container interceptor chain by the `ContainerFactory`. The last interceptor is not added by the container factory, but rather by the container itself because this is the interceptor that interacts with the EJB bean implementation.

The order of the interceptors in the chain is important. The idea behind ordering is that interceptors that are not tied to a particular `EnterpriseContext` instance are positioned before interceptors that interact with caches and pools.

Implementers of the Interceptor interface form a linked -list-like structure through which the `MethodInvocation` object is passed. The first interceptor in the chain is invoked when `ContainerInvoker` passes a `MethodInvocation` to the container. The last interceptor invokes the business method on the bean. There are usually on the order of five interceptors in a chain, depending on the bean type and container configuration. Interceptor semantic complexity ranges from simple to complex. An example of a simple interceptor would be `LoggingInterceptor`, while a complex example is `EntitySynchronizationInterceptor`.

One of the main advantages of an Interceptor pattern is flexibility in the arrangement of interceptors. Another advantage is the clear functional distinction between different interceptors. For example, logic for transaction and security is cleanly separated between the `TXInterceptor` and `SecurityInterceptor`, respectively.

If any of the interceptors fail, the call is terminated at that point. This is a fail-quickly type of semantic. For example, if a secured EJB is accessed without proper permissions, the call will fail as the `SecurityInterceptor` before any transactions are started or instances caches are updated.

`org.jboss.ejb.InstancePool`   An `InstancePool` is used to manage the EJB instances that are not associated with any identity. The pools actually manage subclasses of the `org.jboss.ejb.EnterpriseContext` objects that aggregate unassociated bean instances and related data. Listing 2.17 gives the `InstancePool` interface.

LISTING 2.17   The `org.jboss.ejb.InstancePool` interface

```
public interface InstancePool extends ContainerPlugin
{
    /** Get an instance without identity. Can be used
     *   by finders and create-methods, or stateless beans
```

LISTING 2.17   Continued

```
     *
     * @return      Context /w instance
     * @exception   RemoteException
     */
    public EnterpriseContext get() throws Exception;

    /** Return an anonymous instance after invocation.
     *
     * @param   ctx
     */
    public void free(EnterpriseContext ctx);

    /** Discard an anonymous instance after invocation.
     * This is called if the instance should not be reused,
     * perhaps due to some exception being thrown from it.
     *
     * @param   ctx
     */
    public void discard(EnterpriseContext ctx);
}
```

Depending on the configuration, a container may choose to have a certain size of the pool contain recycled instances, or it may choose to instantiate and initialize an instance on demand.

The pool is used by the InstanceCache implementation to acquire free instances for activation, and it is used by interceptors to acquire instances to be used for Home interface methods (create and finder calls).

org.jboss.ebj.InstanceCache   The container InstanceCache implementation handles all EJB-instances that are in an active state, meaning bean instances that have an identity attached to them. Only entity and stateful session beans are cached, as these are the only bean types that have state between method invocations. The cache key of an entity bean is the bean primary key. The cache key for a stateful session bean is the session id. Listing 2.18 gives the InstanceCache interface.

LISTING 2.18   The org.jboss.ejb.InstanceCache interface

```
public interface InstanceCache extends ContainerPlugin
{
    /**
     *    Gets a bean instance from this cache given the identity.
```

LISTING 2.18 Continued

```
 *    This method may involve activation if the instance is not
 *     in the cache.
 *  Implementation should have O(1) complexity.
 *    This method is never called for stateless session beans.
 *
 * @param id the primary key of the bean
 * @return the EnterpriseContext related to the given id
 * @exception RemoteException in case of illegal calls
 * (concurrent / reentrant), NoSuchObjectException if
 * the bean cannot be found.
 * @see #release
 */
public EnterpriseContext get(Object id)
  throws RemoteException, NoSuchObjectException;

/**
 *    Inserts an active bean instance after creation or activation.
 * Implementation should guarantee proper locking and O(1) complexity.
 *
 * @param ctx the EnterpriseContext to insert in the cache
 * @see #remove
 */
public void insert(EnterpriseContext ctx);

/**
 *    Releases the given bean instance from this cache.
 * This method may passivate the bean to get it out of the cache.
 * Implementation should return almost immediately leaving the
 * passivation to be executed by another thread.
 *
 * @param ctx the EnterpriseContext to release
 * @see #get
 */
public void release(EnterpriseContext ctx);

/** Removes a bean instance from this cache given the identity.
 * Implementation should have O(1) complexity and guarantee
 * proper locking.
 *
 * @param id the primary key of the bean
 * @see #insert
```

LISTING 2.18   Continued

```
*/
public void remove(Object id);

/** Checks whether an instance corresponding to a particular
 * id is active
 *
 * @param id the primary key of the bean
 * @see #insert
 */
public boolean isActive(Object id);


}
```

In addition to managing the list of active instances, the `InstanceCache` is also responsible for activating and passivating instances. If an instance with a given identity is requested, and it is not currently active, the `InstanceCache` must use the `InstancePool` to acquire a free instance, followed by the persistence manager to activate the instance. Similarly, if the InstanceCache decides to passivate an active instance, it must call the persistence manager to passivate it and release the instance to the `InstancePool`.

`org.jboss.ejb.EntityPersistenceManager`   The `EntityPersistenceManager` is responsible for the persistence of `EntityBeans`. This includes the following:

- Creating an EJB instance in a storage

- Loading the state of a given primary key into an EJB instance

- Storing the state of a given EJB instance

- Removing an EJB instance from storage

- Activating the state of an EJB instance

- Passivating the state of an EJB instance

Listing 2.19 gives the `EntityPersistenceManager` interface.

LISTING 2.19   The org.jboss.ejb.EntityPersistenceManager interface

```
public interface EntityPersistenceManager extends ContainerPlugin
{
    /** This method is called whenever an entity is to be created.
        The persistence manager is responsible for calling the
```

LISTING 2.19   Continued

```
        ejbCreate methods on the instance and to handle the results
        properly with respect to the persistent store.
   * @param m  the create method in the home interface that was called
   * @param args  any create parameters
   * @param instance  the instance being used for this create call
   */
  public void createEntity(Method m, Object[] args,
     EntityEnterpriseContext instance) throws Exception;


   /** This method is called when single entities are to be
       found. The persistence manager must find out whether the
       wanted instance is available in the persistence store, and
       if so it shall use the ContainerInvoker plug-in to create
       an EJBObject to the instance, which is to be returned as
       result.

    * @param   finderMethod  the find method in the home interface
        that was called
    * @param   args  any finder parameters
    * @param   instance  the instance to use for the finder call
    * @return  an EJBObject representing the found entity
    */
   public Object findEntity(Method finderMethod, Object[] args,
        EntityEnterpriseContext instance) throws Exception;


   /** This method is called when collections of entities are to
   be found. The persistence manager must find out whether the
   wanted instances are available in the persistence store, and
   if so it shall use the ContainerInvoker plug-in to create EJBObjects
   to the instances, which are to be returned as result.

   * @param   finderMethod  the find method in the home interface
       that was called
   * @param   args  any finder parameters
   * @param   instance  the instance to use for the finder call
   * @return  an EJBObject collection representing the found entities
   */
   public Collection findEntities(Method finderMethod, Object[] args,
        EntityEnterpriseContext instance)  throws Exception;


   /** This method is called when an entity shall be activated.
```

LISTING 2.19   Continued

```
The persistence manager must call the ejbActivate method on
the instance.

 * @param    instance  the instance to use for the activation
 * @exception   RemoteException  thrown if some system exception occurs
 */
public void activateEntity(EntityEnterpriseContext instance)
   throws RemoteException;

/** This method is called whenever an entity shall be load
from the underlying storage. The persistence manager must
load the state from the underlying storage and then call
ejbLoad on the supplied instance.

 * @param   instance  the instance to synchronize
 * @exception   RemoteException  thrown if some system exception occurs
 */
public void loadEntity(EntityEnterpriseContext instance)
   throws RemoteException;

/** This method is called whenever an entity shall be
stored to the underlying storage. The persistence manager
must call ejbStore on the supplied instance and then
store the state to the underlying storage.

 * @param    instance  the instance to synchronize
 * @exception   RemoteException  thrown if some system exception occurs
 */
public void storeEntity(EntityEnterpriseContext instance)
   throws RemoteException;

/** This method is called when an entity shall be
passivated. The persistence manager must call the ejbPassivate
method on the instance.

 * @param    instance  the instance to passivate
 * @exception   RemoteException  thrown if some system exception occurs
 */
public void passivateEntity(EntityEnterpriseContext instance)
   throws RemoteException;
```

LISTING 2.19   Continued

```
    /** This method is called when an entity shall be removed
    from the underlying storage. The persistence manager
    must call ejbRemove on the instance and then remove its
    state from the underlying storage.

    * @param     instance  the instance to remove
    * @exception    RemoteException  thrown if some system exception occurs
    * @exception    RemoveException  thrown if the instance could not be removed
    */
    public void removeEntity(EntityEnterpriseContext instance)
        throws RemoteException, RemoveException;
}
```

As per the EJB 1.1 specification, JBoss supports two entity bean persistence seman-tics: Container Managed Persistence (CMP) and Bean Managed Persistence (BMP). The CMP implementation uses an implementation of the org.jboss.ejb.EntityPersistanceStore interface. By default this is the org.jboss.ejb.plugins.jaws.JAWSPersistenceManager, (JAWS-Just Another Web Store). JAWS performs basic O/R functionality against a JDBC-store. More details about JAWS can be found in the Chapter 5, "JBossCMP." Listing 2.20 gives the EntityPersistanceStore interface.

LISTING 2.20   The org.jboss.ejb.EntityPersistanceStore interface

```
public interface EntityPersistenceStore extends ContainerPlugin
{
    /** This method is called whenever an entity is to be
    created. The persistence manager is responsible for handling
    the results properly with respect to the persistent store.

    The return is the primary key in case of CMP PM
    Null in case of BMP PM (but no store should exist)

    * @param     m  the create method in the home interface that was called
    * @param     args  any create parameters
    * @param     instance  the instance being used for this create call
    * @return    Object, the primary key computed by CMP PM or null for BMP
    * @exception    Exception
    */
    public Object createEntity(Method m, Object[] args,
        EntityEnterpriseContext instance) throws Exception;
```

LISTING 2.20   Continued

```
/** This method is called when single entities are to be
found. The persistence manager must find out whether the
wanted instance is available in the persistence store, if so
it returns the primary key of the object.

 * @param   finderMethod  the find method in the home interface that was called
 * @param   args  any finder parameters
 * @param   instance  the instance to use for the finder call
 * @return     a primary key representing the found entity
 * @exception   RemoteException  thrown if some system exception occurs
 * @exception   FinderException  thrown if some heuristic problem occurs
 */
public Object findEntity(Method finderMethod, Object[] args,
    EntityEnterpriseContext instance) throws Exception;

/** This method is called when collections of entities are
to be found. The persistence manager must find out whether
the wanted instances are available in the persistence store,
and if so it must return a collection of primaryKeys.

 * @param   finderMethod  the find method in the home interface that was called
 * @param   args  any finder parameters
 * @param   instance  the instance to use for the finder call
 * @return     an primary key collection representing the found entities
 * @exception   RemoteException  thrown if some system exception occurs
 * @exception   FinderException  thrown if some heuristic problem occurs
 */
public FinderResults findEntities(Method finderMethod,
    Object[] args, EntityEnterpriseContext instance)
    throws Exception;

/** This method is called when an entity shall be activated.

With the PersistenceManager factorization most EJB calls
should not exists. However this calls permits you to introduce
optimizations in the persistence store. Particularly the
context has a "PersistenceContext" that a PersistenceStore
can use (JAWS does for smart updates) and this is as good a
callback as any other to set it up.
```

LISTING 2.20   Continued

```
     * @param   instance  the instance to use for the activation
     * @exception RemoteException  thrown if some system
        exception occurs
     */
    public void activateEntity(EntityEnterpriseContext instance)
       throws RemoteException;

    /** This method is called whenever an entity shall be loaded
    from the underlying storage. The persistence manager must load
    the state from the underlying storage and then call ejbLoad
    on the supplied instance.

     * @param   instance  the instance to synchronize
     * @exception   RemoteException  thrown if some system
        exception occurs
     */
    public void loadEntity(EntityEnterpriseContext instance)
       throws RemoteException;

    /** This method is called whenever a set of entities should
    be preloaded from the underlying storage. The persistence store
    is allowed to make this a null operation.

     * @param instances the EntityEnterpriseContexts for the
        entities that must be loaded
     * @param keys a PagableKeyCollection previously returned
        from findEntities.
     */
    public void loadEntities(FinderResults keys)
       throws RemoteException;

    /** This method is called whenever an entity shall be
    stored to the underlying storage. The persistence manager
    must call ejbStore on the supplied instance and then
    store the state to the underlying storage.

     * @param   instance  the instance to synchronize
     * @exception   RemoteException  thrown if some system
        exception occurs
     */
    public void storeEntity(EntityEnterpriseContext instance)
       throws RemoteException;
```

LISTING 2.20   Continued

```
/** This method is called when an entity shall be passivate.
The persistence manager must call the ejbPassivate method
on the instance.

See the activate discussion for the reason for exposing
EJB callback calls to the store.

 * @param    instance  the instance to passivate
 * @exception   RemoteException  thrown if some system
    exception occurs
 */
public void passivateEntity(EntityEnterpriseContext instance)
   throws RemoteException;

/** This method is called when an entity shall be removed
from the underlying storage. The persistence manager must
call ejbRemove on the instance and then remove its state
from the underlying storage.

 * @param    instance  the instance to remove
 * @exception  RemoteException  thrown if some system
    exception occurs
 * @exception  RemoveException  thrown if the instance
    could not be removed
 */
public void removeEntity(EntityEnterpriseContext instance)
   throws RemoteException, RemoveException;
}
```

The default BMP implementation of the `EntityPersistenceManager` interface is `org.jboss.ejb.plugins.BMPPersistenceManager`. The BMP persistence manager is fairly simple because all persistence logic is in the entity bean itself. The only duty of the persistence manager is to perform container callbacks.

`org.jboss.ejb.StatefulSessionPersistenceManager`   The `StatefulSessionPersistenceManager` is responsible for the persistence of stateful SessionBeans. This includes the following:

- Creating stateful sessions in a storage

- Activating stateful sessions from a storage

- Passivating stateful sessions to a storage

- Removing stateful sessions from a storage

Listing 2.21 gives the StatefulSessionPersistenceManager interface.

LISTING 2.21   The org.jboss.ejb.StatefulSessionPersistenceManager interface

```
public interface StatefulSessionPersistenceManager extends ContainerPlugin
{
    public void createSession(Method m, Object[] args,
        StatefulSessionEnterpriseContext ctx)
        throws Exception;

    public void activateSession(StatefulSessionEnterpriseContext ctx)
        throws RemoteException;

    public void passivateSession(StatefulSessionEnterpriseContext ctx)
        throws RemoteException;

    public void removeSession(StatefulSessionEnterpriseContext ctx)
        throws RemoteException, RemoveException;

    public void removePassivated(Object key);
}
```

The default implementation of the StatefulSessionPersistenceManager interface is
org.jboss.ejb.plugins.StatefulSessionFilePersistenceManager. As its name
implies, StatefulSessionFilePersistenceManager utilizes the file system to persist
stateful SessionBeans. More specifically, the persistence manager serializes beans in a
flat file whose name is composed of the bean name and session id with a .ser extension. The persistence manager restores a bean's state during activation and respectively stores its state during passivation from the bean's .ser file.

Tracing an EJB Call Through the Container   The preceding sections discussed
specific pieces involved in passing an EJB call invocation to the EJB container. Now it
is time to put all the pieces together to see how a complete method invocation is
passed through the container to the EJB implementation. In particular, look at the
handling of method calls on a CMP entity bean.

The entry point into the container is when the ContainerInvoker calls invoke when
passing in the MethodInvocation object. The container retrieves the first interceptor
in its interceptor chain and calls invoke on the interceptor, passing the
MethodInvocation object. Recall from the standardjboss.xml descriptor that the

container invokers configured for a CMP entity bean, and the ordering of the interceptors is as follows:

1. org.jboss.ejb.plugins.LogInterceptor

2. org.jboss.ejb.plugins.SecurityInterceptor

3. org.jboss.ejb.plugins.TxInterceptorCMT

4. org.jboss.ejb.plugins.EntityLockInterceptor

5. org.jboss.ejb.plugins.EntityInstanceInterceptor

6. org.jboss.ejb.plugins.EntitySynchronizationInterceptor

7. The org.jboss.ejb.EntityContainer.ContainerInterceptor added by the EntityContainer itself.

The start of the call is first optionally logged by the LogInterceptor, depending on the log4j logging priority threshold. The information logged includes the method name and parameters.

The `SecurityInterceptor` then checks to see if the bean has been configured with a security domain. If it has, the caller is first authenticated and then authorized against the configured security domain manager and the ejb-jar.xml method permissions for the bean. The identity of the caller and the caller's credentials are obtained from the `MethodInvocation` object. If the caller fails the security tests, a `java.security.SecurityException` is thrown, and the call is aborted. If there is no security domain specified, the call is simply passed to the next interceptor.

The `TxInterceptorCMT` then decides how to manage transactions for this call. The information needed for this decision comes from the method transaction attributes defined in the `ejb-jar.xml` descriptor. The transaction information is associated with the `MethodInvocation` object if appropriate.

This is followed by the `EntityLockInterceptor`, whose role is to schedule the current thread. Entity beans are single-threaded by default, and so only one thread may be executing inside of the bean implementation class at any given moment. The `EntityLockInterceptor` synchronizes all calling threads.

Until this point in the interceptor chain no bean instance has been associated with the `MethodInvocation`. The `EntityInstanceInterceptor` role is to acquire a context representing the target object from the cache. The interceptor calls the `InstanceCache` with the primary key associated with the `MethodInvocation` to do this. Because the cache does not yet have an instance associated with the given primary key, it first gets a free instance from the instance pool, which it associates with the primary key. It then calls the persistence manager that will activate the instance.

After instance acquisition, the EntitySynchronizationInterceptor manages how this instance is synchronized with the database. The role of this interceptor is to synchronize the state of the cache with the underlying storage. It does this with the ejbLoad and ejbStore semantics of the EJB specification. This is triggered by transaction demarcation in the presence of a transaction. It registers a callback with the underlying transaction monitor through the JTA interfaces. If there is no transaction, the policy is to store state upon returning from invocation. The synchronization polices A, B, C of the specification are taken care of by this interceptor.

Lastly, the container-provided interceptor is invoked. The container always adds itself as the last interceptor at the end of the interceptor chain so that it may delegate business methods to the EJB instance. The instance performs some work, and returns a result. The interceptor chain is now unwound as each interceptor returns from the invoke-operation.

The EntitySynchronizationInterceptor interceptor chooses to store the current state into the database and hence calls storeEntity on the persistence manager, if appropriate depending on the commit and transaction options. The javax.transaction.Synchronization instance created by this interceptor will handle the completion of the transaction.

The EntityInstanceInterceptor then returns the bean instance to the cache.

TxInterceptorCMT interceptor handles the method return according to the transaction settings, possibly committing or rolling back the current transaction.

The SecurityInterceptor never does anything on the call return path, but the LogInterceptor logs the call completion, depending on the log4j logging priority threshold.

Finally, the container invoker returns the result to the client. As you can see, all implementation decisions are performed by various interceptors and plug-ins associated with the container. These decisions are loosely coupled, which allows the deployer of the EJB-application to tweak the behavior of the container to a great degree. This also allows for a number of independent plug-ins to co-exist, each one allowing for slightly, or radically, different behavior.

An example customization would be a persistence manager that used XML files as the backing store instead of a relational database. Another example would security interceptor that used access control lists from a database instead of the ejb-jar.xml descriptor to perform security checks, or multiple security checks could be performed by configuring the container to have multiple security interceptors of different types. All of these options are available by the componentized nature of the container architecture.

Summary

In this chapter, you were introduced to JMX and its use as a component bus by the JBoss server. You were also introduced to the JBoss MBean services notion, which is an extension of the basic JMX MBean concept that adds a set of life cycle operations. An example of how to use MBean services to integrate your custom services was presented. Also presented were the JBoss MBeans that are part of the standard distribution. A summary of each MBean was given along with a description of the MBean's configurable attributes.

You were also introduced to the EJB container architecture. The customizable nature of the container architecture due to its use of plug-in interfaces was emphasized. To demonstrate how the various EJB container components interact, you were walked through the container components as they would be encountered by an EJB method invocation.

In the next chapter, you cover the naming service implementation used by JBoss, the JBossNS component. This includes the role of naming services in J2EE as well as the JBossNS architecture.

ile:
[mkdir] Created dir: /tmp/2.4.4/
[javac] Compiling 154 source file

install:
[copy] Copying 1 file to /tmp/2
[copy] Copying 1 file to /tmp/2

3

JBossNS—The JBoss JNDI Naming Service

This chapter discusses the JBoss JNDI-based naming service as well as the role of JNDI in JBoss and J2EE. An introduction to the basic JNDI API and common usage conventions is covered, and the JBoss specific configuration of J2EE component naming environments defined by the standard deployment descriptors is also addressed. The configuration and architecture of the JBoss naming service component, JBossNS, is examined, as well.

The JBoss naming service is an implementation of the Java Naming and Directory Interface (JNDI). JNDI plays a key role in J2EE because it provides a naming service that allows a user to map a name onto an object. This is a fundamental need in any programming environment because developers and administrators want to be able to refer to objects and services by recognizable names. A good example of a pervasive naming service is the Internet Domain Name System (DNS). The DNS service allows you to refer to hosts using logical names, rather than their numeric Internet addresses. JNDI serves a similar role in J2EE by enabling developers and administrators to create name-to-object bindings for use in J2EE components.

An Overview of JNDI

JNDI is a standard Java API that is bundled with JDK1.3 and higher. JNDI provides a common interface to a variety of existing naming services: DNS, LDAP, Active Directory, RMI registry, COS registry, NIS, and file systems. The JNDI API is divided logically into a client API that is used to access naming services, and a service provider interface (SPI) that allows the user to create JNDI implementations for naming services.

The SPI layer is an abstraction that naming service providers must implement to enable the core JNDI classes to expose the naming service using the common JNDI client interface. An implementation of JNDI for a naming service is referred to as a *JNDI provider*. JBossNS is an example JNDI implementation, based on the SPI classes. Note that the JNDI SPI is not needed by J2EE component developers.

This introduction to JNDI covers the basic concepts and JNDI client API usage.

NOTE

For a thorough introduction and tutorial on JNDI, which covers both the client and service provider APIs, see the Sun tutorial at `http://java.sun.com/products/jndi/tutorial/`.

The JNDI API

The main JNDI API package is the `javax.naming` package. It contains five interfaces, 10 classes, and several exceptions. There is one key class, `InitialContext`, and two key interfaces, `Context` and `Name`.

Names

The notion of a name is of fundamental importance in JNDI. The naming system determines the syntax that the name must follow. The syntax of the naming system allows the user to parse string representations of names into its components. A name is used with a naming system to locate objects. In the simplest sense, a naming system is a collection of objects with unique names. To locate an object in a naming system, you provide a name to the naming system, and the naming system returns the object store under the name.

As an example, consider the Unix file system's naming convention. Each file is named from its path relative to the root of the file system, with each component in the path separated by the forward slash character ("/"). The file's path is ordered from left to right. The pathname, `/usr/jboss/readme.txt`, for example, names a file `readme.txt` in the directory jboss, under the directory usr, located in the root of the file system. JBossNS uses a Unix-style namespace as its naming convention.

The `javax.naming.Name` interface represents a generic name as an ordered sequence of components. It can be a composite name (one that spans multiple namespaces), or a compound name (one that is used within a single hierarchical naming system). The components of a name are numbered. The indexes of a name with N components range from 0 up to, but not including, N. The most significant component is at index 0. An empty name has no components.

A composite name is a sequence of component names tha span multiple name-spaces. An example of a composite name would be the hostname+file commonly used with Unix commands like `scp`. For example, this command copies `localfile.txt` to the file `remotefile.txt` in the `tmp` directory on host `ahost.someorg.org`:

```
scp localfile.txt ahost.someorg.org:/tmp/remotefile.txt
```

The `ahost.someorg.org:/tmp/remotefile.txt` is a composite name that spans the DNS and Unix file system namespaces. The components of the composite name are `ahost.someorg.org` and `/tmp/remotefile.txt`. A component is a string name from the namespace of a naming system. If the component comes from a hierarchical namespace, that component can be further parsed into its atomic parts by using the `javax.naming.CompoundName` class. The JNDI API provides the `javax.naming.CompositeName` class as the implementation of the Name interface for composite names.

A compound name is derived from a hierarchical namespace. Each component in a compound name is an atomic name, meaning a string that cannot be parsed into smaller components. A file pathname in the Unix file system is an example of a compound name.

Contexts

The `javax.naming.Context` interface is the primary interface for interacting with a naming service. The `Context` interface represents a set of name-to-object bindings. Every context has an associated naming convention that determines how the context parses string names into `javax.naming.Name` instances. To create a name-to-object binding, you invoke the `bind` method of a `Context` and then specify a name and an object as arguments. The object can later be retrieved using its name using the `Context` `lookup` method. A `Context` will typically provide operations for binding a name to an object, unbinding a name, and obtaining a listing of all name-to-object bindings. The object you bind into a `Context` can itself be of type `Context`. The `Context` object that is bound is referred to as a subcontext of the `Context` on which the `bind` method was invoked.

As an example, consider a file directory with a pathname /usr, which is a context in the Unix file system. A file directory named relative to another file directory is a subcontext (commonly referred to as a subdirectory). A file directory with a path-name /usr/jboss names a jboss context that is a subcontext of usr. In another example, a DNS domain, such as org, is a context. A DNS domain named relative to another DNS domain is another example of a subcontext. In the DNS domain jboss.org, the DNS domain jboss is a subcontext of org because DNS names are parsed right to left.

Obtaining a Context Using `InitialContext`

All naming service operations are performed on some implementation of the `Context` interface. Therefore, you need a way to obtain a `Context` for the naming service you are interested in using. The `javax.naming.IntialContext` class implements the `Context` interface, and provides the starting point for interacting with a naming service.

When you create an `InitialContext`, it is initialized with properties from the environment. JNDI determines each property's value by merging the values from the following two sources, in order such as:

- The first occurrence of the property from the constructor's environment parameter and (for appropriate properties) the applet parameters and system properties.

- All `jndi.properties` resource files found on the classpath.

For each property found in both of these two sources, the property's value is determined as follows. If the property is one of the standard JNDI properties that specify a list of JNDI factories, all of the values are concatenated into a single, colon-separated list. For other properties, only the first value found is used. The preferred method of specifying the JNDI environment properties is through a jndi.properties file. The reason is that this allows your code to externalize the JNDI provider specific information, and changing JNDI providers will not require changes to your code; thus it avoids the need to recompile to be able to see the change.

The `Context` implementation used internally by the `InitialContext` class is determined at runtime. The default policy uses the environment property "`java.naming.factory.initial`", which contains the class name of the `javax.naming.spi.InitialContextFactory` implementation. You obtain the name of the `InitialContextFactory` class from the naming service provider you are using.

Listing 3.1 gives a sample jndi.properties file a client application would use to connect to a JBossNS service running on the local host at port 1099. The client application would need to have the jndi.properties file available on the application classpath. These are the properties that the JBossNS JNDI implementation requires. Other JNDI providers will have different properties and values.

LISTING 3.1   Sample JBossNS `jndi.properties` File

```
### JBossNS properties
java.naming.factory.initial=org.jnp.interfaces.NamingContextFactory
java.naming.provider.url=jnp://localhost:1099
java.naming.factory.url.pkgs=org.jboss.naming:org.jnp.interfaces
```

J2EE and JNDI—The Application Component Environment

JNDI is a fundamental aspect of the J2EE specifications. One key usage is the isolation of J2EE component code from the environment in which the code is deployed. Use of the application component's environment allows the application component to be customized without the need to access or change the application component's source code. The application component environment is sometimes referred to as the enterprise naming context (ENC). It is the responsibility of the application component container to make an ENC available to the container components in the form of JNDI Context. The ENC is utilized by the participants involved in the life cycle of a J2EE component in the following ways:

- Application component business logic should be coded to access information from its ENC. The component provider uses the standard deployment descriptor for the component to specify the required ENC entries. The entries are declarations of the information and resources the component requires at runtime.

- The container provides tools that allow a deployer of a component to map the ENC references made by the component developer to the deployment environment entity that satisfies the reference.

- The component deployer utilizes the container tools to ready a component for final deployment.

- The component container uses the deployment package information to build the complete component ENC at runtime.

NOTE

The complete specification regarding the use of JNDI in the J2EE platform can be found in Section 5 of the J2EE 1.3 specification. The J2EE specification is available at `http://java.sun.com/j2ee/download.html`.

An application component instance locates the ENC using the JNDI API. An application component instance creates a `javax.naming.InitialContext` object by using the no argument constructor and then looks up the naming environment under the name `java:comp/env`. The application component's environment entries are stored directly in the ENC, or in its subcontexts. Listing 3.2 illustrates the prototypical lines of code a component uses to access its ENC.

LISTING 3.2   ENC Access Sample Code

```
// Obtain the application component's ENC
Context iniCtx = new InitialContext();
Context compEnv = (Context) iniCtx.lookup("java:comp/env");
```

An application component environment is a local environment that is accessible only by the component when the application server container thread of control is interacting with the application component. This means that an EJB Bean1 cannot access the ENC elements of EJB Bean2, and visa-versa. Similarly, Web application Web1 cannot access the ENC elements of Web application Web2 or Bean1 or Bean2 for that matter. Also, arbitrary client code, whether it is executing inside of the application server VM or externally cannot access a component's java:comp JNDI context. The purpose of the ENC is to provide an isolated, read-only namespace that the application component can rely on regardless of the type of environment in which the component is deployed. The ENC must be isolated from other components because each component defines its own ENC content, and components A and B may define the same name to refer to different objects. For example, EJB Bean1 may define an environment entry java:comp/env/red to refer to the hexadecimal value for the RGB color for red, while Web application Web1 may bind the same name to the deployment environment language locale representation of red.

NOTE

There are three levels of naming scope in the JBossNS implementation—names under java:comp, names under java:, and any other name. As discussed, the java:comp context and its subcontexts are only available to the application component associated with the java:comp context. Subcontexts and object bindings directly under java: are only visible within the JBoss server virtual machine. Any other context or object binding is available to remote clients, provided the context or object supports serialization. You'll see how the isolation of these naming scopes is achieved in the section "The JBossNS Architecture" later in this chapter.

An example of where the restricting a binding to the java: context is useful would be a javax.sql.DataSource connection factory that can only be used inside of the JBoss VM where the associated database pool resides. An example of a globally visible name that should accessible by remote client is an EJB home interface.

ENC Usage Conventions

JNDI is used as the API for externalizing a great deal of information from an application component. The JNDI name that the application component uses to access the information is declared in the standard ejb-jar.xml deployment descriptor for EJB components, and the standard web.xml deployment descriptor for Web components. Several different types of information may be stored in and retrieved from JNDI including the following:

- Environment entries as declared by the env-entry elements

- EJB references as declared by ejb-ref and ejb-local-ref elements

- Resource manager connection factory references as declared by the resource-ref elements

- Resource environment references as declared by the resource-env-ref elements

Each type of deployment descriptor element has a JNDI usage convention with regard to the name of the JNDI context under which the information is bound. Also, in addition to the standard deployment descriptor element, there is a JBoss server specific deployment descriptor element that maps the JNDI name as used by the application component to the deployment environment JNDI name.

The ejb-jar.xml ENC Elements

The EJB 2.0 deployment descriptor describes a collection of EJB components and their environment. Each of the three types of EJB components—session, entity, and message-driven—support the specification of an EJB local naming context. The ejb-jar.xml description is a logical view of the environment that the EJB needs to operate. Because the EJB component developer generally cannot know into what environment the EJB will be deployed, the developer describes the component environment in a deployment environment independent manner using logical names. It is the responsibility of a deployment administrator to link the EJB component logical names to the corresponding deployment environment resources.

Figure 3.1 gives a graphical view of the EJB deployment descriptor DTD without the non-ENC elements. Only the session element is shown fully expanded as the ENC elements for entity and message-driven are identical.

NOTE

The full ejb-jar.xml DTD is available from the Sun Web site at
http://java.sun.com/dtd/ejb-jar_2_0.dtd.

The web.xml ENC Elements

The Servlet 2.3 deployment descriptor describes a collection of Web components and their environment. The ENC for a Web application is declared globally for all servlets and JSP pages in the Web application. Because the Web application developer generally cannot know into what environment the Web application will be deployed, the developer describes the component environment in a deployment environment independent manner using logical names. It is the responsibility of a deployment administrator to link the Web component logical names to the corresponding deployment environment resources.

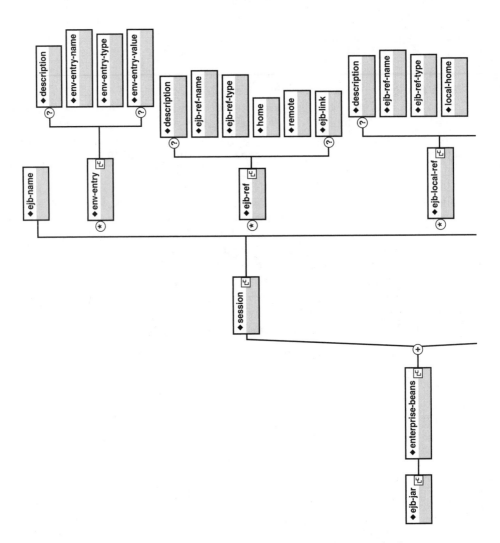

FIGURE 3.1   The ENC elements in the standard EJB 2.0 `ejb-jar.xml` deployment descriptor.

Figure 3.2 gives a graphical view of the Web application deployment descriptor DTD without the non-ENC elements.

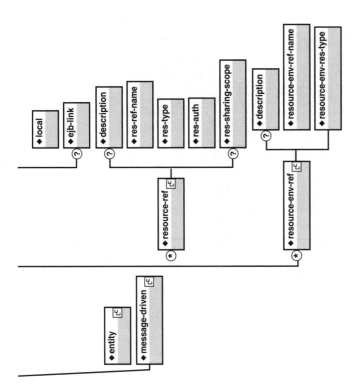

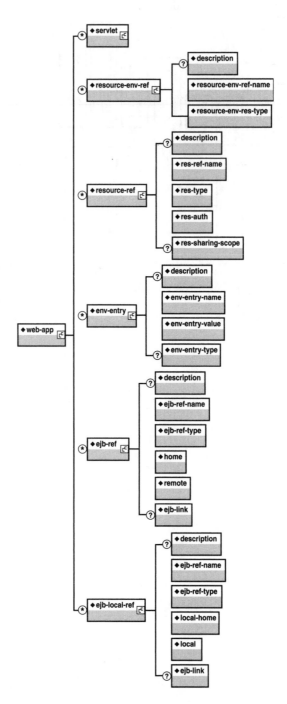

FIGURE 3.2   The ENC elements in the standard servlet 2.3 `web.xml` deployment descriptor.

NOTE

The full web.xml DTD is available from the Sun Web site at http://java.sun.com/dtd/web-app_2_3.dtd.

The jboss.xml ENC Elements

The JBoss EJB deployment descriptor provides the mapping from the EJB component ENC JNDI names to the actual deployed JNDI name. It is the responsibility of the application deployer to map the logical references made by the application component to the corresponding physical resource deployed in a given application server configuration. In JBoss, this is done for the ejb-jar.xml descriptor using the jboss.xml deployment descriptor. Figure 3.3 gives a graphical view of the JBoss EJB deployment descriptor DTD without the non-ENC elements. Only the session element is shown fully expanded as the ENC elements for entity and message-driven are identical.

NOTE

The full jboss.xml DTD is available from the JBoss Web site at http://www.jboss.org/j2ee/dtd/jboss_2_4.dtd.

The jboss-web.xml ENC Elements

The JBoss Web deployment descriptor provides the mapping from the Web application ENC JNDI names to the actual deployed JNDI name. It is the responsibility of the application deployer to map the logical references made by the Web application to the corresponding physical resource deployed in a given application server configuration. In JBoss, this is done for the web.xml descriptor using the jboss-web.xml deployment descriptor. Figure 3.4 gives a graphical view of the JBoss Web deployment descriptor DTD without the non-ENC elements.

NOTE

The full jboss-web.xml DTD is available from the JBoss Web site at http://www.jboss.org/j2ee/dtd/jboss_web.dtd.

Environment Entries

Environment entries are the simplest form of information stored in a component ENC, and are similar to operating system environment variables like those found in Unix or Windows. Environment entries are a name-to-value binding that allows a component to externalize a value and refer to the value using a name.

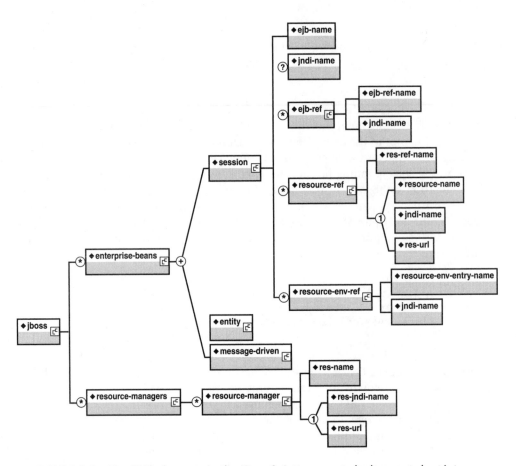

FIGURE 3.3   The ENC elements in the JBoss 2.4 `jboss.xml` deployment descriptor.

An environment entry is declared using an `env-entry` element in the standard deployment descriptors. The `env-entry` element contains the following child elements:

- An optional `description` element that provides a description of the entry

- An `env-entry-name` element giving the name of the entry relative to `java:comp/env`

- An `env-entry-type` element giving the Java type of the entry value that must be one of:

  - `java.lang.Byte`

  - `java.lang.Boolean`

- java.lang.Character

- java.lang.Double

- java.lang.Float

- java.lang.Integer

- java.lang.Long

- java.lang.Short

- java.lang.String

- An env-entry-value element giving the value of entry as a string

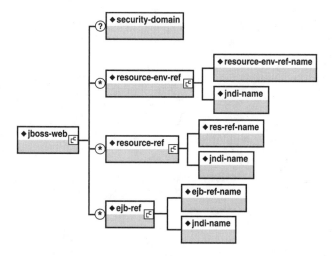

FIGURE 3.4   The ENC elements in the JBoss 2.4 `jboss-web.xml` deployment descriptor.

An example of an env-entry fragment from an `ejb-jar.xml` deployment descriptor
is given in Listing 3.3. There is no JBoss specific deployment descriptor element
because an env-entry is a complete name and value specification. Listing 3.4 shows
a sample code fragment for accessing the maxExemptions and taxRate env-entry
values declared in Listing 3.3.

LISTING 3.3   `ejb-jar.xml` env-entry Fragment

```
...
<session>
 <ejb-name>ASessionBean</ejb-name>
...
```

LISTING 3.3   Continued

```
<env-entry>
  <description>The maximum number of tax exemptions allowed
  </description>
  <env-entry-name>maxExemptions</env-entry-name>
  <env-entry-type>java.lang.Integer</env-entry-type>
  <env-entry-value>15</env-entry-value>
</env-entry>

<env-entry>
  <description>The tax rate
  </description>
  <env-entry-name>taxRate</env-entry-name>
  <env-entry-type>java.lang.Float</env-entry-type>
  <env-entry-value>0.23</env-entry-value>
</env-entry>
</session>
...
```

LISTING 3.4   ENC env-entry Access Code Fragment

```
InitialContext iniCtx = new InitialContext();
Context envCtx = (Context) iniCtx.lookup("java:comp/env");
Integer maxExemptions = (Integer) envCtx.lookup("maxExemptions");
Float taxRate = (Float) envCtx.lookup("taxRate");
```

EJB References

It is common for EJBs and Web components to interact with other EJBs. Because the JNDI name under which an EJB home interface is bound is a deployment time decision, there needs to be a way for a component developer to declare a reference to an EJB that will be linked by the deployer. EJB references satisfy this requirement.

An EJB reference is a link in an application component naming environment that points to a deployed EJB home interface. The name used by the application component is a logical link that isolates the component from the actual name of the EJB home in the deployment environment. The J2EE specification recommends that all references to enterprise beans be organized in the java:comp/env/ejb context of the application component's environment.

An EJB reference is declared using an ejb-ref element in the deployment descriptor. Each ejb-ref element describes the interface requirements that the referencing application component has for the referenced enterprise bean. The `ejb-ref` element contains the following child elements:

- An optional `description` element that provides the purpose of the reference.

- An `ejb-ref-name` element that specifies the name of the reference relative to the `java:comp/env` context. To place the reference under the recommended `java:comp/env/ejb` context, use an `ejb/link-name` form for the `ejb-ref-name` value.

- An `ejb-ref-type` element that specifies the type of the EJB. This must be either Entity or Session.

- A `home` element that gives the fully qualified class name of the EJB home interface.

- A `remote` element that gives the fully qualified class name of the EJB remote interface.

- An optional `ejb-link` element that links the reference to another enterprise bean in the ejb-jar file or in the same J2EE application unit. The `ejb-link` value is the `ejb-name` of the referenced bean. If there are multiple enterprise beans with the same `ejb-name`, the value uses the path name specifying the location of the ejb-jar file that contains the referenced component. The path name is relative to the referencing ejb-jar file. The Application Assembler appends the `ejb-name` of the referenced bean to the path name separated by #. This allows multiple beans with the same name to be uniquely identified.

An EJB reference is scoped to the application component whose declaration contains the `ejb-ref` element. This means that the EJB reference is not accessible from other application components at runtime, and that other application components may define `ejb-ref` elements with the same `ejb-ref-name` without causing a name conflict. Listing 3.5 provides an `ejb-jar.xml` fragment that illustrates the use of the `ejb-ref` element. A code sample that illustrates accessing the `ShoppingCartHome` reference declared in listing 3.5 is given in Listing 3.6.

LISTING 3.5   Example `ejb-jar.xml` `ejb-ref` Descriptor Fragment

```
...
<session>
  <ejb-name>ShoppingCartBean</ejb-name>
  ...
</session>

<session>
```

LISTING 3.5   Continued

```
<ejb-name>ProductBeanUser</ejb-name>
...
<ejb-ref>
  <description>This is a reference to the store products entity
  </description>
  <ejb-ref-name>ejb/ProductHome</ejb-ref-name>
  <ejb-ref-type>Entity</ejb-ref-type>
  <home>org.jboss.store.ejb.ProductHome</home>
  <remote> org.jboss.store.ejb.Product</remote>
</ejb-ref>
</session>

<session>
<ejb-ref>
  <ejb-name>ShoppingCartUser</ejb-name>
  ...
  <ejb-ref-name>ejb/ShoppingCartHome</ejb-ref-name>
  <ejb-ref-type>Session</ejb-ref-type>
  <home>org.jboss.store.ejb.ShoppingCartHome</home>
  <remote> org.jboss.store.ejb.ShoppingCart</remote>
  <ejb-link>ShoppingCartBean</ejb-link>
</ejb-ref>
</session>

<entity>
  <description>The Product entity bean
  </description>
  <ejb-name>ProductBean</ejb-name>
  ...
</entity>
...
```

LISTING 3.6   ENC `ejb-ref` Access Code Fragment

```
InitialContext iniCtx = new InitialContext();
Context ejbCtx = (Context) iniCtx.lookup("java:comp/env/ejb");
ShoppingCartHome home = (ShoppingCartHome) ejbCtx.lookup("ShoppingCartHome");
```

EJB References with `jboss.xml` **and** `jboss-web.xml`
The JBoss server `jboss.xml` EJB deployment descriptor affects EJB references in two ways. First, the `jndi-name` child element of the session and entity elements allows

the user to specify the deployment JNDI name for the EJB home interface. In the absence of a `jboss.xml` specification of the `jndi-name` for an EJB, the home interface is bound under the `ejb-jar.xml` ejb-name value. For example, the session EJB with the `ejb-name` of `ShoppingCartBean` in Listing 3.5 would have its home interface bound under the JNDI name `ShoppingCartBean` in the absence of a `jboss.xml` `jndi-name` specification.

The second use of the `jboss.xml` descriptor with respect to `ejb-refs` is the setting of the destination to which a component's ENC `ejb-ref` refers. The `ejb-link` element cannot be used to refer to EJBs in another enterprise application. If your `ejb-ref` needs to access an external EJB, you can specify the JNDI name of the deployed EJB home using the `jboss.xml` `ejb-ref/jndi-name` element.

The `jboss-web.xml` descriptor is used only to set the destination to which a Web application ENC `ejb-ref` refers. The content model for the JBoss `ejb-ref` is as follows:

- An `ejb-ref-name` element that corresponds to the `ejb-ref-name` element in the `ejb-jar.xml` or `web.xml` standard descriptor

- A `jndi-name` element that specifies the JNDI name of the EJB home interface in the deployment environment

Listing 3.7 provides an example `jboss.xml` descriptor fragment that illustrates the following usage points:

- The `ProductBeanUser` `ejb-ref` link destination is set to the deployment name of `jboss/store/ProductHome`

- The deployment JNDI name of the `ProductBean` is set to `jboss/store/ProductHome`

LISTING 3.7   Example `jboss.xml` `ejb-ref` Fragment

```
...
<session>
<ejb-name>ProductBeanUser</ejb-name>
<ejb-ref>
  <ejb-ref-name>ejb/ProductHome</ejb-ref-name>
  <jndi-name>jboss/store/ProductHome</jndi-name>
</ejb-ref>
</session>

<entity>
  <ejb-name>ProductBean</ejb-name>
  <jndi-name>jboss/store/ProductHome</jndi-name>
```

LISTING 3.7 Continued

```
   ...
</entity>
   ...
```

Resource Manager Connection Factory References

Resource manager connection factory references allow application component code to refer to resource factories using logical names called resource manager connection factory references. Resource manager connection factory references are defined by the resource-ref elements in the standard deployment descriptors. The Deployer binds the resource manager connection factory references to the actual resource manager connection factories that exist in the target operational environment using the jboss.xml and jboss-web.xml descriptors.

Each resource-ref element describes a single resource manager connection factory reference. The resource-ref element consists of the following child elements:

- An optional description element that provides the purpose of the reference.

- A res-ref-name element that specifies the name of the reference relative to the java:comp/env context. The resource type based naming convention for which subcontext to place the res-ref-name into is discussed in the following bulleted list.

- A res-type element that specifies the fully qualified class name of the resource manager connection factory.

- A res-auth element that indicates whether the application component code performs resource signon programmatically, or whether the container signs on to the resource based on the principal mapping information supplied by the Deployer. It must be one of Application or Container.

- An option res-sharing-scope element. This currently is not supported by JBoss.

The J2EE specification recommends that all resource manager connection factory references be organized in the subcontexts of the application component's environment, using a different subcontext for each resource manager type. The recommended resource manager type to subcontext name is as follows:

- JDBC DataSource references should be declared in the java:comp/env/jdbc subcontext.

- JMS connection factories should be declared in the java:comp/env/jms subcontext.

- JavaMail connection factories should be declared in the `java:comp/env/mail` subcontext.

- URL connection factories should be declared in the `java:comp/env/url` subcontext.

Listing 3.8 shows an example web.xml descriptor fragment that illustrates the `resource-ref` element usage. Listing 3.9 provides a code fragment that an application component would use to access the DefaultMail resource defined in Listing 3.8.

LISTING 3.8   `web.xml resource-ref` Descriptor Fragment

```
<web>
...
<servlet>
  <servlet-name>AServlet</servlet-name>
  ...
</servlet>
...
  <!-- JDBC DataSources (java:comp/env/jdbc) -->
  <resource-ref>
      <description>The default DS</description>
      <res-ref-name>jdbc/DefaultDS</res-ref-name>
      <res-type>javax.sql.DataSource</res-type>
      <res-auth>Container</res-auth>
  </resource-ref>
  <!-- JavaMail Connection Factories (java:comp/env/mail) -->
  <resource-ref>
      <description>Default Mail</description>
      <res-ref-name>mail/DefaultMail</res-ref-name>
      <res-type>javax.mail.Session</res-type>
      <res-auth>Container</res-auth>
  </resource-ref>
  <!-- JMS Connection Factories (java:comp/env/jms) -->
  <resource-ref>
      <description>Default QueueFactory</description>
      <res-ref-name>jms/QueFactory</res-ref-name>
      <res-type>javax.jms.QueueConnectionFactory</res-type>
      <res-auth>Container</res-auth>
  </resource-ref>
</web>
```

LISTING 3.9   ENC resource-ref Access Sample Code Fragment

```
Context initCtx = new InitialContext();
javax.mail.Session s = (javax.mail.Session)
  initCtx.lookup("java:comp/env/mail/DefaultMail");
```

Resource Manager Connection Factory References with jboss.xml **and** jboss-web.xml

The purpose of the JBoss jboss.xml EJB deployment descriptor and jboss-web.xml Web application deployment descriptor is to provide the link from the logical name defined by the res-ref-name element to the JNDI name of the resource factory as deployed in JBoss. This is accomplished by providing a resource-ref element in the jboss.xml or jboss-web.xml descriptor. The JBoss resource-ref element consists of the following child elements:

- A res-ref-name element that must match the res-ref-name of a corresponding resource-ref element from the ejb-jar.xml or web.xml standard descriptors

- An optional res-type element that specifies the fully qualified class name of the resource manager connection factory

- A jndi-name element that specifies the JNDI name of the resource factory as deployed in JBoss

Listing 3.10 provides a sample jboss-web.xml descriptor fragment that shows sample mappings of the resource-ref elements given in Listing 3.8.

LISTING 3.10   Sample jboss-web.xml resource-ref Descriptor Fragment

```
<jboss-web>

...

    <resource-ref>
        <res-ref-name>jdbc/DefaultDS</res-ref-name>
        <res-type>javax.sql.DataSource</res-type>
        <jndi-name>java:/DefaultDS</jndi-name>
    </resource-ref>
    <resource-ref>
        <res-ref-name>mail/DefaultMail</res-ref-name>
        <res-type>javax.mail.Session</res-type>
        <jndi-name>java:/Mail</jndi-name>
    </resource-ref>
    <resource-ref>
        <res-ref-name>jms/QueFactory</res-ref-name>
        <res-type>javax.jms.QueueConnectionFactory</res-type>
        <jndi-name>QueueConnectionFactory</jndi-name>
```

LISTING 3.10   Continued

```
    </resource-ref>
...
</jboss-web>
```

Resource Environment References

Resource environment references are elements that refer to administered objects associated with a resource, such as JMS destinations, by using logical names. Resource environment references are defined by the `resource-env-ref` elements in the standard deployment descriptors. The Deployer binds the resource environment references to the actual administered objects location in the target operational environment using the `jboss.xml` and `jboss-web.xml` descriptors.

Each resource-env-ref element describes the requirements that the referencing application component has for the referenced administered object. The `resource-env-ref` element consists of the following child elements:

- An optional `description` element that provides the purpose of the reference.

- A `resource-env-ref-name` element that specifies the name of the reference relative to the `java:comp/env` context. Convention places the name in a subcontext that corresponds to the associated resource factory type. For example, a JMS queue reference named MyQueue should have a `resource-env-ref-name` of `jms/MyQueue`.

- A `resource-env-ref-type` element that specifies the fully qualified class name of the referenced object. For example, in the case of a JMS queue, the value would be `javax.jms.Queue`.

Listing 3.11 provides an example `resource-ref-env` element declaration by a session bean. Listing 3.12 gives a code fragment that illustrates how the session bean would access the queue from its ENC.

LISTING 3.11   An Example `ejb-jar.xml` `resource-env-ref` Fragment

```
<session>
  <ejb-name>MyBean</ejb-name>
  ...
  <resource-env-ref>
    <description>This is a reference to a JMS queue used in the
    processing of Stock info
    </description>
    <resource-env-ref-name>jms/StockInfo</resource-env-ref-name>
    <resource-env-ref-type>javax.jms.Queue</resource-env-ref-type>
```

LISTING 3.11   Continued

```
</resource-env-ref>
...
</session>
```

LISTING 3.12   ENC `resource-env-ref` Access Code Fragment

```
InitialContext iniCtx = new InitialContext();
javax.jms.Queue q = (javax.jms.Queue)
  envCtx.lookup("java:comp/env/jms/StockInfo");
```

Resource Environment References and `jboss.xml`, `jboss-web.xml`
The purpose of the JBoss `jboss.xml` EJB deployment descriptor and `jboss-web.xml`
Web application deployment descriptor is to provide the link from the logical name
defined by the `resource-env-ref-name` element to the JNDI name of the administered object deployed in JBoss. This is accomplished by providing a resource-env-ref
element in the `jboss.xml` or `jboss-web.xml` descriptor. The JBoss `resource-env-ref`
element consists of the following child elements:

- A `resource-env-ref-name` element that must match the `resource-env-ref-`
  `name` of a corresponding `resource-env-ref` element from the `ejb-jar.xml` or
  `web.xml` standard descriptors

- A `jndi-name` element that specifies the JNDI name of the resource as deployed
  in JBoss

Listing 3.13 provides a sample `jboss.xml` descriptor fragment that shows a sample
mapping for the `resource-env-ref` element given in Listing 3.11.

LISTING 3.13   Sample `jboss.xml` `resource-env-ref` Descriptor Fragment

```
<session>
  <ejb-name>MyBean</ejb-name>
  ...
  <resource-env-ref>
    <resource-env-ref-name>jms/StockInfo</resource-env-ref-name>
    <jndi-name>queue/StockInfoQue</jndi-name>
  </resource-env-ref>
  ...
</session>
```

The JBossNS Architecture

The JBossNS architecture is a Java socket/RMI based implementation of the javax.naming.Context interface. It is a client/server implementation that can be accessed remotely. The implementation is optimized so that access from within the same VM in which the JBossNS server is running does not involve sockets. Same VM access occurs through an object reference available as a global singleton. Figure 3.5 illustrates some of the key classes in the JBossNS implementation and their relationships.

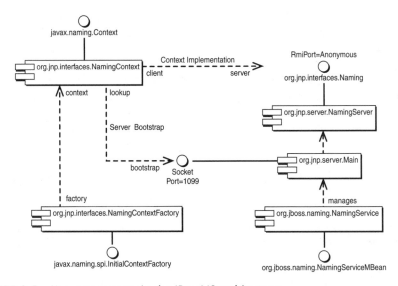

FIGURE 3.5   Key components in the JBossNS architecture.

Start with the NamingService MBean because you have already seen this class when the core JBoss services were discussed. You can then move on to learn how a client's use of InitialContext creates a JBossNS NamingContext.

Recall that the NamingService MBean was introduced when the key MBean services found in the jboss.jcml configuration file in Chapter 2, "JBoss Server Architecture Overview," was discussed. You will now learn about how the NamingService embeds and configures an org.jnp.server.Main instance to start the JBossNS naming server.

The NamingService is an MBean that delegates its functionality to an org.jnp.server.Main MBean. The reason for the duplicate MBeans is because JBossNS started out as a stand-alone JNDI implementation, and can still be run as such. The NamingService MBean embeds the Main instance into the JBoss server so that usage of JNDI with the same VM as the JBoss server does not incur any socket overhead. The configurable attributes of the `NamingService` are really the configurable attributes of the JBossNS `Main` MBean. The setting of any attributes on the `NamingService` MBean simply set the corresponding attributes on the `Main` MBean the `NamingService` contains. When the `NamingService` is started, it starts the contained `Main` MBean to activate the JNDI naming service.

The `NamingService` also creates the java:comp context such that access to this context is isolated based on the context `ClassLoader` of the thread that accesses the java:comp context. This provides the application component private ENC that is required by the J2EE specs. The segregation of java:comp by `ClassLoader` is accomplished by binding a `javax.naming.Reference` to a `Context` that uses the `org.jboss.naming.ENCFactory` as its `javax.naming.ObjectFactory`. When a client performs a lookup of java:comp, or any subcontext, the `ENCFactory` checks the thread context `ClassLoader`, and performs a lookup into a map using the `ClassLoader` as the key. If a `Context` instance does not exist for the `ClassLoader` instance, one is created and associated with the `ClassLoader` in the `ENCFactory` map. Thus, correct isolation of an application component's ENC relies on each component receiving a unique `ClassLoader` that is associated with the component threads of execution.

NOTE

The details of threads and the thread context class loader won't be explored here, but the JNDI tutorial provides a concise discussion that is applicable. See `http://java.sun.com/products/jndi/tutorial/beyond/misc/classloader.html` for the details.

When the `Main` MBean is started, it performs the following tasks:

- Instantiates an `org.jnp.naming.NamingService` instance and sets this as the local VM server instance. This is used by any `org.jnp.interfaces.NamingContext` instances that are created within the JBoss server VM to avoid RMI calls over TCP/IP.

- Exports the `NamingServer` instance's `org.jnp.naming.interfaces.Naming` RMI interface using the configured `RmiPort`, `ClientSocketFactory`, `ServerSocketFactory` attributes.

- Creates a socket that listens on the interface given by the `BindAddress` and `Port` attributes.

- Spawns a thread to accept connections on the socket.

The JBossNS InitialContext Factory

The starting point for any JNDI client access is the creation of an InitialContext object with the environment properties of a naming service established with whom the client wants to communicate. An example of a typical jndi.properties configuration for JBossNS was shown in Listing 3.1.

The properties required for the InitialContext to work with the JBossNS JNDI provider are as follows:

- **java.naming.factory.initial (or Context.INITIAL_CONTEXT_FACTORY)**—The name of the environment property for specifying the initial context factory to use. The value of the property should be the fully qualified class name of the factory class that will create an initial context. If it is not specified, a javax.naming.NoInitialContextException will be thrown when an InitialContext object is created. This must be the org.jnp.interfaces.NamingContextFactory class for JBossNS.

- **java.naming.provider.url (or Context.PROVIDER_URL)**—The name of the environment property for specifying the location of the JBossNS service provider the client will use. The NamingContextFactory class uses this information to know which JBossNS server to connect to. The value of the property should be a URL string. For JBossNS the URL format is *jnp://host:port/[jndi_path]*. The *jnp:* portion of the URL is the protocol and refers to the socket/RMI based protocol used by JBossNS. The *jndi_path* portion of the URL is an option JNDI name relative to the root context, such as apps or apps/tmp. Everything but the host component is optional. The following examples are equivalent because the default port value is 1099:

  - jnp://www.jboss.org:1099/

  - www.jboss.org:1099

  - www.jboss.org

- **java.naming.factory.url.pkgs (or Context.URL_PKG_PREFIXES)**—The name of the environment property for specifying the list of package prefixes to use when loading in URL context factories. The value of the property should be a colon-separated list of package prefixes for the class name of the factory class that will create a URL context factory. For JBossNS this must be org.jboss.naming:org.jnp.interfaces. This property is essential for locating the jnp: and java: URL context factories bundled with the JBossNS provider.

When a client creates an InitialContext with these JBossNS properties available, the org.jnp.interfaces.NamingContextFactory object is used to create the Context instance that will be used in subsequent operations. The NamingContextFactory is the JBossNS implementation of the `javax.naming.spi.InitialContextFactory` interface. When the `NamingContextFactory` class is asked to create a `Context`, it creates an `org.jnp.interfaces.NamingContext` instance with the `InitialContext` environment and name of the context in the global JNDI namespace. It is the `NamingContext` instance that actually performs the task of connecting to the JBossNS server, and implements the `Context` interface. The `Context.PROVIDER_URL` information from the environment indicates from which server to obtain a `NamingServer` RMI reference.

The association of the `NamingContext` instance to a `NamingServer` instance is done in a lazy fashion on the first `Context` operation that is performed. When a `Context` operation is performed and the `NamingContext` has no `NamingServer` associated with it, it looks to see if its environment properties define a `Context.PROVIDER_URL`. A `Context.PROVIDER_URL` defines the host and port of the JBossNS server the `Context` is to use. If there is a provider URL, the `NamingContext` first checks to see if a `Naming` instance keyed by the host and port pair has already been created by checking a `NamingContext` class static map. It simply uses the existing `Naming` instance if one for the host port pair has already been obtained. If no `Naming` instance has been created for the given host and port, the `NamingContext` connects to the host and port using a socket, and retrieves a `Naming` RMI stub from the server by reading a `java.rmi.MarshalledObject` from the socket and invoking its get method. The newly obtained `Naming` instance is cached in the `NamingContext` server map under the host and port pair. If no provider URL was specified in the JNDI environment associated with the context, the `NamingContext` simply uses the in VM `Naming` instance set by the `Main` MBean.

The `NamingContext` implementation of the `Context` interface delegates all operations to the `Naming` instance associated with the `NamingContext`. The `NamingServer` class that implements the `Naming` interface uses a `java.util.Hashtable` as the `Context` store. There is one unique `NamingServer` instance for each distinct JNDI `Name` for a given JBossNS server. There are zero or more transient `NamingContext` instances active at any given moment that refer to a `NamingServer` instance. The purpose of the `NamingContext` is to act as a `Context` to the `Naming` interface adaptor that manages translation of the JNDI names passed to the `NamingContext`. Because a JNDI name can be relative or a URL, it needs to be converted into an absolute name in the context of the JBossNS server to which it refers. This translation is a key function of the `NamingContext`.

Additional Naming MBeans

In addition to the `NamingService` MBean that configures an embedded JBossNS server within JBoss, there are three additional MBean services related to naming that ship with JBoss. They are the `ExternalContext`, `NamingAlias`, and `JNDIView`.

org.jboss.naming.ExternalContext **MBean**

The ExternalContext MBean allows you to federate external JNDI contexts into the JBoss server JNDI namespace. The term external refers to any naming service external to the JBossNS naming service running inside of the JBoss server VM. You can incorporate LDAP servers, file systems, DNS servers, and so on, even if the JNDI provider root context is not serializable. The federation can be made available to remote clients if the naming service supports remote access.

To incorporate an external JNDI naming service, you have to add a configuration of the ExternalContext MBean service to the jboss.jcml configuration file. The configurable attributes of the ExternalContext service are as follows:

- **JndiName** – The JNDI name under which the external context is to be bound.

- **RemoteAccess** – A boolean flag indicating if the external InitialContext should be bound using a Serializable form that allows a remote client to create the external InitialContext. When a remote client looks up the external context via the JBoss JNDI InitialContext, they effectively create an instance of the external InitialContext using the same env properties passed to the ExternalContext MBean. This will only work if the client could do a 'new InitialContext(env)' remotely. This requires that the Context.PROVIDER_URL value of env is resolvable in the remote VM that is accessing the context. This should work for the LDAP example. For the file system example this most likely won't work unless the file system path refers to a common network path. If this property is not given it defaults to false.

- **CacheContext** – The cacheContext flag. When set to true, the external Context is only created when the MBean is started and then stored as an in memory object until the MBean is stopped. If cacheContext is set to false, the external Context is created on each lookup using the MBean properties and InitialContext class. When the uncached Context is looked up by a client, the client should invoke close() on the Context to prevent resource leaks.

- **InitialContext** – The fully qualified class name of the InitialContext implementation to use. Must be one of: javax.naming.InitialContext, javax.naming.directory.InitialDirContext or javax.naming.ldap.InitialLdapContext. In the case of the InitialLdapContext, a null Controls array is used. The default is javax.naming.InitialContex.

- **Properties** – Set the `jndi.properties` information for the external `InitialContext`. This is either a URL string or a classpath resource name. Examples are as follows:

    - `file:///config/myldap.properties`

    - `http://config.mycompany.com/myldap.properties`

    - `/conf/myldap.properties`

    - `myldap.properties`

The `jboss.jcml` fragment shown in Listing 3.14 shows two configurations—one for an LDAP server, and the other for a local file system directory.

LISTING 3.14   `ExternalContext` MBean Configurations File System

```
<!-- Bind a remote LDAP server -->
<mbean code="org.jboss.naming.ExternalContext"
  name=":service=ExternalContext,jndiName=external/ldap/dscape" >
    <attribute name="JndiName">external/ldap/dscape</attribute>
    <attribute name="Properties">dscape.ldap</attribute>
    <attribute name="InitialContext">
      javax.naming.ldap.InitialLdapContext
    </attribute>
    <attribute name="RemoteAccess">true</attribute>
</mbean>
<!-- Bind the /usr/local file system directory -->
<mbean code="org.jboss.naming.ExternalContext"
  name=":service=ExternalContext,jndiName=external/fs/usr/local" >
    <attribute name="JndiName">external/fs/usr/local</attribute>
    <attribute name="Properties">local.props</attribute>
    <attribute name="InitialContext">javax.naming.InitialContext</attribute>
</mbean>
```

The first configuration describes binding an external LDAP context into the JBoss JNDI namespace under the name `external/ldap/dscape`. An example `dscape.ldap` properties file is as follows:

```
java.naming.factory.initial=com.sun.jndi.ldap.LdapCtxFactory
java.naming.provider.url=ldap://ldaphost.displayscape.com:389/o=displayscape.com
java.naming.security.principal=cn=Directory Manager
java.naming.security.authentication=simple
java.naming.security.credentials=secret
```

With this configuration, you can access the external LDAP context located at `ldap://ldaphost.displayscape.com:389/o=displayscape.com` from within the JBoss VM using the following code fragment:

```
InitialContext iniCtx = new InitialContext();
LdapContext ldapCtx = iniCtx.lookup("external/ldap/dscape");
```

Using the same code fragment outside of the JBoss server VM will work in this case because the `RemoteAccess` property was set to true. If it were set to false, it would not work because the remote client would receive a Reference object with an `ObjectFactory` that would not be able to recreate the external `IntialContext`.

The second configuration describes binding a local file system directory `/usr/local` into the JBoss JNDI namespace under the name `external/fs/usr/local`. An example `local.props` properties file is

```
java.naming.factory.initial=com.sun.jndi.fscontext.RefFSContextFactory
java.naming.provider.url=file:///usr/local
```

With this configuration, you can access the external file system context located at `file:///usr/local` from within the JBoss VM using the following code fragment:

```
InitialContext iniCtx = new InitialContext();
Context ldapCtx = iniCtx.lookup("external/fs/usr/local");
```

The `org.jboss.naming.NamingAlias` MBean

The `NamingAlias` MBean is a simple utility service that allows you to create an alias in the form of a JNDI `javax.naming.LinkRef` from one JNDI name to another. This is similar to a symbolic link in the Unix file system. To an alias you add a configuration of the `NamingAlias` MBean to the `jboss.jcml` configuration file. The configurable attributes of the `NamingAlias` service are as follows:

- **FromName** — The location where the `LinkRef` is bound under JNDI.

- **ToName** — The to name of the alias. This is the target name to which the `LinkRef` refers. The name is a URL, or a name to be resolved relative to the InitialContext, or if the first character of the name is., the name is relative to the context in which the link is bound.

An example that can be found in the standard jboss.jcml configuration file is as follows:

```
<mbean code="org.jboss.naming.NamingAlias"
name="DefaultDomain:service=NamingAlias,fromName=QueueConnectionFactory">
  <attribute name="ToName">ConnectionFactory</attribute>
  <attribute name="FromName">QueueConnectionFactory</attribute>
</mbean>
```

This says that the JNDI name `QueueConnectionFactory` should be a binding to a `LinkRef` that points to the binding for the JNDI name `ConnectionFactory`.

The `org.jboss.naming.JNDIView` MBean
The `JNDIView` MBean allows the user to view the JNDI namespace tree as it exists in the JBoss server using the JMX agent view interface. All that is required to use the `JNDIView` service is to add a configuration to `jboss.jcml` file. The `JNDIView` service has no configurable attributes, and so a suitable configuration is:

```
<mbean code="org.jboss.naming.JNDIView" name="DefaultDomain:service=JNDIView"/>
```

To view the JBoss JNDI namespace using the `JNDIView` MBean, you connect to the JMX Agent View using the http interface. The default settings put this at `http://localhost:8082/`. On this page you will see a section that lists the registered MBeans by domain. It should look something like that shown in Figure 3.6, where the `JNDIView` MBean is under the mouse cursor.

Selecting the `JNDIView` link takes you to the `JNDIView` MBean view, which will have a list of the `JNDIView` MBean operations. This view should look similar to that shown in Figure 3.7.

The list operation dumps out the JBoss server JNDI namespace as an html page using a simple text view. As an example, invoking the list operation for the default JBoss-2.4.1 distribution server produced the view shown in Figure 3.8.

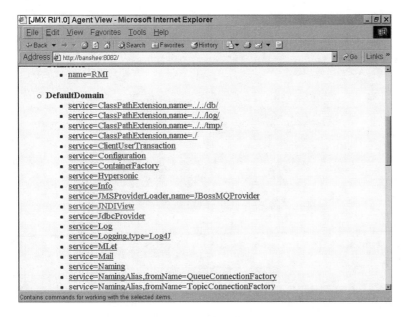

FIGURE 3.6   The HTTP JMX agent view of the configured JBoss MBeans.

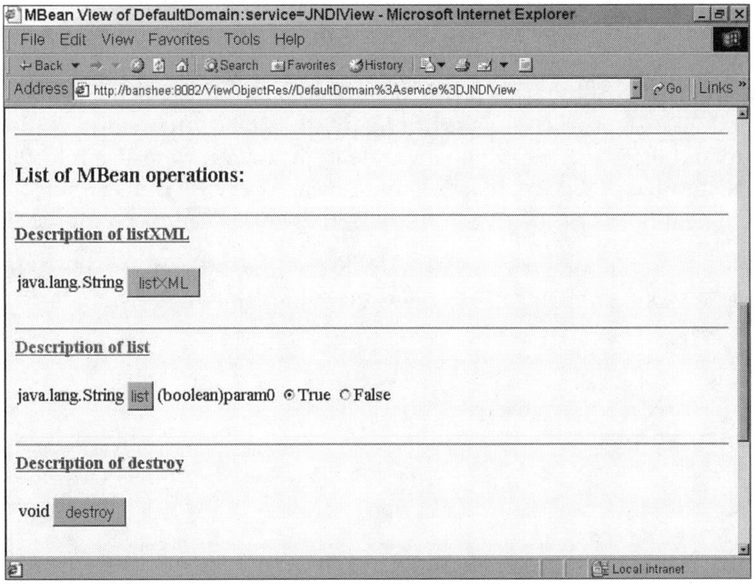

FIGURE 3.7   The HTTP JMX MBean view of the `JNDIView` MBean.

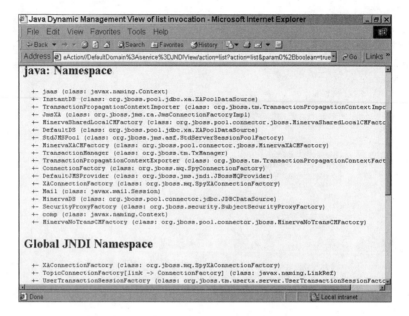

FIGURE 3.8   The HTTP JMX view of the JNDIView list operation output.

Summary

This chapter defined the basic JNDI API and common usage conventions as they apply to J2EE. You learned how to configure the J2EE component ENC using the standard and JBoss specific deployment descriptors. You were also introduced to the JBoss JNDI provider service, JBossNS, and saw an overview of its architecture. Lastly, you saw the MBeans of the JBossNS service that controlled its configuration.

The next JBoss component you will cover is the JBossMQ service. JBossMQ is a Java Message Service-compatible messaging service implementation.

pile:
[mkdir] Created dir: /tmp/2.4.4/
[javac] Compiling 154 source fil
install:
[copy] Copyin
[copy] Copyin
p/2
p/2

4

JBossMQ—The JBoss JMS Messaging Service Implementation

- An Overview of JMS
- An Overview of the JBossMQ Architecture
- Configuring JBossMQ

The Java Message Service (JMS) is an asynchronous message delivery abstraction. JMS plays an important role in enterprise integration scenarios because it allows for decoupled communication. This means that a message sender does not have to have a direct connection to the ultimate recipient of the message, as is the case for remote procedure call- (RPC) based EJBs. JMS has been around as a specification since August of 1998, but only as of EJB 2.0 and J2EE 1.3 has it been incorporated fully into the J2EE standards. The JBoss messaging service (JBossMQ) is an implementation of the JMS 1.0.2 API specification. This chapter provides an overview of JMS and how JMS fits into J2EE. It also provides some simple examples of JMS and MDB usage, discusses the JBossMQ architecture, and covers the configuration of the JBossMQ service as of the JBoss 2.4.4 release.

An Overview of JMS

JMS is an API that describes interface-to-client/server messaging systems. Client/server messaging systems are commonly referred to as message-oriented middleware (MOM), and have been around for many years in the form of proprietary offerings. The purpose of the JMS API is to provide a vendor-independent API for using MOM services from Java. To use JMS as the API for a particular MOM provider, the vendor must provide an implementation of the JMS API. For JBoss, the default JMS provider is

JBossMQ and clients must use the jbossmq-client.jar supplied with the JBoss distribution to use the JBossMQ JMS implementation.

A message-based architecture is useful when the following are present:

- Components do not have tight coupling in the form of references to Java interfaces. Communication is based on standardized or agreed upon message formats, rather than strongly typed interfaces.

- Components are distributed and have unpredictable availability.

- Communication between components can be done in an asynchronous fashion. This means that component 1 can send a message to component 2 and not receive a reply until some future time, if a reply is needed at all.

Such characteristics are common of many enterprise or business-to-business communication patterns.

The JMS Architecture

From a high-level view, messaging systems are conceptually simple. Someone sends a message to a destination, and someone retrieves the message. The messaging system handles the details of how the destinations are managed as well as how the messages are sent and received. This simplicity is reflected in the fact that there are just three basic ideas that show up in the JMS architecture. These ideas are as follows:

- Administered top-level objects that a JMS client accesses using JNDI. These consist of message destinations and connection factories. A destination is a rendezvous point to which messages are sent and retrieved. A connection factory is an entry point into the JMS architecture.

- The messages used for communication between destinations. Messages are the communication content and several different types of messages are supported.

- The JMS provider implementation that ties connection factories, destinations, and messages together. The majority of the JMS API consists of interfaces for which an implementation must be provided. The JMS provider implementation presents the provider messaging system in terms of the JMS API interface abstractions.

Each idea in a high-level fashion is examined in this chapter—first to cover the concepts and then to cover the JMS API specifics.

Message Destinations and Connection Factories

To send a message you need a location to which you can address the message. To receive a message you need a location from which you can pick it up. This rendezvous address is known as a destination in JMS. There are actually two types of destinations in JMS based on two popular messaging models—point-to-point (PTP) and publish/subscribe (pub/sub).

The PTP model is based on the concepts of message queues, senders, and receivers. Each message is addressed to a specific queue, and receiving clients extract messages from the same queue. Queues retain all messages sent to them until the messages are consumed, or until the messages expire. For each message sent to a queue, only a single client can receive or consume the message.

The pub/sub model is based on the concepts of message topics, publishers, and subscribers. A publisher addresses a message to a specific topic to which one or more subscribers listen. Typically, clients must be listening to the topic during the time the publisher sends a message to be able to receive the message. The JMS architecture allows for a variation of this theme based on the notion of a durable topic. A durable topic is a type of topic that has both queue and traditional topic qualities. Messages sent to a durable topic remain in the topic until subscribers retrieve them, and all subscribers receive the published message.

To send a message to a queue, or publish a message to a topic, a client needs to connect to the JMS provider. Likewise, to receive a message from a queue or topic, a client needs to connect to the JMS provider. Connection factories are the mechanism by which clients connect to the JMS provider. Connection factories are the starting point for any JMS client activity.

Queues, topics, and connection factories are all referred to as administered objects by the JMS specification. This means that these objects cannot be created by the interfaces available in the JMS API. Rather, they must be administered in a JMS provider-specific way using a provider-specific mechanism. The only thing that is common across JMS providers is that administered objects are bound into JNDI for subsequent access by JMS clients. Because the JMS specification does not define a standard naming convention for the location of administered objects, the naming convention used depends on the JMS provider. The JMS specification fails to define the administration of destinations and connection factories in a JMS provider–independent manner to make it easy for a messaging system to support the JMS API. There are typically major differences between messaging systems with regard to installation and administration, so the JMS specification simply acknowledges this fact by leaving installation and administration as a JMS provider–specific detail.

Messages

The idea of the message is of central importance to JMS; after all, the purpose of JMS is to allow clients to produce and consume messages. JMS messages are composed of three elements: headers, properties, and bodies. Headers are standardized properties that every message supports. Properties are arbitrary name-to-value bindings similar to a Java `HashMap`. Message bodies are the content of the message that cannot be represented by properties. The various types of messages supported by JMS correspond to common types of body content formats that are used in message systems. The types include byte arrays, maps, streams, and strings.

The JMS Provider

The responsibility of the JMS provider is to provide an implementation of the JMS API. A typical JMS provider is an established middleware vendor that provides a JMS implementation for integration with existing middleware services. Alternatively, as is the case with JBossMQ, the JMS provider is a Java messaging system built on lower-level Java constructs for the sole purpose of providing a JMS compatible messaging system. Providers will vary in any number of qualitative and quantitative aspects, ranging from administration ease of use to performance, scalability, and reliability.

> **NOTE**
>
> A comprehensive listing of JMS providers can be obtained from the JMS home page at http://java.sun.com/products/jms/.

The JMS API

This section takes a more detailed look at the interfaces that correspond to the architectural elements discussed briefly in the previous section. The JMS API itself is rather small, consisting of a single javax.jms package with 44 interfaces, 2 classes, and 13 exceptions. Roughly half of the interfaces deal with PTP while the other half deal with pub/sub. Figure 4.1 gives an overview of the interfaces in the javax.jms package and their relationships. Each component type has a message-model–independent interface that is represented by the white rectangular elements. These are divided into PTP-specific interfaces represented as light-gray circles and pub/sub specific interfaces represented as dark-gray circles. There are no PTP or pub/sub-specific messages. Rather, there are different types of messages based on the body types that are highlighted as white circles.

Connection Factories and Message Destinations Interfaces

At the top of Figure 4.1 are the entry point interfaces to JMS—the connection factories. A client initiates a JMS session by obtaining either a javax.jms.QueueConnectionFactory or a javax.jms.TopicConnectionFactory, depending on whether a PTP or pub/sub model is desired. The sole function of a QueueConnectionFactory is to create javax.jms.QueueConnection objects, while the sole function of a TopicConnectionFactory is to create javax.jms.TopicConnection objects. The creation of a connection can be performed with or without presenting authentication information in the form of a username and password. Whether or not authentication is required is a property of the ConnectionFactory that was set up by the JMS administrator.

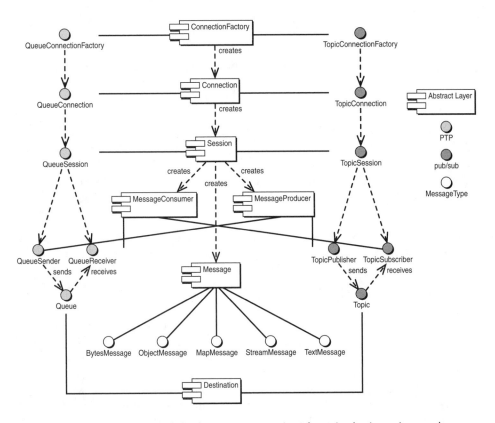

FIGURE 4.1   An overview of the key component interfaces in the javax.jms package.

A connection is a handle to a JMS provider that cannot be used to send or receive messages directly. Its two primary purposes are controlling the flow of messages, which can be started and stopped, and creating sessions. A QueueConnection creates javax.jms.QueueSessions while a TopicConnection creates javax.jms.TopicSessions. A session is a lightweight single-threaded context for producing and consuming messages. A Session is a key object in JMS that provides the following functions:

- Serves as a factory for message producers (javax.jms.QueueSender and javax.jms.TopicPublisher) and message consumers (javax.jms.QueueReceiver and javax.jms.TopicSubscriber)

- Acts as a factory for the various JMS message objects

- Supports a single series of transactions that combine work spanning its producers and consumers into atomic units

- Defines a serial order for the messages it consumes and the messages it produces

- Retains messages it consumes until they have been acknowledged

- Serializes execution of message listeners registered with its message consumers

A JMS client uses a `Session` to create the JMS messages it sends as well as to create message consumers and producers. A message consumer is an entity that receives messages. A message producer is an entity that creates and sends messages.

If a client is interested in sending messages, it will create a `QueueSender` from a `QueueSession` for PTP, or a `TopicPublisher` from a `TopicSession` for pub/sub. Both interfaces are subinterfaces of `javax.jms.MessageProducer` that add methods for sending messages.

If a client is interested in receiving messages it will create a `QueueReceiver` from a `QueueSession` for PTP, or a `TopicSubscriber` from a `TopicSession` for pub/sub. Both interfaces extend the `javax.jms.MessageConsumer` interface and simply add an accessor for the destination from which they receive messages.

A message destination in JMS is represented in the most abstract form by the `javax.jms.Destination` interface. This is a tagging interface that contains no methods. A `Destination` object encapsulates a provider-specific address. There are two subinterfaces of `Destination` that correspond to the two types of messaging paradigms. The destination interface for the PTP messaging paradigm is `javax.jms.Queue`. The destination interface for the pub/sub messaging paradigm is `javax.jms.Topic`. Both `Queue` and `Topic` are interfaces that simply provide the capability to get the name of the queue or topic and display the destination as a string. The `Queue` and `Topic` interfaces serve as opaque addresses that are passed to other JMS API interface methods.

Messages

Messages are the fundamental objects used to pass information between JMS clients. The `javax.jms.Message` interface is the root interface of all other messages, and it defines accessors for all standard message headers and typed property accessors. The property accessors allow you to retrieve a named property as a native Java type—a `java.lang.String`, or a `java.lang.Object`. The JMS API defines a limited support for type conversion of property values, and all properties can be retrieved as a `java.lang.String`.

There are five subinterfaces of `Message` that correspond to the five different types of bodies or content. The five subtypes are as follows:

> `javax.jms.BytesMessage`—The message body contains a stream of raw bytes. This message type is for literally encoding a body to match an existing message format. In many cases, it is

possible to use one of the other body types, which are easier to use. Although the JMS API allows the use of message properties with byte messages, they are typically not used because the inclusion of properties may affect the format.

`javax.jms.MapMessage`—The message body contains a set of name-value pairs, where names are `String` objects and values are Java primitives. The entries can be accessed sequentially or randomly by name. The order of the entries is undefined.

`javax.jms.ObjectMessage`—The message body contains a `java.io.Serializable` Java object.

`javax.jms.StreamMessage`—The message body contains a stream of primitive Java values. It is written and read sequentially using methods similar to the `java.io.DataInputStream` and `java.io.DataOutputStream` classes.

`java.jms.TextMessage`—The message body contains a `String` object. The inclusion of this message type in the JMS specification is based on the assumption that XML will become a popular mechanism for representing content.

A JMS client creates messages from a `javax.jms.Session` instance. The `Session` class is used as the factory for messages in JMS, and it is the only way defined by the JMS specification for obtaining a message.

A PTP Example

All of the JMS API interfaces can now be brought together in the form of a simple PTP example. It illustrates the typical steps required by a JMS client to send and receive messages. Listing 4.1 provides a complete JMS client example program that sends a `TextMessage` to a `Queue` and then asynchronously receives the message from the same `Queue`. The source code for this example can be found in the `src/main/org/jboss/chap5/ex1` directory on the accompanying CD.

NOTE

See Appendix D, "Tools and Book Examples", for a description of installing and using the book examples.

LISTING 4.1　A Simple PTP Example that Demonstrates the Basic Steps for a JMS Client

```
1:package org.jboss.chap5.ex1;
3:import javax.jms.JMSException;
4:import javax.jms.Message;
5:import javax.jms.MessageListener;
6:import javax.jms.Queue;
7:import javax.jms.QueueConnection;
```

LISTING 4.1   Continued

```
8:import javax.jms.QueueConnectionFactory;
9:import javax.jms.QueueReceiver;
10:import javax.jms.QueueSender;
11:import javax.jms.QueueSession;
12:import javax.jms.TextMessage;
13:import javax.naming.InitialContext;
14:import javax.naming.NamingException;
16:import EDU.oswego.cs.dl.util.concurrent.CountDown;
18:/** A complete JMS client example program that sends a
19:TextMessage to a Queue and asynchronously receives the
20:message from the same Queue.
22:@author  Scott.Stark@jboss.org
23:@version $Revision:$
24:*/
25:public class SendRecvClient
26:{
27:    static CountDown done = new CountDown(1);
28:    QueueConnection conn;
29:    QueueSession session;
30:    Queue que;
32:    public static class ExListener implements MessageListener
33:    {
34:        public void onMessage(Message msg)
35:        {
36:            done.release();
37:            TextMessage tm = (TextMessage) msg;
38:            try
39:            {
40:                System.out.println("onMessage, recv text="
41:                    + tm.getText());
42:            }
43:            catch(Throwable t)
44:            {
45:                t.printStackTrace();
46:            }
47:        }
48:    }
50:    public void setupPTP()
51:        throws JMSException, NamingException
52:    {
53:        InitialContext iniCtx = new InitialContext();
```

LISTING 4.1   Continued

```
54:        Object tmp = iniCtx.lookup("QueueConnectionFactory");
55:        QueueConnectionFactory qcf = (QueueConnectionFactory) tmp;
56:        conn = qcf.createQueueConnection();
57:        que = (Queue) iniCtx.lookup("queue/testQueue");
58:        session = conn.createQueueSession(false,
59:           QueueSession.AUTO_ACKNOWLEDGE);
60:        conn.start();
61:    }
63:    public void sendRecvAsync(String text)
64:        throws JMSException, NamingException
65:    {
66:        System.out.println("Begin sendRecvAsync");
67:        // Setup the PTP connection, session
68:        setupPTP();
69:        // Set the async listener
70:        QueueReceiver recv = session.createReceiver(que);
71:        recv.setMessageListener(new ExListener());
72:        // Send a text msg
73:        QueueSender send = session.createSender(que);
74:        TextMessage tm = session.createTextMessage(text);
75:        send.send(tm);
76:        System.out.println("sendRecvAsync, sent text="
77:            + tm.getText());
78:        send.close();
79:        System.out.println("End sendRecvAsync");
80:    }
82:    public void stop()   throws JMSException
83:    {
84:        conn.stop();
85:        session.close();
86:        conn.close();
87:    }
89:    public static void main(String args[]) throws Exception
90:    {
91:        SendRecvClient client = new SendRecvClient();
92:        client.sendRecvAsync("A text msg");
93:        client.done.acquire();
94:        client.stop();
95:        System.exit(0);
96:    }
98:}
```

The key steps performed by the client in the order of execution are as follows:

- Lines 91-92—The main entry point creates a SendRecvClient instance and then invokes the sendRecvAsync method passing in the text that should be sent as the body of the TextMessage.

- Line 68—The first step of the sendRecvAsync method is to perform a typical PTP JMS setup by calling the setupPTP method.

- Lines 53-55—Of the setupPTP method retrieve the QueueConnectionFactory administered object from JNDI under the name "QueueConnectionFactory". The location of the QueueConnectionFactory is a configurable parameter as discussed later in this chapter in the section titled "Configuring JBossMQ".

- Line 56—Creates a QueueConnection from the QueueConnectionFactory to connect to the JMS provider.

- Line 57—looks up a Queue using the name "queue/testQueue". This is one of the Queue destinations defined in the default JBossMQ configuration.

- Lines 58-59—Create a non-transacted QueueSession that automatically acknowledges messages.

- Line 60—The QueueConnection is started so that message delivery will be enabled.

- Line 70—Back in the sendRecvAsync method, creates a QueueReceiver to be used for the asynchronous receipt of messages sent to que.

- Line 71—Assigns the MessageListener instance that will be notified of messages sent to que. The JBossMQ provider will invoke the ExListener class's onMessage method as messages are sent to que.

- Line 73—A QueueSender is created to use for sending messages to que.

- Line 74—A TextMessage is created with the text body passed into the sendRecvAsync method.

- Line 75—Shows the send of the TextMessage to que via the QueueSender.

- Line 78—Closes the QueueSender. It is a good practice to close JMS objects because it allows the JMS provider to reclaim any resources as soon as they are no longer needed.

- Line 93—Back in main, waits for the message sent by the main thread to be received by the listener. Because the message delivery is done asynchronously you have to introduce synchronization code to know when the ExListener receives the message sent on line 75.

Ensure that you have a JBoss server running, and run the example by invoking Ant
with the chap=5 and ex=1 property values. The output you see should look similar to
the following:

```
examples 770>ant -Dchap=5 -Dex=1 run-example

Buildfile: build.xml

run-example:

run-example1:

    [java] Begin sendRecvAsync

    [java] sendRecvAsync, sent text=A text msg

    [java] End sendRecvAsync

    [java] onMessage, recv text=A text msg
```

JMS and J2EE

The addition of the JMS API enhances the J2EE platform by simplifying enterprise
development. The simplification is due to the support JMS has for loosely coupled,
reliable, asynchronous messaging between J2EE components and external non-J2EE
message based systems. JBoss and JBossMQ support the majority of the J2EE 1.3 JMS
requirements. This includes the following:

- The capability for applications, EJB components, and Web components to send
  or synchronously receive JMS messages. Applications can also receive JMS
  messages asynchronously.

- Support for EJB 2.0 message-driven beans (MDB) that allow a business component to asynchronously consume JMS messages and concurrent processing of
  messages by MDBs.

- Message sends and receives can participate in distributed transactions.

- Support for accessing JMS administered objects through the application
  component-naming context or ENC.

Message-Driven Beans

A new type of message-driven enterprise Java bean (MDB) was added in EJB 2.0. It is
a variant of the stateless session bean that can be used to process JMS messages

asynchronously. Unlike other EJB types, an MDB does not have a remote or home interface because clients do not directly invoke it. Rather, an MDB implements the `javax.jms.MessageListener` interface and processes JMS messages delivered to its onMessage method. An example of where MDBs are a natural fit is a workflow application. A workflow is a collection of tasks and actions that model a business process. The completion of a task advances the state of the workflow. Using a message to an MDB to signal the completion of a task is a better approach than invoking a method on a standard EJB because the invocation semantics are more appropriate. To invoke a method on an EJB, the application server must be available and responsive to the synchronous method invocation. To send a message to an MDB a JMS server must be able to queue the message for eventual delivery to the MDB. The key difference between the EJB server and the JMS server is that the JMS server does not have to deliver the message to the ultimate MDB destination and return a response. The JMS server just needs to accept the message and guarantee that it will be delivered. This asynchronous delivery allows for more robust and dynamic systems as the message can be processed when resources are available.

JBoss supports MDBs by using the JBossMQ implementation of the optional JMS application server facilities (ASF) described in section 8 of the JMS 1.0.2 specification.

A JMS provider ASF implementation of `javax.jms.Connection` objects supports the creation of `javax.jms.ConnectionConsumer` instances. The `ConnectionConsumer` interface allows for a pool of `javax.jms.MessageListener` instances that can concurrently consume JMS message. The JBossMQ ASF implementation will be discussed in more detail in the JBossMQ architecture overview.

An MDB Example

This MDB example extends the use of JMS with JBoss. The example is a modification of what was presented in Listing 4.1, which sends multiple text messages to an MDB and then receives modified text messages asynchronously from the MDB. First you will see the MDB and its deployment descriptors and then you will move on to the JMS client. The source code for this example can be found in the `src/main/org/jboss/chap5/ex2` directory on the accompanying CD.

The first step is the coding of the MDB. Listing 4.2 provides the MDB implementation for example2.

LISTING 4.2   The example2 Message-Driven EJB

```
1:package org.jboss.chap4.ex2;
3:import javax.ejb.MessageDrivenBean;
4:import javax.ejb.MessageDrivenContext;
5:import javax.ejb.EJBException;
6:import javax.jms.JMSException;
```

LISTING 4.2   Continued

```
7:import javax.jms.Message;
8:import javax.jms.MessageListener;
9:import javax.jms.Queue;
10:import javax.jms.QueueConnection;
11:import javax.jms.QueueConnectionFactory;
12:import javax.jms.QueueSender;
13:import javax.jms.QueueSession;
14:import javax.jms.TextMessage;
15:import javax.naming.InitialContext;
16:import javax.naming.NamingException;
18:/**
19: *
20: * @author   Scott.Stark@jboss.org
21: * @version $Revision:$
22: */
23:public class TextMDB implements MessageDrivenBean, MessageListener
24:{
25:    private MessageDrivenContext ctx = null;
26:    private QueueConnection conn;
27:    private QueueSession session;
29:    public TextMDB()
30:    {
31:       System.out.println("TextMDB.ctor, this="+hashCode());
32:    }
34:    public void setMessageDrivenContext(MessageDrivenContext ctx)
35:    {
36:       this.ctx = ctx;
37:       System.out.println("TextMDB.setMessageDrivenContext, this="+hashCode());
38:    }
39:
40:    public void ejbCreate()
41:       throws EJBException
42:    {
43:       System.out.println("TextMDB.ejbCreate, this="+hashCode());
44:       try
45:       {
46:          setupPTP();
47:       }
48:       catch(Exception e)
49:       {
50:          throw new EJBException("Failed to init TextMDB", e);
```

LISTING 4.2   Continued

```
51:       }
52:    }
53:    public void ejbRemove()
54:    {
55:       System.out.println("TextMDB.ejbRemove, this="+hashCode());
56:       ctx = null;
57:       try
58:       {
59:          if( session != null )
60:             session.close();
61:          if( conn != null )
62:             conn.close();
63:       }
64:       catch(JMSException e)
65:       {
66:          e.printStackTrace();
67:       }
68:    }
70:    public void onMessage(Message msg)
71:    {
72:       System.out.println("TextMDB.onMessage, this="+hashCode());
73:       try
74:       {
75:          TextMessage tm = (TextMessage) msg;
76:          String text = tm.getText() + "processed by: "+hashCode();
77:          Queue dest = (Queue) msg.getJMSReplyTo();
78:          sendReply(text, dest);
79:       }
80:       catch(Throwable t)
81:       {
82:          t.printStackTrace();
83:       }
84:    }
86:    private void setupPTP()
87:       throws JMSException, NamingException
88:    {
89:       InitialContext iniCtx = new InitialContext();
90:       Object tmp = iniCtx.lookup("java:comp/env/jms/QCF");
91:       QueueConnectionFactory qcf = (QueueConnectionFactory) tmp;
92:       conn = qcf.createQueueConnection();
93:       session = conn.createQueueSession(false,
```

LISTING 4.2   Continued

```
94:          QueueSession.AUTO_ACKNOWLEDGE);
95:      conn.start();
96:    }
97:    private void sendReply(String text, Queue dest)
98:      throws JMSException
99:    {
100:     System.out.println("TextMDB.sendReply, this="+hashCode()
101:        +", dest="+dest);
102:     QueueSender sender = session.createSender(dest);
103:     TextMessage tm = session.createTextMessage(text);
104:     sender.send(tm);
105:     sender.close();
106:   }
108:}
```

Items of note in the `TextMDB` implementation include the following:

- Line 23—The `TextMDB` implements both the `javax.ejb.MessageDrivenBean` interface as well as the `javax.jms.MessageListener` interface. The `MessageDrivenBean` methods correspond to the MDB life-cycle callback methods invoked by the MDB container, while the `MessageListener.onMessage` method is the JMS message delivery callback method seen in all JMS message consumers.

- Line 46—In the `ejbCreate` method, the `TextMDB` invokes the `setupPTP` to perform the same steps to connect to the JMS provider that you saw in the example1 client perform. The `ejbCreate` method is called when an MDB is added to the pool of `MessageListeners` available to handle messages.

- Lines 59-62—In the `ejbRemove` method, the `TextMDB` closes the JMS resources that were allocated in `ejbCreate`. The `ejbRemove` method is called by the application server when an MDB is no longer needed in the `MessageListener` pool.

- Lines 70-84—In the `onMessage` method, the `TextMDB` retrieves the text of the `TextMessage` it receives and annotates the text with its `hashCode` to indicate which MDB received the message. It then retrieves the `Queue` to which replies should be sent using the `TextMessage.getJMSReplyTo` method. The `sendReply` method is invoked to return the annotated text to the indicated `Queue`.

- Lines 97-106—In the `sendReply` method, a `QueueSender` is created from the `TextMDB` QueueSession object with the reply to dest as the target `Queue`. A new `TextMessage` is then created from the annotated `text` value, and the message is sent. Finally, the sender is closed.

- All key methods of the `TextMDB` include a `System.out.println` statement indicating the method and `TextMDB` instance `hashCode`. This allows you to see how the MDB container manages MDB instances in response to JMS message arrivals.

You next need to create the standard ejb-jar.xml and jboss.xml XML deployment descriptors for the MDB. For simple EJBs you often do not need a jboss.xml deployment descriptor. There are two reasons why a jboss.xml descriptor is needed for this MDB. The first reason is that the ejb-jar.xml descriptor does not specify to what queue the TextMDB listens. The queue must be specified by the bean deployer, and this done using the jboss.xml descriptor. Because of this, MDBs must always include a jboss.xml descriptor for the specification of the destination name from which they are to receive messages.

Figure 4.2 shows the MDB portion of the DTD for the jboss.xml descriptor. Under the message-driven element in Figure 4.2, the only element unique to MDBs is the destination-jndi-name element. The value of this element is the deployment environment JNDI name of the `Queue` or `Topic` the MDB is to listen to for messages.

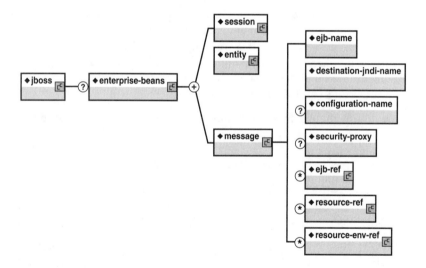

FIGURE 4.2   The MDB portion of the DTD for the jboss.xml descriptor.

The second reason the jboss.xml descriptor is necessary in this example is for resolving the JMS QueueConnectionFactory reference made in the ejb-jar.xml descriptor. The ENC reference in the ejb-jar.xml descriptor needs to be mapped to the deployed JNDI name of the JBossMQ QueueConnectionFactory. This is done using the resource-ref element as seen previously Chapter 3, "JBossNS—The JBoss JNDI Naming Service."

Take a look at the MDB deployment descriptors. Listing 4.3 provides both ejb-jar.xml and jboss.xml deployment descriptors.

LISTING 4.3 The TextMDB ejb-jar.xml and jboss.xml Deployment Descriptors

```
<!--The ejb-jar.xml descriptor -->
<?xml version="1.0"?>
<!DOCTYPE ejb-jar
    PUBLIC "-//Sun Microsystems, Inc.//DTD Enterprise JavaBeans 2.0//EN"
    "http://java.sun.com/dtd/ejb-jar_2_0.dtd"
>

<ejb-jar>
    <enterprise-beans>
        <message-driven>
            <ejb-name>TextMDB</ejb-name>
            <ejb-class>org.jboss.chap5.ex2.TextMDB</ejb-class>
            <transaction-type>Container</transaction-type>
            <acknowledge-mode>AUTO_ACKNOWLEDGE</acknowledge-mode>
            <message-driven-destination>
                <destination-type>javax.jms.Queue</destination-type>
            </message-driven-destination>
            <resource-ref>
                <res-ref-name>jms/QCF</res-ref-name>
                <res-type>javax.jms.QueueConnectionFactory</res-type>
                <res-auth>Container</res-auth>
            </resource-ref>
        </message-driven>
    </enterprise-beans>
</ejb-jar>
<?xml version="1.0"?>

<!--The jboss.xml descriptor -->
<jboss>
    <enterprise-beans>
        <message-driven>
            <ejb-name>TextMDB</ejb-name>
            <destination-jndi-name>queue/B</destination-jndi-name>
            <resource-ref>
                <res-ref-name>jms/QCF</res-ref-name>
```

LISTING 4.3   Continued

```
        <jndi-name>QueueConnectionFactory</jndi-name>
      </resource-ref>
    </message-driven>
  </enterprise-beans>
</jboss>
```

The ejb-jar.xml descriptor declares that the org.jboss.chap5.ex2.TextMDB will receive messages from a java.jms.Queue with container-managed transactions and message auto acknowledgement. It also declares that the java:comp/env/jms/QCF ENC binding should reference a javax.jms.QueueConnectionFactory.

The jboss.xml descriptor fills in the missing pieces. The destination-jndi-name element defines that the Queue from which the TextMDB will receive messages is located under the JNDI name "queue/B". The resource-ref element links the TextMDB java:comp/env/jms/QCF ENC entry to the location of the JBossMQ QueueConnectionFactory.

That completes the example2 MDB. The example2 JMS client is a slight variation of the example1 client. Listing 4.4 gives the example2 client code.

LISTING 4.4   The example2 JMS Client

```
1:package org.jboss.chap4.ex2;
3:import javax.jms.JMSException;
4:import javax.jms.Message;
5:import javax.jms.MessageListener;
6:import javax.jms.Queue;
7:import javax.jms.QueueConnection;
8:import javax.jms.QueueConnectionFactory;
9:import javax.jms.QueueReceiver;
10:import javax.jms.QueueSender;
11:import javax.jms.QueueSession;
12:import javax.jms.TextMessage;
13:import javax.naming.InitialContext;
14:import javax.naming.NamingException;
16:import EDU.oswego.cs.dl.util.concurrent.CountDown;
18:/** A complete JMS client example program that sends N
19:TextMessages to a Queue B and asynchronously receives the
20:messages as modified by TestMDB from QueueB.
22:@author  Scott.Stark@jboss.org
23:@version $Revision:$
24:*/
```

LISTING 4.4   Continued

```
25:public class SendRecvClient
26:{
27:    static final int N = 10;
28:    static CountDown done = new CountDown(N);
29:    QueueConnection conn;
30:    QueueSession session;
31:    Queue queA;
32:    Queue queB;
34:    public static class ExListener implements MessageListener
35:    {
36:       public void onMessage(Message msg)
37:       {
38:          done.release();
39:          TextMessage tm = (TextMessage) msg;
40:          try
41:          {
42:             System.out.println("onMessage, recv text="+tm.getText());
43:          }
44:          catch(Throwable t)
45:          {
46:             t.printStackTrace();
47:          }
48:       }
49:    }
51:    public void setupPTP()
52:       throws JMSException, NamingException
53:    {
54:       InitialContext iniCtx = new InitialContext();
55:       Object tmp = iniCtx.lookup("QueueConnectionFactory");
56:       QueueConnectionFactory qcf = (QueueConnectionFactory) tmp;
57:       conn = qcf.createQueueConnection();
58:       queA = (Queue) iniCtx.lookup("queue/A");
59:       queB = (Queue) iniCtx.lookup("queue/B");
60:       session = conn.createQueueSession(false,
61:          QueueSession.AUTO_ACKNOWLEDGE);
62:       conn.start();
63:    }
65:    public void sendRecvAsync(String textBase)
66:       throws JMSException, NamingException, InterruptedException
67:    {
```

LISTING 4.4   Continued

```
68:    System.out.println("Begin sendRecvAsync");
69:    // Setup the PTP connection, session
70:    setupPTP();
71:    // Set the async listener for queA
72:    QueueReceiver recv = session.createReceiver(queA);
73:    recv.setMessageListener(new ExListener());
74:    // Send a few text msgs to queB
75:    QueueSender send = session.createSender(queB);
76:    for(int m = 0; m < 10; m ++)
77:    {
78:        TextMessage tm = session.createTextMessage(textBase+"#"+m);
79:        tm.setJMSReplyTo(queA);
80:        send.send(tm);
81:        System.out.println("sendRecvAsync, sent text="+tm.getText());
82:    }
83:    System.out.println("End sendRecvAsync");
84:    }
86:    public void stop()   throws JMSException
87:    {
88:        conn.stop();
89:    }
91:    public static void main(String args[]) throws Exception
92:    {
93:        SendRecvClient client = new SendRecvClient();
94:        client.sendRecvAsync("A text msg");
95:        client.done.acquire();
96:        client.stop();
97:        System.exit(0);
98:    }
100:}
```

The differences between the example1 client and this example2 client are the use of two Queues, and the sending and receipt of multiple messages. In the setupPTP method, two Queues are obtained from JNDI—queue/A and queue/B. The queue/A destination will be used to receive messages, and the queue/B destination will be where the client sends messages. The sendRecvAsync method also performs 10 TextMessage sends rather than one, as performed in example1. This means that the main method must wait for 10 messages to be received rather than just one. This is achieved by initializing the EDU.oswego.cs.dl.util.concurrent.CountDown instance with a value of 10 rather than 1.

The reason for sending multiple JMS messages is to test the concurrency of the TextMDB. An application server can employ multiple instances of a given MDB to concurrently process messages. By sending a block of 10 messages, you expect that multiple TextMDB instances will run in parallel to process the messages.

To test the example2 MDB, ensure that you have a JBoss server running, and invoke Ant with the chap=5 and ex=2 property values. The output you see in the client console should look similar to the following:

```
examples 635>ant -Dchap=5 -Dex=2 run-example
Buildfile: build.xml

run-example:

prepare:

example2-jar:

run-example2:
...
     [java] Begin sendRecvAsync
     [java] onMessage, recv text=A text msg#0processed by: 4395216
     [java] sendRecvAsync, sent text=A text msg#0
     [java] sendRecvAsync, sent text=A text msg#1
     [java] sendRecvAsync, sent text=A text msg#2
     [java] sendRecvAsync, sent text=A text msg#3
     [java] sendRecvAsync, sent text=A text msg#4
     [java] sendRecvAsync, sent text=A text msg#5
     [java] onMessage, recv text=A text msg#2processed by: 4395216
     [java] onMessage, recv text=A text msg#3processed by: 494668
     [java] onMessage, recv text=A text msg#4processed by: 494668
     [java] onMessage, recv text=A text msg#5processed by: 4395216
     [java] onMessage, recv text=A text msg#6processed by: 4395216
     [java] onMessage, recv text=A text msg#7processed by: 494668
     [java] onMessage, recv text=A text msg#8processed by: 494668
     [java] onMessage, recv text=A text msg#9processed by: 494668
     [java] onMessage, recv text=A text msg#1processed by: 494668
     [java] sendRecvAsync, sent text=A text msg#6
     [java] onMessage, recv text=A text msg#0processed by: 494668
     [java] onMessage, recv text=A text msg#2processed by: 494668
     [java] onMessage, recv text=A text msg#3processed by: 494668
     [java] onMessage, recv text=A text msg#4processed by: 494668
     [java] onMessage, recv text=A text msg#5processed by: 4395216
```

```
[java] sendRecvAsync, sent text=A text msg#7
[java] onMessage, recv text=A text msg#6processed by: 4395216
[java] onMessage, recv text=A text msg#7processed by: 4395216
[java] sendRecvAsync, sent text=A text msg#8
[java] sendRecvAsync, sent text=A text msg#9
[java] End sendRecvAsync
[java] onMessage, recv text=A text msg#8processed by: 4395216
[java] onMessage, recv text=A text msg#9processed by: 494668
```

```
BUILD SUCCESSFUL
```

```
Total time: 3 seconds
```

There should also be output on the JBoss server console similar to the following:

```
[Container factory] Deploying:file:/.../deploy/example2.jar/
[Verifier] Verifying file:/.../Default/example2.jar/ejb1002.jar
[Container factory] Deploying TextMDB
[ContainerManagement] Initializing
[ContainerManagement] Initialized
[ContainerManagement] Starting
[ContainerManagement] Started
[Container factory] Deployed application: file:/.../example2.jar/
[J2EE Deployer Default] J2EE application: example2.jar is deployed.
[Default] TextMDB.ctor, this=494668
[Default] TextMDB.setMessageDrivenContext, this=494668
[Default] TextMDB.ejbCreate, this=494668
[Default] TextMDB.ctor, this=4395216
[Default] TextMDB.onMessage, this=494668
[Default] TextMDB.setMessageDrivenContext, this=4395216
[Default] TextMDB.sendReply, this=494668, dest=QUEUE.A
[Default] TextMDB.ejbCreate, this=4395216
[OILClientIL] ConnectionReceiverOILClient is connecting to: 172.17.66.54:1791
[Default] TextMDB.onMessage, this=4395216
[Default] TextMDB.sendReply, this=4395216, dest=QUEUE.A
[Default] TextMDB.onMessage, this=4395216
[Default] TextMDB.sendReply, this=4395216, dest=QUEUE.A
[Default] TextMDB.onMessage, this=494668
[Default] TextMDB.sendReply, this=494668, dest=QUEUE.A
[Default] TextMDB.onMessage, this=494668
[Default] TextMDB.sendReply, this=494668, dest=QUEUE.A
[Default] TextMDB.onMessage, this=4395216
[Default] TextMDB.sendReply, this=4395216, dest=QUEUE.A
```

```
[Default] TextMDB.onMessage, this=4395216
[Default] TextMDB.sendReply, this=4395216, dest=QUEUE.A
[Default] TextMDB.onMessage, this=494668
[Default] TextMDB.sendReply, this=494668, dest=QUEUE.A
[Default] TextMDB.onMessage, this=494668
[Default] TextMDB.sendReply, this=494668, dest=QUEUE.A
[Default] TextMDB.onMessage, this=494668
[Default] TextMDB.sendReply, this=494668, dest=QUEUE.A
```

It can be seen from the server console messages that two MDB instances are created to handle the processing of the 10 client messages. This is also evident in the client console message due to the two unique hash code values contained in the processed by: NNNNN message annotations.

An Overview of the JBossMQ Architecture

This section introduces some of the key elements of the JBossMQ server architecture. This is a relatively high-level overview to help you understand how JBossMQ operates and integrates with the JBoss server. The overview focuses on the JBossMQ related MBean services that are responsible for the integration of JBossMQ into the JBoss server.

The core components that comprise the JBossMQ server are discussed first. Figure 4.3 provides an overview of the key JBossMQ services and their high-level relationships.

Figure 4.3 shows the org.jboss.mq.server.JMSServer as the heart of the server components because it is referenced by nearly every other component. The JMSServer is the core of the JMS implementation. The life cycle of the JMSServer is exposed via the org.jboss.mq.server.JBossMQService MBean. This MBean performs the startup and shutdown of the JMSServer in response to JBoss server life-cycle method invocations. The JBossMQService MBean also exposes operations for creating and destroying Queues and Topics at runtime.

Figure 4.3 also shows that the JMSServer delegates user permission checks to the org.jboss.mq.server.StateManager MBean service. This MBean uses an XML file to describe user to password mapping as well as the durable subscriptions.

The handling of persistent messages is delegated to an implementation of the org.jboss.mq.pm.PersistanceManager interface. The choice of which persistence manager the JMSServer uses is based on which MBean service is configured. In Figure 4.3, the org.jboss.mq.pm.rollinglogged.PersistanceManager is shown. This is a file-based persistence manager that is the current default PersistanceManager implementation. Some of the optional persistence manager MBeans are discussed later in this chapter in the section titled "Configuring JBossMQ."

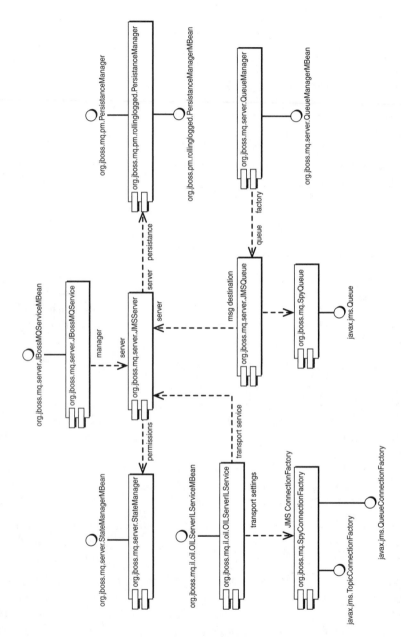

FIGURE 4.3 An overview of the key components in the JBossMQ server components and their relationships.

Recall that Queues and Topics are administered objects for which there is no management API in the JMS specification. Although the JBossMQService exposes operations for destination administration, it would be nice to be able to specify the Queues and Topics as part of the server configuration. This is the purpose of the org.jboss.mq.server.QueueManager MBean shown in Figure 4.3. Each QueueManager MBean creates and binds an org.jboss.mq.SpyQueue into JNDI as an object under the "queue" context using the name assigned as the QueueName attribute. Topics are managed in a similar way by the org.jboss.mq.server.TopicManager MBean, which is not shown in Figure 4.3.

The last core component is the invocation layer service MBean. In Figure 4.3 the optimized invocation layer (OIL) MBean is shown as the org.jboss.mq.il.oil.OILServerILService component. The invocation layer components are responsible for exposing the JMSServer to clients via some message transport. JBossMQ supports a number of different message transports, each of which is configured by a different MBean service. You will look at all of the available message transport services in the section, "Configuring JBossMQ." Figure 4.3 shows the default invocation layer OILServerILService MBean, but none of the related components that deal with message transport.

You can investigate the invocation layer architecture by drilling down into OILServerILService to see its associated message transport components. This gives you a view as presented in Figure 4.4.

The OIL message transport protocol is a custom socket-based protocol that uses a socket on the JMSServer and another on the JMS client to send messages between the two. The JMSServer side socket allows the client to send messages to the JMSServer while the client side socket allows the server to asynchronously deliver messages to the client.

In Figure 4.4 the dark-gray shaded components are those that operate within the JMSServer VM while the light-gray shaded components operate in the JMS client VM. The OILServerILService is the MBean that manages the setup of the OIL components. Its responsibilities include starting the JMSServer-side listening socket that will accept JMS client connections as well as binding an org.jboss.mq.SpyConnectionFactory into JNDI for access by JMS clients. The SpyConnectionFactory instance that the OILServerILService binds into JNDI is associated with an org.jboss.mq.GenericConnectionFactory that handles the creation of the transport specific versions of the org.jboss.mq.il.ServerIL and org.jboss.mq.il.ClientILService interfaces. The GenericConnectionFactory is set up by the OILServerILService to return OIL specific implementations of the transport independent ServerIL and ClientILService interfaces used by the org.jboss.mq.SpyConnection. This is the mechanism used by every invocation layer MBean service to establish a ConnectionFactory for the server invocation layer protocol. This means that the transport protocol a JMS client uses is determined by which `ConnectionFactory` the client accesses. If a client wants to use a particular type of transport, the client needs to know under what JNDI name the invocation layer MBean service binds its `ConnectionFactory`.

Although the `SpyConnectionFactory` is bound into JNDI inside the JMSServer VM, it is accessed by the client within its VM when the client looks up a `QueueConnectionFactory` or `TopicConnectionFactory` to create a `Connection` to the JMS provider. When the client creates a Connection, the creation of the `SpyConnection` causes the creation of `org.jboss.mq.il.oil.OILClientILService` and `org.jboss.mq.il.oil.OILServerIL` instances in the client VM. The `OILClientILService` creates a server socket that the `JMSServer` will use to push messages to the client. The information on how to push messages to the client is sent to the server using the `org.jboss.mq.ConnectionToken` class. This is a serializable pair consisting of a clientID and an `org.jboss.mq.il.oil.OILClientIL` instance. When the `OILClientIL` is used in the JMSServer VM, it establishes a connection back to the `OILClientILService`, if none exists using the port and address information set by the `OILClientILService`.

The `OILServerIL` instance functions similarly to the `OILClientIL`, but it was created in the JMSServer and has the port and address of the `OILServerILService` that created it. When messages are sent to the `JMSServer` over the `SpyConnection`, the `OILServerIL` associated with the connection is used. This causes a socket connection to be made to the `OILServerILService` if none currently exists.

This interaction between server- and client- side components based on factories for interfaces found in the `org.jboss.mq.il` package is the pattern used by all invocation layer implementations. All that varies are the protocol dependent details of how messages are sent to the `JMSServer` side component using the `ServerIL` implementation, and how messages are pushed back to the JMS client using the `ClientIL` implementation.

JBossMQ Application Server Facilities

Up to this point, you have looked at the standard JMS client/server architecture. The JMS specification defines an advanced set of interfaces that allow for concurrent processing of a destination's messages, and collectively this functionality is referred to as application server facilities (ASF). Two of the interfaces that support concurrent message processing, `javax.jms.ServerSessionPool` and `javax.jms.ServerSession`, must be provided by the application server in which the processing occurs. Thus, the set of components that make up the JBossMQ ASF involves both JBossMQ components as well as JBoss server components. A diagram of ASF components is presented in Figure 4.5.

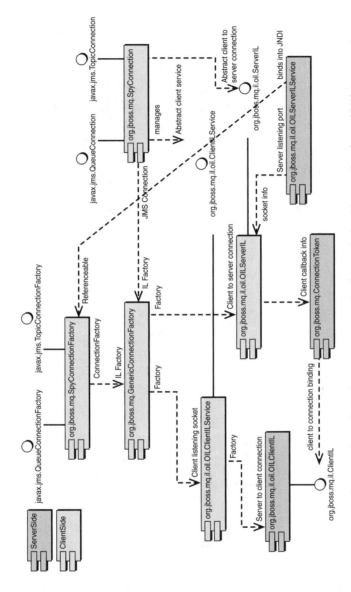

FIGURE 4.4   An overview of the key components in the optimized invocation layer (OIL) transport implementation.

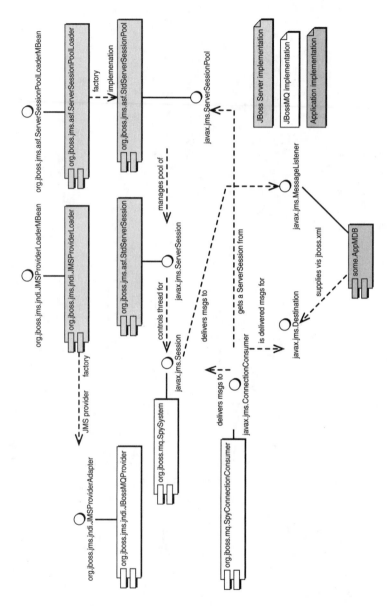

FIGURE 4.5   The JBoss and JBossMQ ASF components and their relationships.

In Figure 4.5, the white circles represent the JMS interfaces that constitute the ASF. The shaded components represent the implementor of the interfaces and which implementation domain they fall into. The light-gray components are implemented by the JBoss server; the white components are implemented by the JBossMQ provider; and the dark-gray components are implemented by the JMS application that wants to perform the concurrent message processing. Here the application is illustrated as an MDB because this is the natural use case of the ASF in J2EE. The JBoss server implements MDBs by utilizing the JMS service's ASF to concurrently process messages sent to MDBs.

The responsibilities of the ASF domains are well defined by the JMS specification and so a discussion of how the ASF components are implemented is not necessary here. However, a discussion of how ASF components used by the JBoss MDB layer are integrated using MBeans that allow either the application server interfaces or the JMS provider interfaces to be replaced with alternate implementations is necessary.

Start with the `org.jboss.jms.jndi.JMSProviderLoader` MBean show in Figure 4.5. This MBean is responsible for loading an instance of the `org.jboss.jms.jndi.JMSProviderAdaptor` interface into the JBoss server and binding it into JNDI. The `JMSProviderAdaptor` interface is an abstraction that defines how to get the root JNDI context for the JMS provider. The abstraction supports getting and setting the JNDI `Context.PROVIDER_URL` for the root `InitialContext`, and the JNDI names of the `QueueConnectionFactory` and `TopicConnectionFactory` bindings in the root context. This is all that is necessary to bootstrap use of a JMS provider. By abstracting this information into an interface, alternate JMS ASF provider implementations can be used with the JBoss MDB container. The `org.jboss.jms.jndi.JBossMQProvider` is the default implementation of `JMSProviderAdaptor` interface and provides the adaptor for the JBossMQ JMS provider. To replace the JBossMQ provider with an alternate JMS ASF implementation, simply create an implementation of the `JMSProviderAdaptor` interface and configure the `JMSProviderLoader` with the class name of the implementation. You will see an example of this in the configuration section.

In addition to being able to replace the JMS provider used for MDBs, you can also replace the `javax.jms.ServerSessionPool` interface implementation. This is possible by configuring the class name of the `org.jboss.jms.asf.ServerSessionPoolFactory` implementation using the `org.jboss.jms.asf.ServerSessionPoolLoader` MBean `PoolFactoryClass` attribute. The default `ServerSessionPoolFactory` factory implementation is the JBoss `org.jboss.jms.asf.StdServerSessionPoolFactory` class.

Configuring JBossMQ

Configuration of JBossMQ is based on the configuration of the JBossMQ MBeans. Several of the JBossMQ MBeans were introduced in the "An Overview of the

JBossMQ Architecture" section earlier in this chapter. The following sections offer a complete description of all JBossMQ MBeans along with their configurable attributes.

org.jboss.mq.server.JBossMQService

The `JBossMQService` MBean embeds the JBossMQ JMS message server into the JBoss server. The JBossMQ server is necessary for EJB 2.0 message-driven beans as well as any other JMS client usage. The `JBossMQService` has no configurable attributes.

The `JBossMQService` does define operations for the runtime administration of queues and topics. Note that the configuration of queues or topics created via these operations is not saved across restarts of the JBoss server.

- `public void createQueue(String name)` throws Exception.
  This creates a `javax.jms.Queue` destination.

- `public void destroyQueue(String name)` throws Exception.
  This destroys an existing `javax.jms.Queue` destination.

- `public void createTopic(String name)` throws Exception.
  This creates a `javax.jms.Topic` destination.

- `public void destroyTopic(String name)` throws Exception.
  This destroys an existing `javax.jms.Topic` destination.

org.jboss.mq.server.StateManager

The `StateManager` MBean is a simple user-to-password and user-to-durable subscription mapping service. It uses an XML file to obtain this mapping information. For a user to create a durable subscription, the user must have an entry in the StateManager.

The single configurable attribute of the `StateManager` service is as follows:

- `StateFile`—This is the name of the `StateManager` XML file. The location of the file is resolved relative to the location of the jboss.jcml file. If no StateFile attribute is specified a default file named jbossmq-state.xml is assumed.

The DTD for the `StateManager` XML file is given graphically in Figure 4.6.

The element meanings are as follows:

- User/Name—The username that corresponds to the
  `Connection.createConnection(username, password)` method.

- User/Password—The password that corresponds to the
  `Connection.createConnection(username, password)` method.

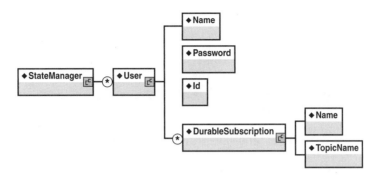

FIGURE 4.6 The DTD for the `StateManager` user-password, user-durable-subscription XML file.

- User/Id—The `clientID` that is associated with the connection for the user-name.

- User/DurableSubscription—A listing of the durable subscriptions associated with the username.

- User/DurableSubscription/Name—The name of the durable subscription. This is the value passed in as the name parameter to the `TopicSession.createDurableSubscriber(Topic, name)` method.

- User/DurableSubscription/TopicName—The name of the Topic current associated with the durable subscription.

org.jboss.mq.pm.rollinglogged.PersistenceManager

The `PersistenceManager` MBean service manages all JBossMQ persistence-related services. It is an implementation of the `org.jboss.mq.pm.PersistenceManager` that uses a file store, and allows up to 1,000 messages to be persisted before it starts discarding the old messages. This is the default persistence manager configured with the JBoss distribution.

The configurable attributes of the service are as follows:

- DataDirectory—The path to the directory where the service will store its data files

- RollOverSize—The maximum number of message to persist before the store file rolls over and old messages are discarded.

`org.jboss.mq.pm.file.PersistanceManager`

This is an alternate `PersistenceManager` MBean service implementation that uses a single file per persistent message. This is a robust implementation, but it is can be quite slow relative to the other implementations because of the overhead involved with opening and closing a file for each message.

The single configurable attribute of the service is as follows:

* DataDirectory—The path to the directory where the service will store its data files

`org.jboss.mq.pm.jdbc.PersistanceManager`

This is an alternate `PersistenceManager` MBean service implementation that stores persistent messages in a JDBC store. It expects a JDBC DataSource that contains two tables that have a schema consistent to the following:

```
CREATE TABLE JMS_MESSAGES
(
  MESSAGEID   CHAR(17) NOT NULL,
  DESTINATION VARCHAR(30) NOT NULL,
  MESSAGEBLOB BLOB,
  PRIMARY KEY (MESSAGEID, DESTINATION)
);
CREATE INDEX JMS_MESSAGES_DEST ON JMS_MESSAGES(DESTINATION);
CREATE TABLE JMS_TRANSACTIONS
(
 ID CHAR(17)
)
```

The single configurable attribute of the service is as follows:

* JmsDBPoolName—The JNDI name of the javax.sql.DataSource to use for obtaining the database connections

`org.jboss.mq.il.oil.OILServerILService`

The `OILServerILService` MBean service configures the optimized invocation layer (OIL) transport mechanism. It is also the default transport by virtue of the fact that is uses the common `QueueConnectionFactory` and `TopicConnectionFactory` as the JNDI location of the connection factories that it binds into JNDI. This is the preferred invocation layer, and should be used by clients external to the JBossMQ server VM. The only potential restriction is that the OIL transport requires that a connection be made from the JBossMQ server back to the client. This may not be possible due to firewall restrictions.

The configurable attributes of the `OILServerILService` service are as follows:

- ConnectionFactoryJNDIRef—The JNDI name under which the combined `javax.jms.QueueConnectionFactory` and `javax.jms.TopicConnectionFactory` instance is bound. This is used by clients to obtain a factory that does not support the JTA two-phase XA distributed transaction protocol.

- XAConnectionFactoryJNDIRef—The JNDI name under which the combined `javax.jms.XAQueueConnectionFactory` and `javax.jms.XATopicConnectionFactory` instance is bound. This is used by clients to obtain a factory that supports the JTA two-phase XA distributed transaction protocol.

- ServerBindPort—The port number to which the OIL service clients connect when they establish a connection to the JBossMQ server. If not specified, the default is an anonymous port assigned by the operating system.

- BindAddress—The interface address on which the OIL service bind its listening port. This is useful for multi-homed hosts. The default is to bind all available interfaces.

org.jboss.mq.il.oil.UILServerILService

The `UILServerILService` MBean service is an unified invocation layer (UIL) transport mechanism similar to the OIL custom socket transport. The difference is that a single socket connection is used between the client and server, and therefore a modified transport scheme is used to allow full duplex sending and receiving of messages. This invocation layer should be used if a client is connecting through a firewall that does not allow connections to originate from the JBossMQ server back into the client. The configurable attributes of the `UILServerILService` service are as follows:

- ConnectionFactoryJNDIRef—The JNDI name under which the combined `javax.jms.QueueConnectionFactory` and `javax.jms.TopicConnectionFactory` instance is bound. This is used by clients to obtain a factory that does not support the JTA two-phase XA distributed transaction protocol.

- XAConnectionFactoryJNDIRef—The JNDI name under which the combined `javax.jms.XAQueueConnectionFactory` and `javax.jms.XATopicConnectionFactory` instance is bound. This is used by clients to obtain a factory that supports the JTA two-phase XA distributed transaction protocol.

- ServerBindPort—The port number to which the UIL service clients connect when they establish a connection to the JBossMQ server. If not specified, the default is an anonymous port assigned by the operating system.

- BindAddress—The interface address on which the UIL service binds its listening port. This is useful for multi-homed hosts. The default is to bind all available interfaces.

org.jboss.mq.il.jvm.JVMServerILService

The JVMServerILService MBean service configures the intra-server VM invocation layer transport mechanism. This is simply an adaptor implementation that incurs only a single method call of overhead in mapping from the ClientIL or ServerIL interfaces onto the JMS server objects. It is a call-by-reference semantic transport that can only be used by JMS clients within the same VM as the JMSServer instance. This invocation layer should be used whenever a JMS client is located inside the same VM as the JBossMQ service as it is the highest performance implementation.

The configurable attributes of the JVMServerILService service are as follows:

- ConnectionFactoryJNDIRef—The JNDI name under which the combined javax.jms.QueueConnectionFactory and javax.jms.TopicConnectionFactory instance are bound. This is used by clients to obtain a factory that does not support the JTA two-phase XA distributed transaction protocol. Note that this should be under the "java:" (for example, java:/ConnectionFactory) context so that it will not be accessible outside of the server VM because it does not support a remote transport. Any attempt to use the factory outside of the JBossMQ server VM will fail.

- XAConnectionFactoryJNDIRef—The JNDI name under which the combined javax.jms.XAQueueConnectionFactory and javax.jms.XATopicConnectionFactory instance is bound. This is used by clients to obtain a factory that supports the JTA two-phase XA distributed transaction protocol. Note that this should be under the "java:" (for example, java:/XAConnectionFactory) context so that it will not be accessible outside of the server VM because it does not support a remote transport. Any attempt to use the factory outside of the JBossMQ server VM will fail.

org.jboss.mq.il.rmi.RMIServerILService

The RMIServerILService MBean service configures an RMI-based invocation layer transport mechanism. Communication between the client and server use standard Java RMI protocol. This is currently somewhat less efficient than the custom protocol used by the OIL and UIL layers due to the synchronous RPC semantics of RMI. It exists because it is easy to implement but should not be used. Future changes in the RMI layer may restore the utility of this invocation layer.

The configurable attributes of the `RMIServerILService` service are as follows:

- ConnectionFactoryJNDIRef—The JNDI name under which the combined `javax.jms.QueueConnectionFactory` and `javax.jms.TopicConnectionFactory` instance is bound. This is used by clients to obtain a factory that does not support the JTA two-phase XA distributed transaction protocol.

- XAConnectionFactoryJNDIRef—The JNDI name under which the combined `javax.jms.XAQueueConnectionFactory` and `javax.jms.XATopicConnectionFactory` instance is bound. This is used by clients to obtain a factory that supports the JTA two-phase XA distributed transaction protocol.

org.jboss.mq.server.TopicManager

The `TopicManager` MBean service manages a `javax.jms.Topic` destination. The `TopicManager` MBean is used to create `javax.jms.Topic` destinations.

The single configurable attribute of the `TopicManager` service is as follows:

- TopicName—The JNDI name under which the `javax.jms.Topic` is bound. This is relative to the "topic" context. Thus, a TopicName of myTopic will be located under the JNDI name "topic/myTopic".

org.jboss.mq.server.QueueManager

The `QueueManager` MBean service manages a `javax.jms.Queue` destination. The `QueueManager` MBean is used to create `javax.jms.Queue` destintations.

The single configurable attribute of the `QueueManager` service is as follows:

- QueueName—The JNDI name under which the `javax.jms.Queue` is bound. This is relative to the queue context. Thus, a QueueName of myQueue will be located under the JNDI name `queue/myQueue`.

org.jboss.jms.jndi.JMSProviderLoader

The `JMSProviderLoader` MBean service creates a JMS provider instance and binds it into JNDI. A JMS provider adaptor is a class that implements the `org.jboss.jms.jndi.JMSProviderAdapter` interface. It is used by the message-driven bean container to access a JMS service provider in a provider independent manner.

The configurable attributes of the `JMSProviderLoader` service are as follows:

- ProviderName—A unique name for the JMS provider. This is used to bind the `JMSProviderAdapter` instance into JNDI under "java:/ProviderName".

- ProviderAdapterClass—The fully qualified class name of the `org.jboss.jms.jndi.JMSProviderAdapter` interface of which to create an instance. To use an alternate JMS provider like Fiorano, you create an implementation of the JMSProviderAdaptor interface that allows the administration of the InitialContext provider url, and the locations of the `QueueConnectionFactory` and `TopicConnectionFactory` in JNDI.

- ProviderURL—The JNDI Context.PROVIDER_URL value to use when creating the JMS provider root `InitialContext`. The resulting `IntialContext` is used to obtain the JMS provider connection factories.

- QueueFactoryRef—The JNDI name under which the provider `javax.jms.QueueConnectionFactory` is bound. This name will be used to look up the `javax.jms.QueueConnectionFactory` from the `InitialContext` created using the ProviderURL attribute value.

- TopicFactoryRef—The JNDI name under which the `javax.jms.TopicConnectionFactory` is bound. This name will be used to look up the `javax.jms.TopicConnectionFactory` from the `InitialContext` created using the ProviderURL attribute value.

org.jboss.jms.asf.ServerSessionPoolLoader

The `ServerSessionPoolLoader` MBean service manages a factory for `javax.jms.ServerSessionPool` objects used by the message-driven bean container.

The configurable attributes of the `ServerSessionPoolLoader` service are as follows:

- PoolName—A unique name for the session pool. This is used to bind the `ServerSessionPoolFactory` instance into JNDI under `java:/PoolName`.

- PoolFactoryClass—The fully qualified class name of the `org.jboss.jms.asf.ServerSessionPoolFactory` interface of which to create an instance.

Summary

This chapter introduced the JMS API and the EJB 2.0 message-driven bean. You were shown an example JMS client and MDB using the JBossMQ JMS provider. An overview of the JBossMQ architecture was presented along with a complete reference for the configuration of the JBossMQ MBeans.

The next chapter, "JBossCMP—The JBoss Container Manager Persistence Layer," covers the JBoss EJB persistence layer component JBossCMP.

bile:
[mkdir] Created dir: /tmp/2.4.4/
[javac] Compiling 154 source file
install:
[copy] Copyin
[copy] Copyin   p/2
                                       p/2

5

IN THIS CHAPTER

- Container Managed Persistence—CMP

- The JBossCMP Architecture

- JAWS—The Default CMP Implementation

- Customizing the Behavior of JAWS

- Configuring JDBC

JBossCMP—The JBoss Container-Managed Persistence Layer

The JBossCMP layer consists of the components that support the EJB 1.1 container-managed persistence (CMP) model. This chapter describes CMP and examines how the JBoss EJB container provides extensible support for CMP. The chapter concludes with an introduction to the default CMP implementation provided with JBoss as well as an explanation of how it can be customized for use with CMP beans.

Container Managed Persistence—CMP

Container-managed persistence is an entity bean model that moves the task of reading and writing an entity bean's persistent state from the bean developer to the EJB container. An entity bean with container-managed persistence relies on the container to perform data access on behalf of the entity bean. The alternative model is bean-managed persistence (BMP) which requires the bean developer to load and store the bean persistent state through code in the entity bean. CMP entity beans are simpler to develop than bean-managed persistence beans because in CMP beans, the bean author focuses on the business logic aspect of the entity bean, while the EJB container handles the persistence requirements. The bean provider must define which fields in the entity bean the container persistence engine should manage. That is the extent of the bean provider's role with regard to persistence. Most application servers provide support for allowing the bean developer to customize how the EJB container manages persistent fields. The customization support available in the default JBoss CMP engine is discussed in the section entitled "Customizing the Behavior of JAWS".

Whether or not CMP is the right model for your entity beans depends primarily on the complexity of any existing relational schema you must use as the source of your entity beans persistent fields. The EJB 1.1 CMP model often cannot be used effectively for highly relational models that spread an object's persistent state over more than one table. In this case, the only real option is to use the BMP entity bean model. You can achieve some of the benefits of the simplicity of the CMP model with BMP if you use a sophisticated object-to-relational mapping tool such as CocoBase.

NOTE

If you want to find more information about CocoBase, check out their Web site at `http://www.thoughtinc.com`.

The JBossCMP Architecture

The JBoss CMP architecture does not depend on a relational JDBC-based store. Persistence management is modeled in an abstract and extensible fashion that allows the use of any persistent store. The key classes that make up the persistence abstraction layer for entity beans are presented in Figure 5.1.

Figure 5.1 shows that the `EntityContainer` relies on an instance of the `org.jboss.ejb.EntityPersistenceManager` interface for persistence management. The `EntityPersistenceManager` abstraction is actually used for both CMP and BMP persistence, but only the CMP implementation is shown in Figure 5.1 as the `org.jboss.ejb.plugins.CMPPersistenceManager` class. The `CMPPersistenceManager` implements the semantics of the EJB 1.1 CMP callback model. The various EJB life cycle callback methods (`ejbLoad`, `ejbStore`, `ejbActivate`, `ejbPassivate`, `ejbRemove`) are invoked by the `CMPPersistenceManager` in response to `EntityPersistenceManager` method invocations. The actual storage of the entity persistent fields is delegated to an `EntityPersistenceStore` implementation that takes care of the details of a particular physical store. For the CMP entity container, it is the implementation of the `EntityPersistenceStore` interface that is externalized by the container configuration and may be replaced by an implementation of your choice. The default implementation of the `EntityPersistenceStore` interface defined in the `standardjboss.xml` configuration file is the `org.jboss.ejb.plugins.jaws.JAWSPersistenceManager`. Customization of the persistence storage of a CMP entity bean comes down to providing a custom implementation of the `EntityPersistenceStore` interface. The following list describes each method, its arguments, return values, and exceptions.

- `Object createEntity(Method m, Object[] args, EntityEnterpriseContext instance)` throws Exception—This method is called whenever an entity is to be created. The persistence manager is responsible for handling the return value as well as any exception generated by the persistent store. The persistence manager first invokes the entity `ejbCreate` method, followed by the `createEntity` method, and then the entity `ejbPostCreate` method. The value the `createEntity` method must return is the primary key object for the newly created entity bean. The method arguments are:

- m—The home interface create method that generated this `createEntity` call

- args—The arguments passed to the home interface create method

- instance—The context associated with the instance being used for this create call

- Object `findEntity`(Method `finderMethod`, Object[] args, EntityEnterpriseContext instance) throws Exception—This method is called when a single entity needs to be found. The persistence store must find out if the desired instance is available in the store, and, if it is, return the primary key of the entity. If the entity cannot be found, a `javax.ejb.ObjectNotFoundException` must be thrown. For any other search-related failure, a `javax.ejb.FinderException` must be thrown. The method arguments are as follows:

  - finderMethod—The home interface find method that generated this findEntity call

  - args—The arguments passed to the home interface find method

  - instance—The context associated with the instance being used for this find call

- FinderResults `findEntities`(Method `finderMethod`, Object[] args, EntityEnterpriseContext instance) throws Exception—This method is called when a collection of entities needs to be found. The persistence store must find out if the desired instances are available in the store, and, if they are, return the matching primary keys as an `org.jboss.util.FinderResults` instance. If the entity cannot be found, an empty `FinderResults` should be returned. A null value must not be returned. If a search related error occurs, a `javax.ejb.FinderException` must be thrown. The method arguments are as follows:

  - finderMethod—The home interface find method that generated this findEntity call

  - args—The arguments passed to the home interface find method

  - instance—The context associated with the instance to use for activation

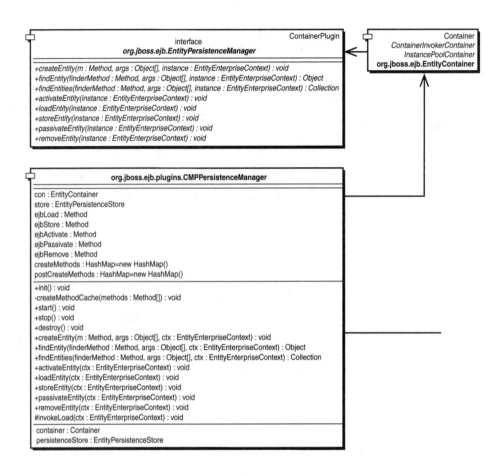

FIGURE 5.1   The JBoss CMP persistence abstraction layer classes.

```
                                                    EnterpriseContext
                          org.jboss.ejb.EntityEnterpriseContext

  ejbObject : EJBObject
  ejbLocalObject : EJBLocalObject
  ctx : EntityContext
  hasRxSynchronization : boolean=false
  -persistenceCtx : Object
  key : cacheKey

  +EntityEnterpriseContext(instance : Object, con : Container)
  +clear() : void
  +discard() : void
  +setCacheKey(key : Object) : void
  +getCacheKey() : CacheKey
  +hasTxSynchronization(value : boolean) : void
  +hasTxSynchronization() : boolean

  #EntityContextImpl

  EJBContext : EJBContext
  EJBObject : EJBObject
  EJBLocalObject : EJBLocalObject
  persistenceContextContext : Object
  valid : boolean
```

```
                                                    ContainerPlugin
                              interface
                      org.jboss.ejb.EntityPersistenceStore

  +createEntity(m : Method, args : Object[], instance : EntityEnterpriseContext) : Object
  +findEntity(finderMethod : Method, args : Object[], instance : EntityEnterpriseContext) : Object
→ +findEntities(finderMethod : Method, args : Object[], instance : EntityEnterpriseContext) : FinderResults
  +activateEntity(instance : EntityEnterpriseContext) : void
  +loadEntity(instance : EntityEnterpriseContext) : void
  +loadEntities(keys : FinderResults) : void
  +storeEntity(instance : EntityEnterpriseContext) : void
  +passivateEntity(instance : EntityEnterpriseContext) : void
  +removeEntity(instance : EntityEnterpriseContext) : void
```

```
                                                    Collection
                          org.jboss.util.FinderResults

  +FinderResults(keys : Collection, queryData:Object, finder : Object, args : Object[])
  +size() : int
  +contains(o : Object) : boolean
  +iterator() : Iterator
  +toArray() : Object[]
  +toArray(array : Object[]) : Object[]
  +add(o : Object) : boolean
  +remove(o : Object
  +containsAll(otherCollection : Collection) : boolean
  +addAll(otherCollection : Collection) : boolean
  +removeAll(otherCollection : Collection) : boolean
  +retainAll(otherCollection : Collection) : boolean
  +clear() : void

  allKeys : Collection
  keys : Collection
  queryData : Object
  finder : Object
  queryArgs : Object[]
  empty : boolean
```

- void `activateEntity(EntityEnterpriseContext instance)` throws `RemoteException`—This method is called when an entity should be activated. This event corresponds to moving an entity instance from the pooled to the ready state and does not really have anything to do with the persistent storage of entity. However, this call permits you to introduce optimizations in the persistence store—particularly if the context has a "PersistenceContext" that a store can use, as JAWS does for smart updates, and this is as good a callback as any other to set it up. The persistence manager invokes this method after `ejbActivate` has been invoked on the entity. On system errors, a `RemoteException` should be thrown. The method argument is as follows:

  - instance—The context associated with the instance being used for this find call.

- void `loadEntity(EntityEnterpriseContext instance)` throws `RemoteException`—This method is called whenever an entity shall be load from the underlying storage. The persistence manager loads the state from the underlying storage by calling the `loadEntity` method and then calls `ejbLoad` on the supplied instance.

  - instance—The context associated with the instance being used for this loadEntity call

- void `loadEntities(FinderResults keys)` throws `RemoteException`—This method is called whenever a set of entities should be preloaded from the underlying storage. The persistence store is allowed to make this a null operation. On system errors, a `RemoteException` should be thrown. The method argument is as follows:

  - keys—A collection of primary keys previously returned from findEntities call

- void `storeEntity(EntityEnterpriseContext instance)` throws `RemoteException`—This method is called whenever an entity needs to be written to the underlying store. The persistence manager must call `ejbStore` on the supplied instance and then store the state by invoking this method. On system errors a `RemoteException` should be thrown. The method argument is as follows:

  - instance—The context associated with the instance to synchronize with the store

- void `passivateEntity(EntityEnterpriseContext instance)` throws `RemoteException`—This method is called when an entity is to be passivated. The persistence manager must call the `ejbPassivate` method on the instance prior to calling this method. See the `activateEntity` method earlier in this chapter for the reason for exposing EJB pool callback calls to the store. On system errors, a `RemoteException` should be thrown. The method argument is as follows:

- instance—The context associated with the instance to passivate

- void removeEntity(EntityEnterpriseContext instance) throws `RemoteException`, `RemoveException`—This method is called when an entity will be removed from the underlying storage. The persistence manager must call `ejbRemove` on the instance prior to invoking this method. If the instance cannot be removed from the store, a `javax.ejb.RemoveException` must be thrown. On system errors a `RemoteException` should be thrown. The method argument is as follows:

  - instance—The context associated with the instance to remove from the store

Because `EntityPersistenceStore` extends the `org.jboss.ejb.ContainerPlugin` interface, the `ContainerPlugin` life-cycle methods must also be implemented. These methods are as follows:

- void init()—Called by the `CMPPersistenceManager` as an initialization request notification.

- void start()—Called by the `CMPPersistenceManager` as a startup request notification.

- void stop()—Called by the `CMPPersistenceManager` as a stop request notification.

- void destroy()—Called by the `CMPPersistenceManager` as a final shutdown request notification.

- void setContainer(Container con)—Called by the `CMPPersistenceManager` to set the `EntityContainer` instance that the store is associated with. The `EntityContainer` can be used to obtain the entity bean metadata and class information.

To help you understand the requirements for implementing a custom store, you will create a simple file based implementation of the `EntityPersistenceStore` interface.

A Custom File-Based Persistence Manager

This section illustrates the steps required to implement a custom store for CMP entity beans. You will create a simple file-based implementation of the `EntityPersistenceStore` interface to demonstrate the basics. Listing 5.1 shows the code for the sample implementation.

LISTING 5.1   The Example File System Based Implementation of the
EntityPersistenceStore Interface

```java
package org.jboss.chap5.ex1;

import java.io.File;
import java.io.InputStream;
import java.io.OutputStream;
import java.io.ObjectInputStream;
import java.io.ObjectOutputStream;
import java.io.FileOutputStream;
import java.io.FileInputStream;
import java.io.IOException;
import java.lang.reflect.Method;
import java.lang.reflect.Field;
import java.rmi.RemoteException;
import java.rmi.ServerException;
import java.util.ArrayList;
import java.util.Collection;
import java.util.Iterator;

import javax.ejb.EJBObject;
import javax.ejb.Handle;
import javax.ejb.EntityBean;
import javax.ejb.CreateException;
import javax.ejb.DuplicateKeyException;
import javax.ejb.FinderException;
import javax.ejb.ObjectNotFoundException;
import javax.ejb.RemoveException;

import org.apache.log4j.Category;

import org.jboss.ejb.Container;
import org.jboss.ejb.EntityContainer;
import org.jboss.ejb.EntityPersistenceStore;
import org.jboss.ejb.EntityEnterpriseContext;
import org.jboss.metadata.EntityMetaData;
import org.jboss.util.FinderResults;

/** An example EntityPersistenceStore implementation that uses a
 file system as the persistent store. An entity bean's cmp fields
 are written/read to/from the file system using Java serialization.
```

LISTING 5.1   Continued

```
@author Scott.Stark@jboss.org
@version $Revision:$
*/
public class FileStore implements EntityPersistenceStore
{
   Category log;
   EntityContainer entityContainer;
   EntityMetaData metaData;
   File storeRootDir;
   Field pkField;
   Field[] cmpFields;

   /** Called to set the EntityContainer we operate on behalf of.
    */
   public void setContainer(Container c)
   {
      entityContainer = (EntityContainer) c;
      metaData = (EntityMetaData) entityContainer.getBeanMetaData();
      log = Category.getInstance("FileStore#"+metaData.getEjbName());
      log.debug("setContainer, c="+c);
   }

   public void init() throws Exception
   {
      String ejbName = metaData.getEjbName();
      // Locate the jboss.home location or the current dir
      String dbPath = System.getProperty("jboss.home", ".");
      dbPath += "/db";
      log.debug("init, using dbPath="+dbPath);
      storeRootDir = new File(dbPath, ejbName);
      if( storeRootDir.exists() == false )
      {
         boolean created = storeRootDir.mkdirs();
         if( created == false )
            throw new IOException("Failed to create storeRootDir: "
               +storeRootDir.getAbsolutePath());
      }
      String pkName = metaData.getPrimKeyField();
      Class beanClass = entityContainer.getBeanClass();
      pkField = beanClass.getField(pkName);
      // Get the public fields of the bean class
```

LISTING 5.1   Continued

```
    ArrayList tmp = new ArrayList();
    Iterator cmpFieldsIter = metaData.getCMPFields();
    while( cmpFieldsIter.hasNext() )
    {
        String name = (String) cmpFieldsIter.next();
        Field f = beanClass.getField(name);
        tmp.add(f);
    }
    cmpFields = new Field[tmp.size()];
    tmp.toArray(cmpFields);
}

public void start()
{
}

public void stop()
{
}

public void destroy()
{
}

public Object createEntity(Method m, Object[] args,
    EntityEnterpriseContext ctx) throws Exception
{
    log.debug("createEntity: m="+m+", args="+args[0]);
    try
    {
        Object bean = ctx.getInstance();
        Object pk = pkField.get(bean);

        // Check exist
        File serFile = getFile(pk);
        if( serFile.exists() == true )
            throw new DuplicateKeyException("Already exists:"+pk);

        // Store to file
        storeEntity(pk, bean);
        return pk;
```

LISTING 5.1   Continued

```
      }
      catch(Exception e)
      {
         throw new CreateException("Could not create entity:"+e);
      }
   }

   public Object findEntity(Method m, Object[] args,
      EntityEnterpriseContext ctx)
      throws RemoteException, FinderException
   {
      log.debug("findEntity: m="+m+", args="+args[0]);
      if( m.getName().equals("findByPrimaryKey") )
      {
         Object pk = args[0];
         File serFile = getFile(pk);
         if( serFile.exists() == false )
            throw new ObjectNotFoundException(pk+" does not exist");

         return pk;
      }
      String msg = "Can't handle finderMethod: "+m;
      throw new FinderException(msg);
   }

   public FinderResults findEntities(Method m, Object[] args,
      EntityEnterpriseContext ctx)
      throws Exception
   {
      log.debug("findEntities: m="+m);
      if( m.getName().equals("findAll") )
      {
         String[] files = storeRootDir.list();
         ArrayList result = new ArrayList();
         for(int i = 0; i < files.length; i++)
         {
            if (files[i].endsWith(".ser"))
            {
               String pk = files[i];
               pk = pk.substring(0,pk.length()-4);
               log.debug("found pk="+pk);
```

LISTING 5.1   Continued

```
                result.add(pk);
            }
        }
        return new FinderResults(result, null, null, null);
    }
    String msg = "Can't handle finderMethod: "+m;
    throw new FinderException(msg);
}

public void loadEntity(EntityEnterpriseContext ctx)
    throws RemoteException
{
    try
    {
        // Read fields from serialized object file
        String pk = ""+ctx.getId();
        log.debug("loadEntity, pk="+pk);
        File serFile = getFile(pk);
        FileInputStream fis = new FileInputStream(serFile);
        ObjectInputStream in = new CMPObjectInputStream(fis);

        Object obj = ctx.getInstance();
        for(int i = 0; i < cmpFields.length; i++)
        {
            Field f = cmpFields[i];
            f.set(obj, in.readObject());
        }
        in.close();
    }
    catch(Exception e)
    {
        throw new ServerException("Load failed", e);
    }
}

public void storeEntity(EntityEnterpriseContext ctx)
    throws RemoteException
{
    storeEntity(ctx.getId(), ctx.getInstance());
}
```

LISTING 5.1   Continued

```java
public void removeEntity(EntityEnterpriseContext ctx)
   throws RemoteException, RemoveException
{
   Object pk = ""+ctx.getId();
   log.debug("removeEntity: pk="+pk);
   File serFile = getFile(pk);
   if( serFile.delete() == false )
      throw new RemoveException("Could not remove file:"+pk);
}

public void loadEntities(FinderResults keys)
{
   // We have no preload phase
}
public void activateEntity(EntityEnterpriseContext ctx)
   throws RemoteException
{
   // We have no passivation logic
}
public void passivateEntity(EntityEnterpriseContext ctx)
   throws RemoteException
{
   // We have no passivation logic
}

protected File getFile(Object id)
{
   String baseName = id.toString();
   return new File(storeRootDir, baseName+".ser");
}

private void storeEntity(Object id, Object obj)
   throws RemoteException
{
   try
   {
      // Write fields to serialized object file
      File serFile = getFile(id);
      log.debug("storeEntity, serFile="+serFile);
      FileOutputStream fos = new FileOutputStream(serFile);
      ObjectOutputStream out = new CMPObjectOutputStream(fos);
```

LISTING 5.1   Continued

```
      for(int i = 0; i < cmpFields.length; i++)
      {
        Field f = cmpFields[i];
        out.writeObject(f.get(obj));
      }
      out.close();
    }
    catch (Exception e)
    {
      throw new ServerException("Store failed", e);
    }
  }

  static class CMPObjectOutputStream
    extends ObjectOutputStream
  {
    public CMPObjectOutputStream(OutputStream out)
      throws IOException
    {
      super(out);
      enableReplaceObject(true);
    }

    protected Object replaceObject(Object obj)
      throws IOException
    {
      if (obj instanceof EJBObject)
        return ((EJBObject)obj).getHandle();

      return obj;
    }
  }

  static class CMPObjectInputStream
    extends ObjectInputStream
  {
    public CMPObjectInputStream(InputStream in)
      throws IOException
    {
      super(in);
      enableResolveObject(true);
```

LISTING 5.1   Continued

```
    }

    protected Object resolveObject(Object obj)
        throws IOException
    {
        if (obj instanceof Handle)
            return ((Handle)obj).getEJBObject();

        return obj;
    }
  }
}
```

This implementation is rather simple and is designed to help you understand the nature of the EntityPersistenceStore interface requirements. The example has a number of fundamental limitations with respect to use in an actual production environment, which is discussed after the implementation and demonstration of its use.

The first five methods of Listing 5.1 are from the org.jboss.ejb.ContainerPlugin interface. The ContainerPlugin interface is used to manage the life cycle of plug-ins associated with an org.jboss.ejb.Container instance. They allow a plug-in to know when it has been associated with a Container and when the Container is initialized, started, stopped, and destroyed. In the FileStore example, you only make use of the setContainer and init methods. The setContainer callback informs the FileStore by which Container instance it will be used. The FileStore uses the setContainer callback to save the EntityContainer reference, obtain the entity bean metadata, and initialize a log4j Category instance with a category name of "FileStore#" concatenated with the entity bean name the EntityContainer is managing. This example uses the log4j API to allow the debugging output from the FileStore to be annotated with a distinct category to isolate the FileStore statements from the rest of the server component logging.

The init method performs three tasks. The first task is the location, and optionally, the creation of the directory into which persistent data for entity beans managed by the EntityContainer will be stored. The directory is the "db/ejbName" subdirectory under the jboss distribution root directory. The second task the init method performs is initialization of a java.lang.reflect.Field instance for the instance variable that serves as the entity bean primary key. The last task is to obtain Field instances for the entity bean instance variables that have been declared as container managed through cmp-field declarations in the ejb-jar.xml descriptor. This information is available from the EntityBeanMetaData associated with the

EntityContainer. The Field instances will be used to read/write values from/to the entity bean instances. Note that you could not have performed the last two steps inside of the setContainer method, as the Class object for the entity bean has not been loaded at the time setContainer is called.

The createEntity method is responsible for creating a new persistent record. It is invoked whenever a client calls a create method on the bean's home interface. The persistent record is created by obtaining the entity bean instance that has been created from the EntityEnterpriseContext using the getInstance method. The primary key for the bean is obtained using reflection via the pkField instance. A File object is created based on the primary key, and a check is made to ensure that the file does not currently exist. Each entity bean is stored in a file with a name equal to the bean's primary key as a string +concatenated with the ".ser" extension. A clash between filenames corresponds to duplicate entity bean primary keys. If a file already exists with the calculated name, a DuplicateKeyException is thrown. If no such file exists, the entity's initial state is saved to disk by calling the storeEntity method and the bean's primary key value is returned. Any Exception that occurs during the save is caught and re-thrown as a CreateException.

The findEntity method is invoked whenever a client calls a single-entity finder method on the bean's home interface. The StoreFile implementation of findEntity only handles the required findByPrimaryKey finder, and this is why the finder method name is checked against "findByPrimaryKey". Location of an entity simply consists of constructing a file from the primary key argument and testing for existence of the file. If the file exists, the input primary key is returned to indicate an entity was found. If the file does not exist, an ObjectNotFoundException is thrown. An attempt to perform any other single-entity finder results in a FinderException being thrown.

The findEntities method is invoked whenever a client calls a multi-entity finder method on the bean's home interface. FileStore implements only the findAll version of the multi-entity finder because this is the easiest version to support. Returning all existing primary keys simply consists of listing all files in the store directory and removing the ".ser" suffix from the filename. An attempt to perform any other multi-entity finder results in a FinderException being thrown.

The loadEntity method is called whenever the container deems it necessary to populate an entity bean instance with the persistent store state. The entity bean's state is loaded by reading its serialized state from its store file using Java serialization and reflection. The entity instance is obtained from the EntityEnterpriseContext using the getInstance method.

The storeEntity method is called whenever the container deems it necessary to save the state of an entity bean instance to the persistent store. This method obtains the entity bean instance and primary key from the EntityEnterpriseContext and then calls the internal storeEntity method to perform the state storage. The internal storeEntity method writes the entity bean's state to its store file using Java serialization and reflection.

The removeEntity method is called whenever a client calls remove on the bean's remote or home interface. Removal of an entity simply entails removal of its persistent store file. A RemoveException is thrown if the file cannot be deleted for any reason.

The remaining EntityPersistenceStore interface methods, loadEntities, activateEntity and passivateEntity are empty methods in the FileStore example, as they serve no purpose in its implementation. An example of where loadEntities would be useful is a JDBC store implementation that preloaded the persistent data for the beans found by the load query. The activateEntity and passivateEntity method may be useful if the persistence store associates an some information with the in memory state of a bean.

A final item of note in the FileStore example is the use of custom ObjectInputStream and ObjectOutputStream subclasses. Recall from your EJB specification reading that CMP fields are restricted to the following: Java primitive types, Serializable types, and references of enterprise beans' remote or home interfaces. The serialized form of remote interfaces does not maintain its association with the EJB instance in the JBoss server. A javax.ejb.Handle does. So, the custom CMPObjectOutputStream and CMPObjectInputStream classes replace EJBObjects with Handles on output and vice-versa on input.

Using the FileStore

Now that you have created a custom persistent store, how do you make use of it? The answer is that you need to modify the default CMP container configuration to use your FileStore class. This requires knowledge about the container configuration section of the jboss.xml descriptor, the details of which are described in Chapter 9, which covers advanced JBoss configuration. Instead of taking a detour and talking in detail about the container configuration options available in the jboss.xml descriptor, this particular example shows you how to use the FileStore by example. You will cover the details of the jboss.xml elements introduced in the example in Chapter 9, "Advanced JBoss Configuration."

To demonstrate the use of the custom FileStore, you need a CMP entity bean. Listing 5.2 provides the home and remote interfaces as well as the bean class for the trivial entity bean you will use as your test case. The entity bean has int, float, double persistent fields, with a String primary key. The int, float, and double fields may be set through mutators. A String description of the entity bean's state is obtained using the getState accessor method. The corresponding ejb-jar.xml and jboss.xml descriptors for the entity bean jar are given in Listing 5.3.

LISTING 5.2   The FileStore Usage Example Entity Bean Home, Remote Interfaces, and Bean Class

```java
/** The FileStore example entity remote interface */
package org.jboss.chap5.ex1;

import java.rmi.RemoteException;
import javax.ejb.EJBObject;

public interface Ex1Entity extends EJBObject
{
    String getState() throws RemoteException;
    public void setIntVar(int i) throws RemoteException;
    public void setFloatVar(float f) throws RemoteException;
    public void setDoubleVar(double d) throws RemoteException;
}


/** The FileStore example entity home interface */
package org.jboss.chap5.ex1;

import java.rmi.RemoteException;
import java.util.Collection;
import javax.ejb.CreateException;
import javax.ejb.EJBHome;
import javax.ejb.FinderException;

public interface Ex1EntityHome extends EJBHome
{
    public Ex1Entity create(String key, int i, float f, double d)
        throws RemoteException, CreateException;

    public Ex1Entity findByPrimaryKey(String name)
        throws RemoteException, FinderException;
    public Collection findAll()
        throws RemoteException, FinderException;

}

/** The FileStore example entity bean implementation */
package org.jboss.chap5.ex1;

import java.rmi.RemoteException;
import javax.ejb.CreateException;
```

LISTING 5.2   Continued

```java
import javax.ejb.EntityBean;
import javax.ejb.EntityContext;

import org.apache.log4j.Category;

public class Ex1EntityBean implements EntityBean
{
    private static final Category log =
        Category.getInstance(Ex1EntityBean.class);
    private EntityContext entityContext;

    public String key;
    public int intVar;
    public float floatVar;
    public double doubleVar;

    public String ejbCreate(String key, int i, float f, double d)
    {
        this.key = key;
        this.intVar = i;
        this.floatVar = f;
        this.doubleVar = d;
        log.debug("ejbCreate: key="+key+", i="+i+", f="+f+", d="+d);
        return null;
    }

    public void ejbPostCreate(String key, int i, float f, double d)
    {
        log.debug("ejbPostCreate: key="+key);
    }

    public void ejbLoad()
    {
        log.debug("ejbLoad:, key="+key);
    }

    public void ejbRemove()
    {
        log.debug("ejbRemove:, key="+key);
    }
```

LISTING 5.2   Continued

```java
public void ejbStore()
{
   log.debug("ejbStore:, key="+key);
}

public void setEntityContext(EntityContext context)
{
   entityContext = context;
   log.debug("setEntityContext:, key="+key);
}

public void unsetEntityContext()
{
   entityContext = null;
   log.debug("unsetEntityContext:, key="+key);
}

public void ejbActivate()
{
}
public void ejbPassivate()
{
}

public String getState()
{
   log.debug("getState:, key="+key);
   StringBuffer sb = new StringBuffer("Ex1EntityBean{");
   sb.append("key=");
   sb.append(key);
   sb.append(";i=");
   sb.append(intVar);
   sb.append(";f=");
   sb.append(floatVar);
   sb.append(";d=");
   sb.append(doubleVar);
   sb.append("}");
   return sb.toString();
}
public void setIntVar(int i)
{
```

LISTING 5.2   Continued

```
      this.intVar = i;
   }
   public void setFloatVar(float f)
   {
      this.floatVar = f;
   }
   public void setDoubleVar(double d)
   {
      this.doubleVar = d;
   }
}
```

LISTING 5.3   The ejb-jar.xml and jboss.xml Descriptors for the FileStore Example
Entity Bean Jar

```
<!-- The ejb-jar.xml descriptor -->
<?xml version="1.0"?>
<!DOCTYPE ejb-jar
   PUBLIC "-//Sun Microsystems, Inc.//DTD Enterprise JavaBeans 2.0//EN"
   "http://java.sun.com/dtd/ejb-jar_2_0.dtd"
>

<ejb-jar>
   <enterprise-beans>
      <entity>
      <ejb-name>Ex1EntityBean</ejb-name>
      <home>org.jboss.chap5.ex1.Ex1EntityHome</home>
      <remote>org.jboss.chap5.ex1.Ex1Entity</remote>
      <ejb-class>org.jboss.chap5.ex1.Ex1EntityBean</ejb-class>
      <persistence-type>Container</persistence-type>
      <prim-key-class>java.lang.String</prim-key-class>
      <reentrant>False</reentrant>
      <cmp-field><field-name>key</field-name></cmp-field>
      <cmp-field><field-name>intVar</field-name></cmp-field>
      <cmp-field><field-name>floatVar</field-name></cmp-field>
      <cmp-field><field-name>doubleVar</field-name></cmp-field>
      <primkey-field>key</primkey-field>
      </entity>
   </enterprise-beans>
</ejb-jar>
```

LISTING 5.3   Continued

```
<!-- The jboss.xml descriptor -->
<?xml version="1.0"?>
<jboss>
   <container-configurations>
     <container-configuration>
       <container-name>Standard CMP EntityBean</container-name>
       <persistence-manager>org.jboss.chap5.ex1.FileStore</persistence-manager>
     </container-configuration>
   </container-configurations>
</jboss>
```

The ejb-jar.xml descriptor defines four CMP fields: key, intVar, floatVar, and
doubleVar with key being the primary key field of type java.lang.String. The
jboss.xml descriptor overrides the "Standard CMP EntityBean" container-configuration element to use the example org.jboss.chap5.example1.FileStore class as
the persistence-manager value. Accept this as magic for the time being; it is
explained in detail in Chapter 9.

The last item needed to complete the FileStore testing is a client application that
accesses the CMP entity bean. Its code is presented in Listing 5.4.

LISTING 5.4   The FileStore Test Case Client Application

```
package org.jboss.chap5.ex1;

import java.util.Collection;
import java.util.Iterator;
import javax.ejb.ObjectNotFoundException;
import javax.naming.InitialContext;

public class Ex1Client
{
   static final int N = 4;

   public static void main(String args[]) throws Exception
   {
      InitialContext iniCtx = new InitialContext();
      Object ref = iniCtx.lookup("Ex1EntityBean");
      Ex1EntityHome home = (Ex1EntityHome) ref;
      Ex1Entity bean = home.create("Bean0", 1, 1.0f, 1.0);
      System.out.println("bean = "+bean.getState());
      bean = home.findByPrimaryKey("Bean0");
```

LISTING 5.4   Continued

```
   System.out.println("findByPrimaryKey(Bean0): "+bean);
   bean.remove();

   try
   {
      bean = home.findByPrimaryKey("Bean0");
      String msg = "findByPrimaryKey did NOT fail as expected";
      throw new IllegalStateException(msg);
   }
   catch(ObjectNotFoundException e)
   {
      System.out.println("findByPrimaryKey failed as expected");
   }

   System.out.println("Creating Bean1..Bean"+N);
   for(int i = 1; i <= N; i ++)
   {
      bean = home.create("Bean"+i, 1+i, 1.0f+i, 1.0+i);
   }
   System.out.println("Finding all beans");
   Collection allBeans = home.findAll();
   Iterator iter = allBeans.iterator();
   while( iter.hasNext() )
   {
      bean = (Ex1Entity) iter.next();
      System.out.println("  "+bean.getState());
   }

   System.out.println("Removing Bean1..Bean"+N);
   for(int i = 1; i <= N; i ++)
   {
      home.remove("Bean"+i);
   }
   System.out.println("Done");
   }
}
```

The client first looks up the Ex1EntityHome and then creates an Ex1Entity instance
with a primary key of "Bean0". Tests of the getState and findByPrimaryKey
methods are performed, and then the bean is removed. The following try/catch
block tests that the bean was actually removed using a call to the findByPrimaryKey

method using the "Bean0" key. If the bean is successfully found an
IllegalStateException is throw as an assertion failure. The remainder of the client
code creates several beans and then tests that the findAll method returns them.

Now you are ready to test the FileStore implementation. To do this, make sure you
have the JBoss server running and execute the Chapter 5, example 1 test code that
was shown in Listing 5.4 by using Ant from your examples root directory as follows:

```
examples 854>ant -Dchap=5 -Dex=1 run-example
Buildfile: build.xml

...


chap5-ex1-jar:

run-example1:
     [copy] Copying 1 file to G:\JBoss-2.4.3\deploy
     [echo] Waiting for deploy...
     [java] bean = Ex1EntityBean{key=Bean0;i=1;f=1.0;d=1.0}
     [java] findByPrimaryKey(Bean0): Ex1EntityBean:Bean0
     [java] findByPrimaryKey failed as expected
     [java] Creating Bean1..Bean4
     [java] Finding all beans
     [java]    Ex1EntityBean{key=Bean1;i=2;f=2.0;d=2.0}
     [java]    Ex1EntityBean{key=Bean2;i=3;f=3.0;d=3.0}
     [java]    Ex1EntityBean{key=Bean3;i=4;f=4.0;d=4.0}
     [java]    Ex1EntityBean{key=Bean4;i=5;f=5.0;d=5.0}
     [java] Removing Bean1..Bean4
     [java] Done


BUILD SUCCESSFUL

Total time: 8 seconds
```

For example 1 you need to also look at the server.log to see the output generated
by the FileStore and the Ex1EntityBean. The tail of the log just after running the
client should resemble the following. Note that many of the lines have been truncated to fit the output into the book format so see your server.log file for the full
output.

```
[Ex1EntityBean] setEntityContext:, key=null
[Ex1EntityBean] ejbCreate: key=Bean0, i=1, f=1.0, d=1.0
[FileStore#Ex1EntityBean] createEntity: m=Ex1Entity create(...)
[FileStore#Ex1EntityBean] storeEntity, serFile=.../Bean0.ser
```

```
[Ex1EntityBean] ejbPostCreate: key=Bean0, i=1, f=1.0, d=1.0
[Ex1EntityBean] ejbStore:, key=Bean0
[FileStore#Ex1EntityBean] storeEntity, serFile=.../Bean0.ser
[Ex1EntityBean] getState:, key=Bean0
[Ex1EntityBean] ejbStore:, key=Bean0
[FileStore#Ex1EntityBean] storeEntity, serFile=.../Bean0.ser
[Ex1EntityBean] setEntityContext:, key=null
[Ex1EntityBean] ejbRemove:, key=Bean0
[FileStore#Ex1EntityBean] removeEntity: pk=Bean0
[Ex1EntityBean] setEntityContext:, key=null
[FileStore#Ex1EntityBean] findEntity: m=Ex1Entity findByPrimaryKey(...)
[Ex1EntityBean] setEntityContext:, key=null
[Ex1EntityBean] ejbCreate: key=Bean1, i=2, f=2.0, d=2.0
[FileStore#Ex1EntityBean] createEntity: m=Ex1Entity create(...)
[FileStore#Ex1EntityBean] storeEntity, serFile=.../Bean1.ser
[Ex1EntityBean] ejbPostCreate: key=Bean1, i=2, f=2.0, d=2.0
[Ex1EntityBean] ejbStore:, key=Bean1
[FileStore#Ex1EntityBean] storeEntity, serFile=.../Bean1.ser
[Ex1EntityBean] setEntityContext:, key=null
[Ex1EntityBean] ejbCreate: key=Bean2, i=3, f=3.0, d=3.0
[FileStore#Ex1EntityBean] createEntity: m=Ex1Entity create(...)
[FileStore#Ex1EntityBean] storeEntity, serFile=.../Bean2.ser
[Ex1EntityBean] ejbPostCreate: key=Bean2, i=3, f=3.0, d=3.0
[Ex1EntityBean] ejbStore:, key=Bean2
[FileStore#Ex1EntityBean] storeEntity, serFile=.../Bean2.ser
[Ex1EntityBean] setEntityContext:, key=null
[Ex1EntityBean] ejbCreate: key=Bean3, i=4, f=4.0, d=4.0
[FileStore#Ex1EntityBean] createEntity: m=Ex1Entity create(...)
[FileStore#Ex1EntityBean] storeEntity, serFile=.../Bean3.ser
[Ex1EntityBean] ejbPostCreate: key=Bean3, i=4, f=4.0, d=4.0
[Ex1EntityBean] ejbStore:, key=Bean3
[FileStore#Ex1EntityBean] storeEntity, serFile=.../Bean3.ser
[Ex1EntityBean] setEntityContext:, key=null
[Ex1EntityBean] ejbCreate: key=Bean4, i=5, f=5.0, d=5.0
[FileStore#Ex1EntityBean] createEntity: m=Ex1Entity create(...)
[FileStore#Ex1EntityBean] storeEntity, serFile=.../Bean4.ser
[Ex1EntityBean] ejbPostCreate: key=Bean4, i=5, f=5.0, d=5.0
[Ex1EntityBean] ejbStore:, key=Bean4
[FileStore#Ex1EntityBean] storeEntity, serFile=.../Bean4.ser
[Ex1EntityBean] setEntityContext:, key=null
[FileStore#Ex1EntityBean] findEntities: m=Collection findAll()
[FileStore#Ex1EntityBean] found pk=Bean1
```

```
[FileStore#Ex1EntityBean] found pk=Bean2
[FileStore#Ex1EntityBean] found pk=Bean3
[FileStore#Ex1EntityBean] found pk=Bean4
[Ex1EntityBean] getState:, key=Bean1
[Ex1EntityBean] ejbStore:, key=Bean1
[FileStore#Ex1EntityBean] storeEntity, serFile=.../Bean1.ser
[Ex1EntityBean] getState:, key=Bean2
[Ex1EntityBean] ejbStore:, key=Bean2
[FileStore#Ex1EntityBean] storeEntity, serFile=.../Bean2.ser
[Ex1EntityBean] getState:, key=Bean3
[Ex1EntityBean] ejbStore:, key=Bean3
[FileStore#Ex1EntityBean] storeEntity, serFile=.../Bean3.ser
[Ex1EntityBean] getState:, key=Bean4
[Ex1EntityBean] ejbStore:, key=Bean4
[FileStore#Ex1EntityBean] storeEntity, serFile=.../Bean4.ser
[Ex1EntityBean] ejbRemove:, key=Bean1
[FileStore#Ex1EntityBean] removeEntity: pk=Bean1
[Ex1EntityBean] ejbRemove:, key=Bean2
[FileStore#Ex1EntityBean] removeEntity: pk=Bean2
[Ex1EntityBean] ejbRemove:, key=Bean3
[FileStore#Ex1EntityBean] removeEntity: pk=Bean3
[Ex1EntityBean] ejbRemove:, key=Bean4
[FileStore#Ex1EntityBean] removeEntity: pk=Bean4
```

The Ex1Client exercises bean creation, removal, and finders. The server.log output illustrates the interaction between the EJB container and its calls to the Ex1EntityBean and the FileStore persistence manager. Because the Ex1Client ultimately removes all the entity beans it creates, the only proof that the FileStore was operating will be the existence of a db/Ex1EntityBean directory under your JBoss server distribution root directory. Experiment with modifying the Ex1Client to have it leave the beans it creates, stop, and restart the server. It then has to find all existing beans to verify that the FileStore is functioning as a persistent store.

Limitations of the FileStore

The FileStore example is a simple, pedagogical example designed to illustrate the basic functionality of an EntityPersistenceStore implementation. The FileStore class has a number of limitations that would need to be addressed for a robust implementation. The most important limitations are with respect to improper transaction semantics. Some of the major limitations of the example include the following:

- Reads and writes are not atomic. If a write fails midway through the entity beans list of persistent fields, the image on disk is an inconsistent mix of the previous values with partially updated values. The same problem exists during the read of the persistent data into the entity bean. The reads and writes need to be made atomic operations.

- Reads and writes are not rolled back on rollback of the current transaction. If a read or write operation succeeds, but the transaction in which the operation is enlisted fails due to some other transacted resource, the `FileStore` does not undo the last operation.

- Only simple primary keys are supported. Support for compound primary keys made of more than one CMP field should also be added. This could be done by introducing a separate key file that contained the compound primary key fields.

- The `findEntities` implementation of `findAll` assumes that the primary key type is `java.lang.String`. This is because the primary keys it returns are derived from the names of the persistent store files. One way to allow for a primary key of any type would be to introduce a ".key" file that contained the serialized content of the primary key.

- The only supported finder methods are `findByPrimaryKey` and `findAll`. Typically, a user wants to be able to locate entities using queries other than identity against a primary key. One way this might be done is to use an XML for the persistent representation and XPATH as the query language.

It is left as an exercise for the reader to address these issues.

JAWS—The Default CMP Implementation

JAWS (Just Another Web Storage) is the default object-to-relational (O-R) mapping tool provided with JBoss for CMP entity beans. JAWS plugs into the JBoss container as the `EntityPersistenceStore` implementation in the default CMP container configuration defined in standard `jboss.xml`. JAWS is essentially a much more sophisticated version of the `FileStore` example you just learned, which uses a JDBC database rather than a file system as its persistent store. The topic of the remainder of this chapter is the customization of JAWS for your particular entity beans and database.

What is O-R Mapping?

O-R mapping technology grew out of the differences between how object-oriented languages represent objects in memory, and how relational databases store data on disk. Objects in the Java language might contain only primitive data types such as int, double, and very simple aggregate objects such as String, making it very easy to express the object's layout on disk. In the case of storing such a simple object in a file, you could just write each primitive data type variable and each String sequentially into the file. Reading such an object back from disk into a memory-based object would be just as easy. However, what about storing more complex objects such as those that contain other objects that contain yet other objects? And, what about storing both simple and complex objects into relational databases?

As the complexity of the objects being stored increases, the intelligence of the O-R mapping tool must also increase. An O-R mapping tool must understand how to traverse the complex object's memory graph, and figure out how to store it to and read it from disk. To add to the complexity, the graph of a single object might contain multiple objects that each references a single, unique object, as well as objects that recursively reference themselves. In these cases, the O-R mapping tool would have to avoid persisting the same object multiple times, perhaps even ending up in an endless loop because of the self-referencing composition! On the other hand, all complex Java objects finally boil down to variables of primitive data types and other simple objects. Therefore, while it can be challenging to persist very complex objects, it is not impossible. JAWS is the free Open Source offering included as the default CMP management tool to ensure that JBoss has a high quality O-R framework.

NOTE

If you still need more capabilities, there are commercial O-R tools that can be used with JBoss. CocoBase, a professional high-end tool available from Thought Inc., is one JBoss Group partner solutions. You can find it at www.thoughtinc.com. Another lightweight, low-cost solution is the MVCSoft Persistence Manager. See the www.jboss.org *partner's section* for additional information on these tools.

Customizing the Behavior of JAWS

JAWS comes pre-configured to use the bundled HypersonicSQL embedded JDBC database and automatic table creation per CMP entity bean. This allows you to experiment with CMP entity beans with no JBoss-specific configuration. However, this is only generally appropriate for relatively simple beans and testing. Fortunately a good deal of JAWS' behavior is customizable using two XML configuration files: standardjaws.xml and jaws.xml. Both files conform to the DTD defined by the jaws_2_4.dtd, which is represented graphically in Figure 5.2. Listing 5.5 shows a portion of the standardjaws.xml descriptor to give you a feel for the nature of the elements. Only the Hypersonic SQL type-mapping is shown in Listing 5.5.

LISTING 5.5   The default standardjaws.xml Descriptor with All but the Hypersonic SQL Type-Mapping Elements Removed

```
<?xml version="1.0" encoding="UTF-8"?>
<jaws>
```

LISTING 5.5   Continued

```
<datasource>java:/DefaultDS</datasource>
<type-mapping>Hypersonic SQL</type-mapping>
<debug>false</debug>

<default-entity>
    <create-table>true</create-table>
    <remove-table>false</remove-table>
    <tuned-updates>false</tuned-updates>
    <read-only>false</read-only>
    <time-out>300</time-out>
    <select-for-update>false</select-for-update>
</default-entity>

<type-mappings>
    <type-mapping>
        <name>Hypersonic SQL</name>
        <mapping>
            <java-type>java.lang.Byte</java-type>
            <jdbc-type>SMALLINT</jdbc-type>
            <sql-type>SMALLINT</sql-type>
        </mapping>
        <mapping>
            <java-type>java.util.Date</java-type>
            <jdbc-type>DATE</jdbc-type>
            <sql-type>DATE</sql-type>
        </mapping>
        <mapping>
            <java-type>java.lang.Boolean</java-type>
            <jdbc-type>BIT</jdbc-type>
            <sql-type>BIT</sql-type>
        </mapping>
        <mapping>
            <java-type>java.lang.Integer</java-type>
            <jdbc-type>INTEGER</jdbc-type>
            <sql-type>INTEGER</sql-type>
        </mapping>
        <mapping>
            <java-type>java.lang.Object</java-type>
            <jdbc-type>JAVA_OBJECT</jdbc-type>
            <sql-type>OBJECT</sql-type>
        </mapping>
```

LISTING 5.5 Continued

```
            <mapping>
                <java-type>java.lang.Short</java-type>
                <jdbc-type>SMALLINT</jdbc-type>
                <sql-type>SMALLINT</sql-type>
            </mapping>
            <mapping>
                <java-type>java.lang.Character</java-type>
                <jdbc-type>CHAR</jdbc-type>
                <sql-type>CHAR</sql-type>
            </mapping>
            <mapping>
                <java-type>java.lang.String</java-type>
                <jdbc-type>VARCHAR</jdbc-type>
                <sql-type>VARCHAR(256)</sql-type>
            </mapping>
            <mapping>
                <java-type>java.sql.Timestamp</java-type>
                <jdbc-type>TIMESTAMP</jdbc-type>
                <sql-type>TIMESTAMP</sql-type>
            </mapping>
            <mapping>
                <java-type>java.lang.Float</java-type>
                <jdbc-type>REAL</jdbc-type>
                <sql-type>REAL</sql-type>
            </mapping>
            <mapping>
                <java-type>java.lang.Long</java-type>
                <jdbc-type>BIGINT</jdbc-type>
                <sql-type>BIGINT</sql-type>
            </mapping>
            <mapping>
                <java-type>java.lang.Double</java-type>
                <jdbc-type>DOUBLE</jdbc-type>
                <sql-type>DOUBLE</sql-type>
            </mapping>
        </type-mapping>
    </type-mappings>
</jaws>
```

The standard jboss.xml file is located in the JBoss server configuration file set directory. It serves as the default values specification. The jaws.xml file is a JBoss server-specific file that you include in your EJB jars inside the META-INF directory along with the required `ejb-jar.xml` and optional `jboss.xml` descriptors. It allows customization of the default JAWS behavior in the same manner that the `jboss.xml` descriptor allows for customization of the standard `jboss.xml` definitions.

When you need to change the default behavior of JAWS, where you do it depends on whether you want to the change to be seen globally or isolated to a particular EJB jar deployment. Changes that should be seen globally should be made in the standard `jboss.xml` descriptor, while EJB jar-specific changes should be made in the jar `META-INF/jaws.xml` descriptor.

The immediate child elements of the `jaws` root element shown in Figure 5.2 define the range of configurable behavior available. The main configuration categories include the following:

- Specification of the `javax.sql.DataSource` location and the Java to SQL type-mapping to use with the `DataSource`

- Global options and defaults

- Entity bean to database mapping and usage options

- Customization of entity bean home interface finder methods

- Java to SQL type-mapping override definitions

Each configuration category and the associated JAWS DTD elements are discussed in the following sections.

Specifying the DataSource and Type-Mapping

The `datasource` element specifies the JNDI name of the `javax.sql.DataSource` binding for obtaining connections to your database. How `DataSource` bindings are configured is addressed in the configuring JDBC section later in this chapter. The default value of "`java:/DefaultDS`" does not need to be changed simply because you are not using the bundled HypersonicSQL database. You would change the `data-source` element value if you have multiple `DataSource` bindings defined; also, if the `DataSource` you want to use does not correspond to the one you have configured as the "`java:/DefaultDS`" binding.

An aspect of JAWS that you are likely to want to change is the Java to SQL type-mapping. If you're not using the embedded HypersonicSQL database as your persistent store, you need to change the type-mapping to one that is compatible with your database. If a there is not a predefined `type-mappings/type-mapping` element in the standardjaws.xml descriptor that matches your database, you can either try one that has equivalent or similar type-mappings, or define a new one.

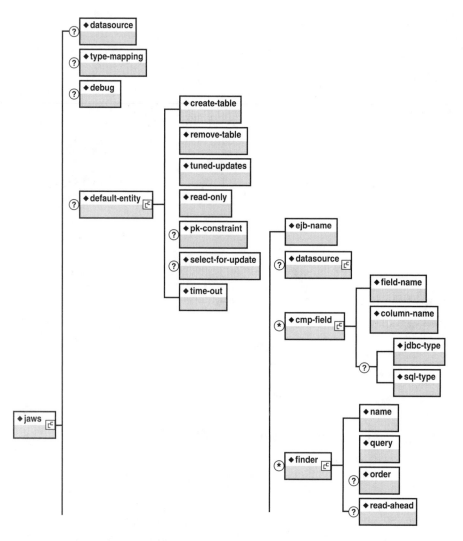

FIGURE 5.2   The JAWS 2.4 XML configuration file DTD.

Java to SQL Type-Mapping Definitions

The type-mapping element defines which collection of mappings from a Java class type to JDBC and SQL types to use with the datasource. Its value is a reference to a name element in the type-mappings/type-mapping-definition section of the XML

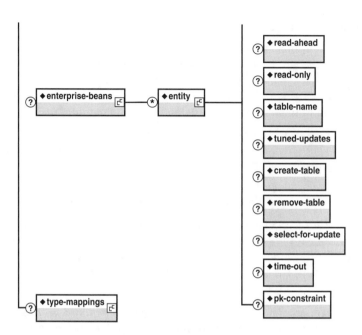

file. The mappings for a large number of databases have been defined and are available in the standardjaws.xml descriptor. If an existing type-mappings/type-mapping-definition does not exist for your database, you need to create an appropriate type-mapping. A type-mapping-definition consists of the name of the definition and zero or more mapping elements that define the Java class type to JDBC and SQL types tuples. The values of the mapping element child elements are as follows:

- The java-type element specifies the fully qualified name of a Java class. This is the Java type of an entity bean cmp-field.

- The jdbc-type element specifies Java class name to JDBC type-mapping. The value of the jdbc-type element is the string name of the java.sql.Types constant to which the Java class should map. This is used to determine what JDBC type to use when encoding an entity bean field value into a JDBC java.sql.PreparedStatement.

- The sql-type element specifies the database SQL declaration for the jdbc-type. This is used when JAWS creates a table for an entity bean.

Global Options and Defaults

There are a number of options that affect the default behavior of JAWS, and are configured via the debug and default-entity elements. The debug element defines whether JAWS logs its SQL activity. When debug is true logging is enabled, and when false (the default), no logging of SQL activity is performed. Setting debug to true is useful when you need to see how JAWS is interacting with your database.

The various child elements of the default-entity element establish global defaults for beans that have no specific entity element specification as well as missing elements of an entity declaration.

Entity Bean to Database Mapping and Usage Options

The default behavior for JAWS is to use a database table per CMP entity bean with each CMP field of the entity bean mapped to a column in the table. The name of the table will be equal to the name of the EJB, and the names of the columns will be those of the CMP fields of the EJB. JAWS will even create the table for you if it does not exist.

This behavior, however, may not be what you want due to pre-existing tables with different naming conventions. You can customize how JAWS maps an entity bean onto a table using the enterprise-beans/entity element specification. There are three classes of child elements in the entity element: bean to table mapping information, JAWS behavior options, and home interface finder specification.

The child elements of the entity element that allow you to control how an entity bean is mapped onto a JDBC table include the following:

- ejb-name—This element specifies the name of the EJB as declared in the ejb-jar.xml descriptor. It must match the value of an ejb-jar/enterprise-beans/entity/ejb-name element from the standard ejb-jar.xml descriptor. In the absence of a table-name element, the value of the ejb-name element is used as the database table name.

- table-name—The name to use as the database table name.

- datasource—The JNDI name of the javax.sql.DataSource binding for obtaining connections to the database which contains the entity bean table.

- cmp-field—This element or elements allows you to override the database column name used for a CMP field. Optionally, you can also override the field type to JDBC and SQL type-mappings. The child elements are as follows:

- field-name—The name of the CMP field as defined in the ejb-jar.xml descriptor. This must match an existing cmp-field/field-name in the ejb-jar.xml descriptor.

- column-name—The name to be used as the database column name for the CMP field.

- jdbc-type—The optional string name of the java.sql.Types constant to which the CMP field class should map.

- sql-type—The optional sql-type element specifies the database SQL declaration for the jdbc-type. It will only be used if JAWS creates the entity bean table.

The discussion of the JAWS behavior options was delayed from the previous section to here because those elements apply to the default behavioral options as well as per entity bean behavioral options. The option related elements and their meanings are as follows:

- read-ahead—This element is a true/false flag indicating whether all data for the entities selected should be loaded immediately. Note that JAWS/JBoss cannot guarantee serializable transactions with the read-ahead set to true.

- read-only—This element is a true/false flag which, when set to true, indicates that changes to the bean's state should not be persisted. The default is false.

- create-table—This element is a true/false flag which, when set to true, indicates that on deploy the entity bean table should be created if it does not exist. If set to false the entity bean table must exist or deployment will fail.

- remove-table—This element is a true/false flag which, when set to true, indicates that on undeploy the entity bean table should be dropped from the database along with all data. The default is false which leaves the table intact after the entity bean is undeployed.

- tuned-updates—This element is a true/false flag which, when set to true, indicates that modifications of the entity bean should generate updated SQL statements that only contain the changed CMP fields. When set to false, the SQL update statement will include all CMP fields.

- select-for-update—This element is a true/false flag which, when set to true, indicates upon loading an entity bean, a 'SELECT ... FOR UPDATE' style of SQL statement should be used. This locks the table row, and can be used to synchronize concurrent use as would be the case when multiple JBoss server instances use the database.

- `time-out`—This element specifies the interval in milliseconds between reloads of `read-only` entity beans. This element does not apply to any entity bean with a `read-only` setting of false.

- `pk-constraint`—This element is a true/false flag which, when set to true and `create-table` is true, indicates that the SQL table create statement must include a primary key constraint on the entity bean primary key columns.

As an example of a customized bean to table mapping for an existing table, consider the following table creation statement:

```
create table Products (productID varchar(64), majorVersion int,
   minorVersion int, description text);
```

Suppose that you have a CMP entity bean named `ProductBean` that contains the following fields you want to be mapped on the this table:

```
String key;
int major;
int minor;
String description;
```

You can specify the mapping from the `ProductBean` EJB to the existing table using the following `jaws.xml` descriptor:

```
<jaws>
   <enterprise-beans>
     <entity>
         <ejb-name>ProductBean</ejb-name>
         <table-name>Products</table-name>
         <create-table>false</create-table>
         <cmp-field>
            <field-name>key</field-name>
            <column-name>productID</column-name>
         </cmp-field>
         <cmp-field>
            <field-name>major</field-name>
            <column-name>majorVersion</column-name>
         </cmp-field>
         <cmp-field>
            <field-name>minor</field-name>
```

```
            <column-name>minorVersion</column-name>
         </cmp-field>
         <cmp-field>
            <field-name>description</field-name>
            <column-name>description</column-name>
         </cmp-field>
      </entity>
   </enterprise-beans>
</jaws>
```

Customization of Entity Bean Home Interface Finder Methods

JAWS handles the creation of finder methods defined in the entity bean home interface. The types of finder methods that JAWS can handle without any customization
include the following:

- findByPrimaryKey—The required single-entity finder method that allows you
  to locate an entity bean by its primary key.

- findAll—A multi-entity finder that returns all existing entity beans. This
  finder method is generated only if declared in the entity bean home interface.

- findBy<*field*>(<*field-type*> value)—JAWS can generate a multi-entity finder
  for finders that query one of the entity bean CMP fields. The <*field*> value
  must be the name of one of the entity bean CMP fields. The <*field-type*>
  value must be the Java type of the CMP field. Such a finder method is generated only if declared in the entity bean home interface.

If you need additional finder methods, you must declare a custom finder using the
jaws.xml descriptor. To do this, specify a finder child element in an enterprise-
beans/entity element. The child elements of the finder element are as follows:

- name—The name of the finder method as declared in the entity bean home
  interface.

- query—The SQL statement portion of the WHERE clause. Inside of this statement, arguments that are passed into the finder method can be referenced as
  {n} where n is the 0 based position of the argument in the finder method argument list.

- order—The optional SQL statement portion of the ORDER BY clause.

- read-ahead—An optional Boolean flag that indicates if all data for found entities should be loaded immediately.

Finder Examples

Given a product entity bean named ProductBean with major and minor CMP fields of type int that correspond to the product version information, suppose you need a finder method to locate all beta products (those with major version <= 1). A custom finder called findBetaVersions could be specified as follows:

```
<jaws>
    <enterprise-beans>
        <entity>
            <ejb-name>ProductBean</ejb-name>
            <finder>
                <name>findBetaVersions</name>
                <query>major &lt;= 0</query>
                <order>key</order>
            </finder>
        </entity>
    </enterprise-beans>
</jaws>
```

The SQL query that would be generated by JAWS for this find would look like:

```
SELECT ProductBean.key FROM ProductBean where major <= 0 ORDER BY key
```

Note that the <= operator had to be specified using the < XML entity because a raw '<' would have been interpreted as the start of a new XML element. Suppose that you also wanted a findOlderProducts finder that selected all products where the major version number was less than the version provided as an argument. The home interface method would look like:

```
Collection findOlderProducts(int version) throws RemoteException
```

and the corresponding custom finder would be coded as:

```
<jaws>
    <enterprise-beans>
        <entity>
            <ejb-name>ProductBean</ejb-name>
            <finder>
                <name>findOlderProducts</name>
                <query>major &lt; {0}</query>
            </finder>
        </entity>
    </enterprise-beans>
</jaws>
```

The SQL prepared statement that would be generated by JAWS for this finder would look similar to the following:

SELECT `ProductBean.key` FROM ProductBean where major < ? ORDER BY keyThe? parameter in the query would be set to the `findOlderProducts` method argument.

Configuring JDBC

A common choice for a persistent store is a JDBC database. JBoss includes an embedded JDBC database called Hypersonic that is configured by default. Additional information on Hypersonic is given in the following section "The Default JDBC Database, Hypersonic SQL". Because it is likely that you have your own database and corresponding JDBC drivers, you need to know how to load a JDBC driver and set up a corresponding `javax.sql.DataSource` for use with the JAWS persistence engine. Two JBoss MBeans handle the loading of JDBC drivers and `DataSource` setup: `org.jboss.jdbc.JdbcProvider` and `org.jboss.jdbc.XADataSourceLoader`.

The `org.jboss.jdbc.JdbcProvider` MBean loads one or more JDBC drivers into the JBoss server VM. The JBoss server classpath must contain the appropriate jars for the JDBC drivers that are to be loaded. Typically, you place the JDBC driver jar files into the `JBOSS_DIST/lib/ext` to satisfy this requirement.

The configurable attributes for the `JdbcProvider` include the drivers. Drivers are a comma-separated list of the JDBC fully qualified class names that are to be loaded when the service starts. Each driver is loaded by calling `Class.forName`(name), where name is the fully qualified class name of the JDBC driver.

You will go through an example of configuring the MySQL Open Source database as a demonstration of using a JDBC database with JBoss. The example will use the MySQL database because its configuration is not included in the standard JBoss distribution.

> **NOTE**
>
> You can obtain the latest version of the MySQL database from its home page at
> `http://www.mysql.com/`. The JDBC driver for MySQL can be obtained from
> `http://mmmysql.sourceforge.net/`.

The first step is to configure JBoss to load your database JDBC driver. In this example setup, you will be using version 2.0.6 of the MySQL JDBC driver. The corresponding jar file is named mm.mysql-2.0.6.jar. You need to make the JDBC driver classes available to the JBoss server by adding the mm.mysql-2.0.6.jar to the server classpath. The easiest way to do this is to simply drop the jar into the JBoss server lib/ext directory. All jars located in this directory are added to the classpath used by the server on startup.

Once that is accomplished, you need to add the name of the JDBC `java.sql.Driver` interface implementation class to the `JdbcProvider` MBean configuration. For the MySQL JDBC driver, the `Driver` class implementation is called `org.gjt.mm.mysql.Driver`. Add this to the `JdbcProvider` configuration by adding the class name to the Drivers attribute as shown here:

```
<mbean code="org.jboss.jdbc.JdbcProvider"
  name="DefaultDomain:service=JdbcProvider">
    <attribute name="Drivers">org.hsqldb.jdbcDriver,
      org.gjt.mm.mysql.Driver
    </attribute>
</mbean>
```

The Driver's attribute value is a comma-separated list of class names that implement the `Driver` interface, which should be loaded on startup. Adding the `org.gjt.mm.mysql.Driver` name to JdbcProvider configuration will cause the MySQL JDBC driver to be loaded into the VM when the JBoss server starts, in addition to the default Hypersonic JDBC driver(`org.hsqldb.jdbcDriver`). The driver will then be accessible to the `XADataSourceLoader` MBean. The next step is the configuration of the MySQL `DataSource`.

DataSources

A `javax.sql.DataSource` object is a factory for `java.sql.Connection` objects. You obtain a `DataSource` instance by accessing its binding using a JNDI lookup. The `org.jboss.jdbc.XADataSourceLoader` MBean manages connection pools and creates a `DataSource` binding for a JDBC driver. Connections obtained from the resulting `DataSource` are automatically registered with any transaction associated with the current thread and support two-phase commit. You configure the MBean with the properties appropriate for the JDBC driver for which you want to establish a `DataSource`. The configurable attributes of the `XADataSourceLoader` MBean include the following:

- `PoolName`—The name to assign to the pool. This is used to bind the pool into JNDI under `java:/name`.

- `DataSourceClass`—The fully qualified class name of the `javax.sql.XADataSource` implementation. If your JDBC driver does not include support for XADataSource, use `org.jboss.pool.jdbc.xa.wrapper.XADataSourceImpl` for this value. The `XADataSourceImpl` class acts as an `XADataSource` proxy for non-XADataSource JDBC drivers.

- Properties—Any properties required to connect to the data source. This should be expressed in a String of the form name1=value1;name2=value2;name3=value3 and so on.

- URL—The JDBC URL used to connect to the data source.

- JDBCUser—The user name used to connect to the data source.

- Password—The user password used to connect to the data source.

- MinSize—The minimum size of the pool. The pool always starts with one instance; but if shrinking is enabled, the pool will never fall below this size. It has no effect if shrinking is not enabled. The default is 0.

- MaxSize—The maximum size of the pool. Once the pool has grown to hold this number of instances, it will not add any more instances. If one of the pooled instances is available when a request comes in, it will be returned. If none of the pooled instances are available, the pool will either block until an instance is available, or return null (see the Blocking parameter). If you set this to zero, the pool size will be unlimited. The default is 0.

- GCMinIdleTime—If garbage collection is enabled, the amount of time (in milliseconds) that must pass before a connection in use is garbage collected—forcibly returned to the pool. The default is 1200000 (20 minutes).

- GCEnabled—Whether the pool should check for connections that have not been returned to the pool after a long period of time. This would catch things such as a client that disconnects suddenly without closing database connections gracefully, or queries that take an unexpectedly long time to run. This is not generally useful in an EJB environment, though it may be for stateful session beans that keep a DB connection as part of their state. This is in contrast to the idle timeout, which closes connection that have been idle in the pool. The default is false.

- GCInterval—How often garbage collection and shrinking should run (in milliseconds), if they are enabled. The default is 120000 (2 minutes).

- InvalidateOnError—Sets the response for errors. If this flag is set and an error event occurs, the connection is removed from the pool entirely. Otherwise, the object is returned to the pool of available objects. For example, a SQL error may not indicate a bad database connection (flag not set), while a TCP/IP error probably indicates a bad network connection (flag set). The default is false.

- TimestampUsed—Sets whether object clients can update the last used time. If so, the last used time will be updated for significant actions (executing a query, navigating on a ResultSet, and so on). If not, the last used time will only be updated when the object is given to a client and returned to the pool. This time is important if shrinking or garbage collection are enabled (particularly the latter). The default is false.

- `Blocking`—Controls the behavior of the pool when all the connections are in use. If set to true, then a client that requests a connection will wait until one is available. If set to false, the pool will return null immediately, and the client may retry. If you set blocking to false, your client must be prepared to handle null results! The default is true.

- `BlockingTimeout`—Sets how long to wait in milliseconds for a free connection when blocking, -1 indicates to wait forever. The default is -1.

- `IdleTimeout`—Set the idle timeout for unused connections. If a connection has been unused in the pool for this amount of time, it will be released the next time garbage collection and shrinking are run (see GCInterval). The default is 30 minutes.

- `IdleTimeoutEnabled`—Whether the pool should close idle connections. This prevents the pool from keeping a large number of connections open indefinitely after a spike in activity. Any connection that has been unused in the pool for longer than this amount of time will be closed. If you do not want the pool to shrink so rapidly, you can set the `MaxIdleTimeoutPercent` and then some connections will be recreated to replace the closed ones. This is in contrast to garbage collection, which returns connections to the pool that have been checked out of the pool but not returned for a long period of time. The default is false.

- `MaxIdleTimeoutPercent`—Sets the idle timeout percent as a fraction between 0 and 1. If a number of connections are determined to be idle, they will all be closed and removed from the pool. However, if the ratio of objects released to objects in the pool is greater than this fraction, some new objects will be created to replace the closed objects. This prevents the pool size from decreasing too rapidly. Set to 0 to decrease the pool size by a maximum of 1 object per test, or 1 to never replace objects that have exceeded the idle timeout. The pool will always replace enough closed connections to stay at the minimum size. The default is 1.

- `LoggingEnabled`—Whether the pool should record activity to the JBoss log. This includes events like connections being checked out and returned. It is generally only useful for troubleshooting purposes, such as to find a connection leak. The default is false.

- `TransactionIsolation`—Sets the Transaction isolation level on the SQL Connection. Valid values are TRANSACTION_NONE, TRANSACTION_READ_UNCOMMITTED, TRANSACTION_READ_COMMITTED , TRANSACTION_REPEATABLE_READ, TRANSACTION_SERIALIZABLE. The choice of the level allows one to choose a trade-off between performance and transaction isolation. The values listed are from poor to full isolation; but from good to poor performance. Refer to `java.sql.Connection` for more information. The default is to use the JDBC driver default.

Generally only the first five to seven attributes need to be specified as the default values for the remaining attributes are appropriate. The following is an annotated listing of the `XADataSourceLoader` attributes that you will use for the MySQL setup.

- `PoolName`—You will set this value to MySQLDS. This means that the MySQL DataSource will be available from within the server VM under the JNDI name `java:/MySQLDS`.

- `DataSourceClass`—You will use the `org.jboss.pool.jdbc.xa.wrapper.XADataSourceImpl` because the MySQL driver does not provide XADataSource support.

- `URL`—You will connect to the sample database on a local MySQL server; therefore, our JDBC URL will be `jdbc:mysql://localhost/sample`.

- `JDBCUser`—The default MySQL install requires no username when connecting from the localhost, so leave this empty.

- `Password`—The default MySQL install requires no password when connecting from the localhost, so leave this empty.

- `MinSize`—Use 0 for this example to enable the number of active database connections to drop to zero.

- `MaxSize`—Use 5 for this example to restrict the maximum number of active database connections to five.

Creating a `XADataSourceLoader` MBean configuration with these attribute settings gives you the following configuration to add to the `jboss.jcml` file:

```
<mbean code="org.jboss.jdbc.XADataSourceLoader"
  name="DefaultDomain:service=XADataSource,name=MySQLDS">
    <attribute name="PoolName">MySQLDS</attribute>
    <attribute name="DataSourceClass">
      org.jboss.pool.jdbc.xa.wrapper.XADataSourceImpl
    </attribute>
    <attribute name="URL">jdbc:mysql://localhost/sample</attribute>
    <attribute name="JDBCUser"></attribute>
    <attribute name="Password"></attribute>
    <attribute name="MinSize">0</attribute>
    <attribute name="MaxSize">5</attribute>
  </mbean>
```

That concludes the steps required to configure a database `DataSource`. The online documentation on the `www.jboss.org` Web site lists some example `jboss.jcml` configurations for common databases, so if you need a JDBC `DataSource` configuration for you database, that is the best place to start.

The Default JDBC Database, Hypersonic SQL

JBoss comes bundled with an embeddable Open Source database called Hypersonic SQL (http://sourceforge.net/projects/hsqldb). It is configured using the `org.jboss.jdbc.HypersonicDatabase` MBean service, which integrates the Hypersonic database into the JBoss server. On startup the `HypersonicDatabase` MBean initializes an in memory database.

The configurable attributes for the `HypersonicDatabase` service include the following:

- `Database`—The name of database. This translated into a file path under the JBOSS_DIST/db/hypersonic JBoss distribution directory. The default value is "default".

- `Port`—The listening port number to use for the Hypersonic database server connection.

- `Silent`—A Boolean flag indicating if the server should not display diagnostic messages. The default value is true indicating that no messages should be displayed.

- `Trace`—A Boolean flag indicating if the server should display JDBC trace messages. The default value is false indicating that no messages should be displayed.

Summary

In this chapter you were introduced to the JBoss persistence layer abstraction and shown how a custom persistence layer could be provided using a file system based store as an example. JAWS, the default JBoss CMP persistence manager, was also discussed and customization of the JAWS engine using the jaws.xml descriptor was presented. Configuration of a JDBC database pool using the `XADataSourceLoader` MBean was examined.

In the following Chapter 6, "JBossTX—The JBoss Transaction Manager," you will learn about the JBoss transaction manager as well as the JBossTX architecture.

bile:
[mkdir] Created dir: /tmp/2.4.4/
[javac] Compiling 154 source fil
install:
[copy] Copyin
[copy] Copyin

p/2
p/2

6

JBossTX – The JBoss Transaction Manager

This chapter discusses transaction management in JBoss and the JBossTX architecture. The JBossTX architecture allows for any Java Transaction API (JTA) transaction manager implementation to be used. JBossTX includes a fast in-VM implementation of a JTA compatible transaction manager that is used as the default transaction manager. This chapter provides an overview of the key transaction concepts and notions in the JTA to provide sufficient background for the JBossTX architecture discussion. It then covers the interfaces that make up the JBossTX architecture, and concludes with a discussion of the MBeans available for integration of alternate transaction managers.

Transaction/JTA Overview

For the purpose of this discussion, a transaction can be defined as a unit of work containing one or more operations involving one or more shared resources having Atomicity, Consistency, Isolation and Durability (ACID) properties. ACID can be defined as follows:

- Atomicity—A transaction must be atomic, meaning that either all or none the work done in the transaction must be performed. Doing only part of a transaction is not allowed.

- Consistency—When a transaction is completed, the system must be in a stable and consistent condition. Here consistent is with respect to all modifications of state that have been attempted by work done in the context of a transaction. If the transaction fails, there cannot be any side effects of partially completed work that would leave the system in a non-derministic or inconsistent state.

- Isolation—Different transactions must be isolated from each other. This means that the partial work done in one transaction is not visible to other transactions until the transaction is committed, and that each process in a multi-user system can be programmed as if it were the only process accessing the system. A commit of a transaction is simply the successful completion of all units of work done in the context of the transaction.

- Durability—The changes made during a transaction are made persistent when it is committed. When a transaction is committed, its changes will not be lost, even if the server crashes afterwards.

To illustrate these concepts, consider a simple banking account application. The banking application has a database with a number of accounts. The result of a transfer between accounts must leave the net sum of all accounts the same before and after the transfer. An amount of money M is moved from account A to account B by subtracting money M from account A and adding money M to account B. This operation must be done in a transaction, and all four ACID properties are important.

The atomicity property means that both the withdrawal and deposit are performed as an indivisible unit. If, for some reason, both cannot be done, nothing will be done.

The consistency property means that after the transaction, the sum of the amounts of all accounts must still be 0.

The isolation property is important when more than one bank clerk uses the system at the same time. A withdrawal or deposit could be implemented as a three-step process. First, the amount of the account is read from the database. Next, something is subtracted from or added to the amount read from the database. Finally, the new amount is written to the database. Without transaction isolation, several bad things could happen. For example, if two processes read the amount of account A at the same time, and each independently added or subtracted something before writing the new amount to the database, the first change would be incorrectly overwritten by the last.

The durability property is also important. If a money transfer transaction is committed, the bank must trust that some subsequent failure cannot undo the money transfer.

Pessimistic and Optimistic Locking

Transactional isolation is usually implemented by locking whatever is accessed in a transaction. There are two different approaches to transactional locking—pessimistic locking and optimistic locking.

With pessimistic locking, locks are applied in a fail-safe way. In the banking application example, an account is locked as soon as it is accessed in a transaction. Attempts to use the account in other transactions while it is locked will result in the other process being delayed until the account lock is released, or the transaction will be rolled back. The lock exists until the transaction has either been committed or rolled back.

The disadvantage of pessimistic locking is that a resource is locked from the time it is first accessed in a transaction until the transaction is finished, making it inaccessible to other transactions during that time. If most transactions simply look at the resource and never change it, an exclusive lock may be excessive because it may cause lock contention; thus, optimistic locking may be a better approach.

With optimistic locking, a resource is not actually locked when it is first is accessed by a transaction. Instead, the state of the resource at the time when it would have been locked with the pessimistic locking approach is saved. Other transactions are able to concurrently access the resource, and the possibility of conflicting changes is possible. At commit time, when the resource is about to be updated in persistent storage, the state of the resource is read from storage again and compared to the state that was saved when the resource was first accessed in the transaction. If the two states differ, a conflicting update was made, and the transaction will be rolled back.

In the banking application account transfer example, the original balance of an account is saved when the account is first accessed in a transaction. Call this value B0. Because the work to be done in the context of the transaction will change the account balance, the balance is read from the store again just before the persistent balance is about to be updated with the post transfer balance value. Call the second value B1. If the two balance values B0 and B1 are not the same, the transaction will fail itself because another transaction has modified the account balance and any logic based on the B0 value are invalid. If B0 and B1 are the same, the new balance value is written to persistent storage.

The Components of a Distributed Transaction

There are a number of participants in a distributed transaction. These include the following:

- Transaction Manager—This component is distributed across the transactional system. It manages and coordinates the work involved in the transaction. The transaction manager is exposed by the `javax.transaction.TransactionManager` interface in JTA.

- Transaction Context—A transaction context identifies a particular transaction. In JTA the corresponding interface is `javax.transaction.Transaction`.

- Transactional Client—A transactional client can invoke operations on one or more transactional objects in a single transaction. The transactional client that started the transaction is called the transaction originator. A transaction client is either an explicit or implicit user of JTA interfaces, and has no interface representation in the JTA.

- Transactional Object—A transactional object is an object whose behavior is affected by operations performed on it within a transactional context. A transactional object can also be a transactional client. Most Enterprise Java Beans are transactional objects.

- Recoverable Resource—A recoverable resource is a transactional object whose state is saved to persistent storage if the transaction is committed, and whose state can be reset to what it was at the beginning of the transaction if the transaction is rolled back. At commit time, the transaction manager uses a two-phase protocol when communicating with the recoverable resource. This ensures transactional integrity when more than one recoverable resource is involved in the transaction being committed. Transactional databases and message brokers like JBossMQ are examples of recoverable resources. A recoverable resource is represented using the `javax.transaction.xa.XAResource` interface in JTA.

The Two-Phase XA Protocol

When a transaction is about to be committed, it is the responsibility of the transaction manager to ensure that either all of it is committed, or that all of is rolled back. If only a single recoverable resource is involved in the transaction, the task of the transaction manager is simple—to tell the resource to commit the changes to stable storage.

When more than one recoverable resource is involved in the transaction, management of the commit gets more complicated. Simply asking each of the recoverable resources to commit changes to stable storage is not enough to maintain the atomic property of the transaction. The reason for this is that if one recoverable resource has committed and another fails to commit, part of the transaction would be committed and the other part rolled back.

To get around this problem, the two-phase XA protocol is used. The XA protocol involves an extra preparation phase before the actual commit phase. Before asking any of the recoverable resources to commit the changes, the transaction manager asks all the recoverable resources to prepare to commit. When a recoverable resource indicates it is prepared to commit the transaction, it has ensured that it can commit the transaction. The resource is still able to rollback the transaction, if necessary.

So the first phase consists of the transaction manager asking all the recoverable resources to prepare to commit. If any of the recoverable resources fails to prepare, the transaction will be rolled back. But if all recoverable resources indicate they were able to prepare to commit, the second phase of the XA protocol begins. This consists of the transaction manager asking all the recoverable resources to commit the transaction. Because all the recoverable resources have indicated they are prepared, this step cannot fail.

Heuristic Exceptions

In a distributed environment communications failures can happen. If communication between the transaction manager and a recoverable resource is not possible for an extended period of time, the recoverable resource may decide to unilaterally commit or rollback changes done in the context of a transaction. Such a decision is called a heuristic decision. It is one of the worst errors that can happen in a transaction system, as it can lead to parts of the transaction being committed while other parts are rolled back, thus violating the atomicity property of transaction and possibly leading to data integrity corruption.

Because of the dangers of heuristic exceptions, a recoverable resource that makes a heuristic decision is required to maintain all information about the decision in stable storage until the transaction manager tells it to forget about the heuristic decision. The actual data about the heuristic decision that is saved in stable storage depends on the type of recoverable resource, and is not standardized. The idea is that a system manager can look at the data, and possibly edit the resource to correct any data integrity problems.

There are several different kinds of heuristic exceptions defined by the JTA. The `javax.transaction.HeuristicCommitException` is thrown when a recoverable resource is asked to rollback to report that a heuristic decision was made and all relevant updates have been committed. On the opposite end is the `javax.transaction.HeuristicRollbackException`, which is thrown by a recoverable resource when it is asked to commit to indicate that a heuristic decision was made and all relevant updates have been rolled back.

The `javax.transaction.HeuristicMixedException` is the worst heuristic exception. It is thrown to indicate that parts of the transaction were committed, while other parts were rolled back. The transaction manager throws this exception when some recoverable resources did a heuristic commit, while other recoverable resources did a heuristic rollback.

Transaction IDs and Branches

In JTA, the identity of transactions is encapsulated in objects implementing the `javax.transaction.xa.Xid` interface. The transaction ID is an aggregate of the following three parts:

- The integer format identifier indicates the transaction family and tells how the other two parts should be interpreted. A value of 0 indicates that the X/Open specification format.

- The global transaction id identifies the global transaction within the transaction family.

- The branch qualifier denotes a particular branch of the global transaction.

Transaction branches are used to identify different parts of the same global transaction. Whenever the transaction manager involves a new, recoverable resource in a transaction it creates a new transaction branch.

JBoss Transaction Internals

The JBoss application server is written to be independent of the actual transaction manager used. JBoss uses the JTA `javax.transaction.TransactionManager` interface as its view of the server transaction manager. Thus, JBoss may use any transaction manager that implements the JTA TransactionManager interface. Whenever a transaction manager is used, it is obtained from the well-known JNDI location `java:/TransactionManager`. This is the globally available access point for the server transaction manager.

If transaction contexts are to be propagated with RMI/JRMP calls, the transaction manager must also implement two simple interfaces for the import and export of transaction propagation contexts (TPCs). The interfaces are `org.jboss.tm.TransactionPropagationContextImporter` and `org.jboss.tm.TransactionPropagationContextFactory`.

Being independent of the actual transaction manager used also means that JBoss does not specify the format of type of the transaction propagation contexts used. In JBoss, a TPC is of type `Object`, and the only requirement is that the TPC must implementation the `java.io.Serializable` interface.

When using the RMI/JRMP protocol for remote calls, the TPC is carried as a field in the `org.jboss.ejb.plugins.jrmp.client.RemoteMethodInvocation` class that is used to forward remote method invocation requests.

Adapting a Transaction Manager to JBoss

A transaction manager has to implement the Java Transaction API to be easily integrated with JBoss. As almost everything in JBoss, the transaction manager is managed as an MBean. Like all JBoss services, it should implement `org.jboss.util.ServiceMBean` to ensure proper life-cycle management.

The primary requirement of the transaction manager service on startup is that it binds its implementation of the three required interfaces into JNDI. These interfaces and their JNDI locations include the following:

- The `javax.transaction.TransactionManager` interface—This interface is used by the application server to manage transactions on behalf of the transactional objects that use container managed transactions. It must be bound under the JNDI name `java:/TransactionManager`.

- The transaction propagation context factory interface `org.jboss.tm.TransactionPropagationContextFactory`—This is called by JBoss whenever a transaction propagation context is needed for transporting a transaction with a remote method call. It must be bound under the JNDI name `java:/TransactionPropagationContextExporter`.

- The transaction propagation context importer interface `org.jboss.tm.TransactionPropagationContextImporter`—This interface is called by JBoss whenever a transaction propagation context from an incoming remote method invocation has to be converted to a transaction that can be used within the receiving JBoss server VM. It must be bound under the JNDI name `java:/TransactionPropagationContextImporter`.

Establishing these JNDI bindings is all the transaction manager service needs to do to install its implementation as the JBoss server transaction manager.

The Default Transaction Manager

By default, JBoss is configured to use the fast in-VM transaction manager. This transaction manager is exceptionally fast, but does have the following limitations:

- It does not do transactional logging, and is thus incapable of automated recovery after a server crash.

- While it does support propagating transaction contexts with remote calls, it does not support propagating transaction contexts to other virtual machines, so all transactional work must be done in the same virtual machine as the JBoss server.

The corresponding default transaction manager MBean service is the `org.jboss.tm.TransactionManagerService` MBean. It has the following two configurable attributes:

- The default transaction timeout in seconds. The default value is 300 seconds.

- The class to use for `javax.transaction.xa.Xid` instances. This is a workaround for XA JDBC drivers that only works with their own Xid implementation. Examples of such drivers are the older Oracle XA drivers. If not specified, a JBoss implementation of the Xid interface is used.

The Tyrex Transaction Manager

Tyrex is a full-blown Common Object Request Broker Architecture (CORBA) based transaction manager that supports transaction context propagation between different server VMs.

> **NOTE**
>
> CORBA is a vendor and language independent RPC architecture. It is similar in functionality to Java's RMI, but it uses a standard write protocol called IIOP and allows for different languages to be used. Support for IIOP is exists in Java and is being mandated by the latest version of the EJB 2.0 specification. For additional details on CORBA and IIOP see the Object Management Group home page at http://www.omg.org.

A JBoss MBean service has been written for this transaction manager that enables its use in JBoss without using the IIOP wire protocol. The Tyrex MBean class is included in the default bundle as org.jboss.tm.plugins.tyrex.TransactionManagerService.

The MBean has only one configurable attribute called ConfigFileName, which is the location of the Tyrex domain configuration file as either a URL string or a classpath resource. If no ConfigFileName value is specified, it defaults to domain.xml. The Tyrex MBean is included in the default jboss.jcml configuration file just after he standard JBoss transaction manager MBean, but is commented out. To switch to the Tyrex transaction manager, you need simply to comment out, or remove the default JBoss MBean and uncomment the Tyrex plugin. The Tyrex MBean configuration looks similar to the following:

```
<mbean code="org.jboss.tm.plugins.tyrex.TransactionManagerService"
  name="DefaultDomain:service=TransactionManager">
  <attribute name="ConfigFileName">domain.xml</attribute>
</mbean>
```

To properly configure the Tyrex MBean service, you need to set up the domain.xml configuration file correctly. Download the Tyrex distribution from tyrex.exolab.org Web site for the required configuration documentation.

UserTransaction Support

The JTA javax.transaction.UserTransaction interface allows applications to explicitly control transactions. For enterprise session beans that manage transaction themselves (BMT), a UserTransaction can be obtained by calling the getUserTransaction method on the bean context object, javax.ejb.SessionContext.

NOTE

For BMT beans, do not obtain the `UserTransaction` interface using a JNDI lookup. Doing this violates the EJB specification, and the returned `UserTransaction` object does not have the hooks the EJB container needs to make important checks.

To use the `UserTransaction` interface in code other than a BMT EJB, the `org.jboss.tm.usertx.server.ClientUserTransactionService` MBean must be configured and started. This MBean publishes a `UserTransaction` implementation under the JNDI name `UserTransaction`. This MBean is configured by default in the standard JBoss distributions and has no configurable attributes.

When the `UserTransaction` is obtained with a JNDI lookup from a stand-alone client, such as a client operating in a virtual machine other than the server's, a simple `UserTransaction` suitable for thin clients is returned. This `UserTransaction` implementation controls only the transactions on the server from which the `UserTransaction` object was obtained. Local transactional work performed in the client is not done within the transactions started by this `UserTransaction` object.

When a `UserTransaction` object is obtained by looking up the JNDI name `UserTransaction` in the same virtual machine as JBoss, a simple interface to the JTA `TransactionManager` is returned. This is suitable for Web components running in Web containers embedded in JBoss. When components are deployed in an embedded Web server, the deployer will make a JNDI link from the standard `java:comp/UserTransaction` ENC name to the global `UserTransaction` binding. This is done so that the Web components can look up the `UserTranaction` instance under JNDI name as specified by the J2EE.

Summary

In this chapter you were introduced to the notion of a transaction and the ACID properties of a transaction were defined. The notion of a distributed transaction and the participants as defined by the JTA were given. Lastly, the mechanism for integrating a transaction manager into JBoss was specified through a description of the default JBoss transaction manager MBean service.

Next you will cover the JBoss components that make up the J2EE connector architecture implementation, JBossCX.

ile:
[mkdir] Created dir: /tmp/2.4.4/j
[javac] Compiling 154 source file

install:
[copy] Copyin
[copy] Copyin

7

JBossCX—The JBoss Connector Architecture

This chapter discusses the JBoss server implementation of the J2EE Connector Architecture (JCA). JCA is a resource manager integration API whose goal is to standardize access to non-relational resources in the same way the JDBC API standardized access to relational data. This chapter introduces the utility of the JCA APIs and then describes the state of JCA in JBoss 2.4.x.

CA Overview

J2EE 1.3 contains a connector architecture (JCA) specification that allows for the integration of transacted and secure resource adaptors into a J2EE application server environment. The JCA specification describes the notion of such resource managers as Enterprise Information Systems (EIS). Examples of EIS include enterprise resource planning packages, mainframe transaction processing, non-Java legacy applications, and so on.

> **NOTE**
>
> The full JCA specification is available from the JCA home page
> at http://java.sun.com/j2ee/connector/.

The reason for the focus of the JCA specification on EIS is primarily because the notions of transactions, security, and scalability are requirements in enterprise software systems.

However, the JCA is applicable to any resource that needs to integrate into JBoss in a secure, scalable, and transacted manner.

The connector architecture defines a standard Service Provider Interface (SPI) for integrating the transaction, security, and connection management facilities of an application server with those of a resource manager. The SPI defines the system level contract between the resource adaptor and the application server.

The connector architecture also defines a Common Client Interface (CCI) for accessing resources. The CCI is targeted at EIS development tools and frameworks. The CCI provides a way to minimize the EIS specific code required by such tools. Typically, J2EE developers access a resource using such a tool or a resource specific interface rather than using CCI directly because the CCI is not a type specific API. To be used effectively the CCI must be used in conjunction with metadata that describes how to map from the generic CCI API to the resource manager specific data types used internally by the resource manager.

Connector architecture enables a resource vendor to provide a standard adaptor for its product. A resource adaptor is a system-level software driver that is used by a Java application to connect to resource. The resource adaptor plugs into an application server and provides connectivity between the resource manager, the application server, and the enterprise application. A resource vendor need only implement a JCA compliant adaptor once to allow use of the resource manager in any JCA capable application server.

An application server vendor extends its architecture once to support the connector architecture, and is then assured of seamless connectivity to multiple resource managers. Likewise, a resource manager vendor provides one standard resource adaptor and the resource has the capability to plug into any application server that supports the connector architecture.

A graphical depiction of the JCA participants is given in Figure 7.1.

Figure 7.1 illustrates that the application server is extended to provide support for the JCA SPI. This extension allows a resource adaptor to integrate with the server connection pooling, transaction management, and security management facilities. This integration API defines a system contract that consists of the following:

- Connection management—A contract that allows the application server to pool resource connections. The purpose of the pool management is to allow for scalability. Resource connections are typically expensive objects to create, and pooling them allows for more effective reuse and management.

- Transaction Management—A contract that allows the application server transaction manager to manage transactions that engage resource managers.

- Security Management—A contract that enables secured access to resource managers.

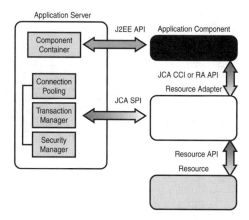

FIGURE 7.1   An overview of the interaction between the key participants defined by the JCA specification.

The resource adaptor implements the resource manager side of the system contract. This entails using the application server connection pooling, providing transaction resource information, and using the security integration information. The resource adaptor also exposes the resource manager to the application server components. This can be done using the CCI or a resource adaptor specific API.

The application component integrates into the application server using a standard J2EE container to component contract. For an EJB component, this contract is defined by the EJB specification. The application component interacts with the resource adaptor in the same way as it would with any other standard resource factory; for example, a javax.sql.DataSource JDBC resource factory. The only difference with a JCA resource adaptor is that the client has the option of using the resource adaptor independent CCI API if the resource adaptor supports this.

Figure 7.2 illustrates the relationship between the JCA architecture participants in terms of how they relate to the JCA SPI, CCI and JTA packages.

The JBossCX architecture provides the implementation of the application server specific classes. Figure 7.2 shows that this comes down to the implementation of the javax.resource.spi.ConnectionManager and javax.resource.spi.ConnectionEventListener interfaces.

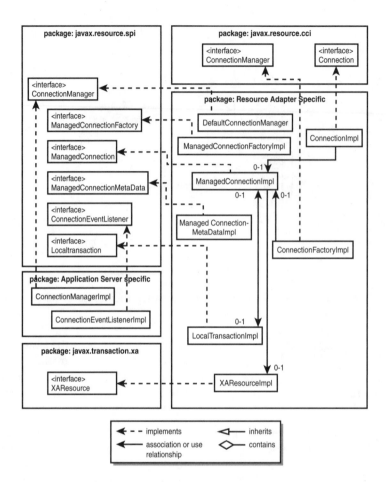

FIGURE 7.2   A class diagram for the connection management architecture.

An Overview of the JBossCX Architecture

The JBossCX framework provides the application server architecture extension required for the use of JCA resource adaptors. This is primarily a connection pooling and management extension along with a number of MBeans for loading resource adaptors into the JBoss server. Figure 7.3 expands the generic view given by Figure 7.2 to illustrate how the JBossCX layer implements the application server specific extension along with an example JMS resource adaptor that is bundled with JBoss.

The starting point for discussing the components in the JBoss server portion of Figure 7.3 are the two MBeans, `org.jboss.resource.ConnectionManagerFactoryLoader` and `org.jboss.resource.ConnectionFactoryLoader`.

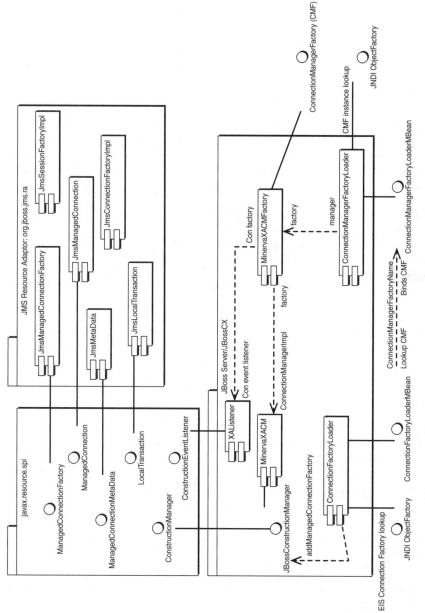

FIGURE 7.3 The key JBossCX classes that comprise the JBoss server JCA system level contract implementation.

ConnectionManagerFactoryLoader **MBean**

The `ConnectionManagerFactoryLoader` is responsible for binding an
`org.jboss.resource.ConnectionManagerFactory` instance into JNDI so that an
`org.jboss.resource.ConnectionFactoryLoader` MBean can access it. A
`ConnectionManagerFactory` implementation is responsible for creating
`org.jboss.resource.JBossConnectionManager` instances for use by the JBoss server.
The `JBossConnectionManager` interface is a subinterface of
`javax.resource.spi.ConnectionManager` that adds support for re-enlisting connections under new transactions and shutting down the `JBossConnectionManager`. You
define one or more `ConnectionManagerFactoryLoader` MBeans in the `jboss.jcml` file
to define the types of `ConnectionManager` implementations that are available for use
in the JBoss server. The configurable attributes of the
`ConnectionManagerFactoryLoader` MBean are as follows:

- `FactoryName`—The name of the connection manager factory. This is the name
  under which the connection manager factory will be bound in JNDI. Note that
  this name will be prefixed with `java:/` so that the binding will only be available inside of the JBoss server VM.

- `FactoryClass`—The fully qualified class name of the
  `org.jboss.resource.JBossConnectionManager` interface implementation to use
  as the connection manager factory. The available implementations will be
  discussed in the next paragraph.

- `Properties`—The properties to set on the connection manager factory instance.
  This is in the `java.util.Properties.load` format (one property per line in the
  form name=value).

- `TransactionManagerName`—The JNDI name of the
  `javax.transaction.TransactionManager` instance to use. If not specified, this
  defaults to '`java:/TransactionManager`'.

There are three implementations of the `ConnectionManagerFactory` interface
bundled with the standard JBoss server distribution. They are as follows:

- `org.jboss.pool.connector.jboss.MinervaNoTransCMFactory`—A factory for
  `JBossConnectionManager` instances suitable for use with resource adaptors that
  do not support transactions

- `org.jboss.pool.connector.jboss.`
  `MinervaSharedLocalCMFactory`—A factory for `JBossConnectionManager`
  instances suitable for use with resource adaptors that support local transactions
  rather than the two phase JTA XA protocol

- `org.jboss.pool.connector.jboss.MinervaXACMFactory`—A factory for
  `JBossConnectionManager` instances suitable for use with resource adaptors that
  support JTA XA transactions

The default JBoss `jboss.jcml` configuration file defines a `ConnectionManagerFactoryLoader` for each of the three `ConnectionManagerFactory` implementations. You would typically not need to define a `ConnectionManagerFactoryLoader` MBean yourself unless you want to provide an alternate implementation of one of the `JBossConnectionManagers`.

As an example of how these classes are related, Figure 7.3 shows a `ConnectionManagerFactoryLoader` associated with a `MinervaXACMFactory`, which is in turn associated with a `MinervaXACM` instance and a `XAListener` instance. The `MinervaXACM` is the `JBossConnectionManager` implementation that the `MinervaXACMFactory` creates. The `XAListener` instance is the `javax.resource.spi.ConnectionEventListener` callback interface implementation for `MinervaXACM`. Taken together, a `ConnectionManagerFactoryLoader` and its classes associated through the MBean configuration comprise the classes required by the JCA for the application server side of the system level contract.

The last piece of the resource adaptor integration puzzle is how a resource adaptor is loaded into the JBoss server and associated with a particular `ConnectionManager` instance. There are two elements to this task. One task is the creation of a resource adaptor archive (RAR) as defined by the JCA specification. The other task is to configure a `ConnectionFactoryLoader` MBean to specify the RAR deployment properties, including the security settings, resource adaptor properties, and the `ConnectionManager` type to use. You will be presented the `ConnectionFactoryLoader` MBean configuration and then and then look at creating a RAR for a skeleton resource adaptor.

ConnectionFactoryLoader **MBean**

For a resource adaptor's resource to be made available to application server components, a connection factory must be bound into JNDI. This is the standard pattern for all resources, and it is a requirement of the JCA specification that resource adaptors provide a connection factory that can be bound into JNDI. The `ConnectionFactoryLoader` MBean is the JBoss deployment tool provided to allow a RAR administrator to configure all aspects of a resource adaptor deployment.

For each resource adaptor that is to be deployed in a JBoss server, a `ConnectionFactoryLoader` MBean configuration must be defined and the attributes appropriate to the adaptor must be specified. The configurable attributes of the `ConnectionFactoryLoader` MBean are as follows:

- `FactoryName`—The JNDI name of the connection factory. This is the name under which the connection factory is bound in JNDI for access by application server components.

- `RARDeployerName`—The name of the MBean that deploys the resource adaptor to which this configuration relates. Currently, JBoss lazily configures the adaptor separately from the RAR deployment step, and the two steps are tied together via a JMX notification. The `ConnectionFactoryLoader` MBean needs to know the name of the MBean that deploys RARs so that it can register for JMX notifications to be able to configure the adaptor connection factory when the RAR is deployed. The default value of `JCA:service=RARDeployer` should only be changed if the RAR deployer MBean name is changed.

- `ResourceAdapterName`—The name of the resource adaptor for which this connection factory creates connections. This is the name given in the resource adaptor's <display-name> deployment descriptor element. It is used to filter JMX notifications to catch the deployment of the RAR.

- `Properties`—The properties to set on the resource adaptor to configure it to connect to a particular resource instance. This is in the `java.util.Properties.load` format (one property per line in the form name=value). The types of properties depend completely on the resource adaptor.

- `ConnectionManagerFactoryName`—The name of the connection manager factory to use. This is the name given in a previously defined `ConnectionManagerFactoryLoader` MBean. It should be one of the standard `ConnectionManagerFactory` implementations: `MinervaNoTransCMFactory`, `MinervaSharedLocalCMFactory` or `MinervaXACMFactory`.

- `ConnectionManagerProperties`—The properties (in `java.util.Properties.load` format) to set on the connection manager for this connection factory. These properties control settings such as connection pooling parameters.

- `PrincipalMappingClass`—The name of the class that implements the `org.jboss.resource.security.PrincipalMapping` interface. This class is responsible for mapping from the principal on behalf of whom the application component method is executing to the principal that is used for validating access to the resource.

- `PrincipalMappingProperties`—The properties (in `java.util.Properties.load` format) to pass to the principal mapping implementation specified above via the `PrincipalMapping.setProperties` method.

A Sample Skeleton JCA Resource Adaptor

To conclude the discussion of the JBossCX framework, you will create and deploy a single non-transacted resource adaptor that provides a skeleton implementation that stubs out the required interfaces and logs all method calls. The details of the requirements of a resource adaptor provider are not discussed here because these are presented in detail in the JCA specification. The purpose of the adaptor is to demonstrate the steps required to create and deploy a RAR in JBoss and to see how JBoss interacts with the adaptor.

NOTE

The source to the example adaptor can be found in the `src/main/org/jboss/chap7/ex1` directory of the book examples.

All of the resource adaptor classes in Figure 7.4 are from the `org.jboss.chap7.ex1` package. You will build the adaptor, deploy it to the JBoss server, and run an example client against an EJB that uses the resource adaptor to demonstrate the basic steps in a complete context. You'll then take a look at the JBoss server log to see how the JBossCX framework interacts with the resource adaptor to help you better understand the components in the JCA system level contract.

To build the example and deploy the RAR to the JBoss server `deploy/lib` directory, execute the following Ant command in the book examples directory:

```
examples 808>ant -Dchap=7 build-chap
Buildfile: build.xml
...
chap7-ex1-rar:
     [copy] Copying 1 file to G:\JBoss-2.4.3\deploy\lib

prepare:

chap7-ex1-jar:
BUILD SUCCESSFUL
```

Next, create a custom configuration of the JBoss server that includes a modified `jboss.jcml` file and log4j.properties file by executing the CD's Chapter 7 configuration build as follows:

```
examples 1127>ant -Dchap=7 config
Buildfile: build.xml

config:

config:
     [copy] Copying 14 files to G:\JBoss-2.4.3\conf\chap7
     [copy] Copying 2 files to G:\JBoss-2.4.3\conf\chap7
BUILD SUCCESSFUL
```

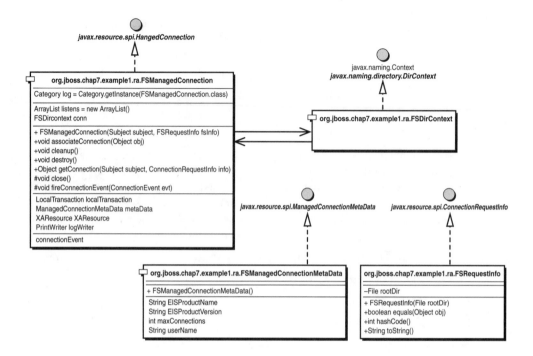

FIGURE 7.4   A class diagram for the example file system resource adaptor.

This creates a chap7 configuration file set under the JBoss distribution `conf` directory. The example `jboss.jcml` file defines a `ConnectionFactoryLoader` MBean configuration for the example resource adaptor. This portion of the jboss.jcml file is presented in Listing 7.1

LISTING 7.1   The jboss.jcml `ConnectionFactoryLoader` MBean Configuration Fragment for the Example Resource Adaptor

```
<!-- The chap7 example1 filesystem resource adaptor -->
<mbean code="org.jboss.resource.ConnectionFactoryLoader"
       name="JCA:service=ConnectionFactoryLoader,name=NoTransFS">
  <attribute name="FactoryName">NoTransFS</attribute>
  <attribute name="RARDeployerName">JCA:service=RARDeployer</attribute>
  <attribute name="ResourceAdapterName">File System Adapter</attribute>
  <attribute name="ConnectionManagerFactoryName">
    MinervaNoTransCMFactory
  </attribute>
  <attribute name="ConnectionManagerProperties" />
```

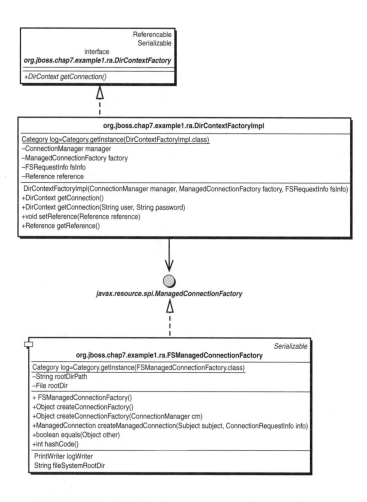

LISTING 7.1   Continued

```
<!-- Principal mapping configuration -->
<attribute name="PrincipalMappingClass">
   org.jboss.resource.security.ManyToOnePrincipalMapping
</attribute>
<attribute name="PrincipalMappingProperties">
  userName=jduke
  password=theduke
</attribute>
</mbean>
```

The key attributes of Listing 7.1 are as follows:

- FactoryName=NoTransFS—The adaptor factory will be bound into JNDI under the name java:/NoTransFS.

- ResourceAdapterName=File System Adapter—The name of the display-name element of the resource adaptor rar.xml descriptor. These must match for the JMX notification to be received by the ConnectionFactoryLoader.

- ConnectionManagerFactoryName=MinervaNoTransCMFactory— Because this is a non-transaction capable resource adaptor, you must choose the corresponding ConnectionManagerFactory type.

- PrincipalMappingClass= org.jboss.resource.security.ManyToOnePrincipalMapping—Choose the default implementation of the PrincipalMapping interface that maps all caller principals onto the principal name and password given by the PrincipalMappingProperties set.

- PrincipalMappingProperties=userName= jduke;password=theduke—The properties for the PrincipalMappingClass that assign the resource principal the name jduke with a password of theduke as the principal credentials.

Start up the JBoss server using the chap7 configuration file set, and the console should display output similar to the following:

```
bin 1426>run.bat chap7
JBOSS_CLASSPATH=;run.jar;../lib/crimson.jar
jboss.home = G:\JBoss-2.4.4
Using JAAS LoginConfig: file:/G:/JBoss-2.4.4/conf/chap7/auth.conf
Using configuration "chap7"
[root] Started Log4jService, config=
   file:/G:/JBoss-2.4.4/conf/chap7/log4j.properties
...
[AutoDeployer] Auto deploy of
   file:/G:/JBoss-2.4.4/deploy/lib/chap7-ex1.rar
[RARDeployer] Attempting to deploy RAR at
   'file:/G:/JBoss-2.4.4/deploy/lib/chap7-ex1.rar'
[RARMetaData] License terms present. See deployment descriptor.
[NoTransFS] Not setting config property 'Password'
[NoTransFS] Not setting config property 'UserName'
[NoTransFS] Using default value '/tmp/db/fs_store' for config
   property 'FileSystemRootDir'
```

```
[NoTransFS] Bound connection factory for resource adaptor
  'File System Adapter' to JNDI name 'java:/NoTransFS'
[AutoDeployer] Started
```

This output indicates that the resource adaptor has been successfully deployed and its connection factory has been bound into JNDI under the name 'java:/NoTransFS'. Now test access of the resource adaptor by a J2EE component. To do this, you have created a trivial stateless session bean that has a single method called echo. Inside of the echo method, the EJB accesses the resource adaptor connection factory, creates a connection, and then immediately closes the connection. The echo method code is shown in Listing 7.2.

LISTING 7.2   The Stateless Session Bean echo Method Code That Shows the Access of the Resource Adaptor Connection Factory

```java
public String echo(String arg)
{
    log.debug("echo, arg="+arg);
    try
    {
        InitialContext iniCtx = new InitialContext();
        Context enc = (Context) iniCtx.lookup("java:comp/env");
        Object ref = enc.lookup("ra/DirContextFactory");
        log.debug("echo, ra/DirContextFactory="+ref);
        DirContextFactory dcf = (DirContextFactory) ref;
        log.debug("echo, found dcf="+dcf);
        DirContext dc = dcf.getConnection();
        log.debug("echo, lookup dc="+dc);
        dc.close();
    }
    catch(NamingException e)
    {
        log.error("Failed during JNDI access", e);
    }
    return arg;
}
```

The EJB is not using the CCI interface to access the resource adaptor. Rather, it is using the resource adaptor-specific API based on the proprietary DirContextFactory interface that returns a JNDI DirContext object as the connection object. The example EJB is simply exercising the system contract layer by looking up the resource adaptor connection factory, creating a connection to the resource, and closing the connection. The EJB does not actually do anything with the connection because this would only exercise the resource adaptor implementation; this is a non-transactional resource.

Run the test client that calls the `EchoBean.echo` method by running Ant as follows from the examples directory:

```
examples 814>ant -Dchap=7 -Dex=1 run-example
Buildfile: build.xml
...
run-example1:
     [copy] Copying 1 file to G:\JBoss-2.4.3\deploy
     [echo] Waiting for deploy...
     [java] Created Echo
     [java] Echo.echo('Hello') = Hello
```

Now examine the output that has been logged by the resource adaptor to understand the interaction between the adaptor and the JBossCX layer. The output is in the `log/chap7.log` file of the JBoss server distribution. The events seen in the log are summarized using a sequence diagram. Figure 7.5 shows the events that occur during the deployment of the resource adaptor.

The process starts when the `RARDeployer` MBean sends a notification that it has installed the resource adaptor found in the chap7-ex1.rar. The notification is processed by the `handleNotification` method of the `ConnectionFactoryLoader` MBean. The events that occur within the `handleNotification` method are as follows:

1.1—If the notification is a deployment event, the `loadConnectionFactory` method is called with the `org.jboss.resource.RARMetaData` object that was passed in with the event notification.

1.1.1—The `ClassLoader` object associated with the `RARMetaData` is obtained. This will be used to load the resource adaptor classes. This `ClassLoader` is assigned by the `RARDeployer`, and has access to all of the classes in the RAR deployment.

1.1.2—The name of the `ManagedConnectionFactory` implementation class is obtained from the `RARMetaData`.

1.1.3—The `ManagedConnectionFactory` implementation class is loaded using the 1.1.1 `ClassLoader` instance.

1.1.4—The `ManagedConnectionFactory` implementation class is instantiated by invoking `newInstance` on the implementation class loaded in 1.1.3. This means that the implementation class must have a public no-arg constructor.

1.1.5—A `java.util.Map` of the properties defined in the RAR `ra.xml` descriptor is obtained from the `RARMetaData` instance. This represents the collection of `config-property` elements that were declared in the `ra.xml` descriptor.

1.1.6.1—An iteration over the properties loaded in 1.1.5 is performed and JavaBean style reflection is used to determine which properties have setters methods in the ManagedConnectionFactory instance. The diagram is illustrating that the FSManagedConnectionFactory class only has one setter for the FileSystemRootDir property. In general, any number of properties can be set by defining config-property elements in the ra.xml descriptor, and implementing a JavaBean setter style method.

1.1.7—The class defined in the PrincipalMappingClass attribute of the ConnectionFactoryLoader MBean is loaded using the ClassLoader from 1.1.1. This is a class that implements the org.jboss.resource.security.PrincipalMapping interface.

1.1.8—The PrincipalMapping implementation class is instantiated by invoking newInstance on the class loaded in 1.1.7. This means that the implementation class must have a public no-arg constructor.

1.1.9—The ManagedConnectionFactory created in 1.1.4 is made available to the PrincipalMapping instance via the setManagedConnectionFactory method.

1.1.10—The value of the ConnectionFactoryLoader MBean PrincipalMappingProperties attribute is passed to the PrincipalMapping instance via the setProperties method.

1.1.11—The RARMetaData value is passed to the PrincipalMapping instance via the setRARMetaData method.

1.1.12—The org.jboss.resource.ConnectionManagerFactory instance to be used with the resource adaptor is located in JNDI. This is done using the name defined as the ConnectionFactoryLoader MBean ConnectionManagerFactoryName attribute value. In this case this locates an org.jboss.pool.connector.jboss.MinervaNoTransCMFactory instance since the jboss.jcml configuration specifies 'MinervaNoTransCMFactory' as the ConnectionManagerFactoryName value.

1.1.13—A JBossConnectionManager instance is created by invoking the addManagedConnectionFactory method on the ConnectionManagerFactory located in 1.1.12. This is the javax.resource.spi.ConnectionManager instance that will be associated with the resource adaptor.

1.1.14—A resource adaptor connection factory is created by invoking the createConnectionFactory method on the ManagedConnectionFactory instance. The ConnectionManager instance created in 1.1.13 is passed along with the method invocation.

1.1.14.1—The FSManagedConnectionFactory creates an instance of the example resource adaptor connection factory. This is a DirConectFactoryImpl instance. The DirConectFactoryImpl is provided the ConnectionManager instance as an argument to its constructor. The DirConectFactoryImpl will need this for creating connections.

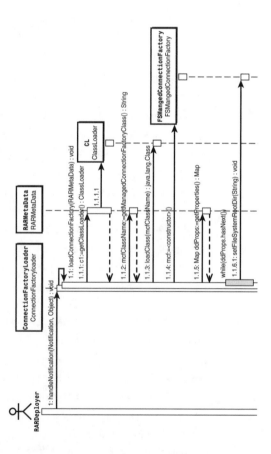

FIGURE 7.5   A sequence diagram illustrating the key interactions between the JBossCX framework and the example resource adaptor during deployment.

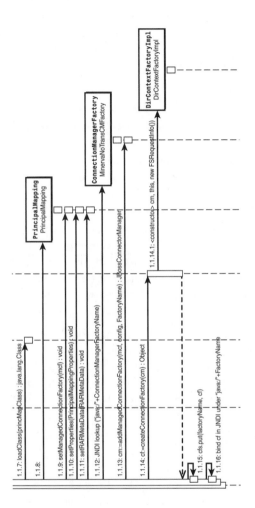

1.1.15—The resource adaptor connection factory is placed into a static `HashMap` of connection factory instances using the JNDI name of the factory as the key. This is used by the `javax.naming.spi.ObjectFactory.getObjectInstance` method implementation when a component does a lookup on the resource adaptor connection factory location.

1.1.16—The resource adaptor connection factory is bound into JNDI under the name `'java:/'`+FactoryName where FactoryName is the value of the `ConnectionFactoryLoader` MBean FactoryName attribute. For this example, the full JNDI name is `'java:/NoTransFS'` because `'NoTransFS'` is the value of the FactoryName attribute. The actual value bound into JNDI is a `javax.naming.Reference` with the `ConnectionFactoryLoader` as the `ObjectFactory` implementation.

These are the steps involved with making the resource adaptor connection factory available to application server components. The remaining log messages are the result of the example client invoking the `EchoBean.echo` method and this method's interaction with the resource adaptor connection factory. Figure 7.6 is a sequence diagram that summarizes the events that occur when the `EchoBean` accesses the resource adaptor connection factory from JNDI and creates a connection.

The starting point is the client's invocation of the `EchoBean.echo` method. For the sake of conciseness of Figure 7.6, the client is shown directly invoking the `EchoBean.echo` method when in reality the JBoss EJB container handles the invocation. There are three distinct interactions between the EchoBean and the resource adaptor; the lookup of the connection factory, the creation of a connection, and the close of the connection.

The lookup of the resource adaptor connection factory is illustrated by the 1.1 sequences of events. The events are:

1.1—The echo method performs a JNDI lookup of the resource adaptor connection factory.

1.1.1—The JNDI framework requests that value associated with the reference bound into JNDI using the reference `ObjectFactory`. The `ObjectFactory` is the `ConnectionFactoryLoader` MBean configured for the resource adaptor.

1.1.1.1—The `ConnectionFactoryLoader` locates the resource adaptor connection factory from the class map of connection factories using the name passed into the `getObjectInstance` method.

1.1.1.1.1—This signifies the location of the resource adaptor connection factory.

The resulting Object returned by the lookup of 1.1 is cast to the `DirContextFactory` type so that it can be used to create a connection.

After the EchoBean has obtained the `DirContextFactory` for the resource adaptor, it creates a connection to the resource manager. This is illustrated by the 1.2 sequences of events, which are as follows:

1.2—The getConnection method is invoked on the DirContextFactory obtained from the JNDI lookup.

1.2.1—The DirContextFactoryImpl class asks its associated ConnectionManager to allocate a connection. It passes in the ManagedConnectionFactory and FSRequestInfo that were associated with the DirContextFactoryImpl during its construction.

1.2.1.1—The ConnectionManager asks its object pool for a connection object. Because no connections have been created, the pool must create a new connection. This connection is created by requesting a new managed connection from the ManagedConnectionFactory. The javax.security.auth.Subject associated with the pool as well as the FSRequestInfo data are passed as arguments to the createManagedConnection method invocation.

1.2.1.1.1—The FSManagedConnectionFactory creates a new FSManagedConnection instance and passes in the Subject and FSRequestInfo data.

1.2.1.2—A javax.resource.spi.ConnectionListener instance is created. The type of listener created is based on the type of ConnectionManager. In this case it is an BaseConnectionManager$NoTransactionListener instance from the org.jboss.pool.connector package.

1.2.1.3—The listener is asked to register with its connection.

1.2.1.3.1—The listener registers as a javax.resource.spi.ConnectionEventListener with the ManagedConnection instance created in 1.2.1.1.

1.2.1.4—The ManagedConnection is asked for the underlying resource manager connection. The Subject and FSRequestInfo data are passed as arguments to the getConnection method invocation.

1.2.1.4.1—The FSManagedConnection creates the example resource adaptor connection type by creating a FSDirContext instance.

The resulting connection object returned by the lookup of 1.2 is cast to a javax.naming.directory.DirContext instance because this is the public interface defined by the resource adaptor.

After the EchoBean has obtained the DirContext for the resource adaptor, it simply closes the connection to indicate its interaction with the resource manager is complete. This is illustrated by the 1.3 sequences of events, which are as follows:

1.3—The EchoBean invokes close on the DirContext to indicate the no further use of the connection will occur.

1.3.1—The FSDirContext instance invokes close on its associated FSManagedConnection to allow it to inform its listeners that close has been invoked.

1.3.1.1—The FSManagedConnection creates a javax.resource.spi.ConnectionEvent and then invokes its fireConnectionEvent method to inform all registered ConnectionEventListeners of the event.

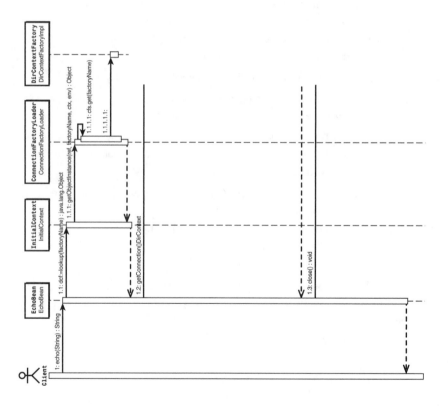

FIGURE 7.6   A sequence diagram illustrating the key interactions between the JBossCX framework and the example resource adaptor that result when the EchoBean accesses the resource adaptor connection factory.

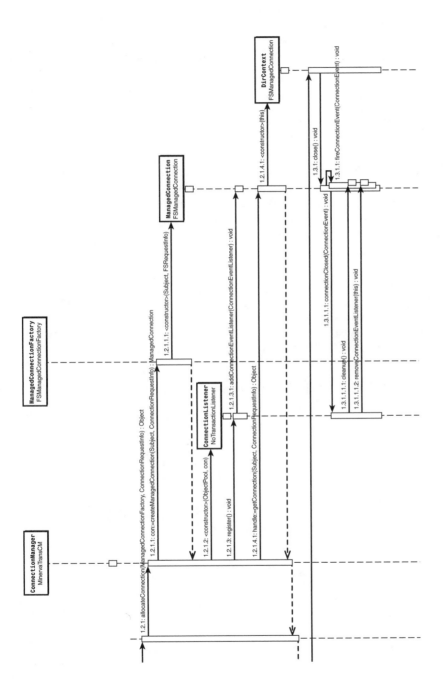

1.3.1.1.1—The `NoTransactionListener` is notified of the close event via its `connectionClosed` method.

1.3.1.1.1.1—The `NoTransactionListener` places the `ManagedConnection` back into the connection pool. This results in a cleanup invocation of the `FSManagedConnection` instance.

1.3.1.1.1.2—The `NoTransactionListener` removes itself as a `ConnectionEventListener` of the `FSManagedConnection` instance.

Your investigation into the interaction between the JBossCX layer and a trivial resource adaptor should give you sufficient understanding of the steps required to configure any resource adaptor. The example adaptor can also serve as a starting point for the creation of your own custom resource adaptors if you need to integrate non-JDBC resources into the JBoss server environment.

Summary

This chapter introduced the JCA architecture and the JBoss implementation of the application server system contract. The JBossCX MBeans that support the integration of JCA resource adaptors was presented, and an example file system resource adaptor was created. This illustrated both the usage of the JBossCX MBeans and the interaction between the JBossCX JCA components and a resource adaptor.

In the following chapter, you will cover the JBoss security architecture and the default implementation provided by the JBossSX framework.

ile:
    [mkdir] Created dir: /tmp/2.4.4/
    [javac] Compiling 154 source file

install:
    [copy] Copyin
    [copy] Copyin

8

JBossSX—The JBoss Security Extension Framework

Security is a fundamental part of any enterprise application. You need to be able to restrict who is allowed to access your applications and control what operations application users may perform. The J2EE specifications define a simple role-based security model for EJBs and Web components. The JBoss component framework that handles security is the JBossSX extension framework. The JBossSX security extension provides support for both the role-based declarative J2EE security model as well as integration of custom security via a security proxy layer. The default implementation of the declarative security model is based on Java Authentication and Authorization Service (JAAS) login modules and subjects. The security proxy layer allows custom security that cannot be described using the declarative model to be added to an EJB in a way that is independent of the EJB business object.

J2EE Declarative Security Overview

The security model advocated by the J2EE specification is a declarative model. It is declarative in that you describe the security roles and permissions using a standard XML descriptor rather than embedding security into your business component. This isolates security from business-level code because security tends to be a more a function of where the component is deployed, rather than an inherent aspect of the component's business logic. For example, consider an ATM component that is to be used to access a bank account. The security requirements, roles, and permissions will vary independent of how one accesses the bank account based on what bank is managing the account, where the ATM machine is deployed, and so on.

Securing a J2EE application is based on the specification of the application security requirements via the standard J2EE deployment descriptors. You secure access to EJBs and Web components in an enterprise application by using the ejb-jar.xml and web.xml deployment descriptors. Figures 8.1 and 8.2 illustrate the security-related elements in the EJB 2.0 and Servlet 2.2 deployment descriptors, respectively.

Security References

Both EJBs and servlets may declare one or more `security-role-ref` elements. This element is used to declare that a component is using the `role-name` value as an argument to the `isCallerInRole(String)` method. Using the `isCallerInRole` method, a component can verify if the caller is in a role that has been declared with a `security-role-ref/role-name` element. The `role-name` element value must link to a `security-role` element through the `role-link` element. The typical use of `isCallerInRole` is to perform a security check that cannot be defined using the role based `method-permission` elements. However, use of `isCallerInRole` is discouraged because this results in security logic embedded inside of the component code. Example descriptor fragments that illustrate `security-role-ref` usage are presented in Listing 8.1.

LISTING 8.1   Example ejb-jar.xml and web.xml Descriptor Fragments that Illustrate the `security-role-ref` Element Usage

```
<!-- A sample ejb-jar.xml fragment -->
<ejb-jar>
 <enterprise-beans>
    <session>
      <ejb-name>ASessionBean</ejb-name>
      ...
        <security-role-ref>
        <role-name>TheRoleICheck</role-name>
        <role-link>TheApplicationRole</role-link>
      </security-role-ref>
    </session>
 </enterprise-beans>
 ...
```

LISTING 8.1   Continued

```
</ejb-jar>

<!-- A sample web.xml fragment -->
<web-app>
  <servlet>
    <servlet-name>AServlet</servlet-name>
    ...
      <security-role-ref>
        <role-name>TheServletRole</role-name>
        <role-link>TheApplicationRole</role-link>
      </security-role-ref>
  </servlet>
...
</web-app>
```

Security Identity

EJBs can optionally declare a `security-identity` element. New to EJB 2.0 is the capability to specify what identity an EJB should use when it invokes methods on other components. The invocation identity can be that of the current caller, or it can be a specific role. The application assembler uses the `security-identity` element with a `use-caller-identity` child element to indicate the current caller's identity should be propagated as the security identity for method invocations made by the EJB. Propagation of the caller's identity is the default used in the absence of an explicit `security-identity` element declaration.

Alternatively, the application assembler can use the `run-as/role-name` child element to specify that a specific security role given by the `role-name` value should be used as the security identity for method invocations made by the EJB. Note that this does not change the caller's identity as seen by `EJBContext.getCallerPrincipal()`. Rather, the caller's security roles are set to the single role specified by the `run-as/role-name` element value. One use case for the `run-as` element is to prevent external clients from accessing internal EJBs. This is accomplished by assigning the internal EJB `method-permission` elements that restrict access to a role never assigned to an external client. EJBs that need to use internal EJB are then configured with a `run-as/role-name` equal to the restricted role. An example descriptor fragment that illustrates `security-identity` element usage is presented in Listing 8.2.

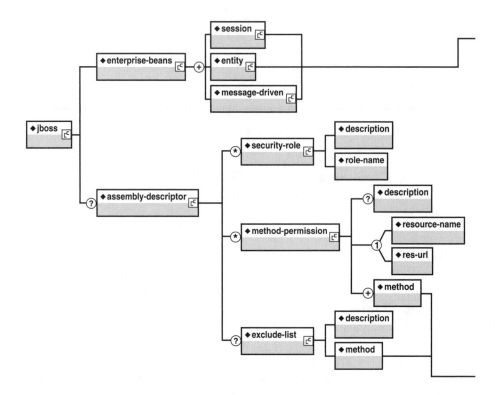

FIGURE 8.1　A subset of the EJB 2.0 deployment descriptor content model that shows the security-related elements.

LISTING 8.2　An Example ejb-jar.xml Descriptor Fragment that Illustrates the security-identity Element Usage

```
<!-- A sample ejb-jar.xml fragment -->
<ejb-jar>
<enterprise-beans>
    <session>
      <ejb-name>ASessionBean</ejb-name>
      ...
        <security-identity>
          <use-caller-identity/>
        </security-identity>
    </session>
    <session>
      <ejb-name>RunAsBean</ejb-name>
      ...
```

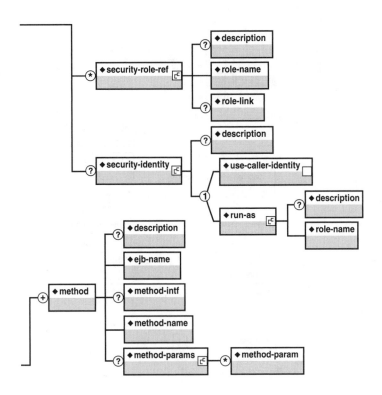

LISTING 8.2   Continued

```
        <security-identity>
         <run-as>
            <description>A private internal role</description>
            <role-name>InternalRole</role-name>
         </run-as>
        </security-identity>
      </session>
</enterprise-beans>
...
</ejb-jar>
```

The same security identity capability has been introduced for servlets since the J2EE 2.3 servlet specification, but this capability is currently unsupported in JBoss 2.4.

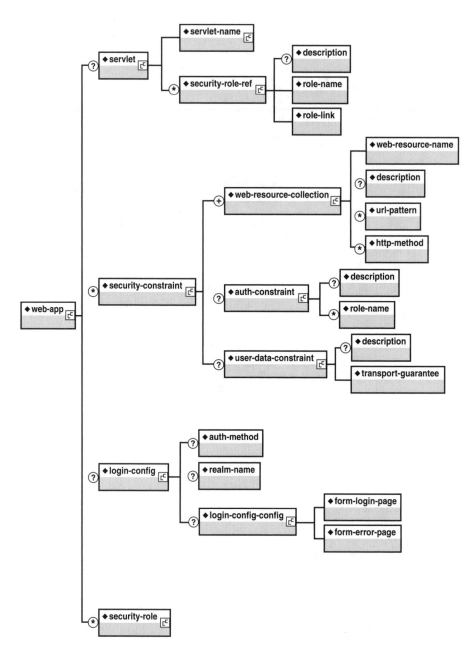

FIGURE 8.2   A subset of the Servlet 2.2 deployment descriptor content model that shows the security-related elements.

Security Roles

The security role name referenced by either the `security-role-ref` or `security-identity` element needs to map to one of the application's declared roles. An application assembler defines logical security roles by declaring `security-role` elements. The `role-name` value is a logical application role name like Administrator, Architect, SalesManager, and so on.

> **NOTE**
>
> What is a role? The J2EE specifications note that it is important to keep in mind that the security roles in the deployment descriptor are used to define the logical security view of an application. Roles defined in the J2EE deployment descriptors should not be confused with the user groups, users, principals, and other concepts that exist in the target enterprise's operational environment. The deployment descriptor roles are application constructs with application domain specific names. For example, a banking application might use role names such as BankManager, Teller, and Customer.

In JBoss, a `security-role` is only used to map `security-role-ref`/`role-name` values to the logical role to which the component declared role name refers. The user's assigned roles are a dynamic function of the application's security manager, as you will see when the JBossSX implementation is discussed in detail in section "The JBossSX Security Extension Architecture." JBoss does not require the definition of `security-role` elements to be able to declare method permissions. Therefore, the specification of `security-role` elements is simply a good practice to ensure portability across application servers and for deployment descriptor maintenance. Example descriptor fragments that illustrate `security-role` usage are presented in Listing 8.3.

LISTING 8.3   Example ejb-jar.xml and web.xml descriptor Fragments that Illustrate the `security-role` Element Usage

```
<!-- A sample ejb-jar.xml fragment -->
<ejb-jar>
...
  <assembly-descriptor>
    <security-role>
      <description>The single application role</description>
      <role-name>TheApplicationRole</role-name>
    </security-role>
  </assembly-descriptor>
</ejb-jar>

<!-- A sample web.xml fragment -->
<web-app>
```

LISTING 8.3   Continued

```
...
<security-role>
  <description>The single application role</description>
  <role-name>TheApplicationRole</role-name>
</security-role>
</web-app>
```

EJB Method Permissions

An application assembler can set the roles that are allowed to invoke an EJB's home and remote interface methods through method-permission element declarations. Each method-permission element contains one or more role-name child elements that define the logical roles that are allowed access to the EJB methods, as identified by method child elements. As of EJB 2.0, you can now specify an unchecked element instead of the role-name element to declare that any authenticated user can access the methods identified by method child elements. In addition, you can declare that no one should have access to a method with the exclude-list element. If an EJB has methods that have not been declared as accessible by a role using a method-permission element, the EJB methods default to being excluded from use. This is equivalent to defaulting the methods into the exclude-list.

The three supported styles of method element declarations are as follows:

- Style 1—Used for referring to all of the home and component interface methods of the named enterprise bean.

    ```
    <method>
      <ejb-name>EJBNAME</ejb-name>
      <method-name>*</method-name>
    </method>
    ```

- Style 2—Used for referring to a specified method of the home or component interface of the named enterprise bean. If there are multiple methods with the same overloaded name, this style refers to all of the overloaded methods.

    ```
    <method>
      <ejb-name>EJBNAME</ejb-name>
      <method-name>METHOD</method-name>
    </method>
    ```

- Style 3—Used to refer to a specified method within a set of methods with an overloaded name. The method must be defined in the specified enterprise bean's home or remote interface. The method-param element values are the fully qualified name of the corresponding method parameter type. If there are multiple methods with the same overloaded signature, the permission applies to all of the matching overloaded methods.

```
<method>
  <ejb-name>EJBNAME</ejb-name>
  <method-name>METHOD</method-name>
  <method-params>
    <method-param>PARAMETER_1</method-param>
    ...
    <method-param>PARAMETER_N</method-param>
  </method-params>
</method>
```

The optional `method-intf` element can be used to differentiate methods with the same name and signature that are defined in both the home and remote interfaces of an enterprise bean. Listing 8.4 provides examples of the `method-permission` element usage.

LISTING 8.4   An Example ejb-jar.xml Descriptor Fragment that Illustrates the `method-permission` Element Usage

```
<ejb-jar>
  <assembly-descriptor>
    <method-permission>
      <description>The employee and temp-employee roles may
       access any method of the EmployeeService bean
      </description>
      <role-name>employee</role-name>
      <role-name>temp-employee</role-name>
      <method>
        <ejb-name>EmployeeService</ejb-name>
        <method-name>*</method-name>
      </method>
    </method-permission>

    <method-permission>
      <description>The employee role may access the
       findByPrimaryKey, getEmployeeInfo, and the
       updateEmployeeInfo(String) method of the AardvarkPayroll
       bean
      </description>
      <role-name>employee</role-name>
```

LISTING 8.4   Continued

```
<method>
  <ejb-name>AardvarkPayroll</ejb-name>
  <method-name>findByPrimaryKey</method-name>
</method>

<method>
  <ejb-name>AardvarkPayroll</ejb-name>
  <method-name>getEmployeeInfo</method-name>
</method>

<method>
  <ejb-name>AardvarkPayroll</ejb-name>
  <method-name>updateEmployeeInfo</method-name>
  <method-params>
      <method-param>java.lang.String</method-param>
  </method-params>
</method>
</method-permission>

<method-permission>
  <description>The admin role may access any method
  of the EmployeeServiceAdmin bean
  </description>
  <role-name>admin</role-name>
  <method>
    <ejb-name>EmployeeServiceAdmin</ejb-name>
    <method-name>*</method-name>
  </method>
</method-permission>

<method-permission>
  <description>Any authenticated user may access any method
  of the EmployeeServiceHelp bean
  </description>
  <unchecked/>
  <method>
    <ejb-name>EmployeeServiceHelp</ejb-name>
    <method-name>*</method-name>
  </method>
</method-permission>
```

LISTING 8.4   Continued

```
    <exclude-list>
      <description>No fireTheCTO methods of the EmployeeFiring
      bean may be used in this deployment
      </description>
      <method>
        <ejb-name>EmployeeFiring</ejb-name>
        <method-name>fireTheCTO</method-name>
      </method>
    </exclude-list>
  </assembly-descriptor>
</ejb-jar>
```

Web Content Security Constraints

In a Web application, security is defined by the roles allowed access to content by a URL pattern that identifies the protected content. This set of information is declared using the web.xml security-constraint element. The content to be secured is declared using one or more web-resource-collection elements. Each web-resource-collection element contains an optional series of url-pattern elements followed by an optional series of http-method elements. The url-pattern element value specifies a URL pattern against which a request URL must match for the request to correspond to an attempt to access secured content. The http-method element value specifies a type of HTTP request to allow.

The optional user-data-constraint element specifies the requirements for the transport layer of the client to server connection. The requirement may be for content integrity (preventing data tampering in the communication process) or for confidentiality (preventing reading while in transit). The transport-guarantee element value specifies the degree to which communication between client and server should be protected. Its values are NONE, INTEGRAL, or CONFIDENTIAL. A value of NONE means that the application does not require any transport guarantees. A value of INTEGRAL means that the application requires the data sent between the client and server be sent in such a way that it can't be changed in transit. A value of CONFIDENTIAL means that the application requires the data be transmitted in a fashion that prevents other entities from observing the contents of the transmission. In most cases, the presence of the INTEGRAL or CONFIDENTIAL flag indicates that the use of SSL is required.

The optional login-config is used to configure the authentication method that should be used, the realm name that should be used for this application, and the attributes that are needed by the form login mechanism. The auth-method child element specifies the authentication mechanism for the Web application. As a prerequisite to gaining access to any Web resources that are protected by an authorization constraint, a user must have authenticated using the configured mechanism. Legal values for auth-method are BASIC, DIGEST, FORM, or CLIENT-CERT. The realm-name child element specifies the realm name to use in HTTP BASIC and DIGEST authorization. The form-login-config child element specifies the log in as well as error pages that should be used in form-based login. If the auth-method value is not FORM, form-login-config and its child elements are ignored.

As an example, the web.xml descriptor fragment given in Listing 8.5 indicates that any URL lying under the Web application /restricted path requires an AuthorizedUser role. There is no required transport guarantee, and the authentication method used for obtaining the user identity is BASIC HTTP authentication.

LISTING 8.5   A web.xml Descriptor Fragment that Illustrates the Use of the security-constraint and Related Elements

```
<web-app>
...
  <security-constraint>
    <web-resource-collection>
      <web-resource-name>Secure Content</web-resource-name>
      <url-pattern>/restricted/*</ url-pattern></
    <web-resource-collection>
    <auth-constraint>
      <role-name>AuthorizedUser</role-name>
    </auth-constraint>
    <user-data-constraint>
     <transport-guarantee>NONE</transport-guarantee>
    </user-data-constraint>
  </security-constraint>
...
<login-config>
    <auth-method>BASIC</auth-method>
    <realm-name>The Restricted Zone</realm-name>
</login-config>
...
<security-role>
   <description>The role required to access restricted content
   </description>
   <role-name>AuthorizedUser</role-name>
</security-role>
...
</web-app>
```

Enabling Declarative Security in JBoss

The J2EE security elements that have been covered thus far describe only the security requirements from the application's perspective. Because J2EE security elements declare logical roles, the application deployer maps the roles from the application domain onto the deployment environment. The J2EE specifications omit these application-server-specific details. In JBoss, mapping the application roles onto the deployment environment entails specifying a security manager that implements the J2EE security model using JBoss server-specific deployment descriptors. The details behind the security configuration are discussed when the generic JBoss server security interfaces are described in section "Enabling Declarative Security in JBoss Revisited."

An Introduction to JAAS

The default implementation of the JBossSX framework is based on the JAAS API. Because this is a relatively new API, one which has not seen wide spread use, its important that you understand the basic elements of the JAAS API to understand the implementation details of JBossSX. This section provides an introduction to JAAS to prepare you for the JBossSX architecture discussion.

> **NOTE**
>
> Additional details on the JAAS package can be found at the JAAS home page here at
> `http://java.sun.com/products/jaas/`.

What is JAAS?

The JAAS 1.0 API consists of a set of Java packages designed for user authentication and authorization. It implements a Java version of the standard Pluggable Authentication Module (PAM) framework and compatibly extends the Java 2 Platform's access control architecture to support user-based authorization. JAAS was first released as an extension package for JDK 1.3 and is bundled with the current JDK 1.4 beta. Because the JBossSX framework uses only the authentication capabilities of JAAS to implement the declarative role-based J2EE security model, this introduction focuses on only that topic.

> **NOTE**
>
> Much of this section's material is derived from the JAAS 1.0 Developers Guide, so if you're familiar with its content you can skip ahead to the JBossSX architecture discussion, "The JBoss Security Model," later in this chapter.

JAAS authentication is performed in a pluggable fashion. This permits Java applications to remain independent from underlying authentication technologies and allows the JBossSX security manager to work in different security infrastructures. Integration with a security infrastructure can be achieved without changing the JBossSX security manager implementation. All that needs to change is the configuration of the authentication stack that JAAS uses.

The JAAS Core Classes

The JAAS core classes can be broken down into three categories: common, authentication, and authorization. The following list presents only the common and authentication classes because these are the specific classes used to implement the functionality of JBossSX covered in this chapter.

Common classes:

- Subject (`javax.security.auth.Subject`)

- Principal (`java.security.Principal`)

Authentication classes:

- Callback (`javax.security.auth.callback.Callback`)

- CallbackHandler (`javax.security.auth.callback.CallbackHandler`)

- Configuration (`javax.security.auth.login.Configuration`)

- LoginContext (`javax.security.auth.login.LoginContext`)

- LoginModule (`javax.security.auth.spi.LoginModule`)

Subject and Principal

To authorize access to resources, applications first need to authenticate the request's source. The JAAS framework defines the term subject to represent a request's source. The Subject class is the central class in JAAS. A Subject represents information for a single entity, such as a person or service. It encompasses the entity's principals, public credentials, and private credentials. The JAAS APIs use the existing Java 2 `java.security.Principal` interface to represent a principal, which is essentially just a typed name.

During the authentication process, a Subject is populated with associated identities, or Principals. A Subject may have many Principals. For example, a person may have a name Principal (John Doe), a social security number Principal (123-45-6789), and a username Principal (johnd), all of which help distinguish the Subject from other `Subjects`. To retrieve the `Principals` associated with a `Subject`, two methods are available:

```
public final class Subject implements java.io.Serializable
{
...
  public Set getPrincipals();
  public Set getPrincipals(Class c);
}
```

The first method returns all `Principals` contained in the `Subject`. The second method returns only those `Principals` that are instances of `Class` c or one of its subclasses. An empty set is returned if the `Subject` has no matching `Principals`. Note that the `java.security.acl.Group` interface is a subinterface of `java.security.Principal`, and so an instance in the principals set may represent a logical grouping of other principals or groups of principals.

Authentication of a Subject

Authentication of a `Subject` requires a JAAS login. The login procedure consists of the following steps:

1. An application instantiates a `LoginContext` passing in the name of the login configuration and a `CallbackHandler` to populate the `Callback` objects, as required by the configuration `LoginModules`.

2. The `LoginContext` consults a `Configuration` to load all of the `LoginModules` included in the named login configuration. If no such named configuration exists the other configuration is used as a default.

3. The application invokes the `LoginContext.login` method.

4. The login method invokes all the loaded `LoginModules`. As each `LoginModule` attempts to authenticate the `Subject`, it invokes the `handle` method on the associated `CallbackHandler` to obtain the information required for the authentication process. The required information is passed to the `handle` method in the form of an array of `Callback` objects. Upon success, the `LoginModules` associate relevant `Principals` and credentials with the `Subject`.

5. The `LoginContext` returns the authentication status to the application. Success is represented by a return from the `login` method. Failure is represented through a `LoginException` being thrown by the `login` method.

6. If authentication succeeds, the application retrieves the authenticated `Subject` using the `LoginContext.getSubject` method.

7. After the scope of the `Subject` authentication is complete, all `Principals` and related information associated with the `Subject` by the `login` method may be removed by invoking the `LoginContext.logout` method.

The LoginContext class provides the basic methods for authenticating Subjects and offers a way to develop an application independent of the underlying authentication technology. The LoginContext consults a Configuration to determine the authentication services configured for a particular application. LoginModules classes represent the authentication services. Therefore, you can plug different LoginModules into an application without changing the application itself. Listing 8.6 provides code fragments that illustrate the steps required by an application to authenticate a Subject.

LISTING 8.6   An Illustration of the Steps of the Authentication Process from the Application Perspective

```
CallbackHandler handler = new MyHandler();
LoginContext lc = new LoginContext("some-config", handler);
try
{
  lc.login();
  Subject subject = lc.getSubject();
}
catch(LoginException e)
{
  System.out.println("authentication failed");
  e.printStackTrace();
}


// Perform work as authenticated Subject
  ...


// Scope of work complete, logout to remove authentication info
try
{
  lc.logout();
}
catch(LoginException e)
{
  System.out.println("logout failed");
  e.printStackTrace();
}


// A sample MyHandler class
class MyHandler implements CallbackHandler
{
  public void handle(Callback[] callbacks) throws
    IOException, UnsupportedCallbackException
```

LISTING 8.6   Continued

```
{
    for (int i = 0; i < callbacks.length; i++)
    {
        if (callbacks[i] instanceof NameCallback)
        {
            NameCallback nc = (NameCallback)callbacks[i];
            nc.setName(username);
        }
        else if (callbacks[i] instanceof PasswordCallback)
        {
            PasswordCallback pc = (PasswordCallback)callbacks[i];
            pc.setPassword(password);
        }
        else
        {
            throw new UnsupportedCallbackException(callbacks[i],
                "Unrecognized Callback");
        }
    }
}
}
```

Developers integrate with an authentication technology by creating an implementation of the `LoginModule` interface. This allows different authentication technologies to be plugged into an application by administrator. Multiple `LoginModules` can be chained together to allow for more than one authentication technology as part of the authentication process. For example, one `LoginModule` may perform username/password-based authentication, while another may interface to hardware devices such as smart card readers or biometric authenticators. The life cycle of a `LoginModule` is driven by the `LoginContext` object against which the client creates and issues the `login` method. The process consists of a two phases. The steps of the process are as follows:

1. The `LoginContext` creates each configured `LoginModule` using its public no-arg constructor.

2. Each `LoginModule` is initialized with a call to its `initialize` method. The `Subject` argument is guaranteed to be non-null. The signature of the `initialize` method is `public void initialize(Subject subject, CallbackHandler callbackHandler, Map sharedState, Map options);`.

3. The `login` method is then called to start the authentication process. An example method implementation might prompt the user for a username and

password and then verify the information against data stored in a naming service, such as NIS or LDAP. Alternative implementations might interface to smart cards and biometric devices, or simply extract user information from the underlying operating system. The validation of user identity by each `LoginModule` is considered phase 1 of JAAS authentication. The signature of the login method is `boolean login() throws LoginException;`.

4. If the `LoginContext`'s overall authentication succeeds, `commit` is invoked on each `LoginModule`. If phase 1 succeeded for a `LoginModule`, the `commit` method continues with phase 2: associating relevant `Principals`, public credentials, and/or private credentials with the `Subject`. If phase 1 fails for a `LoginModule`, `commit` removes any previously stored authentication state, such as usernames or passwords. The signature of the `commit` method is `boolean commit() throws LoginException;`.

5. If the `LoginContext`'s overall authentication failed, the `abort` method is invoked on each `LoginModule`. The abort method removes/destroys any authentication state created by the `login` or `initialize` methods. The signature of the `abort` method is `boolean abort() throws LoginException;`.

6. Removal of the authentication state after a successful login is accomplished when the application invokes `logout` on the `LoginContext`. This in turn results in a `logout` method invocation on each `LoginModule`. The `logout` method removes the `Principals` and credentials originally associated with the `Subject` during the `commit` operation. Credentials should be destroyed upon removal. The signature of the `logout` method is `boolean logout() throws LoginException;`.

When a `LoginModule` must communicate with the user to obtain authentication information, it uses a `CallbackHandler` object. Applications implement the `CallbackHandler` interface and pass it to the `LoginContext`, which forwards it directly to the underlying `LoginModules`. `LoginModules` use the `CallbackHandler` both to gather input from users, such as a password or smart-card PIN number, and to supply information to users, such as status information. By allowing the application to specify the `CallbackHandler`, underlying `LoginModules` remain independent from the different ways applications interact with users. For example, a `CallbackHandler`'s implementation for a GUI application might display a window to solicit user input. On the other hand, a `CallbackHandler`'s implementation for a non-GUI environment, such as an application server, might simply obtain credential information using an application server API. The `CallbackHandler` interface has one method to implement:

```
void handle(Callback[] callbacks)
throws java.io.IOException, UnsupportedCallbackException;
```

The last authentication class to cover is the `Callback` interface. This is a tagging interface for which several default implementations are provided, including `NameCallback` and `PasswordCallback` that were shown in Listing 8.6. `LoginModules` use a `Callback` to request information required by the authentication mechanism the `LoginModule` encapsulates. `LoginModules` pass an array of `Callbacks` directly to the `CallbackHandler.handle` method during the authentication's login phase. If a `CallbackHandler` does not understand how to use a `Callback` object passed into the handle method, it throws an `UnsupportedCallbackException` to abort the login call.

The JBoss Security Model

Similar to the rest of the JBoss architecture, security at the lowest level is defined as a set of interfaces for which alternate implementations may be provided. There are three basic interfaces that define the JBoss server security layer—`org.jboss.security.AuthenticationManager`, `org.jboss.security.RealmMapping`, and `org.jboss.security.SecurityProxy`. Figure 8.3 shows a class diagram of the security interfaces and their relationship to the EJB container architecture.

The white classes represent the security interfaces while the grey classes represent the EJB container layer. The two interfaces required for the implementation of the J2EE security model are the `org.jboss.security.AuthenticationManager` and `org.jboss.security.RealmMapping`. Figure 8.4 shows how the security interfaces are referenced by the JBoss core components and implemented by the JBossSX components.

The roles of the security interfaces presented in Figure 8.3 are summarized in the following list:

- `AuthenticationManager` is an interface responsible for validating credentials associated with principals. Principals are identities and examples include usernames, employee numbers, social security numbers, and so on. Credentials are proof of the identity and examples include passwords, session keys, digital signatures, and so on. The `isValid` method is invoked to see if a user identity and associated credentials as known in the operational environment are valid proof of the user identity.

- `RealmMapping` is an interface responsible for principal mapping and role mapping. The `getPrincipal` method takes a user identity as known in the operational environment and returns the application domain identity. The `doesUserHaveRole` method validates that the user identity in the operation environment has been assigned the indicated role from the application domain.

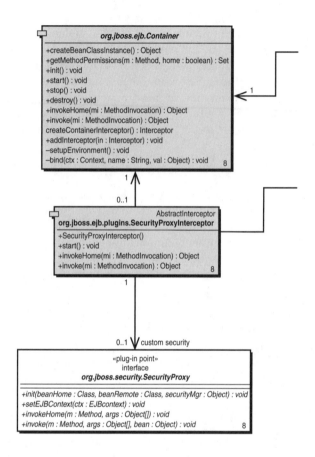

FIGURE 8.3   The key security model interfaces and their relationship to the JBoss server EJB container elements.

- SecurityProxy is an interface describing the requirements for a custom SecurityProxyInterceptor plug-in. A SecurityProxy allows for the externalization of custom security checks on a per-method basis for both the EJB home and remote interface methods.

- SubjectSecurityManager is a subinterface of AuthenticationManager that simply adds accessor methods for obtaining the security domain name of the security manager and the current thread's authenticated Subject. In future releases this interface will simply be integrated into the SecurityDomain interface.

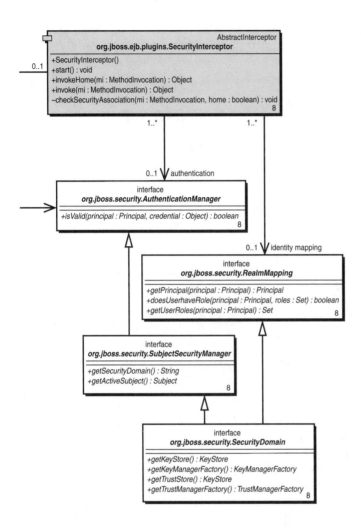

- SecurityDomain is an extension of the AuthenticationManager, RealmMapping, and SubjectSecurityManager interfaces. It is a move to a comprehensive security interface, based on the JAAS Subject, a java.security.KeyStore, and the JSSE com.sun.net.ssl.KeyManagerFactory and com.sun.net.ssl.TrustManagerFactory interfaces. This interface is still a work in progress. It will be the basis of a multi-domain security architecture that will better support ASP-style deployments of applications and resources.

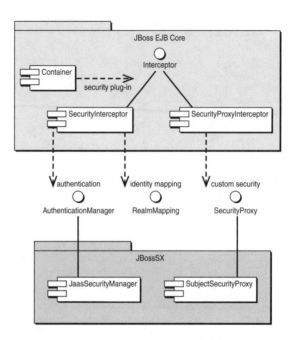

FIGURE 8.4   The relationship between the JBossSX framework implementation classes and the JBoss server EJB container layer.

Note that the `AuthenticationManager`, `RealmMapping` and `SecurityProxy` interfaces have no association to JAAS related classes. Although the JBossSX framework is heavily dependent on JAAS, the basic security interfaces required for implementation of the J2EE security model are not. The JBossSX framework is simply an implementation of the basic security plug-in interfaces that are based on JAAS. The component diagram presented in Figure 8.4 illustrates this fact. The implication of this plug-in architecture is that you are free to replace the JAAS-based JBossSX implementation classes with your own custom security manager implementation that does not make use of JAAS, if you so desire. You'll see how to do this when you look at the JBossSX MBeans available for the configuration of JBossSX in the section titled "The JBossSX Security Extension Architecture".

Enabling Declarative Security in JBoss Revisited

Recall that the discussion of the J2EE standard security model in section "J2EE Declarative Security Overview," ended with a requirement for the use of JBoss server-specific deployment descriptor to enable security. The details of this configuration is presented here, as this configuration is part of the generic JBoss security model. Figure 8.5 shows the JBoss-specific EJB and Web application deployment descriptor's security-related elements.

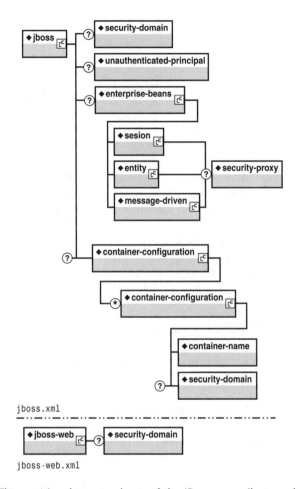

jboss.xml

jboss-web.xml

FIGURE 8.5   The security element subsets of the JBoss server jboss.xml and jboss-web.xml deployment descriptors.

The value of a security-domain element specifies the JNDI name of the security manager interface implementation that JBoss uses for the EJB and Web containers. This is an object that implements both the AuthenticationManager and RealmMapping interfaces. When specified as a top-level element, it defines what security domain is in effect for all EJBs in the deployment unit. This is the typical usage because mixing security managers within a deployment unit complicates inter-component operation and administration.

To specify the security-domain for an individual EJB, you specify the security-domain at the container configuration level.

This will override any top-level security-domain element.

The unauthenticated-principal element specifies the name to use for the Principal object returned by the EJBContext.getUserPrincpal method when an unauthenticated user invokes an EJB. Note that this conveys no special permissions to an unauthenticated caller. Its primary purpose is to allow unsecured servlets and JSP pages to invoke unsecured EJBs, and allow the target EJB to obtain a non-null Principal for the caller using the getUserPrincipal method. This is a J2EE specification requirement.

The security-proxy element identifies a custom security proxy implementation that allows per-request security checks outside the scope of the EJB declarative security model without embedding security logic into the EJB implementation. This may be an implementation of the org.jboss.security.SecurityProxy interface, or just an object that implements methods in the home or remote interface of the EJB to secure without implementing any common interface. If the given class does not implement the SecurityProxy interface, the instance must be wrapped in a SecurityProxy implementation that delegates the method invocations to the object. The org.jboss.security.SubjectSecurityProxy is an example implementation used by the default JBossSX installation.

Take a look at a simple example of a custom SecurityProxy in the context of a trivial stateless session bean. The custom SecurityProxy validates that no one invokes the bean's echo method with a four-letter word as its argument. This is a check that is not possible with role-based security—you cannot define a FourLetterEchoInvoker role because the security context is the method argument, not a property of the caller. The code for the custom SecurityProxy is given in Listing 8.7, and the full source code is available in the src/main/org/jboss/chap8/ex1 directory of the book examples on the CD. The associated jboss.xml descriptor that installs the EchoSecurityProxy as the custom proxy for the EchoBean is given in Listing 8.8.

LISTING 8.7   The Example 1 Custom EchoSecurityProxy Implementation that Enforces the Echo Argument-Based Security Constraint

```
package org.jboss.chap8.ex1;

import java.lang.reflect.Method;
import javax.ejb.EJBContext;

import org.apache.log4j.Category;

import org.jboss.security.SecurityProxy;

/** A simple example of a custom SecurityProxy implementation
that demonstrates method argument-based security checks.
```

LISTING 8.7   Continued

```
 * @author Scott.Stark@jboss.org
 * @version $Revision:$
 */
public class EchoSecurityProxy implements SecurityProxy
{
    Category log = Category.getInstance(EchoSecurityProxy.class);
    Method echo;

    public void init(Class beanHome, Class beanRemote,
        Object securityMgr)
        throws InstantiationException
    {
        log.debug("init, beanHome="+beanHome
            + ", beanRemote="+beanRemote
            + ", securityMgr="+securityMgr);
        // Get the echo method for equality testing in invoke
        try
        {
            Class[] params = {String.class};
            echo = beanRemote.getDeclaredMethod("echo", params);
        }
        catch(Exception e)
        {
            String msg = "Failed to finde an echo(String) method";
            log.error(msg, e);
            throw new InstantiationException(msg);
        }
    }
    public void setEJBContext(EJBContext ctx)
    {
        log.debug("setEJBContext, ctx="+ctx);
    }
    public void invokeHome(Method m, Object[] args)
        throws SecurityException
    {
        // We don't validate access to home methods
    }
    public void invoke(Method m, Object[] args, Object bean)
        throws SecurityException
```

LISTING 8.7   Continued

```
{
    log.debug("invoke, m="+m);
    // Check for the echo method
    if( m.equals(echo) )
    {
        // Validate that the msg arg is not four-letter word
        String arg = (String) args[0];
        if( arg == null || arg.length() == 4 )
            throw new SecurityException("No four-letter words");
    }
    // We are not responsible for doing the invoke
}
}
```

LISTING 8.8   The jboss.xml Descriptor that Configures the `EchoSecurityProxy` as the Custom Security Proxy for the `EchoBean`

```
<jboss>
    <security-domain>java:/jaas/other</security-domain>

    <enterprise-beans>
        <session>
            <ejb-name>EchoBean</ejb-name>
            <security-proxy>org.jboss.chap8.ex1.EchoSecurityProxy
            </security-proxy>
        </session>
    </enterprise-beans>
</jboss>
```

The `EchoSecurityProxy` checks that the method to be invoked on the bean instance corresponds to the `echo(String)` method loaded the `init` method. If there is a match, the method argument is obtained and its length compared against four or null. Either case results in a `SecurityException` being thrown. Certainly this is a contrived example, but only in its application. It is a common requirement that applications must perform security checks based on the value of method arguments. The point of the example is to demonstrate how custom security beyond the scope of the standard declarative security model can be introduced independent of the bean implementation. This allows the specification and coding of the security requirements to be delegated to security experts. Because the security proxy layer can be done independent of the bean implementation, security can be changed to match the deployment environment requirements.

The first step to testing the custom security proxy is to configure the JBoss server with a configuration file set that enables unauthenticated users access to unsecured beans. To execute this step run the following Ant command from the book examples root directory:

NOTE

For information on installing and using Ant, see Appendix D, "Tools and Book Examples."

```
examples 1015>ant -Dchap=8 config
Buildfile: build.xml

config:

config:
    [copy] Copying 14 files to G:\JBoss-2.4.4\conf\chap8
    [copy] Copying 3 files to G:\JBoss-2.4.4\conf\chap8

BUILD SUCCESSFUL

Total time: 1 second
```

This creates a chap8 configuration file set under the JBoss distribution conf directory. Next, start the JBoss server using the chap8 configuration. You do this using either the run.bat or run.sh script, and pass the chap8 configuration name to the script as follows:

```
bin 1116>run.bat chap8
JBOSS_CLASSPATH=;run.jar;../lib/crimson.jar
jboss.home = G:\JBoss-2.4.4
Using JAAS LoginConfig: file:/G:/JBoss-2.4.4/conf/chap8/auth.conf
Using configuration "chap8"
...
```

Now test the custom proxy by running a client that attempts to invoke the EchoBean.echo method with the arguments "Hello" and "Four" as illustrated in this fragment:

```
public class ExClient
{
```

```
public static void main(String args[]) throws Exception
{
  InitialContext iniCtx = new InitialContext();
  Object ref = iniCtx.lookup("EchoBean");
  EchoHome home = (EchoHome) ref;
  Echo echo = home.create();
  System.out.println("Created Echo");
  System.out.println("Echo.echo('Hello') = "+echo.echo("Hello"));
  System.out.println("Echo.echo('Four') = "+echo.echo("Four"));
  }
}
```

The first call should succeed, while the second should fail because "Four" is a four-letter word. Run the client as follows using Ant:

```
examples 1144>ant -Dchap=8 -Dex=1 run-example
Buildfile: build.xml

...

chap8-ex1-jar:

run-example1:
 [copy] Copying 1 file to G:\JBoss-2.4.4\deploy
 [echo] Waiting for 5 seconds for deploy...
 [java] Created Echo
 [java] Echo.echo('Hello') = Hello
 [java] java.rmi.ServerException: RemoteException occurred in
server thread; nested exception is:
 [java]     javax.transaction.TransactionRolledbackException:
SecurityProxy.invoke exception, principal=null, msg=No four-letter words;
nested exception is:
 [java]     java.lang.SecurityException: SecurityProxy.invoke
exception, principal=null, msg=No four-letter words; nested exception is:
 [java]     java.rmi.RemoteException: SecurityProxy.invoke exception,
principal=nullmsg=No four-letter words; nested exception is:
 ...
 [java]     at $Proxy1.echo(Unknown Source)
 [java]     at org.jboss.chap8.ex1.ExClient.main(ExClient.java:20)
 [java] Exception in thread "main"
 [java] Java Result: 1
```

The result is that the echo('Hello') method call succeeds as expected and the echo('Four') method call results in a rather messy looking exception, which is also expected. The above output has been truncated to fit in the book so you should see quite a bit more than is shown here. The key part to the exception is that the `SecurityException`("No four-letter words") generated by the `EchoSecurityProxy` was thrown to abort the attempted method invocation as desired.

The JBossSX Security Extension Architecture

The preceding discussion of the general JBoss security layer stated that the JBossSX security extension framework is an implementation of the security layer interfaces. This is the primary purpose of the JBossSX framework. The details of the implementation are interesting in that it offers a great deal of customization for integration into existing security infrastructures. A security infrastructure can be anything from a database or LDAP server to a sophisticated security software suite. The integration flexibility is achieved using the pluggable authentication model available in the JAAS framework.

The heart of the JBossSX framework is `org.jboss.security.plugins.JaasSecurityManager`. This is the default implementation of the `AuthenticationManager` and `RealmMapping` interfaces. Figure 8.6 shows how the JaasSecurityManager integrates into the EJB and Web container layers based on the `security-domain` element of the corresponding component deployment descriptor.

Figure 8.6 depicts an enterprise application that contains both EJBs and Web content secured under the security domain jwdomain. The EJB and Web containers have a request interceptor architecture that includes a security interceptor, which enforces the container security model. At deployment time, the `security-domain` element value in the jboss.xml and jboss-web.xml descriptors is used to obtain the security manager instance associated with the container. The security interceptor then uses the security manager to perform its role. When a secured component is requested, the security interceptor delegates security checks to the security manager instance associated with the container.

The JBossSX `JaasSecurityManager` implementation, shown in Figure 8.6 as the JaasSecurityMgr component, performs security checks based on the information associated with the `Subject` instance that results from executing the JAAS login modules configured under the name matching the `security-domain` element value.

How the JaasSecurityManager Uses JAAS

The `JaasSecurityManager` uses the JAAS packages to implement the `AuthenticationManager` and `RealmMapping` interface behavior. In particular, its behavior derives from the execution of the login module instances that are configured under the name that matches the security domain to which the

JaasSecurityManager has been assigned. The login modules implement the security domain's principal authentication and role-mapping behavior. Thus, you can use the JaasSecurityManager across different security domains simply by plugging in different login module configurations for the domains.

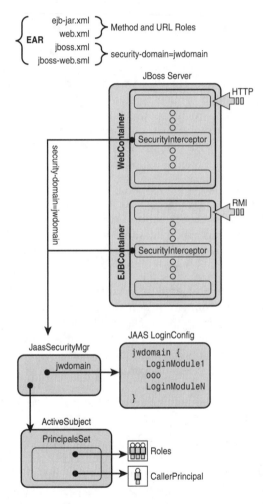

FIGURE 8.6   The relationship between the security-domain component deployment descriptor value, the component container, and the JaasSecurityManager.

To illustrate the details of the JaasSecurityManager's usage of the JAAS authentication process, walk through a client invocation of an EJB home method invocation. The prerequisite setting is as follows: The EJB has been deployed in the JBoss server, its home interface methods have been secured using method-permission elements in the ejb-jar.xml descriptor, and it has been assigned a security domain named "jwdo-main" using the jboss.xml descriptor security-domain element. Figure 8.7 provides a view of the client to server communication.

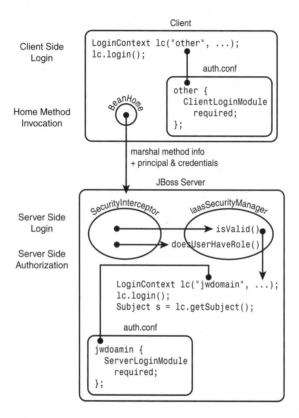

FIGURE 8.7   An illustration of the steps involved in the authentication and authorization of a secured EJB home method invocation.

The labeled events shown in Figure 8.7 are described in the following paragraphs.

The client first has to perform a JAAS login to establish the principal and credentials for authentication, and this is labeled *Client Side Login* in Figure 8.7. This is how clients establish their login identities in JBoss. Support for presenting the login infor-mation via JNDI InitialContext properties is not provided. A JAAS login entails creating a LoginContext instance and passing the name of the configuration to use. In Figure 8.7, the configuration name is "other". This one-time log in associates the login principal and credentials with all subsequent EJB method invocations. Note that the process might not authenticate the user. The nature of the client-side login depends on the login module configuration that the client uses. In Figure 8.7, the `"other"` client-side login configuration entry is set up to use the ClientLoginModule module (an `org.jboss.security.ClientLoginModule`). This is the default client side module that simply binds the username and password to the JBoss EJB invocation layer for later authentication on the server. The identity of the client is not authenticated on the client.

Later, the client obtains the EJB home interface and attempts to create a bean. This event is labeled as *Home Method Invocation* in Figure 8.7. This results in a home interface method invocation being sent to the JBoss server. The invocation includes the method arguments passed by the client along with the user identity and credentials from the client-side JAAS log in.

On the server side, the security interceptor first requires authentication of the user invoking the call, which, as on the client side, involves a JAAS login. This event is labeled as *Server Side Login* in Figure 8.7. The security domain under which the EJB is secured determines the choice of login modules. The security domain name is used as the login configuration entry name passed to the `LoginContext` constructor. In Figure 8.7, the EJB security domain is `"jwdomain"`. If the JAAS login authenticates the user, a JAAS `Subject` is created that contains the following in its PrincipalsSet:

NOTE

This usage pattern of the `Subject` Principals set is the standard usage that JBossSX expects of server-side login modules. To ensure proper conformance to this pattern, any custom login module you write should subclass the JBossSX `AbstractServerLoginModule` class, one of its subclasses, or at least follow the pattern as documented in the custom login module section titled "Writing Custom Login Modules," presented later in this chapter.

- A `java.security.Principal` that corresponds to the client identity as known in the deployment security environment.

- A `java.security.acl.Group` named `"Roles"` that contains the role names from the application domain to which the user has been assigned. `org.jboss.security.SimplePrincipal` objects are used to represent the role names; `SimplePrincipal` is a simple string-based implementation of `Principal`. These roles are used to validate the roles assigned to methods in ejb-jar.xml and the `EJBContext.isCallerInRole(String)` method implementation.

- An optional `java.security.acl.Group` named `"CallerPrincipal"`, which contains a single `org.jboss.security.SimplePrincipal` that corresponds to the identity of the application domain's caller. The `"CallerPrincipal"` sole group member will be the value returned by the `EJBContext.getCallerPrincipal()` method. The purpose of this mapping is to allow a `Principal` as known in the operational security environment to map to a `Principal` with a name known to the application. In the absence of a `"CallerPrincipal"`, mapping the deployment security environment principal is used as the `getCallerPrincipal` method value. That is, the operational principal is the same as the application domain principal.

The final step of the security interceptor check is to verify that the authenticated user has permission to invoke the requested method. This is labeled as *Server Side Authorization* in Figure 8.7. Performing the authorization entails the following steps:

- Obtain the names of the roles allowed to access the EJB method from the EJB container. The role names are determined by ejb-jar.xml descriptor `role-name` elements of all `method-permission` elements containing the invoked method.

- If no roles have been assigned, or the method is specified in an `exclude-list` element, access to the method is denied. Otherwise, the `JaasSecurityManager.doesUserHaveRole(Principal, Set)` method is invoked by the security interceptor to see if the caller has one of the assigned role names. The `doesUserHaveRole` method implementation iterates through the role names and checks if the authenticated user's Subject `Roles` group contains a `SimplePrincipal` with the assigned role name. Access is allowed if any role name is a member of the `Roles` group. Access is denied if none of the role names are members.

- If the EJB was configured with a custom security proxy, the method invocation is delegated to it. If the security proxy wants to deny access to the caller, it will throw a `java.lang.SecurityException`. If no `SecurityException` is thrown, access to the EJB method is allowed and the method invocation passes to the next container interceptor. Note that the `SecurityProxyInterceptor` handles this check, and this interceptor is not shown in Figure 8.7.

Every secured EJB method invocation, or secured Web content access, requires the authentication and authorization of the caller because security information is handled as a stateless attribute of the request that must be presented and validated on each request. This can be an expensive operation if the JAAS login involves client-to-server communication. Because of this, the JaasSecurityManager supports the notion of an authentication cache that is used to store principal and credential information from previous successful logins. You can specify the authentication cache instance to use as part of the JaasSecurityManager configuration as you will see when the associated MBean service is discussed in section "The JaasSecurityManagerService MBean". In the absence of any user-defined cache, a default cache that maintains credential information for a configurable period of time is used.

The JaasSecurityManagerService MBean

The JaasSecurityManagerService MBean service manages security managers. Although its name begins with Jaas, the security managers it handles need not use JAAS in their implementation. The name arose from the fact that the default security manager implementation is the JaasSecurityManager. The primary role of the JaasSecurityManagerService is to externalize the security manager implementation. You can change the security manager implementation by providing an alternate implementation of the AuthenticationManager and RealmMapping interfaces. Of course this is optional because, by default, the JaasSecurityManager implementation is used.

The second fundamental role of the JaasSecurityManagerService is to provide a JNDI javax.naming.spi.ObjectFactory implementation to allow for simple code-free management of the JNDI name-to-security manager implementation mapping. It has been mentioned that security is enabled by specifying the JNDI name of the security manager implementation via the security-domain deployment descriptor element. When you specify a JNDI name, there has to be an object binding there to use. To simplify the setup of the JNDI name-to-security manager bindings, the JaasSecurityManagerService manages the association of security manager instances to names by binding a next naming system reference with itself as the JNDI ObjectFactory under the name java:/jaas. This allows you to use a naming convention of the form java:/jaas/XYZ as the value for the security-domain element, and the security manager instance for the XYZ security domain will be created as needed for you. The security manager for the domain XYZ is created on the first lookup against the java:/jaas/XYZ binding by creating an instance of the class specified by the SecurityManagerClassName attribute using a constructor that takes the name of the security domain. For example, consider the following container security configuration snippet:

```
<jboss>
    <!-- Configure all containers to be secured under the
      "hades" security domain -->
    <security-domain>java:/jaas/hades</security-domain>
    ...
</jboss>
```

Any lookup of the name java:/jaas/hades will return a security manager instance that has been associated with the security domain named hades. This security manager will implement the AuthenticationManager and RealmMapping security interfaces and will be of the type specified by the JaasSecurityManagerService SecurityManagerClassName attribute.

The JaasSecurityManagerService MBean is configured by default for use in the standard JBoss distribution, and you can often use the default configuration as is.

The configurable attributes of the `JaasSecurityManagerService` include the following:

- SecurityManagerClassName—The name of the class that provides the security manager implementation. It requires both the `org.jboss.security.AuthenticationManager` and `org.jboss.security.RealmMapping` interfaces. This defaults to JAAS-based `org.jboss.security.plugins.JaasSecurityManager`.

- SecurityProxyFactoryClassName—The name of the class that provides the `org.jboss.security.SecurityProxyFactory` implementation, and defaults to `org.jboss.security.SubjectSecurityProxyFactory`.

- AuthenticationCacheJndiName—Specifies the location of the security credential cache policy. This is first treated as an `ObjectFactory` location capable of returning `CachePolicy` instances on a per-security-domain basis. This is done by appending the name of the security domain to this name when looking up the `CachePolicy` for a domain. If this fails, the location is treated as a single CachePolicy for all security domains. As a default, a timed cache policy is used.

- DefaultCacheTimeout—Specifies the default timed cache policy timeout in seconds, and defaults to 1800 seconds (30 minutes). The value you use for the timeout is a tradeoff between frequent authentication operations and how long credential information may be out of synch with respect to the security information store. This has no affect if the AuthenticationCacheJndiName has been changed from the default value.

- DefaultCacheResolution—Specifies the default timed cache policy resolution in seconds. This controls the interval between checks for timeouts, and defaults to 60 seconds (1 minute). This has no affect if the AuthenticationCacheJndiName has been changed from the default value.

The `JaasSecurityManagerService` also supports a mechanism that allows any security domain authentication cache to be flushed at runtime. This can be done to drop all cached credentials when the underlying store has been updated and you want the store state to be used immediately. The MBean operation signature is as follows:

```
public void flushAuthenticationCache(String securityDomain);
```

This can be invoked programmatically using the following code snippet:

```
MBeanServer server = ...;
String jaasMgrName = "Security:name=JaasSecurityManager";
ObjectName jaasMgr = new ObjectName(jaasMgrName);
Object[] params = {domainName};
```

```
String[] signature = {"java.lang.String"};
server.invoke(jaasMgr, "flushAuthenticationCache", params,
    signature);
```

Using and Writing JBossSX Login Modules

The JaasSecurityManager implementation allows complete customization of the authentication mechanism usingthe JAAS login module configuration. By defining the login module configuration entry that corresponds to the security domain name you have used to secure access to your J2EE components, you define the authentication mechanism and integration implementation.

The JBossSX framework includes a number of bundled login modules suitable for integration with standard security infrastructure store protocols such as LDAP and JDBC. It also includes standard base class implementations that help enforce the expected `LoginModule` to `Subject` usage pattern that was described in the "How the JaasSecurityManager Uses JAAS" section. These implementations allow for easy integration of your own authentication protocol, if none of the bundled login modules prove suitable.

org.jboss.security.auth.spi.IdentityLoginModule

The `IdentityLoginModule` is a simple login module that associates the principal specified in the module options with any subject authenticated against the module. It creates a `SimplePrincipal` instance using the name specified by the `principal` option. Although this is certainly not an appropriate login module for production strength authentication, it can be of use in development environments when you want to test the security associated with a given principal and associated roles.

The supported login module configuration options include the following:

- principal=string—The name to use for the `SimplePrincipal` all users are authenticated as. The principal name defaults to guest.

- roles=string-list—The names of the roles that will be assigned to the user principal. The value is a comma-delimited list of role names.

- password-stacking=useFirstPass—When password-stacking option is set, this module first looks for a shared username under the property name `javax.security.auth.login.name` in the login module shared state `Map`. If found, this is used as the principal name. If not found, the principal name set by this login module is stored under the property name `javax.security.auth.login.name`.

A sample login configuration entry that would authenticate all users as the principal named "jduke" and assign role names of "TheDuke", and "AnimatedCharacter" is as follows:

```
testIdentity {
    org.jboss.security.auth.spi.IdentityLoginModule required
        principal=jduke
        roles=TheDuke,AnimatedCharater;
};
```

To add this entry to a JBoss server login cofiguration found in the default configuration file set you would modify the `conf/default/auth.conf` file of the JBoss distribution.

org.jboss.security.auth.spi.UsersRolesLoginModule

The `UsersRolesLoginModule` is another simple login module that supports multiple users and user roles, and is based on two Java Properties formatted text files. The username-to-password mapping file is called `users.properties` and the username to roles mapping file is called `roles.properties`. The properties files are loaded during initialization using the `initialize` method thread context class loader. This means that these files can be placed into the J2EE deployment jar, the JBoss configuration directory, or any directory on the JBoss server or system classpath. The primary purpose of this login module is to easily test the security settings of multiple users and roles using properties files deployed with the application.

The users.properties file uses a `username=password` format with each user entry on a separate line as shown here:

```
username1=password1
username2=password2

...
```

The roles.properties file uses a `username=role1,role2,...` format with an optional group name value. For example:

```
username1=role1,role2,...
username1.RoleGroup1=role3,role4,...
username2=role1,role3,...
```

The `username.XXX` form of property name is used to assign the username roles to a particular named group of roles where the XXX portion of the property name is the group name. The "username=..." form is an abbreviation for "username.Roles=...", where the "Roles" group name is the standard name the JaasSecurityManager expects to contain the roles which define the users permissions.

The following would be equivalent definitions for the jduke username:

```
jduke=TheDuke,AnimatedCharacter
jduke.Roles=TheDuke,AnimatedCharacter
```

The supported login module configuration options include the following:

- unauthenticatedIdentity=name—Defines the principal name that should be assigned to requests that contain no authentication information. This can be used to allow unprotected servlets to invoke methods on EJBs that do not require a specific role. Such a principal has no associated roles, and so can only access either unsecured EJBs or EJB methods that are associated with the unchecked permission constraint.

- password-stacking=useFirstPass—When password-stacking option is set, this module first looks for a shared username and password under the property names `javax.security.auth.login.name` and `javax.security.auth.login.password` respectively in the login module shared state `Map`. If found, these are used as the principal name and password. If not found, the principal name and password are set by this login module and stored under the property names `javax.security.auth.login.name` and `javax.security.auth.login.password` respectively.

A sample login configuration entry that assigned unauthenticated users the principal name "nobody" is:

```
testUsersRoles {
    org.jboss.security.auth.spi.UsersRolesLoginModule required
        unauthenticatedIdentity=nobody;
};
```

To add this entry to a JBoss server login cnfiguration found in the default configuration file set you would modify the `conf/default/auth.conf` file of the JBoss distribution.

org.jboss.security.auth.spi.LdapLoginModule

The `LdapLoginModule` is a LoginModule implementation that authenticates against an LDAP server using JNDI login using the login module configuration options. You would use the `LdapLoginModule` if your username and credential information are store in an LDAP server that is accessible using a JNDI LDAP provider.

The LDAP connectivity information is provided as configuration options that are passed through to the environment object used to create JNDI initial context. The standard LDAP JNDI properties used include the following:

- java.naming.factory.initial—The classname of the InitialContextFactory implementation. This defaults to the Sun LDAP provider implementation `com.sun.jndi.ldap.LdapCtxFactory`.

- java.naming.provider.url—The ldap URL for the LDAP server.

- java.naming.security.authentication—The security level to use. This defaults to simple.

- java.naming.security.protocol—The transport protocol to use for secure access, such as ssl.

- java.naming.security.principal—The principal for authenticating the caller to the service. This is built from other properties as described below.

- java.naming.security.credentials—The value of the property depends on the authentication scheme. For example, it could be a hashed password, clear-text password, key, certificate, and so on.

The supported login module configuration options include the following:

- principalDNPrefix=string—A prefix to add to the username to form the user distinguished name. See principalDNSuffix for more info.

- principalDNSuffix=string—A suffix to add to the username when forming the user distinguished name. This is useful if you prompt a user for a username, and you don't want the user to have to enter the fully distinguished name. Using this property and principalDNSuffix the userDN will be formed as:

```
String userDN = principalDNPrefix + username + principalDNSuffix;
```

- useObjectCredential=true|false|—Indicates that the credential should be obtained as an opaque Object using the `org.jboss.security.auth.callback.ObjectCallback` type of `Callback` rather than as a char[] password using a JAAS `PasswordCallback`. This allows for passing non-char[] credential information to the LDAP server.

- rolesCtxDN=string—The distinguished name to the context to search for user roles.

- roleAttributeID=string—The name of the attribute that contains the user roles. This defaults to roles.

- uidAttributeID=string—The name of the attribute in the object containing the user roles that corresponds to the userid. This is used to locate the user roles, and defaults to uid.

- matchOnUserDN=true|false—A flag indicating if the search for user roles should match on the user's fully distinguished name. If false, just the username is used as the match value against the uidAttributeName attribute. If true, the full userDN is used as the match value.

- unauthenticatedIdentity=string—The principal name that should be assigned to requests that contain no authentication information. This behavior is inherited from the `UsernamePasswordLoginModule` superclass.

- password-stacking=useFirstPass—When the password-stacking option is set, this module first looks for a shared username and password under the property names `javax.security.auth.login.name` and `javax.security.auth.login.password` respectively in the login module shared state `Map`. If found, these are used as the principal name and password. If not found, the principal name and password are set by this login module and stored under the property names `javax.security.auth.login.name` and `javax.security.auth.login.password` respectively.

The authentication of a user is performed by connecting to the LDAP server based on the login module configuration options. Connecting to the LDAP server is done by creating an `InitialLdapContext` with an environment composed of the LDAP JNDI properties described previously in this section. The Context.SECURITY_PRINCIPAL is set to the distinguished name of the user as obtained by the callback handler in combination with the principalDNPrefix and principalDNSuffix option values. The Context.SECURITY_CREDENTIALS property is either set to the `String` password or the `Object` credential depending on the useObjectCredential option.

Once authentication has succeeded by virtue of being able to create an InitialLdapContext instance, the user's roles are queried by performing a search on the rolesCtxDN location with search attributes set to the roleAttributeName and uidAttributeName option values. The roles names are obtaining by invoking the `toString` method on the role attributes in the search result set.

A sample login configuration entry is:

```
testLdap {
    org.jboss.security.auth.spi.LdapLoginModule required
    java.naming.factory.initial=com.sun.jndi.ldap.LdapCtxFactory
    java.naming.provider.url="ldap://ldaphost.jboss.org:1389/"
    java.naming.security.authentication=simple
    principalDNPrefix=uid=
```

```
    uidAttributeID=userid
    roleAttributeID=roleName
    principalDNSuffix=,ou=People,o=jboss.org
    rolesCtxDN=cn=JBossSX Tests,ou=Roles,o=jboss.org
};
```

To add this entry to a JBoss server login configuration found in the default configuration file set you would modify the `conf/default/auth.conf` file of the JBoss distribution.

To help you understand all of the options of the LdapLoginModule, consider the sample LDAP server data shown in Figure 8.8. This figure corresponds to the testLdap login configuration just shown.

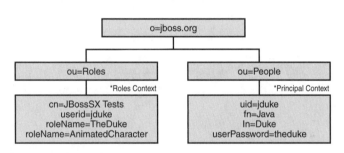

FIGURE 8.8   An LDAP server configuration compatible with the testLdap sample configuration.

Take a look at the testLdap login module configuration in comparision to the Figure 8.8 schema. The `java.naming.factory.initial`, `java.naming.factory.url` and `java.naming.security` options indicate the Sun LDAP JNDI provider implementation will be used, the LDAP server is located on host ldaphost.jboss.org on port 1389, and that simple username and password will be used to authenticate clients connecting to the LDAP server.

When the `LdapLoginModule` performs authentication of a user, it does so by connecting to the LDAP server specified by the `java.naming.factory.url`. The `java.naming.security.principal` property is built from the principalDNPrefix, passed in username and principalDNSuffix as described above. For the testLdap configuration example and a username of 'jduke', the `java.naming.security.principal` string would be 'uid=jduke,ou=People,o=jboss.org'. This corresponds to the LDAP context on the lower right of Figure 8.8 labeled as Principal Context. The `java.naming.security.credentials` property would be set to the passed in password and it would have to match the userPassword attribute of the Principal Context. How a secured LDAP context stores the authentication credential information depends on the LDAP server, so your LDAP server may handle the validation of the `java.naming.security.credentials` property differently.

Once authentication succeeds, the roles on which authorization will be based are retrieved by performing a JNDI search of the LDAP context whose distinguished name is given by the `rolesCtxDN` option value. For the testLdap configuration this is 'cn=JBossSX Tests,ou=Roles,o=jboss.org' and corresponds to the LDAP context on the lower left of Figure 8.8. The search attempts to locate any subcontexts that contain an attribute whose name is given by the `uidAttributeID` option, and whose value matches the username passed to the login module. For any matching context, all values of the attribute whose name is given by the `roleAttributeID` option are obtained. For the testLdap configuration the attribute name that contains the roles is called roleName. The resulting roleName values are stored in the JAAS `Subject` associated with the `LdapLoginModule` as the `Roles` group principals that will be used for role-based authorization. For the LDAP schema shown in Figure 8.8, the roles that will be assigned to the user 'jduke' are 'TheDuke' and 'AnimatedCharacter'.

org.jboss.security.auth.spi.DatabaseServerLoginModule

The `DatabaseServerLoginModule` is a JDBC-based login module that supports authentication and role mapping. You would use this login module if you have your username, password, and role information in a JDBC accessible database. The `DatabaseServerLoginModule` is based on two logical tables:

```
Table Principals(PrincipalID text, Password text)
Table Roles(PrincipalID text, Role text, RoleGroup text)
```

The `Principals` table associates the user `PrincipalID` with the valid password and the `Roles` table associates the user `PrincipalID` with its role sets. The roles used for user permissions must be contained in rows with a `RoleGroup` column value of `Roles`. The tables are logical in that you can specify the SQL query that the login module uses. All that is required is that the `java.sql.ResultSet` has the same logical structure as the `Principals` and `Roles` tables described previously. The actual names of the tables and columns are not relevant as the results are accessed based on the column index. To clarify this notion, consider a database with two tables, `Principals` and `Roles`, as already declared. The following statements build the tables to contain a `PrincipalID` 'java' with a Password of 'echoman' in the `Principals` table, a `PrincipalID` 'java' with a role named 'Echo' in the 'Roles' `RoleGroup` in the `Roles` table, and a `PrincipalID` 'java' with a role named 'caller_java' in the 'CallerPrincipal' `RoleGroup` in the `Roles` table:

```
INSERT INTO Principals VALUES('java', 'echoman')
INSERT INTO Roles VALUES('java', 'Echo', 'Roles')
INSERT INTO Roles VALUES('java', 'caller_java', 'CallerPrincipal')
```

The supported login module configuration options include the following:

- dsJndiName—The JNDI name for the DataSource of the database containing the logical "Principals" and "Roles" tables. This defaults to "java:/DefaultDS".

- principalsQuery—The prepared statement query equivalent to "select Password from Principals where PrincipalID=?". If not specified, the statement will be used exactly as prepared.

- rolesQuery—The prepared statement query equivalent to "select Role, RoleGroup from Roles where PrincipalID=?". If not specified, the statement will be used exactly as prepared.

- unauthenticatedIdentity=string—The principal name that should be assigned to requests that contain no authentication information.

- password-stacking=useFirstPass—When the password-stacking option is set, this module first looks for a shared username and password under the property names javax.security.auth.login.name and javax.security.auth.login.password, respectively, in the login module shared state Map. If found, these are used as the principal name and password. If not found, the principal name and password are set by this login module and stored under the property names javax.security.auth.login.name and javax.security.auth.login.password, respectively.

As an example DatabaseServerLoginModule configuration, consider a custom table schema such as the following:

```
CREATE TABLE Users(username VARCHAR(64) PRIMARY KEY, passwd VARCHAR(64))
CREATE TABLE UserRoles(username VARCHAR(64), userRoles VARCHAR(32))
```

The corresponding DatabaseServerLoginModule configuration would be:

```
testDB {
    org.jboss.security.auth.spi.DatabaseServerLoginModule required
      dsJndiName="java:/MyDatabaseDS"
      principalsQuery="select passwd from Users username where username=?"
      rolesQuery="select userRoles, 'Roles' from UserRoles where username=?"
      ;
};
```

To add this to a JBoss server login configuration found in the default configuration file set you would add this entry to the `conf/default/auth.conf` file of the JBoss distribution.

org.jboss.security.auth.spi.ProxyLoginModule

The `ProxyLoginModule` is a login module that loads a delegate `LoginModule` using the current thread context class loader. The purpose of this module is to work around the current JAAS 1.0 class loader limitation that requires `LoginModules` to be on the system classpath. Some custom `LoginModules` use classes that are loaded from the JBoss server lib/ext directory, and these are not available if the LoginModule is placed on the system classpath. To work around this limitation use the `ProxyLoginModule` to bootstrap the custom LoginModule. The `ProxyLoginModule` has one required configuration option called moduleName. It specifies the fully qualified class name of the LoginModule implementation that is to be bootstrapped. Any number of additional configuration options may be specified, and are passed to the bootstrapped login module.

As an example, consider a custom login module that makes use of some service that is loaded from the JBoss lib/ext directory. The class name of the custom login module is `com.biz.CustomServiceLoginModule`. A suitable `ProxyLoginModule` configuration entry for bootstrapping this custom login module would be:

```
testProxy {
    org.jboss.security.auth.spi.ProxyLoginModule required
      moduleName=com.biz.CustomServiceLoginModule
      customOption1=value1
      customOption2=value2
      customOption3=value3;
};
```

org.jboss.security.ClientLoginModule

The `ClientLoginModule` is an implementation of `LoginModule` for use by JBoss clients for the establishment of the caller identity and credentials. This simply sets the `org.jboss.security.SecurityAssociation.principal` to the value of the `NameCallback` filled in by the `CallbackHandler`, and the `org.jboss.security.SecurityAssociation.credential` to the value of the `PasswordCallback` filled in by the `CallbackHandler`. This is the only supported mechanism for a client to establish the current thread's caller. Both standalone client applications and server environments, acting as JBoss EJB clients where the security environment has not been configured to use JBossSX transparently, need to use the `ClientLoginModule`. Of course, you could always set the `org.jboss.security.SecurityAssociation` information directly, but this is considered an internal API that is subject to change without notice.

Note that this login module does not perform any authentication. It merely copies the login information provided to it into the JBoss server EJB invocation layer for subsequent authentication on the server. If you need to perform client-side authentication of users, you would need to configure another login module in addition to the `ClientLoginModule`.

The supported login module configuration options include the following:

- multi-threaded=true|false—When the multi-threaded option is set to true, each login thread has its own principal and credential storage. This is useful in client environments where multiple user identities are active in separate threads. When set to true, each separate thread must perform its own login. When set to false, the login identity and credentials are global variables that apply to all threads in the VM. The default for this option is false.

- password-stacking=useFirstPass—When the password-stacking option is set, this module first looks for a shared username and password using `javax.security.auth.login.name` and `javax.security.auth.login.password` respectively in the login module shared state `Map`. This allows a module that was configured prior to this to establish a valid username and password that should be passed to JBoss. You would use this option if you want to perform client-side authentication of clients using some other login module such as the `LdapLoginModule`.

The default configuration entry found in the JBoss distribution `client/auth.conf` file is:

```
other {
    // Put your login modules that work without jBoss here

    // jBoss LoginModule
    org.jboss.security.ClientLoginModule required;

    // Put your login modules that need jBoss here
};
```

Writing Custom Login Modules

If the login modules bundled with the JBossSX framework do not work with your security environment, you can write your own custom login module implementation that does.

Recall from the section on the `JaasSecurityManager` architecture that the `JaasSecurityManager` expected a particular usage pattern of the `Subject` principals set. You need to understand the JAAS Subject class's information storage features and the expected usage of these features to be able to write a login module that works with the JaasSecurityManager. This section examines this requirement and introduces two abstract base LoginModule implementations that can help you implement your own custom login modules.

You can obtain security information associated with a Subject in six ways using the following methods:

```
java.util.Set getPrincipals()
java.util.Set getPrincipals(java.lang.Class c)
java.util.Set getPrivateCredentials()
java.util.Set getPrivateCredentials(java.lang.Class c)
java.util.Set getPublicCredentials()
java.util.Set getPublicCredentials(java.lang.Class c)
```

For Subject identities and roles, JBossSX has selected the most natural choice: the principals sets obtained via getPrincipals() and getPrincipals(java.lang.Class). The usage pattern is as follows:

- User identities (username, social security number, employee ID, and so on) are stored as java.security.Principal objects in the Subject Principals set. The Principal implementation that represents the user identity must base comparisons and equality on the name of the principal. A suitable implementation is available as the org.jboss.security.SimplePrincipal class. Other Principal instances may be added to the Subject Principals set as needed.

- The assigned user roles are also stored in the Principals set, but they are grouped in named role sets using java.security.acl.Group instances. The Group interface defines a collection of Principals or Groups, and is a subinterface of java.security.Principal. Any number of role sets can be assigned to a Subject. Currently, the JBossSX framework uses two well-known role sets with the names Roles and CallerPrincipal. The Roles Group is the collection of Principals for the named roles as known in the application domain under which the Subject has been authenticated. This role set is used by methods like the EJBContext.isCallerInRole(String), which EJBs can use to see if the current caller belongs to the named application domain role. The security interceptor logic that performs method permission checks also uses this role set. The CallerPrincipal Group consists of the single Principal identity assigned to the user in the application domain. The EJBContext.getCallerPrincipal() method uses the CallerPrincipal to allow the application domain to map from the operation environment identity to a user identity suitable for the application. If a Subject does not have a CallerPrincipal Group, the application identity is the same as operational environment identity.

Support for the Subject **Usage Pattern**

To simplify correct implementation of the Subject usage patterns, JBossSX includes two abstract login modules that handle the population of the authenticated Subject with a template pattern that enforces correct Subject usage. The most generic of the two is the org.jboss.security.auth.spi.AbstractLoginModule class. It provides a concrete implementation of the javax.security.auth.spi.LoginModule interface and offers abstract methods for the key tasks specific to an operation environment security infrastructure. The key details of the class are highlighted in the following class fragment. The Javadoc comments detail the responsibilities of subclasses.

```
package org.jboss.security.auth.spi;
/** This class implements the common functionality required for a
JAAS server-side LoginModule, and implements the JBossSX standard
Subject usage pattern of storing identities and roles. Subclass
this module to create your own custom LoginModule and override the
login(), getRoleSets(), and getIdentity() methods.
*/
public abstract class AbstractServerLoginModule
     implements javax.security.auth.spi.LoginModule
{
    protected Subject subject;
    protected CallbackHandler callbackHandler;
    protected Map sharedState;
    protected Map options;

    ...
    /** Initialize the login module. This stores the subject,
    callbackHandler and sharedState, and options for the login
    session. Subclasses should override if they need to process
    their own options. A call to super.initialize(...) must be
    made in the case of an override.
    @param subject, the Subject to update after a successful login.
    @param callbackHandler, the CallbackHandler that will be used
     to obtain the user identity and credentials.
    @param sharedState, a Map shared between all configured login
     module instances
    @param options,
        @option password-stacking: if true, the login identity will
        be taken from the javax.security.auth.login.name value of
        the sharedState map, and the proof of identity from the
        javax.security.auth.login.password value of the sharedState
        map.
    */
```

```
public void initialize(Subject subject,
  CallbackHandler callbackHandler,
  Map sharedState,
  Map options)
{
  ...
}

/** Looks for javax.security.auth.login.name and
javax.security.auth.login.password values in the sharedState
map if the useFirstPass option was true and returns true
if they exist. If they do not or are null, this method returns
false. Subclasses should override to perform the required
credential validation steps.
*/
public boolean login() throws LoginException
{
  ...
}

/** Overridden by subclasses to return the Principal that
corresponds to the user primary identity.
*/
abstract protected Principal getIdentity();

/** Overridden by subclasses to return the Groups that
correspond to the role sets assigned to the user. Subclasses
should create at least a Group named "Roles" that contains
the roles assigned to the user.
A second common group is "CallerPrincipal" that provides
the application identity of the user rather than the security
domain identity.
@return Group[] containing the sets of roles
*/
abstract protected Group[] getRoleSets() throws LoginException;
}
```

The second abstract base login module suitable for custom login modules is the
org.jboss.security.auth.spi.UsernamePasswordLoginModule. The login module
further simplifies custom login module implementation by enforcing a string-based

username as the user identity, and a char[] password as the authentication credential. It also supports the mapping of anonymous users (indicated by a null username and password) to a Principal with no roles. The key details of the class are highlighted in the following class fragment. The Javadoc comments detail the responsibilities of subclasses.

```java
package org.jboss.security.auth.spi;
/** An abstract subclass of AbstractServerLoginModule that imposes
 a an identity == String username, credentials == String password
 view on the login process. Subclasses override the
 getUsersPassword() and getUsersRoles() methods to return the
 expected password and roles for the user.
*/
public abstract class UsernamePasswordLoginModule
     extends AbstractServerLoginModule
{
   /** The login identity */
   private Principal identity;
   /** The proof of login identity */
   private char[] credential;
   /** The principal to use when a null username and password
    are seen */
   private Principal unauthenticatedIdentity;

   ...

   /** Override the superclass method to look for an
   unauthenticatedIdentity property. This method first invokes
   the super version.
   @param options,
     @option unauthenticatedIdentity: the name of the principal
       to assign and authenticate when a null username and password
       are seen.
   */
   public void initialize(Subject subject,
      CallbackHandler callbackHandler,
      Map sharedState,
      Map options)
   {
      super.initialize(subject, callbackHandler, sharedState,
```

```
        options);
      // Check for unauthenticatedIdentity option.
      Object option = options.get("unauthenticatedIdentity");
      String name = (String) option;
      if( name != null )
         unauthenticatedIdentity = new SimplePrincipal(name);
   }


   ...


   /** A hook that allows subclasses to change the validation of
   the input password against the expected password. This version
   checks that neither inputPassword or expectedPassword are null
   and that inputPassword.equals(expectedPassword) is true;
   @return true if the inputPassword is valid, false otherwise.
   */
   protected boolean validatePassword(String inputPassword,
      String expectedPassword)
   {
      if( inputPassword == null || expectedPassword == null )
         return false;
      return inputPassword.equals(expectedPassword);
   }


   /** Get the expected password for the current username
   available via the getUsername() method. This is called from
   within the login() method after the CallbackHandler has
   returned the username and candidate password.
   @return the valid password String
   */
   abstract protected String getUsersPassword()
      throws LoginException;
}
```

The choice of subclassing the AbstractLoginModule versus
UsernamePasswordLoginModule is simply based on whether a String based username
and String credential are usable for the authentication technology you are writing
the login module for. If the String based semantic is valid, then subclass
UsernamePasswordLoginModule, else subclass AbstractLoginModule.

The steps you are required to perform when writing a custom login module can be
summarized as such: When writing a custom login module that integrates with your

security infrastructure, you should start by subclassing `AbstractLoginModule` or `UsernamePasswordLoginModule` to ensure that your login module provides the authenticated `Principal` information in the form expected by the JBossSX security manager.

When subclassing the AbstractLoginModule, you need to override the following:

- `void initialize(Subject, CallbackHandler, Map, Map)` if you have custom options to parse.

- `boolean login()` to perform the authentication activity.

- `Principal getIdentity()` to return the Principal object for the user authenticated by the `login()` step.

- `Group[] getRoleSets()` to return at least one `Group` named `Roles` that contains the roles assigned to the `Principal` authenticated during `login()`. A second common `Group` is named `CallerPrincipal` which provides the user's application identity rather than the security domain identity.

When subclassing the UsernamePasswordLoginModule, you need to override the following:

- `void initialize(Subject, CallbackHandler, Map, Map)` if you have custom options to parse.

- `String getUsersPassword()` to return the expected password for the current username available via the `getUsername()` method. The `getUsersPassword()` method is called from within `login()` after the `CallbackHandler` returns the username and candidate password.

- `Group[] getRoleSets()` to return at least one `Group` named `Roles` that contains the roles assigned to the `Principal` authenticated during `login()`. A second common `Group` is named `CallerPrincipal` and provides the user's application identity rather than the security domain identity.

The Secure Remote Password (SRP) Protocol

The Security Remote Password (SRP) protocol is an implementation of a public key exchange handshake described in the Internet standards working group request for comments 2945 (RFC2945) available from ftp://ftp.isi.edu/in-notes/rfc2945.txt. The RFC2945 abstract highlights that SRP is a cryptographically strong authentication mechanism that is based on simple string passwords, and can be used as a secure replacement for existing unsecured password authentication procedures. The heart of SRP is a key exchange algorithm that does not require key servers and certificates singed by trusted sources unlike SSL. These properties make SRP an ideal drop-in replacement for password based authentication mechanisms that don't provide the same level of security as SRP.

SRP is similar in concept and security to other public key exchange algorithms, such as Diffie-Hellman and RSA. SRP is based on simple string passwords in a way that does not require a clear text password to exist on the server. This is in contrast to other public key-based algorithm that require client certificates and the corresponding certificate management infrastructure.

NOTE

The complete RFC2945 specification can be obtained at `http://www.rfc-editor.org/rfc.html`. Additional information on the SRP algorithm and its history can be found at `http://www-cs-students.stanford.edu/~tjw/srp/`.

NOTE

Algorithms like Diffie-Hellman and RSA are known as public key exchange algorithms. The concept of public key algorithms is that you have two keys, one public that is available to everyone, and one that is private and known only to you. When someone wants to send encrypted information to you, encrypt the information using your public key. Only you are able to decrypt the information using your private key. Contrast this with the more traditional shared password based encryption schemes that require the sender and receiver to know the shared password. Public key algorithms eliminate the need to share passwords.

The JBossSX framework includes an implementation of SRP that consists of the following elements:

- An implementation of the SRP handshake protocol that is independent of any particular client/server protocol.

- An RMI implementation of the handshake protocol as the default client/server SRP implementation.

- A client-side JAAS `LoginModule` implementation that uses the RMI implementation for use in authenticating clients in a secure fashion.

- A JMX MBean for managing the RMI server implementation. The MBean allows the RMI server implementation to be plugged into a JMX framework and externalizes the configuration of the verification information store. It also establishes an authentication cache that is bound into the JBoss server JNDI namespace.

- A server-side JAAS LoginModule implementation that uses the authentication cache managed by the SRP JMX MBean.

Figure 8.9 shows a diagram of the key components involved in the JBossSX implementation of the SRP client/server framework.

On the client side, SRP shows up as a custom JAAS `LoginModule` implementation that communicates to the authentication server through an `org.jboss.security.srp.SRPServerInterface` proxy. A client enables authentication using SRP by configuring a login configuration entry that includes the `org.jboss.security.srp.jaas.SRPLoginModule`. This module supports the following configuration options:

- principalClassName—The fully qualified class name of the `java.security.Principal` implementation to use. The implementation must provide a public constructor that accepts a single String argument representing the name of the principal. This defaults to `org.jboss.security.SimplePrincipal`.

- srpServerJndiName—The JNDI name of the `SRPServerInterface` object to use for communicating with the SRP authentication server. If both srpServerJndiName and srpServerRmiUrl options are specified, the srpServerJndiName is tried before srpServerRmiUrl.

- srpServerRmiUrl—The RMI protocol URL string for the location of the `SRPServerInterface` proxy to use for communicating with the SRP authentication server.

The `SRPLoginModule` needs to be configured along with the standard `ClientLoginModule` to allow the SRP authentication credentials to be used for validation of access to security J2EE components. An example login configuration entry that demonstrates such a setup is:

```
srp {
    org.jboss.security.srp.jaas.SRPLoginModule required
    srpServerJndiName="SRPServerInterface"
    ;

    org.jboss.security.ClientLoginModule required
    password-stacking="useFirstPass"
    ;
};
```

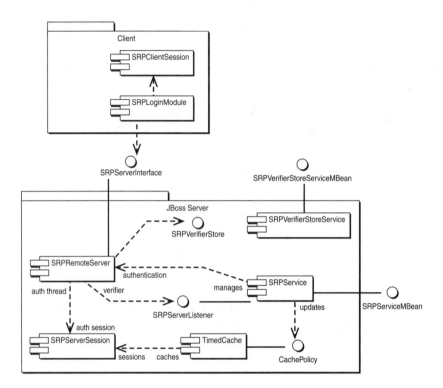

FIGURE 8.9   The JBossSX components of the SRP client-server framework.

On the JBoss server side, there are objects, managed by two Mbeans, that collectively make up the SRP server. The primary service is the
org.jboss.security.srp.SRPService MBean, and it is responsible for exposing an RMI
accessible version of the SRPServerInterface as well as updating the SRP authentication session cache. The configurable SRPService MBean attributes include the following:

- JndiName—The JNDI name from which the SRPServerInterface proxy should
  be available. This is the location where the SRPService binds the serializable
  dynamic proxy to the SRPServerInterface. It defaults to
  srp/SRPServerInterface.

- VerifierSourceJndiName—The JNDI name of the SRPVerifierSource implementation that should be used by the SRPService. It defaults to
  srp/DefaultVerifierSource.

- AuthenticationCacheJndiName—The JNDI name under which the authentication org.jboss.util.CachePolicy implementation to be used for caching

authentication information is bound. The SRP session cache is made available for use through this binding. It defaults to `srp/AuthenticationCache`.

- ServerPort—RMI port for the `SRPRemoteServerInterface`, and defaults to 10099.

- ClientSocketFactory—An optional custom `java.rmi.server.RMIClientSocketFactory` implementation class name used during the export of the `SRPServerInterface`. The default is `RMIClientSocketFactory`.

- ServerSocketFactory—An optional custom `java.rmi.server.RMIServerSocketFactory` implementation class name used during the export of the `SRPServerInterface`. The default is `RMIServerSocketFactory`.

- AuthenticationCacheTimeout—Specifies the timed cache policy timeout in seconds. This defaults to 1800 seconds (30 minutes).

- AuthenticationCacheResolution—Specifies the timed cache policy resolution in seconds. This controls the interval between checks for timeouts. This defaults to 60 seconds (1 minute).

The one input setting is the VerifierSourceJndiName attribute. This is the location of the SRP password information store implementation that must be provided and made available through JNDI. The `SRPVerifierStoreService` is an example MBean service that binds an implementation of the `SRPVerifierStore` interface that uses a file of serialized objects as the persistent store. Although not realistic for a production environment, it does allow for testing of the SRP protocol, and provides an example of the requirements for an `SRPVerifierStore` service. The configurable `SRPVerifierStoreService` MBean attributes include the following:

- JndiName—The JNDI name from which the `SRPVerifierStore` implementation should be available. It defaults to `srp/DefaultVerifierSource`.

- StoreFile—The location of the user password verifier serialized object store file, such as a URL or a resource name to be found in the classpath. It defaults to `SRPVerifierStore.ser`.

The `SRPVerifierStoreService` MBean also supports addUser and delUser operations for addition and deletion of users. The signatures are:

```
public void addUser(String username, String password) throws IOException;
public void delUser(String username) throws IOException;
```

An example configuration of these services is presented with an SRP authentication example in the section "An SRP Example."

Inside of the SRP Algorithm

The appeal of the SRP algorithm is that is allows for mutual authentication of client and server using simple text passwords without a secure communication channel. You might be wondering how this is done. Figure 8.10 (see page 304-305) presents a sequence diagram of the authentication protocol as implemented by JBossSX.

The highlights of what is taking place for the key message exchanges presented in Figure 8.10 are as follows. If you want the complete details and theory behind the algorithm, refer to the SRP references mentioned in a note earlier. There are six steps that are performed to complete authentication:

1. The client-side `SRPLoginModule` retrieves the `SRPServerInterface` instance for the remote authentication server from the naming service.

2. The client-side `SRPLoginModule` requests the SRP parameters associated with the username attempting the login. There are a number of parameters involved in the SRP algorithm that must be chosen when the user password is first transformed into the verifier form used by the SRP algorithm. Rather than hardcoding the parameters (which could be done with minimal security risk), the JBossSX implementation allows a user to retrieve this information as part of the exchange protocol. The `getSRPParameters(username)` call retrieves the SRP parameters for the given username.

3. The client-side `SRPLoginModule` begins an SRP session by creating a `SRPClientSession` object using the login username, clear-text password, and SRP parameters obtained from step 2. The client then creates a random number A that is used to build the private SRP session key. The client initializes the server side of the SRP session by invoking the `SRPServerInterface.init` method and passing in the username and client generated random number A. The server returns it's own random number B. This step corresponds to the exchange of public keys.

4. The client-side `SRPLoginModule` creates a challenge M1 to the server by invoking `SRPClientSession.response` method passing the server random number B as an argument. This challenge is sent to the server via the `SRPServerInterface.verify` method and server's response is saved as M2. This step corresponds to an exchange of challenges. At this point the server has verified that the user is who they say they are.

5. The client-side `SRPLoginModule` obtains the private SRP session key that has been generated as a result of the previous messages exchanges. This is saved as a private credential in the login Subject. The server challenge response M2 from step 4 is verified by invoking the `SRPClientSession.verify` method. If this succeeds, mutual authentication of the client to server and server to client have been completed.

6. The client-side `SRPLoginModule` saves the login username and M1 challenge into the `LoginModule` sharedState `Map`. This is used as the `Principal` name and credentials by the standard JBoss `ClientLoginModule`. The M1 challenge is used in place of the password as proof of identity on any method invocations on J2EE components. The M1 challenge is a cryptographically strong hash associated with the SRP session. Its interception via a third partly cannot be used to obtain the user's password.

Although SRP has many interesting properties, it is still an evolving component in the JBossSX framework and has limitations of which you should be aware. Issues of note include the following:

- Because of how JBoss detaches the method transport protocol from the component container where authentication is performed, an unauthorized user could snoop the SRP M1 challenge and effectively use the challenge to make requests as the associated username. SSL can be used to prevent such masquerade uses of the opaque credential.

- The SRPService maintains a cache of SRP sessions that time out after a configurable period. Once they time out, any subsequent J2EE component access will fail because there is currently no mechanism for transparently renegotiating the SRP authentication credentials. You must either set the authentication cache timeout very long (up to 2,147,483,647 seconds, or approximately 68 years), or handle re-authentication in your code on failure.

- There can only be one SRP session for a given username. Because the negotiated SRP session produces a private session key that can be used for encryption/decryption between the client and server, the session is effectively a stateful one. The current association of the SRP session to the username limits one session per username. In the future this may be extended to support multiple user sessions.

At the end of this authentication protocol, the `SRPServerSession` has been placed into the `SRPService` authentication cache for subsequent use by the `SRPCacheLoginModule`. To use end-to-end SRP authentication for J2EE component calls, you need to configure the security domain under which the components are secured to use the `org.jboss.security.srp.jaas.SRPCacheLoginModule`. The `SRPCacheLoginModule` has a single configuration option named cacheJndiName that sets the JNDI location of the SRP authentication `CachePolicy` instance. This must correspond to the AuthenticationCacheJndiName attribute value of the `SRPService` MBean. The `SRPCacheLoginModule` authenticates user credentials by obtaining the client challenge from the `SRPServerSession` object in the authentication cache and comparing this to the challenge passed as the user credentials. Figure 8.11 illustrates the operation of the `SRPCacheLoginModule.login` method implementation.

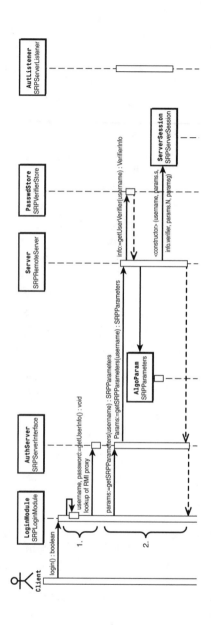

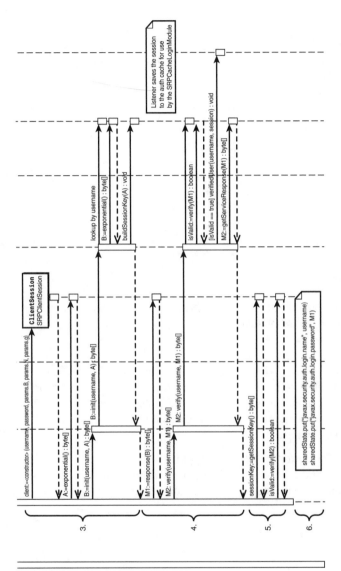

FIGURE 8.10   The SRP client-server authentication algorithm sequence diagram.

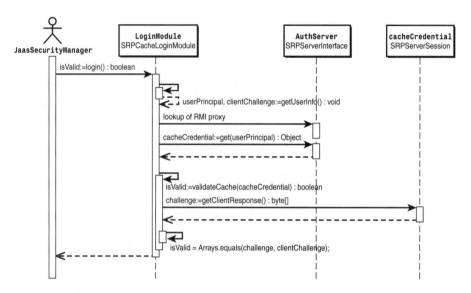

FIGURE 8.11   A sequence diagram illustrating the interaction of the SRPCacheLoginModule with the SRP session cache.

An SRP Example

Quite a bit of material has been covered on SRP; now its time to demonstrate SRP in practice with an example. The example demonstrates client-side authentication of the user via SRP as well as subsequent secured access to a simple EJB using the SRP session challenge as the user credential.

The first step required is to configure the JBoss server with a configuration file set that enables the SRP MBeans and adds a login configuration entry for the SRPCacheLoginModule. To execute this step, run the following Ant command from the book examples root directory:

```
examples 1015>ant -Dchap=8 config
Buildfile: build.xml

config:

config:
    [copy] Copying 14 files to G:\JBoss-2.4.4\conf\chap8
    [copy] Copying 3 files to G:\JBoss-2.4.4\conf\chap8

BUILD SUCCESSFUL

Total time: 1 second
```

This creates a chap8 configuration file set under the JBoss distribution conf directory. Next, start the JBoss server using the chap8 configuration. You do this using either the run.bat or run.sh script and pass the chap8 configuration name to the script as follows:

```
bin 1116>run.bat chap8
JBOSS_CLASSPATH=;run.jar;../lib/crimson.jar
jboss.home = G:\JBoss-2.4.4
Using JAAS LoginConfig: file:/G:/JBoss-2.4.4/conf/chap8/auth.conf
Using configuration "chap8"
...
[SRPVerifierStoreService] Starting
[SRPVerifierStoreService] Created SerialObjectStore at:
  G:\JBoss-2.4.4\bin\chap8_store.ser
[SRPVerifierStoreService] Started
[SRPService] Starting
[SRPRemoteServer] setVerifierStore, ...
[SRPService] Bound SRPServerProxy at srp/SRPServerInterface
[SRPService] Bound AuthenticationCache at srp/AuthenticationCache
[SRPService] Started
[Service Control] Started 48 services
[Default] JBoss 2.4.4 Started in 0m:6s
```

You can see at the end of the console output that the SRPVerifierStoreService and SRPService have been started. Run the example 2 client by executing the following command:

```
examples 1018>ant -Dchap=8 -Dex=2 run-example
Buildfile: build.xml
...
chap8-ex2-jar:
run-example2:
     [java] Accessing the Security:service=SRPVerifierStore MBean server
     [java] Creating username=jduke, password=theduke
     [java] User jduke added
     [copy] Copying 1 file to G:\JBoss-2.4.4\deploy
     [echo] Waiting for deploy...
     [java] Logging in using the 'srp' configuration
     [java] Created Echo
     [java] Echo.echo()#1 = This is call 1
     [java] Echo.echo()#2 failed with exception:
         Authentication exception, principal=jduke
BUILD SUCCESSFUL
Total time: 31 seconds
```

In the examples directory, you will find a file called ex2-trace.log. This is a detailed trace of the client side of the SRP algorithm. The tail of the JBoss server.log contains the server-side trace of the SRP algorithm. The traces show step-by-step the construction of the public keys, challenges, session key, and verification.

Note that the client has taken a long time to run relative to the other simple examples. The reason for this is the construction of the client's public key. This involves the creation of a cryptographically strong random number, and this process takes quite a bit of time the first time. If you were to log out and log in again within the same VM, the process would be much faster. Also note that "Echo.echo()#2" fails with an Authentication exception. The client code sleeps for 15 seconds after making the first call to demonstrate the behavior of the SRPService cache expiration. The SRPService cache policy timeout has been set to a mere 10 seconds to force this issue. As stated earlier, you need to make the cache timeout very long, or handle re-authentication on failure.

Listing 8.9 describes the configuration changes that were required to enable the use of the SRP authentication protocol. If you look at the bottom of the conf/chap8/jboss.jcml file, under the JBoss server root directory, you will see the following entries shown in Listing 8.9.

LISTING 8.9   The jboss.jcml SRP MBean Service Configuration Entries used with Example 2

```
<!-- ======================================================== -->
<!-- Add your custom MBeans here                        -->
<!-- ======================================================== -->

<mbean code="org.jboss.security.srp.SRPVerifierStoreService"
    name="Security:service=SRPVerifierStore">
  <attribute name="JndiName">srp/Chap8VerifierStore</attribute>
  <attribute name="StoreFile">chap8-store.ser</attribute>
</mbean>

<mbean code="org.jboss.security.srp.SRPService"
    name="Security:service=SRPService">
  <attribute name="JndiName">srp/SRPServerInterface</attribute>
  <attribute name="VerifierSourceJndiName">
    srp/Chap8VerifierStore
  </attribute>
  <attribute name="AuthenticationCacheJndiName">
    srp/AuthenticationCache
```

LISTING 8.9   Continued

```
    </attribute>
    <attribute name="AuthenticationCacheTimeout">10</attribute>
    <attribute name="AuthenticationCacheResolution">5</attribute>
    <attribute name="ServerPort">12345</attribute>
</mbean>
```

This configures the SRPVerifierStoreService and SRPService MBean services using a number of non-default values for the supported attributes to demonstrate their use. The one item of note is that the JndiName attribute of the SRPVerifierStoreService is equal to the VerifierSourceJndiName attribute of the SRPService. This is required because the SRPService needs an implementation of the SRPVerifierStore interface for accessing user password verification information. Providing this implementation is the purpose of the SRPVerifierStoreService.

The other JBoss server configuration change was the addition of a login module configuration entry that used the SRPCacheLoginModule. If you look at the conf/chap8/auth.conf file you will see the two entries given in Listing 8.10.

LISTING 8.10   The JBoss Server auth.conf JAAS Login Configuration File used with Example 2

```
srp {
    org.jboss.security.auth.spi.ProxyLoginModule required
        moduleName=org.jboss.security.srp.jaas.SRPCacheLoginModule
        cacheJndiName="srp/AuthenticationCache"
        ;

    org.jboss.security.auth.spi.UsersRolesLoginModule required
        password-stacking=useFirstPass
        ;
};

// The default server login module
other {
    org.jboss.security.auth.spi.UsersRolesLoginModule required
        unauthenticatedIdentity="nobody";
};
```

It is the "srp" login configuration entry that is of interest. There are three issues to note about this configuration. First, note that you had to use the ProxyLoginModule to bootstrap the `SRPCacheLoginModule`. The reason for this is that the `SRPCacheLoginModule` used the `org.jboss.util.TimedCache` class located in the lib/ext/jboss.jar archive. This jar is not loaded by the system class loader, and thus would not be available if the `SRPCacheLoginModule` was loaded by the system class loader.

Also, the cacheJndiName="srp/AuthenticationCache" configuration option tells the `SRPCacheLoginModule` the location of the `CachePolicy` that contains the `SRPServerSession` for users who have authenticated against the `SRPService`.

Finally, the configuration includes a `UsersRolesLoginModule` with the password-stacking=useFirstPass configuration option. It is required to use a second login module with the `SRPCacheLoginModule` because SRP is only an authentication technology. A second login module needs to be configured to accept the authentication credentials validated by the `SRPCacheLoginModule` to set the principal's roles that determines the principal's permissions.

The example entity bean you want to secure using this configuration includes a jboss.xml descriptor with a `security-domain` element value of srp. It also includes a user.properties file that is ignored and a roles.properties file that is used by the `UsersRolesLoginModule` to establish the roles for the user after authentication by the `SRPCacheLoginModule`.

An appropriate auth.conf file must also be created on the client side. Listing 8.11 shows the client side "srp" login configuration entry.

LISTING 8.11   The JBoss Client auth.conf JAAS Login Configuration File used with Example 2

```
srp {
    org.jboss.security.srp.jaas.SRPLoginModule required
    srpServerJndiName="srp/SRPServerInterface"
    ;

    org.jboss.security.ClientLoginModule required
    password-stacking="useFirstPass"
    ;
};
```

The client configuration makes use of the `SRPLoginModule` with a srpServerJndiName option value that corresponds to the JBoss server component `SRPService` JndiName attribute value. Also needed is the `ClientLoginModule` configured with the password-stacking="useFirstPass" value to propagate the user authentication credentials to the EJB invocation layer.

Running JBoss With a Java 2 Security Manager

By default the JBoss server does not start with a Java 2 security manager. If you want to restrict privileges of code using Java 2 permissions, you need to configure the JBoss server to run under a security manager. This is done by configuring the Java VM options in the run.bat or run.sh scripts in the JBoss server distribution bin directory. The two required VM options are as follows:

- java.security.manager—This is used without any value to specify that the default security manager should be used. This is the preferred security manager. You can also pass a value to the java.security.manager option to specify a custom security manager implementation. The value must be the fully qualified class name of a subclass of java.lang.SecurityManager. This form specifies that the policy file should augment the default security policy as configured by the VM installation.

- java.security.policy—This is used to specify the policy file that will augment the default security policy information for the VM. This option takes two forms: `java.security.policy=policyFileURL` and `java.security.policy==policyFileURL`. This form specifies that only the indicated policy file should be used. The policyFileURL value can be any URL for which a protocol handler exists, or a file path specification.

Listing 8.12 illustrates a fragment of the standard run.bat start script for Win32 that shows the addition of these two options to the command line used to start JBoss.

LISTING 8.12   The Modifications to the Win32 run.bat Start Script to Run JBoss with a Java 2 Security Manager

```
...

set CONFIG=%1
@if "%CONFIG%" == "" set CONFIG=default
set PF=../conf/%CONFIG%/server.policy
set OPTS=-Djava.security.manager
set OPTS=%OPTS% -Djava.security.policy=%PF%
echo JBOSS_CLASSPATH=%JBOSS_CLASSPATH%
java %JAXP% %OPTS% -classpath "%JBOSS_CLASSPATH%" org.jboss.Main %*
```

Listing 8.13 shows a fragment of the standard run.sh start script for Unix/Linux systems that shows the addition of these two options to the command line used to start JBoss.

LISTING 8.13   The Modifications to the Unix/Linux run.sh Start Script to Run JBoss with a Java 2 Security Manager

```
...

CONFIG=$1
if [ "$CONFIG" == "" ]; then CONFIG=default; fi
PF=../conf/$CONFIG/server.policy
OPTS=-Djava.security.manager
OPTS="$OPTS -Djava.security.policy=$PF"
echo JBOSS_CLASSPATH=$JBOSS_CLASSPATH
java $HOTSPOT $JAXP $OPTS -classpath $JBOSS_CLASSPATH org.jboss.Main $@
```

Both start scripts are setting the security policy file to the server.policy file located in the JBoss configuration file set directory that corresponds to the configuration name passed as the first argument to the script. This allows you to maintain a security policy per configuration file set without having to modify the start script.

Enabling Java 2 security is the easy part. The difficult part of Java 2 security is establishing the allowed permissions. If you look at the server.policy file that is contained in the default configuration file set, you'll see that it contains the following permission grant statement:

```
grant {
        // Allow everything for now
        permission java.security.AllPermission;
};
```

This effectively disables security permission checking for all code as it says any code can do anything, which is not a reasonable default. What is a reasonable set of permissions is entirely up to you. Here is a little-known tidbit on debugging security policy settings. There are various debugging flags that you can set to determine what security manager is using your security policy file as well as what policy files are contributing permissions. Running the VM as follows shows the possible debugging flag settings:

```
bin 1205>java -Djava.security.debug=help

all        turn on all debugging
access     print all checkPermission results
jar        jar verification
policy     loading and granting
scl        permissions SecureClassLoader assigns
```

The following can be used with access:

```
stack      include stack trace
domain     dumps all domains in context
failure    before throwing exception, dump stack
           and domain that didn't have permission
```

Running with -Djava.security.debug=all provides the most output, but the output volume is torrential. This might be a good place to start, if you don't understand a given security failure at all. A less verbose setting that helps debug permission failures is to use -Djava.security.debug=access,failure. This is still relatively verbose, but not nearly as bad as the all mode because the security domain information is only displayed on access failures.

Using SSL with JBoss Using JSSE

A prerequisite to using SSL is that you have the JSSE package installed as define by the JSSE installation guide. If you don't have the JSSE package, you can download it from http://java.sun.com/products/jsse/index.html. To test that you have JSEE installed, you need to be able to compile and run this simple installation test case:

```java
import java.net.*;
import javax.net.ServerSocketFactory;
import javax.net.ssl.*;

public class JSSE_install_check
{
    public static void main(String[] args) throws Exception
    {
        ServerSocketFactory factory =
            SSLServerSocketFactory.getDefault();
        SSLServerSocket sslSocket = (SSLServerSocket)
            factory.createServerSocket(12345);

        String [] cipherSuites = sslSocket.getEnabledCipherSuites();
        for(int i = 0; i < cipherSuites.length; i++)
        {
            System.out.println("Cipher Suite " + i +
            " = " + cipherSuites[i]);
        }
    }
}
```

An example of a successful run is:

```
bin 1218>java -version
java version "1.3.1_01"
Java(TM) 2 Runtime Environment, Standard Edition (build 1.3.1_01)
Java HotSpot(TM) Client VM (build 1.3.1_01, mixed mode)
bin 1219>java JSSE_install_check
Cipher Suite 0 = SSL_DHE_DSS_WITH_DES_CBC_SHA
Cipher Suite 1 = SSL_DHE_DSS_WITH_3DES_EDE_CBC_SHA
Cipher Suite 2 = SSL_DHE_DSS_EXPORT_WITH_DES40_CBC_SHA
Cipher Suite 3 = SSL_RSA_WITH_RC4_128_MD5
Cipher Suite 4 = SSL_RSA_WITH_RC4_128_SHA
Cipher Suite 5 = SSL_RSA_WITH_DES_CBC_SHA
Cipher Suite 6 = SSL_RSA_WITH_3DES_EDE_CBC_SHA
Cipher Suite 7 = SSL_RSA_EXPORT_WITH_RC4_40_MD5
```

Once you have JSSE properly configured, you need a public key/private key pair in the form of an X509 certificate for use by the JBoss server. For the purpose of this example, a self-signed certificate using the JDK 1.3 keytool has been created and includes the resulting keystore file in the chap8 configuration directory as chap8.keystore. It was created using the following command and input:

```
examples 1121>keytool -genkey -alias rmi+ssl -keyalg RSA
  -keystore chap8.keystore -validity 3650
Enter keystore password:  rmi+ssl
What is your first and last name?
  [Unknown]:  Chapter8 SSL Example
What is the name of your organizational unit?
  [Unknown]:  JBoss Book
What is the name of your organization?
  [Unknown]:  JBoss Group, LLC
What is the name of your City or Locality?
  [Unknown]:  Issaquah
What is the name of your State or Province?
  [Unknown]:  WA
What is the two-letter country code for this unit?
  [Unknown]:  US
Is <CN=Chapter8 SSL Example, OU=JBoss Book, O="JBoss Group, LLC", L=Issaquah, ST
=WA, C=US> correct?
  [no]:  yes

Enter key password for <rmi+ssl>
        (RETURN if same as keystore password):
```

This produces a keystore file called chap8.keystore. A keystore is a database of security keys. There are two different types of entries in a keystore:

- key entries—Each entry holds very sensitive cryptographic key information, which is stored in a protected format to prevent unauthorized access. Typically, a key stored in this type of entry is a secret key, or a private key accompanied by the certificate chain for the corresponding public key. The keytool and jarsigner tools only handle the latter type of entry, such as private keys and their associated certificate chains.

- trusted certificate entries—Each entry contains a single public key certificate belonging to another party. It is called a trusted certificate because the keystore owner trusts that the public key in the certificate indeed belongs to the identity identified by the subject (owner) of the certificate. The issuer of the certificate vouches for this by signing the certificate.

Listing the conf/chap8/chap8.keystore file contents using the keytool shows one self-signed certificate:

```
bin 1281>keytool -list -v -keystore ../conf/chap8/chap8.keystore
Enter keystore password:  rmi+ssl

Keystore type: jks
Keystore provider: SUN

Your keystore contains 1 entry:

Alias name: rmi+ssl
Creation date: Thu Nov 08 19:50:23 PST 2001
Entry type: keyEntry
Certificate chain length: 1
Certificate[1]:
Owner: CN=Chapter8 SSL Example, OU=JBoss Book, O="JBoss Group, LLC",
 L=Issaquah, ST=WA, C=US
Issuer: CN=Chapter8 SSL Example, OU=JBoss Book, O="JBoss Group, LLC",
 L=Issaquah, ST=WA, C=US
Serial number: 3beb5271
Valid from: Thu Nov 08 19:50:09 PST 2001 until: Sun Nov 06
 19:50:09 PST 2011
Certificate fingerprints:
 MD5:  F6:1B:2B:E9:A5:23:E7:22:B2:18:6F:3F:9F:E7:38:AE
 SHA1: F2:20:50:36:97:86:52:89:71:48:A2:C3:06:C8:F9:2D:F7:79:00:36


*******************************************
*******************************************
```

With JSSE installed and a keystore with the certificate you will use for the JBoss server, you are ready to configure JBoss to use SSL for EJB access. This is done by configuring the EJB container RMI socket factories. The JBossSX framework includes implementations of the `java.rmi.server.RMIServerSocketFactory` and `java.rmi.server.RMIClientSocketFactory` interfaces that enable the use of RMI over SSL encrypted sockets. The implementation classes are `org.jboss.security.ssl.RMISSLServerSocketFactory` and `org.jboss.security.ssl.RMISSLClientSocketFactory`, respectively. There are two steps to enable the use of SSL for RMI access to EJBs. The first is to enable the use of a keystore as the database for the SSL server certificate, which is done by configuring an `org.jboss.security.plugins.JaasSecurityDomain` MBean. The jboss.jcml file in the chap8 configuration file set directory already includes the following MBean entry:

```
<!-- The SSL domain setup -->
<mbean code="org.jboss.security.plugins.JaasSecurityDomain"
    name="Security:name=JaasSecurityDomain,domain=RMI+SSL">
  <constructor>
    <arg type="java.lang.String" value="RMI+SSL"/>
  </constructor>
  <attribute name="KeyStoreURL">chap8.keystore</attribute>
  <attribute name="KeyStorePass">rmi+ssl</attribute>
</mbean>
```

The `JaasSecurityDomain` is a subclass of the standard `JaasSecurityManager` class that adds the notions of a keystore as well JSSE KeyManagerFactory and TrustManagerFactory access. It extends the basic security manager to allow support for SSL and other cryptographic operations that require security keys. This configuration simply loads the chap8.keystore from the JBoss server configuration using the indicated password.

With this setup you are now able to perform the second step, which is to define an EJB container configuration that uses the JBossSX RMI socket factories that support SSL.

To do this you need to define a custom EJB container configuration using the jboss.xml descriptor. This requires knowledge that is not fully discussed until Chapter 9, "Advanced JBoss Configuration Using `jboss.xml`". The configuration required to enable RMI over SSL access to stateless session bean is provided for you in Listing 8.14. You will use this configuration in a stateless session bean example.

LISTING 8.14   The jboss.xml Container Configuration to Enable SSL with Stateless Session Beans

```xml
<?xml version="1.0"?>
<jboss>
   <container-configurations>
      <container-configuration>
         <container-name>Standard Stateless SessionBean</container-name>
         <!-- Override the container socket factories -->
         <container-invoker-conf>
            <Optimized>true</Optimized>
            <RMIObjectPort>4445</RMIObjectPort>
            <RMIClientSocketFactory>
               org.jboss.security.ssl.RMISSLClientSocketFactory
            </RMIClientSocketFactory>
            <RMIServerSocketFactory>
               org.jboss.security.ssl.RMISSLServerSocketFactory
            </RMIServerSocketFactory>
            <ssl-domain>java:/jaas/RMI+SSL</ssl-domain>
         </container-invoker-conf>
      </container-configuration>
   </container-configurations>
</jboss>
```

It is the container-invoker-conf element that is doing all of the work. The key elements are as follows:

- RMIObjectPort—This specifies that the serverlistening port should be 4445 rather than the default of 4444. This must be changed so that both SSL and non-SSL stateless session beans may coexist.

- RMIClientSocketFactory—This specifies the client side of the RMI server socket factory. The org.jboss.security.ssl.RMISSLClientSocketFactory class is one that know how to obtain the required JSSE information from a JaasSecurityDomain KeyStore.

- RMIServerSocketFactory—This specifies the server side of the RMI server socket factory. The org.jboss.security.ssl.RMISSLServerSocketFactory class is one that know how to obtain the required JSSE information from a JaasSecurityDomain KeyStore.

- ssl-domain—This specifies the JNDI name of the JaasSecurityDomain that the SSL socket factories should use to obtain the KeyStore information needed for JSSE.

The example 3 code is located under the src/main/org/jboss/chap8/ex3 directory of
the book examples located on the CD. This is another simple stateless session bean
with an echo method that returns its input argument. It is hard to tell when SSL is
in use unless it fails, so run the example 3 client in two different ways to demonstrate that the EJB deployment is, in fact, using SSL. Start the JBoss server using the
chap8 configuration and then run example 3a as follows:

```
examples 1130>ant -Dchap=8 -Dex=3a run-example
Buildfile: build.xml
...
run-example3a:
    [copy] Copying 1 file to G:\JBoss-2.4.4\deploy
    [echo] Waiting for 15 seconds for deploy...
java.rmi.MarshalException: Error marshaling transport header;
    nested exception is:
    javax.net.ssl.SSLException: untrusted server cert chain
javax.net.ssl.SSLException: untrusted server cert chain
    at com.sun.net.ssl.internal.ssl.SSLSocketImpl.a
    at com.sun.net.ssl.internal.ssl.ClientHandshaker.a
    at com.sun.net.ssl.internal.ssl.ClientHandshaker.processMessage
    at com.sun.net.ssl.internal.ssl.Handshaker.process_record
    at com.sun.net.ssl.internal.ssl.SSLSocketImpl.a
    at com.sun.net.ssl.internal.ssl.SSLSocketImpl.a
    at com.sun.net.ssl.internal.ssl.AppOutputStream.write
    at java.io.BufferedOutputStream.flushBuffer
    at java.io.BufferedOutputStream.flush
    at java.io.DataOutputStream.flush
    at sun.rmi.transport.tcp.TCPChannel.createConnection
    at sun.rmi.transport.tcp.TCPChannel.newConnection
    at sun.rmi.server.UnicastRef.invoke
    at org.jboss.ejb.plugins.jrmp.server.JRMPContainerInvoker_Stub.invokeHome
    at org.jboss.ejb.plugins.jrmp.interfaces.HomeProxy.invokeHome
    at org.jboss.ejb.plugins.jrmp.interfaces.HomeProxy.invoke
    at $Proxy0.create(Unknown Source)
    at org.jboss.chap8.ex3.ExClient.main(ExClient.java:25)
Exception in thread "main"
Java Result: 1
```

The resulting exception is expected, and is the purpose of the 3a version of the
example. Note that the exception stack trace has been edited to fit into the book
format, so expect some difference. The key item to notice about the exception is it
clearly shows you are using the Sun JSSE classes to communicate with the JBoss EJB
container. The exception is saying that the self-signed certificate you are using as the

JBoss server certificate cannot be validated as signed by any of the default certificate authorities. This is expected because the default certificate authority keystore that ships with the JSSE package only includes well known certificate authorities such as VeriSign, Thawte, and RSA Data Security. To get the EJB client to accept your self-signed certificate as valid, you need to tell the JSSE classes to use your chap8.keystore as its truststore. A truststore is just a keystore that contains public key certificates used to sign other certificates. To do this, run example 3 using -Dex=3 rather than -Dex=3a to pass the location of the correct truststore using the javax.net.ssl.trustStore system property:

```
examples 1118>ant -Dchap=8 -Dex=3 run-example
Buildfile: build.xml
...
run-example3:
     [copy] Copying 1 file to G:\JBoss-2.4.4\deploy
     [echo] Waiting for 5 seconds for deploy...
     [java] DEBUG [Thread-0] (RMISSLClientSocketFactory.java:69) - SSL handshake
Completed, cipher=SSL_RSA_WITH_RC4_128_SHA, peerHost=172.17.66.54
     [java] 0 [Thread-0] DEBUG org.jboss.security.ssl.RMISSLClientSocketFactory
  - SSL handshakeCompleted, cipher=SSL_RSA_WITH_RC4_128_SHA, peerHost=172.17.66.54
     [java] Created Echo
     [java] Echo.echo()#1 = This is call 1
BUILD SUCCESSFUL
Total time: 15 seconds
```

This time the only indication that an SSL socket is involved is because of the "SSL handshakeCompleted" message. This is coming from the RMISSLClientSocketFactory class as a debug level log message. If you did not have the client configured to print out log4j debug level messages, there would be no direct indication that SSL was involved. If you note the run times and the load on your system CPU, there definitely is a difference. SSL, like SRP, involves the use of cryptographically strong random numbers that take time to seed the first time they are used. This shows up as high CPU utilization and start up times.

One consequence of this is that if you are running on a system that is slower than the one used to run the examples for the book, such as when running example 3a, you may seen an exception similar to the following:

```
javax.naming.NameNotFoundException: EchoBean not bound
 at sun.rmi.transport.StreamRemoteCall.exceptionReceivedFromServer
 at sun.rmi.transport.StreamRemoteCall.executeCall
 at sun.rmi.server.UnicastRef.invoke
 at org.jnp.server.NamingServer_Stub.lookup
 at org.jnp.interfaces.NamingContext.lookup
```

```
    at org.jnp.interfaces.NamingContext.lookup
    at javax.naming.InitialContext.lookup
    at org.jboss.chap8.ex3.ExClient.main(ExClient.java:23)
Exception in thread "main"
Java Result: 1
```

The problem is that the JBoss server has not finished deploying the example EJB in the time the client allowed. This is due to the initial setup time of the secure random number generator used by the SSL server socket. If you see this issue, simply rerun the example again or increase the deployment wait time in the chap8 build.xml Ant script.

Summary

J2EE Declarative Security Overview including the deployment descriptor security related elements for both EJBs and Web components. The use of the jboss.xml and jboss-web.xml descriptors to enable security was also discussed.

The generic JBoss security plug-in architecture was introduced. The interfaces that supported the J2EE declarative security model were discussed. Also discussed and demonstrated was the custom security interface that allowed one to enforce security constructs that cannot be described by the J2EE declarative model.

An introduction to JAAS that highlighted the authentication classes was given. The default JAAS based security manager plug-in implementation was discussed. This included its architecture, use of JAAS and MBean configuration. The standard supporting JAAS login module implementations shipped with JBoss were presented and their options detailed. You were also shown two abstract login modules supplied with JBoss that help in writing your own custom login modules.

The SRP protocol was also described. Both the algorithm and the JBoss implementation were discussed. An example was presented and a critique of the current JBoss implementation was given.

Lastly, the use of SSL with EJBs was described. A sample configuration was presented and an example of using SSL with a stateless session bean was given.

In Chapter 9, "Advanced JBoss Configuration Using `jboss.xml`," you will cover the jboss.xml descriptor. A complete description of the advanced configuration capabilities of the jboss.xml descriptor will be presented.

```
ile:
[mkdir] Created dir: /tmp/2.4.4/j
[javac] Compiling 154 source file

install:
  [copy] Copyin
  [copy] Copyin
```

9

IN THIS CHAPTER

p/2.
n/2

Advanced JBoss Configuration Using jboss.xml

The jboss.xml Descriptor

The jboss.xml descriptor is the mechanism by which all configurable aspects of the JBoss EJB container are specified. In addition to the allowing a deployer to specify the EJB ENC and security bindings that have been covered in previous chapters, the jboss.xml descriptor allows for customization of most of the EJB container behavior. You will begin your introduction to the JBoss advanced configuration options by viewing the complete jboss.xml descriptor DTD. This is split across Figures 9.1 and 9.2 due to the size of the DTD image.

You have already seen nearly every element of the jboss.xml descriptor shown in Figure 9.1. The exceptions are the top-level enforce-ejb-restricitions element and the configuration-name element under each of the EJB element types. The enforce-ejb-restrictions element is a true/false flag that indicates whether the EJB programming restrictions defined in the EJB specification should be enforced by the JBoss EJB container. This is currently unsupported, and setting it has no affect. The JBoss container does not enforce the EJB programming restrictions.

The configuration-name element is a link to a container-configurations/container-configuration element in Figure 9.2. It specifies which container configuration to use for the referring EJB. The link is from a configuration-name element to a `container-name` element. You are able to specify container configurations per class of EJB by including a `container-configuration` element in the EJB definition. Typically, the user does not define completely new container configurations, although this is supported. The typical usage of a `jboss.xml` level `container-configuration` is to override one or more aspects of a `container-configuration` coming from the `standardjboss.xml` descriptor. This is done by first specifying the name of an existing `standardjboss.xml` `container-configuration/container-name` as the value for the EJB `configuration-name` element. The desired `standardjboss.xml` descriptor `container-configuration` elements are then overridden by including a `jboss.xml` `container-configuration` that specifies the elements that are to be overridden. You have already seen an example of this in Chapter 8, "JbossSX—The JBoss Security Extension Framework," when you set up custom RMI socket factories that supported SSL. Listing 9.1 reproduces the `jboss.xml` descriptor that was used to do this.

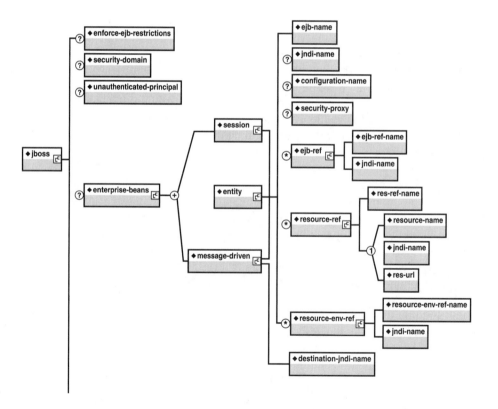

FIGURE 9.1   The jboss.xml descriptor DTD EJB related elements.

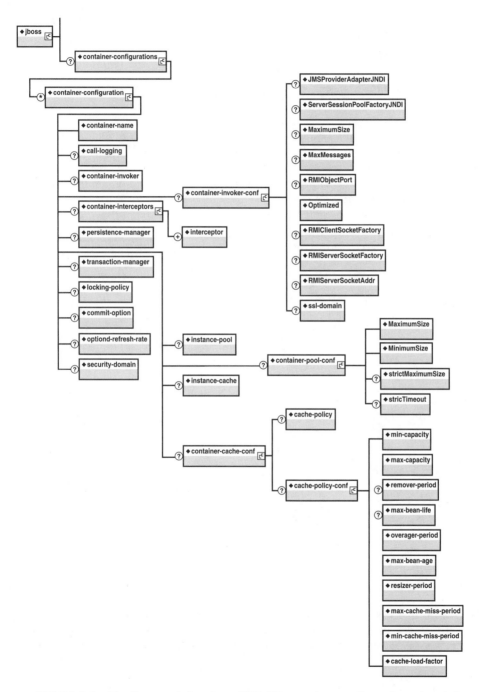

FIGURE 9.2   The jboss.xml descriptor DTD EJB container configuration related elements.

LISTING 9.1   The Chapter 8 `jboss.xml` Container Configuration to Enable SSL with Stateless Session Beans

```
<?xml version="1.0"?>
<jboss>
    <container-configurations>
        <container-configuration>
            <container-name>Standard Stateless SessionBean</container-name>
            <!-- Override the container socket factories -->
            <container-invoker-conf>
                <Optimized>true</Optimized>
                <RMIObjectPort>4445</RMIObjectPort>
                <RMIClientSocketFactory>
                    org.jboss.security.ssl.RMISSLClientSocketFactory
                </RMIClientSocketFactory>
                <RMIServerSocketFactory>
                    org.jboss.security.ssl.RMISSLServerSocketFactory
                </RMIServerSocketFactory>
                <ssl-domain>java:/jaas/RMI+SSL</ssl-domain>
            </container-invoker-conf>
        </container-configuration>
    </container-configurations>
</jboss>
```

The first thing you might notice is that no EJB section containing a `configuration-name` element is present, as per the first step of the procedure just described. For example, you might have expected the following at the start of Listing 9.1:

```
<jboss>
  <enterprise-beans>
    <session>
      <ejb-name>EchoBean</ejb-name>
      <configuration-name>Standard Stateless SessionBean
      </configuration-name>
    </session>
  </enterprise-beans>
  ...
```

The reason that this was not necessary is because you were overriding the EJB's standard container configuration for stateless session beans. The JBoss EJB container factory needs a container configuration when it deploys an EJB. If the EJB has not provided a container configuration specification in the deployment unit ejb-jar, the container factory chooses a container configuration from the `standardjboss.xml` descriptor based on the type of the EJB. So, in reality, there is an implicit `configuration-name` element for every type of EJB, and the mappings from the EJB type to default container configuration name are as follows:

- container-managed persistence entity = Standard CMP EntityBean

- bean-managed persistence entity = Standard BMP EntityBean

- stateless session = Standard Stateless SessionBean

- stateful session = Standard Stateful SessionBean

- message driven = Standard Message Driven Bean

It is not necessary to indicate which container configuration an EJB is using if you are overriding the default for the bean type. It probably provides for a more self-contained descriptor to include the `configuration-name` element, but this is a matter of style.

Now that you know how to specify which container configuration an EJB is using, and that you can define a deployment unit level override, the question is what are all of those `container-configuration` child elements? This question will be addressed element by element in the following sections. A number of the elements specify interface class implementations whose configuration is affected by other elements, so before starting in on the configuration elements you need to understand the `org.jboss.metadata.XmlLoadable` interface.

The `XmlLoadable` interface is a simple interface that consists of a single method. The interface definition is:

```
import org.w3c.dom.Element;
public interface XmlLoadable {
    public void importXml(Element element) throws Exception;
}
```

Classes implement this interface to allow their configuration to be specified via an XML document fragment. The root element of the document fragment is what would be passed to the `importXml` method. You'll see a few examples of this as the container configuration elements are described later in this chapter.

The `container-name` Element

The `container-name` element specifies a unique name for a given configuration. EJBs link to a particular container configuration by setting their `configuration-name` element to the value of the `container-name` for the container configuration.

The `call-logging` Element

The `call-logging` element expects a Boolean (true or false) as its value to indicate whether or not the `LogInterceptor` should log method calls to a container. This is obsolete with the change to log4j, which provides a fine-grained logging API. You'll look at the log4j API in Chapter 11, "Using JBoss."

The `container-invoker` and `container-invoker-conf` Elements

The `container-invoker` element specifies the class name of the `org.jboss.ejb.ContainerInvoker` implementation to use. The `ContainerInvoker` implementation is responsible for receiving remote method invocations for EJBs and forwarding the requests to the EJB container with which it is associated. Basically, the container invoker is the object that exposes a particular method invocation protocol. Currently there are two `ContainerInvoker` implementation choices available—`org.jboss.ejb.plugins.jrmp.server.JRMPContainerInvoker` for RMI/JRMP access to session and entity beans, and `org.jboss.ejb.plugins.jms.JMSContainerInvoker` for JMS access to message driven beans.

The `container-invoker` class is configured using the `container-invoker-conf` element, provided that the class that implements the `ContainerInvoker` interface also implements the `XmlLoadable` interface. If it does, it is simply passed the XML document `container-invoker-conf` element to use as it chooses. The child elements of the `container-invoker-conf` element break down into two groups, which correspond to the two current `ContainerInvoker` implementation classes. For the `JRMPContainerInvoker`, the following `container-invoker-conf` child elements are meaningful:

- `Optimized` controls the bean method call argument and return value copy semantics within the JVM in which JBoss is running. It can take the value true or false. If the value is false, the container will behave per the EJB specification and all method arguments and return values of methods will be passed using RMI copy-by-value semantics, regardless of whether the client is running remotely or in the same VM as the JBoss server. If the value of `Optimized` is true, method arguments and return values will be passed by reference rather than by value. This is much more efficient, and can result in substantial performance improvements; however, it can also result in unexpected behavior if the objects passed to an EJB are stored as instance variables without first making a copy. Similarly, if a method return value is an instance variable of an EJB, a direct reference to the internal state of the EJB is returned and modifications to this value violate the security, transaction, and multi-threaded contract the EJB container provides. Essentially the `Optimized` element allows any bean to behave as an EJB 2.0 local object and all caveats related to pass by reference semantics apply.

- `RMIObjectPort` sets the RMI server socket listening port number. This is the port RMI clients will connect to when communicating through the EJB home interface.

- `RMIClientSocketFactory` specifies a fully qualified class name for the `java.rmi.server.RMIClientSocketFactory` interface to use during export of the EJB home interface.

- `RMIServerSocketFactory` specifies a fully qualified class name for the `java.rmi.server.RMIServerSocketFactory` interface to use during export of the EJB home interface.

- `RMIServerSocketAddr` specifies the interface address that will be used for the RMI server socket listening port. This can be either a DNS hostname or a dot-decimal Internet address. Because the `RMIServerSocketFactory` does not support a method that accepts an `InetAddress` object, this value is passed to the `RMIServerSocketFactory` implementation class using reflection. A check for the existence of a ➥`public void setBindAddress(java.net.InetAddress addr)` ➥ method is made, and if one exists, the `RMIServerSocketAddr` value is passed to the `RMIServerSocketFactory` implementation. If the `RMIServerSocketFactory` implementation does not support such a method, the `RMIServerSocketAddr` value will be ignored.

- `ssl-domain`, specifies the JNDI name of an `org.jboss.security.SecurityDomain` interface implementation to associate with the `RMIServerSocketFactory` implementation. The value will be passed to the `RMIServerSocketFactory` using reflection to locate a method with a signature of `public void setSecurityDomain(org.jboss.security.SecurityDomain d)`. If no such method exists, the `ssl-domain` will be ignored.

For the `JMSContainerInvoker`, the following `container-invoker-conf` child elements are meaningful:

- `JMSProviderAdapterJNDI` specifies the JNDI name of the `org.jboss.jms.jndi.JMSProviderAdapter` implementation to use to set up the JMS layer.

- `ServerSessionPoolFactoryJNDI` specifies the JNDI name of the `org.jboss.jms.asf.ServerSessionPoolFactory` implementation to use for creating the `javax.jms.ServerSessionPool` that will be used to manage the concurrency of the MDBs.

- `MaximumSize` specifies the upper limit to the number of concurrent MDBs that will be allowed for the JMS destination associated with a given MDB deployment. This defaults to 15 if not specified.

- MaxMessages specifies the maxMessages parameter value for the createConnectionConsumer method of javax.jms.QueueConnection and javax.jms.TopicConnection interfaces, as well as the maxMessages parameter value for the createDurableConnectionConsumer method of javax.jms.TopicConnection. It is the maximum number of messages that can be assigned to a server session at one time. This defaults to 1 if not specified. This value should not be modified from the default unless your JMS provider indicates this is supported.

An example of a custom configuration of the JRMPContainerInvoker for stateless session beans was given in Listing 9.1. Listing 9.2 gives an example JMSContainerInvoker configuration to specify an alternate JMS provider and restrict the maximum number of MDBs in a deployment to 1.

LISTING 9.2   An Example `jboss.xml` JMSContainerInvoker Configuration for Message Driven Beans

```
<?xml version="1.0"?>
<jboss>
    <container-configurations>
        <container-configuration>
            <container-name>Standard Message Driven Bean</container-name>
                <container-invoker>org.jboss.ejb.plugins.jms.JMSContainerInvoker
                </container-invoker>
                <container-invoker-conf>
                  <JMSProviderAdapterJNDI>SonicMQProvider</JMSProviderAdapterJNDI>
                  <ServerSessionPoolFactoryJNDI>StdJMSPool
                  </ServerSessionPoolFactoryJNDI>
                  <MaximumSize>1</MaximumSize>
                  <MaxMessages>1</MaxMessages>
                </container-invoker-conf>
        </container-configuration>
    </container-configurations>
</jboss>
```

The `container-interceptors` Element

The container-interceptors element specifies one or more interceptor elements to be configured as the method interceptor chain for the container. The value of the interceptor element is a fully qualified class name of an org.jboss.ejb.Interceptor interface implementation. The container interceptors form a linked list-like structure through which EJB method invocations pass. The first interceptor in the chain is invoked when `ContainerInvoker` passes a method invocation to the container. The last interceptor invokes the business method on the bean. The `Interceptor` interface was covered in detail in Chapter 2 when the container plug-in framework was discussed.

> **NOTE**
>
> Generally, care must be taken when changing an existing standard EJB interceptor configuration because the EJB contract regarding security, transactions, persistence, and thread safety derives from the interceptors. You should have an understanding of the EJB specification as it pertains to the security, transactions, persistence, and thread safety contracts before modifying the `container-interceptors`.

The `instance-pool` and `container-pool-conf` Elements

The `instance-pool` element specifies the fully qualified class name of an `org.jboss.ejb.InstancePool` interface implementation to use as the container `InstancePool`. The `InstancePool` interface was covered in Chapter 2 when the container plug-in framework was discussed. The `container-pool-conf` is passed to the `InstancePool` implementation class given by the `instance-pool` element if it implements `XmlLoadable` interface. All current JBoss `InstancePool` implementations derive from the `org.jboss.ejb.plugins.AbstractInstancePool` class and the `InstancePool` provides support for the `MinimumSize` and `MaximumSize` `container-pool-conf` child elements. The `MinimumSize` element gives the minimum number of instances to keep in the pool, while the `MaximumSize` specifies the maximum number of pool instances that are allowed. The `Synchronized` child element is a true/false flag used by the specialty `org.jboss.ejb.plugins.SingletonStatelessSessionInstancePool` class that supports a single stateless session instance or a singleton pattern. If `Synchronized` is true, only one method invocation thread at a time is allowed to access the singleton session bean. If `Synchronized` is false, the singleton may have multiple method invocation threads active at any given moment and the session bean would have to be coded in a thread-safe manner.

The `instance-cache` and `container-cache-conf` Elements

The `instance-cache` element specifies the fully qualified class name of the `org.jboss.ejb.InstanceCache` interface implementation. This element is only meaningful for entity and stateful session beans as these are the only EJB types that have an associated identity. If you need to review the requirements of the `InstanceCache` implementation see the Chapter 2 discussion on the container plug-in framework.

The `container-cache-conf` element is passed to the `InstanceCache` implementation if it supports the `XmlLoadable` interface. If it does not, the `container-cache-conf` element will silently be ignored. All current JBoss `InstanceCache` implementations derive from the `org.jboss.ejb.plugins.AbstractInstanceCache` class. The `AbstractInstanceCache` implementations provide support for the `XmlLoadable` interface and use the `cache-policy` child element as the fully qualified class name of an `org.jboss.util.CachePolicy` implementation that acts as the instance cache store. The `cache-policy-conf` child element is passed to the `CachePolicy` implementation if it supports the `XmlLoadable` interface. If it does not, the `cache-policy-conf` element will silently be ignored.

There are two JBoss implementations of `CachePolicy` used by the standard`jboss.xml` configuration that support the current array of `cache-policy-conf` child elements. The classes are `org.jboss.ejb.plugins.LRUEnterpriseContextCachePolicy` and `org.jboss.ejb.plugins.LRUStatefulContextCachePolicy`. The `LRUEnterpriseContextCachePolicy` is used by entity bean containers, while the `LRUStatefulContextCachePolicy` is used by stateful session bean containers. Both cache policies implement a least recently used (LRU) policy and support the following `cache-policy-conf` child elements:

- `min-capacity` specifies the minimum capacity in terms of object instances for this cache.

- `max-capacity` specifies the maximum capacity of the cache, in terms of object instances, which cannot be less than `min-capacity`.

- `overager-period` specifies the period in seconds between runs of the overager task. The purpose of the overager task is to see if the cache contains beans with an age greater than the `max-bean-age` element value. Any beans meeting this criterion will be passivated.

- `max-bean-age` specifies the maximum period of inactivity in seconds a bean can have before it will be passivated by the overager process.

- `resizer-period` specifies the period in seconds between runs of the resizer task. The purpose of the resizer task is to contract or expand the cache capacity based on the remaining three element values in the following way. When the resizer task executes, it checks the current period between cache misses; if the period is less than the `min-cache-miss-period` value, the cache is expanded up to the `max-capacity` value using the `cache-load-factor`. If instead the period between cache misses is greater than the `max-cache-miss-period` value, the cache is contracted using the `cache-load-factor`.

- `max-cache-miss-period` specifies the time period in seconds in which a cache miss should signal that the cache capacity be contracted. It is equivalent to the minimum miss rate that will be tolerated before the cache is contracted.

- `min-cache-miss-period` specifies the time period in seconds in which a cache miss should signal that the cache capacity be expanded. It is equivalent to the maximum miss rate that will be tolerated before the cache is expanded.

- `cache-load-factor` specifies the factor by which the cache capacity is contracted and expanded. The factor should be less than 1. When the cache is contracted, the capacity is reduced so that the current ratio of beans to cache capacity is equal to the `cache-load-factor` value. When the cache is expanded, the new capacity is determined as current-capacity * 1/`cache-load-factor`. The actual expansion factor may be as high as 2 based on an internal algorithm that is based on the number of cache misses. The higher the cache miss rate, the closer the true expansion factor will be to 2.

The `LRUStatefulContextCachePolicy` also supports the remaining child elements:

- `remover-period` specifies the period in seconds between runs of the remover task. The remover task removes passivated beans that have not been accessed in more than the `max-bean-life` seconds. This task prevents stateful session beans that were not removed by users from filling up the passivation store.

- `max-bean-life` specifies the maximum period of inactivity in seconds that a bean can exist before being removed from the passivation store.

An alternative cache policy implementation is the `org.jboss.ejb.plugins.NoPassivationCachePolicy` class, which simply never passivates instances. It uses an in-memory HashMap implementation that never discards instances unless they are explicitly removed. This class does not support any of the `cache-policy-conf` configuration elements. You might consider using this policy if you know that you will have large numbers of objects that will fit into memory to avoid unnecessary passivation.

The `persistence-manager` Element

The `persistence-manager` element value specifies the fully qualified class name of the persistence manager implementation. The type of the implementation depends on the type of EJB. For stateful session beans it must be an implementation of the `org.jboss.ejb.StatefulSessionPersistenceManager` interface. For BMP entity beans it must be an implementation of the `org.jboss.ejb.EntityPersistenceManager` interface, while for CMP entity beans it must be an implementation of the `org.jboss.ejb.EntityPersistenceStore` interface.

The `transaction-manager` Element

The `transaction-manager` element is now obsolete and no longer used. The JTA implementation class is now obtained from the well-known JNDI location `"java:/TransactionManager"`.

The `locking-policy` Element

The `locking-policy` element gives the fully qualified class name of the EJB lock implementation to use. This class must implement the `org.jboss.ejb.BeanLock` interface. The current JBoss versions include the following:

- `org.jboss.ejb.plugins.lock.MethodOnlyEJBLock` is an implementation that does not perform any pessimistic transactional locking. It does provide locking for single-threaded non-reentrant beans.

- `org.jboss.ejb.plugins.lock.QueuedPessimisticEJBLock` is an implementation that holds threads awaiting the transactional lock to be freed in a fair FIFO queue. Non-transactional threads are also put into this wait queue as well. Unlike the `SimplePessimisticEJBLock` that notifies all threads on transaction completion, this class pops the next waiting transaction from the queue, and notifies only those waiting threads associated with that transaction. This class should perform better than `SimplePessimisticEJBLock` when contention is high. This implementation is the current default used by the standard configurations.

- `org.jboss.ejb.plugins.lock.SimplePessimisticEJBLock` is an implementation that is similar to `QueuedPessimisticEJBLock`, but threads are simply blocked by waiting on the lock, and are notified using the `notifyAll` broadcast. We have no reason to use `SimplePessimisticEJBLock` instead of `QueuedPessimisticEJBLock`.

The `commit-option` and `optiond-refresh-rate` Element

The `commit-option` value specifies the EJB entity bean persistent storage commit option. It must be one of A, B, C, or D. The meanings of the option values areas follows:

- A—The container caches the bean's state between transactions. This option assumes that the container is the only user accessing the persistent store. This assumption allows the container to synchronize the in-memory state from the persistent storage only when absolutely necessary. This occurs before the first business method executes on a found bean or after the bean is passivated and reactivated to serve another business method. This behavior is independent of whether the business method executes inside a transaction context.

- B—The container caches the bean's state between transactions; however, unlike option A, the container does not assume exclusive access to the persistent store. The container, therefore, will synchronize the in-memory state at the beginning of each transaction. This means that business methods executing in a transaction context don't see much benefit from the container caching the bean, whereas business methods executing outside a transaction context (transaction attributes Never, NotSupported, or Supports) access the cached (and potentially invalid) state of the bean.

- C—The container does not cache bean instances. The in-memory state must be synchronized on every transaction start. For business methods executing outside a transaction, the synchronization is still performed; but the ejbLoad executes in the same transaction context as that of the caller.

- D—This is a JBoss-specific feature that is not described in the EJB specification. It is a lazy read scheme where bean state is cached between transactions as with option A, but the state is periodically resynchronized with that of the persistent store. The time between reloads may be configured using the optiond-refresh-rate element.

The optiond-refresh-rate element can be used to specify the time in seconds between reloads of the state cache maintained when the commit-option value is D. If not specified, the default time between cache reloads is 30 seconds.

The security-domain, role-mapping-manager, and authentication-module Elements

The security-domain element specifies the JNDI name of the object that implements the org.jboss.security.AuthenticationManager and org.jboss.security.RealmMapping interfaces. The role-mapping-manager and authentication-module elements are legacy notions that allowed you to specify the implementations of the AuthenticationManager and RealmMapping independently, but this is no longer supported.

Summary

This chapter focused on the configurable aspects of the JBoss EJB container. The jboss.xml descriptor DTD was presented in its entirety and you were introduced to the jboss.xml and standardjboss.xml descriptor elements that are used to customize the JBoss EJB container behavior.

You next cover how servlet containers are incorporated into JBoss using an abstract MBean integration service.

```
ile:
 [mkdir] Created dir: /tmp/2.4.4/
 [javac] Compiling 154 source fil
install:
 [copy] Copyin
 [copy] Copyin
```

10

Integrating Web Containers

This chapter describes the steps for integrating a third party Web container into the JBoss application server framework. A Web container is a J2EE server component that enables access to servlets and JSP pages. Example servlet containers include Tomcat and Jetty.

Integrating a servlet container into JBoss consists of mapping web-app.xml JNDI information into the JBoss JNDI namespace using an optional jboss-web.xml descriptor as well as delegating authentication and authorization to the JBoss security layer. The org.jboss.web.AbstractWebContainer class exists to simplify these tasks. The focus of the first part of this chapter is how to integrate a Web container using the AbstractWebContainer class. The chapter concludes with a discussion on how to configure the use of secure socket layer (SSL) encryption with the JBoss/Tomcat bundle, as well as how to configure Apache with the JBoss/Tomcat bundle.

The AbstractWebContainer Class

The org.jboss.web.AbstractWebContainer class is an implementation of a template pattern for Web container integration into JBoss. Web container providers that want to integrate their container into a JBoss server should create a subclass of AbstractWebContainer and provide the Web container specific setup and Web application archive (WAR) deployment steps. The AbstractWebContainer provides support for parsing the standard J2EE web.xml Web application deployment descriptor JNDI and security elements as well as support for parsing the JBoss specific jboss-web.xml descriptor. Parsing of these deployment descriptors is performed to generate an integrated JNDI environment and security context. You have already seen the elements of the jboss-web.xml descriptor in previous chapters. Figure 10.1 provides a complete view of the jboss-web.xml descriptor DTD for reference.

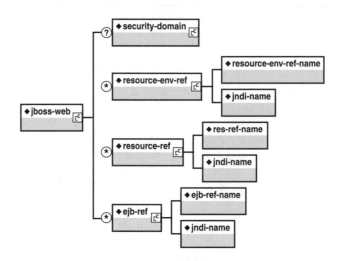

FIGURE 10.1   The complete jboss-web.xml descriptor DTD.

The AbstractWebContainer is an abstract class that implements the org.jboss.web.AbstractWebContainerMBean interface used by the JBoss J2EE deployer to delegate the task of installing WAR files that need to be deployed. Listing 10.1 presents some of the key AbstractWebContainer methods.

LISTING 10.1   Key Methods of the AbstractWebContainer Class

```
1:public abstract class AbstractWebContainer
2:    extends ServiceMBeanSupport
3:    implements AbstractWebContainerMBean
4:{
5:    public static interface WebDescriptorParser
6:    {
7:        public void parseWebAppDescriptors(ClassLoader loader,
8:            Element webApp, Element jbossWeb) throws Exception;
9:    }
10:
11:    public void setConfig(Element config)
12:    {
```

LISTING 10.1   Continued

```
13:      ...
14:    }
15
16:    public synchronized void deploy(String ctxPath, String warUrl)
17:       throws DeploymentException
18:    {
19:       Thread thread = Thread.currentThread();
20:       ClassLoader appClassLoader = thread.getContextClassLoader();
21:       // Create a classloader for the war to ensure a unique ENC
22:       URL[] empty = {};
23:       URLClassLoader warLoader = URLClassLoader.newInstance(empty,
24:          appClassLoader);
25:       thread.setContextClassLoader(warLoader);
26:       WebDescriptorParser webAppParser = new DescriptorParser();
27:       WebApplication warInfo = performDeploy(ctxPath, warUrl,
28:          webAppParser);
29:       deploymentMap.put(warUrl, warInfo);
30:       thread.setContextClassLoader(appClassLoader);
31:    }
32
33:    protected abstract WebApplication performDeploy(String ctxPath,
34:       String warUrl, WebDescriptorParser webAppParser)
35:       throws Exception;
36
37:    public synchronized void undeploy(String warUrl)
38:       throws DeploymentException
39:    {
40:       performUndeploy(warUrl);
41:       // Remove the web Web application ENC...
42:       deploymentMap.remove(warUrl);
43:    }
44
45:    protected abstract void performUndeploy(String warUrl)
46:       throws Exception;
47
48:    public WebApplication getDeployedApp(String warUrl)
49:    {
50:       WebApplication appInfo = (WebApplication) deploymentMap.get(warUrl);
51:       return appInfo;
52:    }
53
```

LISTING 10.1   Continued

```
54:   public Iterator getDeployedApplications()
55:   {
56:      return deploymentMap.values().iterator();
57:   }
58:
59:   protected void parseWebAppDescriptors(ClassLoader loader,
60:      Element webApp, Element jbossWeb) throws Exception
61:   {
62:      ...
63:      addEnvEntries(...);
64:      linkResourceEnvRefs(...);
65:      linkResourceRefs(...);
66:      linkEjbRefs(...);
67:      linkSecurityDomain(...);
68:   }
69:
70:   protected void addEnvEntries(Iterator envEntries, Context envCtx)
71:      throws ClassNotFoundException, NamingException
72:   {
73:      ...
74:   }
75:
76:   protected void linkResourceEnvRefs(Iterator resourceRefs, Context envCtx)
77:      throws NamingException
78:   {
79:      ...
80:   }
81:
82:   protected void linkResourceRefs(Iterator resourceRefs, Context envCtx)
83:      throws NamingException
84:   {
85:      ...
86:   }
87:
88:   protected void linkEjbRefs(Iterator ejbRefs, Context envCtx)
89:      throws NamingException
90:   {
91:      ...
92:   }
93:
```

LISTING 10.1 Continued

```
94:    protected void linkSecurityDomain(String securityDomain, Context envCtx)
95:       throws NamingException
96:    {
97:       ...
98:    }
99:}
```

Lines 11-14 correspond to the setConfig method. This method is a stub method that subclasses can override if they want to support an arbitrary extended configuration beyond that which is possible through MBean attributes. The config argument is the parent DOM element for an arbitrary hierarchy given by the child element of the Config attribute in the mbean element specification of the jboss.jcml file. You'll see an example use of this method and config value when you look at the MBean that supports embedding Tomcat into JBoss.

Lines 16-31 correspond to the deploy method. This method is a template pattern method implementation. The arguments to the deploy method include ctxPath, which is the context-root element value from the J2EE application.xml descriptor. This may be null if the war is being deployed outside of an EAR(enterprise application archive). The warUrl argument is the URL string to the WAR that is to be deployed.

The first step of the deploy method is to save the current thread context ClassLoader and then create another URLClassCloader (warLoader) using the saved ClassLoader as its parent. This warLoader is used to ensure a unique JNDI ENC (enterprise naming context) for the WAR will be created. This is done by the code on lines 19-24. Chapter 3, "JBossNS—The JBoss Naming Service," mentioned that the java:comp context's uniqueness was determined by the ClassLoader that created the java:comp context. The warLoader ClassLoader is set as the current thread context ClassLoader before the performDeploy call is made on line 25. Next, the Web container-specific subclass is asked to perform the actual deployment of the WAR through the performDeploy call on line 26. The returned WebApplication object is stored in the deployed application map using the warUrl as the key on line 29. The final step at line 30 is to restore the thread context ClassLoader to the one that existed at the start of the method.

Lines 33-35 give the signature for the abstract performDeploy method. This method is called by the deploy method and must be overridden by subclasses to perform the Web container specific deployment steps. A WebApplication object must be returned that contains the Web application class loader, web.xml web-app document element, and the jboss-web.xml jboss-web document element provided that a jboss-web.xml descriptor existed in the WAR. The ctxPath argument is the context-root element value for the Web module from the J2EE application.xml descriptor. This may be null if the WAR is not being deployed as part of an enterprise application. The warUrl argument is the string for the URL of the Web application WAR to deploy. The webAppParser argument is a callback handle the subclass must use to invoke the parseWebAppDescriptors method to set up the Web application JNDI environment. This callback provides a hook for the subclass to establish the Web application JNDI environment before any servlets are created that are to be loaded on startup of the WAR. A subclass' performDeploy method implementation needs to be arranged so that it can call the parseWebAppDescriptors before starting any servlets that need to access JNDI for JBoss resources like EJBs, resource factories, and so on. One important setup detail that needs to be handled by a subclass implementation is to use the current thread context ClassLoader as the parent ClassLoader for any Web container-specific ClassLoader created. Failure to do this results in problems for Web applications that attempt to access EJBs or JBoss resources through the JNDI ENC.

Lines 37-43 correspond to the undeploy method. This is a template pattern method implementation. Line 40 of this method calls the subclass performUndeploy method to perform the container-specific undeployment steps. Next, at line 42, the warUrl is unregistered from the deployment map. The warUrl argument is the string URL of the WAR as originally passed to the deploy method.

Lines 45-46 give the signature of the abstract performUndeploy method. This method is called as part of the undeploy() method template as shown on line 40. A call to performUndeploy asks the subclass to perform the Web container-specific undeployment steps.

Lines 59-68 correspond to the parseWebAppDescriptors method. This is invoked from within the subclass performDeploy method when it invokes the webAppParser.parseWebAppDescriptors callback to parse the web-app.xml and jboss-web.xml deployment descriptors for the WAR deployment. The method creates the Web application ENC (java:comp/env) env-entry, resource-env-ref, resource-ref, and ejb-ref element values declared in the web.xml descriptor. The creation of the env-entry values does not require a jboss-web.xml descriptor. The creation of the resource-env-ref, resource-ref, and ejb-ref elements does require a jboss-web.xml descriptor for the JNDI name of the deployed resources/EJBs. Because the ENC context is private to the Web application, the Web application ClassLoader is used to identify the ENC. The loader argument is the ClassLoader for the Web application, and may not be null. The webApp argument is the root web-app element of the web.xml descriptor and may not be null. The jbossWeb argument is the root jboss-web element of the jboss-web.xml descriptor, and may be null to indicate that no jboss-web.xml descriptor exists in the WAR. The implementation of the parseWebAppDescriptors obtains the meta-data objects from the WAR deployment descriptors and then creates the JNDI ENC bindings by calling methods shown on lines 63-67.

The addEnvEntries method on lines 70-74 creates the java:comp/env Web application env-entry bindings that were specified in the web.xml descriptor.

The linkResourceEnvRefs method on lines 76-80 maps the java:comp/env/xxx Web application JNDI ENC resource-env-ref web.xml descriptor elements onto the deployed JNDI names using the mappings specified in the jboss-web.xml descriptor.

The linkResourceRefs method on lines 82-86 maps the java:comp/env/xxx Web application JNDI ENC resource-ref web.xml descriptor elements onto the deployed JNDI names using the mappings specified in the jboss-web.xml descriptor.

The linkEjbRefs method on lines 88-92 maps the java:comp/env/ejb Web application JNDI ENC ejb-ref web.xml descriptor elements onto the deployed JNDI names using the mappings specified in the jboss-web.xml descriptor.

The linkSecurityDomain method on lines 94-98 creates a java:comp/env/security context that contains a securityMgr binding pointing to the AuthenticationManager implementation and a realmMapping binding pointing to the RealmMapping implementation that is associated with the security domain for the Web application. Also created is a subject binding that provides dynamic access to the authenticated Subject associated with the request thread. If the jboss-web.xml descriptor contained a security-domain element, the bindings are javax.naming.LinkRefs to the JNDI name specified by the security-domain element, or subcontexts of this name. If there was no security-domain element, the bindings are to org.jboss.security.plugins.NullSecurityManager instance that simply allows all authentication and authorization checks.

Creating an AbstractWebContainer Subclass

To integrate a Web container into JBoss, you need to create a subclass of AbstractWebContainer and implement the required performDeploy(String, String, WebDescriptorParser) and performUndeploy(String) methods as described in the preceding section. The following additional integration points should be considered as well.

Using the Thread Context Class Loader

Although this issue was noted in the performDeploy method description, it is repeated here because it is such a critical detail. During the setup of a WAR container, the current thread context ClassLoader must be used as the parent ClassLoader for any Web container-specific ClassLoader that is created. Failure to do this results in problems for Web applications that attempt to access EJBs or JBoss resources through the JNDI ENC. The problems range from JNDI naming exceptions concerning missing bindings, java:comp/env for example, to java.lang.ClassNotFoundExceptions or java.lang.ClassCastExceptions depending on whether or not the EJBs are bundled with the WAR.

Integrating Logging Using log4j

JBoss uses the Apache log4j logging API as its internal logging API. For a Web container to integrate well with JBoss, it needs to provide a mapping between the Web container logging abstraction to the log4j API. As a subclass of `AbstractWebContainer`, the integration class has access to the log4j interface via the `super.log` instance variable or equivalently, the superclass `getLog` method. This is an instance of the `org.jboss.logging.Logger` class that wraps the log4j category. The name of the log4j category is the name of the container subclass.

Delegating Web Container Authentication and Authorization to JBossSX

Ideally, both Web application as well as EJB authentication and authorization are handled by the same security manager. To enable this for your Web container, you must hook into the JBoss security layer. This typically requires a request interceptor that maps from the Web container security callouts to the JBoss security API. Integration with the JBossSX security framework is based on the establishment of a java:comp/env/security context as described in the `linkSecurityDomain` method comments in the section, "The AbstractWebContainer Class." The security context provides access to the JBossSX security manager interface implementations associated with the Web application for use by subclass request interceptors. An outline of the steps for authenticating a user using the security context is presented in Listing 10.2 in quasi psuedo-code. Listing 10.3 provides the equivalent process for the authorization of a user.

LISTING 10.2   A Psuedo-Code Description of Authenticating a User Via the JBossSX API and the java:comp/env/security JNDI Context

```
// Get the username and password from the request context...
HttpServletRequest request = ...;
String username = getUsername(request);
String password = getPassword(request);
// Get the JBoss security manager from the ENC context
InitialContext iniCtx = new InitialContext();
AuthenticationManager securityMgr = (AuthenticationManager)
    iniCtx.lookup("java:comp/env/security/securityMgr");
SimplePrincipal principal = new SimplePrincipal(username);
if( securityMgr.isValid(principal, password) )
{
    // Indicate the user is allowed access to the Web content...
    // Propagate the user info to JBoss for any calls into made by the servlet
    SecurityAssociation.setPrincipal(principal);
    SecurityAssociation.setCredential(password.toCharArray());
}
else
```

LISTING 10.2   Continued

```
{
    // Deny access...
}
```

The `SecurityAssociation.setPrincipal` and `SecurityAssociation.setCredential` methods assign their respective argument to thread local variables for the current thread. This information remains a property of the thread until it is explicitly cleared or reset. Also, these variables are not currently protected with Java2 security permissions so access to the current principal and their credentials are available to anyone who knows where to look. The next release of JBoss will introduce additional Java2 permission checks to allow access to these thread local variables to be restricted.

LISTING 10.3   A Psuedo-Code Description of Authorization a User Via the JBossSX API and the java:comp/env/security JNDI Context

```
// Get the username and required roles from the request context...
HttpServletRequest request = ...;
String username = getUsername(request);
String[] roles = getContentRoles(request);
// Get the JBoss security manager from the ENC context
InitialContext iniCtx = new InitialContext();
RealmMapping securityMgr = (RealmMapping)
    iniCtx.lookup("java:comp/env/security/realmMapping");
SimplePrincipal principal = new SimplePrincipal(username);
Set requiredRoles = new HashSet(java.util.Arrays.asList(roles));
if( securityMgr.doesUserHaveRole(principal, requiredRoles) )
{
    // Indicate user has the required roles for the Web content...
}
else
{
    // Deny access...
}
```

JBoss/Tomcat-4.x Bundle Notes

This section discusses configuration issues specific to the JBoss/Tomcat-4.x integration bundle. At the time of this writing, the Tomcat-4.x release, also known by the name Catalina, is the latest Apache Java servlet container. It supports the Servlet 2.3/JSP 1.2 specifications. The JBoss/Tomcat integration layer is undergoing changes to provide better integration and control through the MBean service that embeds Tomcat into JBoss. This is a move away from supporting the external Tomcat server.xml configuration file.

The MBean used to embed the Tomcat-4.x series of Web containers is the `org.jboss.web.catalina.EmbeddedCatalinaServiceSX` service. It is a subclass of the `AbstractWebContainer` class. Its configurable attributes include the following:

- Port sets the listening port number for the primary Catalina HTTP connector. A value of 0 indicates that any available port should be used. This defaults to 8080.

- BindAddress sets the specific network address for the primary Catalina HTTP connector. This can be used on a multi-homed host to establish a server socket that will only accept connect requests on one of its addresses. This defaults to all available addresses.

- EngineClass sets the class name of the server container engine class, which must be an implementation of the `org.apache.Catalina.Engine` interface. This defaults to `org.apache.catalina.core.StandardEngine`.

- AcceptCount sets the primary Catalina HTTP connector listening port backlog limit. This defaults to 10.

- MinProcessors sets the minimum number of HTTP request processors to start on initialization. This defaults to 5.

- MaxProcessors sets the maximum number of HTTP request processors allowed. If this is < 0, an unlimited number of processors are allowed. This defaults to 20.

- EnableLookups sets the enable DNS lookups flag. This affects the RemoteHost HttpServletRequest property value. If EnableLookups is true, the requesting hostname is resolved using a DNS address to hostname lookup. If EnableLookups is false, the requesting hostname is left as a dot-decimal address. This defaults to false.

- SecurityDomain sets the JNDI name of the `org.jboss.security.SecurityDomain` implementation to use for JSSE enabled SSL. There is no default value.

- ConnectorType sets the type of the primary connector. Currently only http and warp are supported. Additional connectors may be set through the Config attribute of the MBean configuration.

- Config an attribute that provides support for extended configuration using constructs from the standard Tomcat server.xml file to specify additional connectors, and so on. The current support for the type of configuration that can be specified includes the Catalina server.xml Server/Service/Connector and its child elements. You'll see examples of using this feature to enable SSL and the Apache AJP 1.3 Connector in the following sections.

Using SSL With the JBoss/Tomcat Bundle

There are three ways you can configure HTTP over SSL for the embedded Tomcat servlet container. If you want to only allow access over SSL encrypted connections, you can configure the primary connector using the EmbeddedCatalinaServiceSX SecurityDomain attribute. Set the SecurityDomain attribute to the JNDI name of the org.jboss.security.SecurityDomain implementation from which JSSE should obtain the SSL KeyStore. This requires establishing a SecurityDomain using the org.jboss.security.plugins.JaasSecurityDomain MBean. These two steps are similar to the procedure used in Chapter 8, "JbossSX—The JBoss Security Extension Framework," to enable RMI with SSL encryption. A jboss.jcml configuration file fragment that illustrates the setup of SSL via this approach, and which uses the same JaasSecurityDomain setup as Chapter 8, is given in Listing 10.4.

LISTING 10.4   The JaasSecurityDoman and EmbeddedCatalinaSX MBean Configurations for Setting up Tomcat-4.x to Use SSL as Its Primary Connector Protocol

```
<server>
...
 <!— The SSL domain setup —>
 <mbean code="org.jboss.security.plugins.JaasSecurityDomain"
     name="Security:name=JaasSecurityDomain,domain=RMI+SSL">
   <constructor>
      <arg type="java.lang.String" value="RMI+SSL"/>
   </constructor>
   <attribute name="KeyStoreURL">chap8.keystore</attribute>
   <attribute name="KeyStorePass">rmi+ssl</attribute>
 </mbean>
...
  <!— The embedded Tomcat-4.x setup with a single SSL HTTP
    connector enabled —>
  <mbean code="org.jboss.web.catalina.EmbeddedCatalinaServiceSX"
      name="DefaultDomain:service=EmbeddedTomcat">
   <attribute name="Port">8443</attribute>
   <attribute name="SecurityDomain">java:/jaas/RMI+SSL</attribute>
  </mbean>
</server>
```

Alternatively, if you want to support both access using non-SSL and SSL, you can do this by adding a Connector configuration to the EmbeddedCatalinaSX MBean. This can be done as documented in the Catalina SSL-HowTo available on the Apache Web site at http://jakarta.apache.org/tomcat/tomcat-4.0-doc/ssl-howto.html, or by using a JBoss specific connector socket factory that allows you to obtain the JSSE server certificate information from a JBossSX SecurityDomain. A jboss.jcml configuration file fragment that illustrates the setup of SSL using the latter approach is given in Listing 10.5.

LISTING 10.5   The JaasSecurityDoman and EmbeddedCatalinaSX MBean Configurations for Setting Up Tomcat-4.x to Use Both Non-SSL and SSL enabled HTTP Connectors

```
<server>
...
 <!— The SSL domain setup —>
 <mbean code="org.jboss.security.plugins.JaasSecurityDomain"
     name="Security:name=JaasSecurityDomain,domain=RMI+SSL">
   <constructor>
      <arg type="java.lang.String" value="RMI+SSL"/>
   </constructor>
   <attribute name="KeyStoreURL">chap8.keystore</attribute>
   <attribute name="KeyStorePass">rmi+ssl</attribute>
 </mbean>
...
  <!— The embedded Tomcat-4.x setup with non-SSL and SSL HTTP
    connectors enabled —>
  <mbean code="org.jboss.web.catalina.EmbeddedCatalinaServiceSX"
      name="DefaultDomain:service=EmbeddedTomcat">
    <attribute name="Config">
      <Connector
className="org.apache.catalina.connector.http.HttpConnector"
          port="8443" minProcessors="5" maxProcessors="75"
          enableLookups="true"
          acceptCount="10" scheme="https" secure="true">
        <Factory
className="org.jboss.web.catalina.security.SSLServerSocketFactory"
            securityDomainName="java:/jaas/RMI+SSL"/>
      </Connector>
    </attribute>
  </mbean>
</server>
```

All approaches work, so what you choose is a matter of preference. Note that if you try to test this configuration using the self-signed certificate from the Chapter 8—chap8.keystore—and attempt to access content over an https connection, your browser will likely display a warning dialog box indicating that it does not trust the certificate authority that signed the certificate of the server to which you are connecting. For example, when the first configuration example was tested, Internet Explorer (IE) 5.5 displays the initial Security Alert dialog box shown in Figure 10.2. Click Yes to open the Certificate dialog box and the General tab as shown in Figure 10.3. This is the expected behavior because anyone can generate a self-signed certificate with any information she wants, and a Web browser should warn when such a secure site is encountered.

FIGURE 10.2   The Internet Explorer 5.5 Security Alert dialog box.

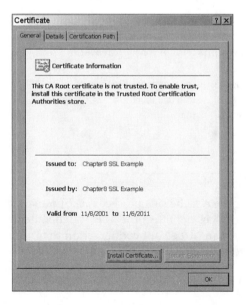

FIGURE 10.3   The Internet Explorer 5.5 SSL Certificate dialog box.

Using Apache With the JBoss/Tomcat-4.x Bundle

Apache is an Open Source Web server that is widely used and available on numerous platforms. Apache has no inherent support for Java servlets, so it is often used in combination with Tomcat. Apache has a modular architecture that you can customize. One of the available customization modules is a connector module called mod_jk. It allows Apache to delegate servlet and JSP page requests to a Tomcat Web container.

NOTE

Binaries and source code for Apache can be obtained from the Apache home page at http://www.apache.org/.

To enable the use of Apache as a front-end Web server that delegates servlet requests to a JBoss/Tomcat bundle, you need to configure an appropriate connector in the EmbeddedCatalinaSX MBean definition. For example, to configure the use of the Ajpv13 protocol connector with the Apache mod_jk module, you would use a configuration such as that given in Listing 10.6.

LISTING 10.6   An Example EmbeddedCatalinaSX MBean Configuration that Supports Integration with Apache Using the Ajpv13 Protocol Connector

```
<server>
...
  <!— The embedded Tomcat-4.x setup with AJP13 connector —>
  <mbean code="org.jboss.web.catalina.EmbeddedCatalinaServiceSX"
      name="DefaultDomain:service=EmbeddedTomcat">
   <attribute name="Config">
      <Connector className="org.apache.ajp.tomcat4.Ajp13Connector"
            port="8009" minProcessors="5" maxProcessors="75"
            acceptCount="10" />
   </attribute>
  </mbean>
</server>
```

The configuration of the Apache side proceeds as it normally would—bundling Tomcat inside of JBoss does not affect the how Apache interacts with Tomcat. For example, a fragment of an httpd.conf configuration to test the Listing 10.6 setup might look similar to the following:

```
...
LoadModule    jk_module    libexec/mod_jk.so
AddModule     mod_jk.c
```

```
<IfModule mod_jk.c>
    JkWorkersFile /tmp/workers.properties
    JkLogFile     /tmp/mod_jk.log
    JkLogLevel    debug
    JkMount       /jbosstest/* ajp13
</IfModule>
```

Other Apache to Tomcat configurations would follow the same pattern. All that would change is the Connector element definition placed into the EmbeddedCatalinaSX MBean configuration.

Summary

In this chapter you learned about the Web container integration layer JBoss provides. The focus was on the AbstractWebContainer MBean service and how you would subclass it to integrate any Web container you choose. The JBoss/Tomcat-4.x bundle was also discussed. You were shown the configuration of the EmeddedCatalinaSX MBean in addition to how to use SSL and Apache with the the Tomcat-4.x Web container when it is embedded into the JBoss server.

The following chapter examines JBoss from the perspective of running enterprise applications and then goes through the steps required to deploy non-trivial applications.

ile:
[mkdir] Created dir: /tmp/2.4.4/
[javac] Compiling 154 source file
install:
[copy] Copyin   p/2.
[copy] Copyin   p/2

11

Using JBoss

- Building and Running Enterprise Applications with JBoss

- Migrating the Java Pet Store 1.1.2 Application to JBoss

- Using the JBossTest Unit Test Suite

Until this point the focus of this book has been largely on the architecture and configuration of the various JBoss server components. The focus of this chapter switches to running J2EE applications using JBoss. The chapter starts with a discussion of a sample mail management application, then dicusses porting the J2EE blueprints 1.1.2 Java Pet Store application to JBoss, and concludes by covering the JBossTest unit test suite.

Building and Running Enterprise Applications with JBoss

This section goes through the details of creating an e-mail forwarding application that uses a number of J2EE components as well as a custom MBean service. This provides a detailed example of building, configuring, and deploying a non-trivial application under JBoss. The concept of the application is to monitor an IMAP mail account for new mail that matches a set of criteria, and applies a new mail action to the matching messages. The implementation that is discussed simply forwards an abbreviated transcript of any new mail messages to another e-mail address through an SMTP gateway using JavaMail. for example, this allows a traveling user to receive text message summaries of new e-mail on their cell phone.

An overview of the e-mail forwarding application architecture is given in Figure 11.1.

NOTE

The source code for the application is located in the
src/main/org/jboss/chap11 directory of the book examples on the CD.

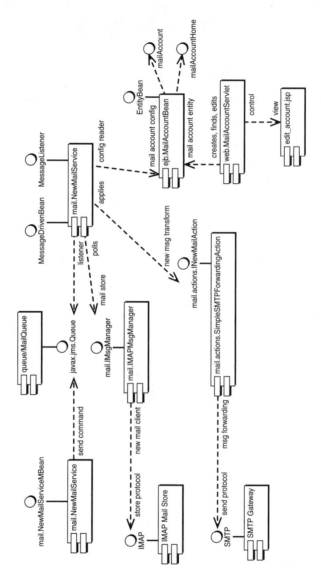

FIGURE 11.1   An overview of the e-mail forwarding application architecture.

Starting with the `NewMailService`, this is a custom MBean that acts as a new mail check command generator. It sends a JMS message to the queue/MailQueue destination at a timed interval specified by one of its attributes. The `MailHandlerMDB` is the listener of the queue/MailQueue destination. On receipt of a new mail check command message, the `MailHandlerMDB` queries for all `MailAccounts` that are due for a check of their IMAP mail stores for new messages. For each `MailAccount` instance that needs a new mail check, the `MailHandlerMDB` creates a `javax.mail.Session` and `javax.mail.Store` using the account information. The `MailHandlerMDB` then polls the mail store for new messages using an `IMsgManager` instance. The check for new messages includes any search criterion filter associated with the `INewMailAction` for the `MailAccount`. If new messages exist, the `INewMailAction` is then invoked to apply its action logic to the matching messages.

For this example application, the implementation of `INewMailAction` is called `SimpleSMTPFowardingAction`. The `SimpleSMTPFowardingAction` takes any messages that match the search filter that has been associated with the action, and creates a summary text message that includes two lines per message. The two lines are the message sender's e-mail address and the message subject. This summary text message is then forwarded to the action forwarding e-mail address using the action SMTP gateway server property.

The purpose of the `IMsgManager` abstraction is to hide the mechanism by which new messages are identified in a mail store. Different mail store protocols have varying levels of support for determining new mail messages. For example, IMAP(Internet message access protocol version 4) has direct support for the notion of new messages, while POP3(post office protocol version 3) does not. Therefore, an abstraction above the mail store is necessary to allow for the identification of new mail messages, and the `IMsgManager` interface provides this abstraction. An implementation of the `IMsgManager` interface access the associated mail store using the JavaMail APIs. This is combined with mail store-specific logic to support identification of new mail messages. The `IMsgManager` interface supports limiting the set new mail messages to messages that match a search criterion. For example, you may only want to be notified of new mail from a particular user, or of mail that contains certain key words in the subject.

The management of `MailAccount` entity beans is the function of the `MailAccountServlet`. The `MailAccountServlet` provides a Web interface that allows users to create, find, and edit mail forwarding account information. The MailAccountServlet uses the edit_account.jsp JSP page as the view for displaying the create, find, and edit operation data. The edit_account.jsp page simply translates the account data into an HTML form. It is a simple model/view/control pattern implementation where the `MailAccount` entity bean serves as the model data, the `MailAccountServlet` is the controller, and the edit_account.jsp page serves as the application view.

One question you may be asking is why use a message driven bean (MDB) instead of a stateless session bean. There are two reasons. The first is that this demonstrates the utility of message driven beans as a mechanism for loose coupling between services. A common problem users face is how to package a custom MBean service with one more EJB from an enterprise application. The problem is that MBean services are loaded using the JBoss server application main class loader, and EJBs are loaded using a class loader that delegates to the main class loader. For an MBean to be a client of an EJB, the MBean must have access to the home and remote interfaces of the EJB. This means that these classes must be available to the main class loader. You can split up the EJB jar to place its client-facing classes into a separate jar that is made available to the main class loader, but this can prevent redeployment of the EJBs. Sometimes this limitation is acceptable, and sometimes it is not. If it is not acceptable, one way around the problem is to introduce a weakly typed coupling between the service and the EJBs. Using JMS to drive an MDB in a command pattern is one way to do this. Another method would be to generate a SOAP message and send this to a servlet that also implemented a command pattern. This would require more setup than the MDB approach as SOAP is not supported by the default JBoss distributions.

The second reason for using an MDB is scalability. If you were to offer a mail forwarding service based on this application, you could find yourself needing to manage many client accounts. Checking for new mail is a relatively slow operation, and you would need to employ many servers to handle large numbers of clients. This can be done easily with JMS even in the absence of support for clustering by JBoss. One way to do this would be to configure several JBoss servers running JMS with the `MailHandlerMDB` deployed in each server. Each server would use a slightly different deployment descriptor for the `MailHandlerMDB` jar that varied in its topic message selector. Another JBoss server would serve as the master that runs the custom `NewMailService` MBean. When the `NewMailService` awakens to send the new mail message command, it would create several JMS messages that specified a range of user accounts to poll. These messages would then be sent to a JMS topic and be distributed to the various JBoss servers where the `MailHandlerMDB`s are deployed. This is an example of using the JMS topic one-to-many message distribution model to achieve a simple clustering implementation.

The MailAccount, MailHandlerMDB and NewMailService Component Details

With a broad overview and rational for the type of architecture used for the mail forwarding application behind you, you can now look at the three main components in more detail.

Figure 11.2 presents a class diagram of the `MailAccount` CMP entity bean, its home and remote interfaces, and the `AccountInfo` bulk data accessor object. The

MailAccount bean is a rather trivial persistent view of mail account information for a user. A simple CMP persistence model works well here because you have no interest in a relational view of the account information.

The CMP fields of the MailAccount bean are as follows:

- mailServer—The account mail server where messages are stored.

- mailProtocol—The protocol used by the mail server. Only IMAP is supported in this version of the application.

- mailProtocolPort—The port number on which the mail server is listening, if not the default for the protocol.

- mailFolders—A list of mail folder names for the account. If null, all subscribed folders will be used.

- username—The user name to use when accessing the mail server.

- password—The password for username on the mail server.

- emailAddress—The e-mail address associated with username. This is used as the from e-mail address on forwarded messages.

- checkFrequency—The mail check frequency in seconds. This can only extend the interval between checks for new mail. An account is checked at the maximum of the periods of the NewMailService MBean and the account specified period.

- newMailAction—The mail action is the action that is applied to any new mail messages. The action may include a javax.mail.search.SearchTerm that further filters new mail for arbitrary criteria, such as who sent the mail, keywords in the subject, and so on. The current version of the application only supports the use of the SimpleSMTPFowardingAction described earlier.

- nextExpirationCheck—The time at which the account should next be checked for new messages. The units of the nextExpirationCheck field are the same as the System.currentTimeMillis method value, milliseconds, between the current time and midnight, January 1, 1970 UTC.

The only methods of the remote interface are the bulk setter and getter of the MailAccount fields in the form of the AccountInfo object, and the setNextExpirationCheck method that updates the next time at which the account should be checked for new mail. The home interface defines the required findByPrimaryKey finder that locates a MailAccount by the username field. It also defines two custom finders that allow you to locate MailAccounts by nextExpirationCheck values in a given range as well as by nextExpirationCheck and username range. The current version of the application only uses the findByNewMsgExpiration(begin, end) form of the custom finder.

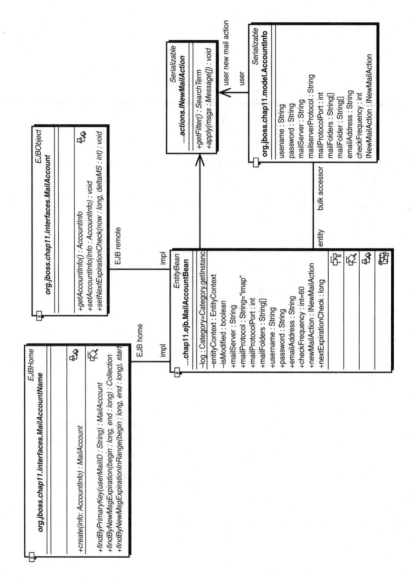

FIGURE 11.2   The MailAccount CMP entity bean and the AccountInfo bulk accessor representation classes.

Figure 11.3 presents the `MailHandlerMDB` class and the classes with which it directly interacts. The `MailHandlerMDB` is driven by JMS messages sent to the JMS queue to which the MDB listens. The `onMessage` method looks for a command property and invokes the dispatch method with the name of the command and the message. In the current application the only command that is handled is a request to check for new messages. The logic for this command handler is coded in the MDB as the `checkForNewMsgs` method. A more flexible implementation of the MDB command pattern would externalize this logic using a stateless session bean to allow the command dispatch logic to be separated from the command implementation.

The `checkForNewMsgs` method queries for all `MailAccount` instances with `nextExpirationCheck` values that lie between the current time and the last time `onMessage` method was invoked by querying the `MailAccountHome` interface `findByNewMsgExpiration` finder. For all accounts meeting this criterion, the `AccountInfo` data is obtained and the `checkForNewMsg(AccountInfo)` method called to poll the associated account mail store. After opening the account mail store, an `IMsgManager` instance for the mail store protocol is obtained by doing a lookup against the `java:comp/env/mail/IMsgManager` context with a subcontext name equal to the protocol name as specified by the account information. You'll see that the `NewMailService` is responsible for installing a protocol-based factory to support this. The `IMsgManager` instance is initialized with mail store default folder and any folder names from the account info. A lightweight check (how lightweight depends on the mail store protocol) for new messages is performed by invoking the `IMsgManager.hasNewMessages` method. If the mail store indicates that new messages are present, a query for all news messages contained in the specified folders that also meet the search criterion associated with account `INewMailAction` is performed using the `IMsgManager.getNewMessage(SearchTerm)` method. Any messages returned are delegated to the account `INewMailAction.apply(Message[])` method. All connections to the mail store are then closed.

On return from the `checkForNewMsg(AccountInfo)` method, either due to a normal completion of the method or a failure due to an exception, the `MailAccount` `nextExpirationCheck` value is updated to the next scheduled check. Note that this could mean that new messages will be missed. An attempt could be made to make this as robust as possible, but in general, in the absence of a JCA connector for the mail store, the new message check is not part of the MDB JMS transaction and because of this cannot be made 100% reliable. This is usually acceptable as mail is a somewhat unreliable protocol that lacks guaranteed message delivery semantics.

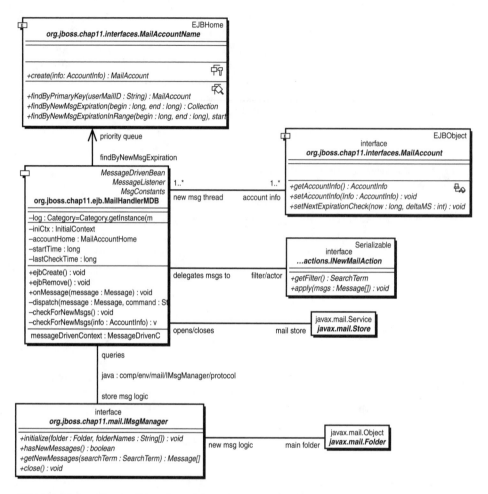

FIGURE 11.3   The MailHandlerMDB and associated classes.

The final major component from the application is the `NewMailService` MBean. The class diagram for the `NewMailService` is show in Figure 11.4. The `NewMailService` is responsible for driving the processing of the new mail message checks and binding the implementation of the `IMsgManager` interface for each supported mail store protocol into JNDI. In the current application implementation, the task of driving the `MailHandlerMDB` processing is a trivial timer-based task that uses the `java.util.Timer` and `java.util.TimedTask` classes. The logic behind this task could be considerably more complicated, and could entail partitioning the client accounts into ranges for distributed processing by a cluster of `MailHandlerMDB` deployments listening to a JMS topic.

The mechanism for providing implementations of the `IMsgManager` interface for each supported mail store protocol is a custom JNDI `ObjectFactory` binding under java:/IMsgManager. The `IMsgManagerObjectFactory` provides the `ObjectFactory` implementation that supports this. This is a common pattern that allows a custom service to provide either a static or dynamic implementation of an interface to a J2EE component. It works well because of the standardized ENC notion supported by all J2EE components. An application assembler defines a link to a resource factory or resource environment reference that is linked to the actual context that supports the desired object by the application deployer using a JBoss server deployment descriptor. The `IMsgManagerObjectFactory` is an example that allows the use of the java:/IMsgManager context as a dynamic factory for `IMsgManager` instances based on the mail store protocol. The usage construct is that one performs a lookup against the java:/IMsgManager context for a binding using the name of the desired protocol. When the java:/IMsgManager context is accessed, the `IMsgManagerObjectFactory.getObjectInstance` method is invoked by the JNDI framework to obtain the `javax.naming.Context` implementation. The implementation returned is a dynamic `java.lang.reflect.Proxy` that implements that `Context` interface using the `IMsgManagerObjectFactory` as the `java.lang.reflect.InvocationHandler` implementation. The only `Context` methods that are supported by the implementation are the `lookup`, `list`, and `toString` methods. When you do a lookup against the `Context` implementation, the name passed to look up is treated as the name of the mail store protocol, and the appropriate `IMsgManager` is constructed and returned as the `Context` binding for the protocol name.

Hopefully this discussion on the `MailAccount`, `MailHandlerMDB` and `NewMailService` gives you sufficient background to tackle the application code on your own. The `MailAccountServlet` is a rather simple controller implementation that is discussed later in this chapter as you go through a demo of the application using the Web interface in the "Testing the Mail Forwarding Application" section.

Building and Assembling the Mail Forwarding Application

The complete mail forwarding application consists of a jar containing the `NewMailService` MBean as well as the EJB jar and Web application archive combined into an EAR. To build and package the application components, you need to create an appropriate Ant build file, write the deployment descriptors, and define the MBean configuration. The compilation phase for all of the book examples is defined in the build.xml in the examples directory, so take a look at its classpath definitions for compiling and running clients to see the scope of required JBoss jars. Listing 11.1 presents the build.xml classpath definitions.

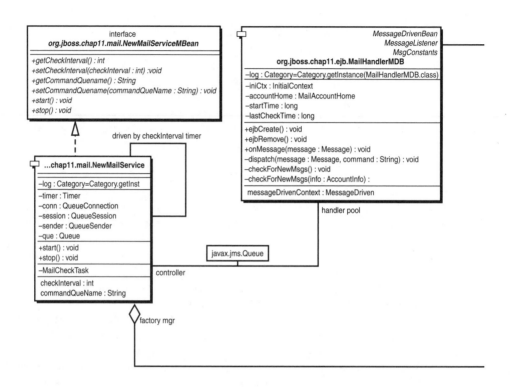

FIGURE 11.4   The NewMailService MBean and associated classes.

LISTING 11.1   The Book Examples build.xml File build.path and client.path Classpaths
Demonstrating the Standard Requirements for Compiling and Running with JBoss

```
<project name="JBossBook examples" default="build-all" basedir=".">

  <!-- Allow override from local properties file -->
  <property file=".ant.properties" />
  <!-- Override with your JBoss/Web server bundle dist root -->
  <property name="dist.root" value="G:/JBoss-2.4.4_Tomcat-3.2.3" />
  <property name="jboss.dist" value="${dist.root}/jboss"/>
  <property name="jboss.deploy.dir" value="${jboss.dist}/deploy"/>
  <!-- Change if your not using tomcat -->
```

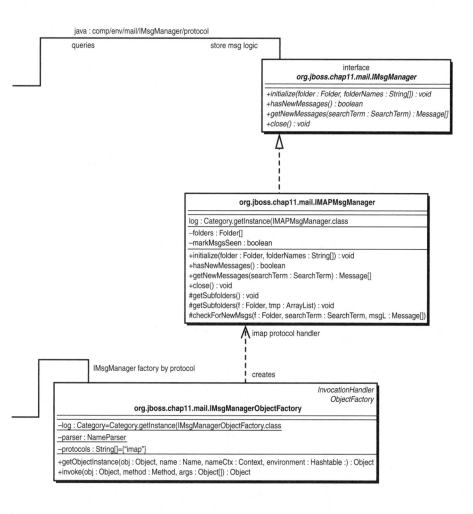

java : comp/env/mail/IMsgManager/protocol

queries   store msg logic

interface
org.jboss.chap11.mail.IMsgManager

+*initialize(folder : Folder, folderNames : String[]) : void*
+*hasNewMessages() : boolean*
+*getNewMessages(searchTerm : SearchTerm) : Message[]*
+*close() : void*

org.jboss.chap11.mail.IMAPMsgManager

log : Category.getInstance(IMAPMsgManager.class

–folders : Folder[]
–markMsgsSeen : boolean

+initialize(folder : Folder, folderNames : String[]) : void
+hasNewMessages() : boolean
+getNewMessages(searchTerm : SearchTerm) : Message[]
+close() : void
#getSubfolders() : void
#getSubfolders(f : Folder, tmp : ArrayList) : void
#checkForNewMsgs(f : Folder, searchTerm : SearchTerm, msgL : Message[])

imap protocol handler

IMsgManager factory by protocol   creates

InvocationHandler
ObjectFactory
org.jboss.chap11.mail.IMsgManagerObjectFactory

–log : Category=Category.getInstance(IMsgManagerObjectFactory.class
–parser : NameParser
–protocols : String[]={"imap"}

+getObjectInstance(obj : Object, name : Name, nameCtx : Context, environment : Hashtable :) : Object
+invoke(obj : Object, method : Method, args : Object[]) : Object

---

LISTING 11.1 Continued

```
<property name="servlet.jar"
    value="${dist.root}/tomcat/lib/servlet.jar"/>


<property name="src.dir" value="${basedir}/src/main"/>
<property name="src.resources" value="${basedir}/src/resources"/>
<property name="build.dir" value="${basedir}/build"/>
<property name="build.classes.dir" value="${build.dir}/classes"/>


<path id="build.path">
  <pathelement location="${jboss.dist}/client/jboss-j2ee.jar"/>
```

LISTING 11.1   Continued

```
    <pathelement location="${jboss.dist}/client/jaas.jar"/>
    <pathelement
      location="${jboss.dist}/client/jbosssx-client.jar"/>
    <pathelement location="${jboss.dist}/client/jboss-client.jar"/>
    <pathelement location="${jboss.dist}/client/jnp-client.jar"/>
    <pathelement location="${jboss.dist}/client/log4j.jar"/>
    <pathelement
      location="${jboss.dist}/client/oswego-concurrent.jar"/>
    <pathelement location="${jboss.dist}/lib/jmxri.jar"/>
    <pathelement location="${jboss.dist}/lib/ext/activation.jar"/>
    <pathelement location="${jboss.dist}/lib/ext/jboss.jar"/>
    <pathelement location="${jboss.dist}/lib/ext/mail.jar"/>
    <pathelement location="${servlet.jar}"/>
    <pathelement location="${build.classes.dir}"/>
  </path>

  <path id="client.path">
    <pathelement location="${jboss.dist}/client/jboss-j2ee.jar"/>
    <pathelement location="${jboss.dist}/client/jaas.jar"/>
    <pathelement
      location="${jboss.dist}/client/jbossmq-client.jar"/>
    <pathelement
      location="${jboss.dist}/client/jbosssx-client.jar"/>
    <pathelement
      location="${jboss.dist}/client/jboss-client.jar"/>
    <pathelement location="${jboss.dist}/client/jnp-client.jar"/>
    <pathelement location="${jboss.dist}/client/log4j.jar"/>
    <pathelement
      location="${jboss.dist}/client/oswego-concurrent.jar"/>
    <pathelement location="${build.classes.dir}"/>
    <pathelement location="${src.resources}"/>
  </path>
...
    <!-- Compile all java source under src/main -->
    <target name="compile" depends="init">
    <mkdir dir="${build.classes.dir}"/>
    <javac srcdir="${src.dir}"
           destdir="${build.classes.dir}"
           classpathref="${classpath_id}"
           debug="on"
           deprecation="on"
           optimize="off"
```

LISTING 11.1   Continued

```
        includes="org/jboss/**"
    />
    </target>
...
```

Note that because you are compiling all of the examples in a single step this requires more jars than a standard client because the functionality of the examples covers all aspects of the standard J2EE components as well as custom JBoss extensions. There are a few reasons why all classes are not included in a single jar or at least a fewer number of jars. In terms of the JBoss jars, the modularity of JBoss allows you to replace any of the standard frameworks with versions of your own, at least in theory. Therefore, aggregating all these framework classes into a single jar would hinder such plug-and-play replacement. For the non-JBoss jars, the packages are the original distributions from Sun or the third-party that produced them and must remain in their original form as per the distribution license.

In Listing 11.1, the path element with the id="build.path" value defines the class-path used by the compile target to build all book example code. The jars included in the build.path definition are as follows:

- client/jboss-j2ee.jar—This jar includes the standard J2EE interfaces and classes from the javax package namespace. This includes the standard EJB, JMS, JCA, and JTA packages.

- client/jaas.jar—This jar includes the JAAS javax.security extension classes.

- client/jbosssx-client.jar—This jar includes the JBossSX classes required by client using the JAAS login mechanism as well as the client side SRP classes.

- client/jboss-client.jar—This jar includes all of the JBoss EJB client classes.

- client/jnp-client.jar—This jar includes the JBossNS client classes.

- client/log4j.jar—This jar includes the Apache log4j classes.

- client/oswego-concurrent.jar—This jar includes the concurrency classes from Doug Lea of "Concurrent Programming in Java" book fame.

NOTE

Java has relatively low-level operation for multi-threaded programming. Doug Lea, Java expert, has created a package of higher-level utility classes useful for multi-thread programming. This package is freely available with full source code from http://gee.cs.oswego.edu/dl/classes/EDU/oswego/cs/dl/util/concurrent/intro.html. The oswego-concurrent.jar contains the 1.3.1 version of these classes.

- lib/jmxri.jar—This is the JMX reference implementation jar and contains the javax.management package classes.

- lib/ext/activation.jar—This jar includes the JavaBean activation extension package(javax.activation) classes. It is needed for use with JavaMail.

- lib/ext/jboss.jar—This is the JBoss server core jar. It contains all core JBoss classes and is needed by custom services.

- lib/ext/mail.jar—This is the JavaMail extension package which includes the javax.mail classes.

- servlet.jar—This is the Servlet extension package which includes the javax.servlet classes. It is needed when compiling servlets.

An Additional common jar that may be required for compilation is as follows:

- lib/jboss-jdbc_ext.jar—This jar contains the JDBC 2.0 extension classes from the javax.sql package. These classes are separated from the jboss-j2ee.jar due to the restriction that JAAS 1.0 requires login modules to be on the system class-path and the org.jboss.security.auth.spi.DatabaseServerLoginModule uses the javax.sql classes.

With all these jars how do you know which ones to include? Either you learn, include them all, or start with a basic collection and when compilation errors occur due to missing classes, search the jars for the needed package. It is not really that difficult. The classpath needed to run a Java client is a subset of the build path because the build includes components that run inside of the JBoss server. The one exception to this is the client/jbossmq-client.jar needed by JBossMQ client applications. The reason this jar is needed at runtime but not during compilation is because the JMS API consists almost entirely of interfaces. The classes that appear in a JMS client are all from the standard javax.jms package and so compilation only requires these standard interfaces. However, running the client requires an implementation of these interfaces and so a JMS provider specific jar is required.

After compiling the application classes you need to package them for deployment to the JBoss server. This entails creating the standard J2EE deployment descriptors and any JBoss specific deployment descriptors required to map application component references to the corresponding deployment environment binding. Listing 11.2 gives the ejb-jar.xml descriptor for the MailAccount CMP entity bean as well as the MailHandlerMDB message driven bean.

LISTING 11.2   The ejb-jar.xml Descriptor for the Mail Forwarding Application Enterprise Beans

```
<?xml version="1.0"?>
<!DOCTYPE ejb-jar
```

LISTING 11.2   Continued

```
    PUBLIC "-//Sun Microsystems, Inc.//DTD Enterprise JavaBeans 2.0//EN"
    "http://java.sun.com/dtd/ejb-jar_2_0.dtd"
>


<ejb-jar>
    <enterprise-beans>
      <entity>
        <ejb-name>MailAccountBean</ejb-name>
        <home>org.jboss.chap11.interfaces.MailAccountHome</home>
        <remote>org.jboss.chap11.interfaces.MailAccount</remote>
        <ejb-class>org.jboss.chap11.ejb.MailAccountBean</ejb-class>
        <persistence-type>Container</persistence-type>
        <prim-key-class>java.lang.String</prim-key-class>
        <reentrant>False</reentrant>
        <cmp-field>
          <field-name>mailServer</field-name>
        </cmp-field>
        <cmp-field>
          <field-name>mailProtocol</field-name>
        </cmp-field>
        <cmp-field>
          <field-name>mailProtocolPort</field-name>
        </cmp-field>
        <cmp-field>
          <field-name>mailFolders</field-name>
        </cmp-field>
        <cmp-field>
          <field-name>username</field-name>
        </cmp-field>
        <cmp-field>
          <field-name>password</field-name>
        </cmp-field>
        <cmp-field>
          <field-name>emailAddress</field-name>
        </cmp-field>
        <cmp-field>
          <field-name>checkFrequency</field-name>
        </cmp-field>
        <cmp-field>
          <field-name>newMailAction</field-name>
        </cmp-field>
```

LISTING 11.2   Continued

```
            <cmp-field>
              <field-name>nextExpirationCheck</field-name>
            </cmp-field>
            <primkey-field>username</primkey-field>
          </entity>

          <message-driven>
            <ejb-name>MailHandlerMDB</ejb-name>
            <ejb-class>org.jboss.chap11.ejb.MailHandlerMDB</ejb-class>
            <transaction-type>Container</transaction-type>
            <acknowledge-mode>AUTO_ACKNOWLEDGE</acknowledge-mode>
            <message-driven-destination>
              <destination-type>javax.jms.Queue</destination-type>
            </message-driven-destination>
            <ejb-ref>
              <ejb-ref-name>ejb/MailAccountHome</ejb-ref-name>
              <ejb-ref-type>Entity</ejb-ref-type>
              <home>org.jboss.chap11.interfaces.MailAccountHome</home>
              <remote>org.jboss.chap11.interfaces.MailAccount</remote>
              <ejb-link>MailAccountBean</ejb-link>
            </ejb-ref>
            <resource-env-ref>
              <resource-env-ref-name>mail/IMsgManager
              </resource-env-ref-name>
              <resource-env-ref-type>org.jboss.chap11.mail.IMsgManager
              </resource-env-ref-type>
            </resource-env-ref>
          </message-driven>
        </enterprise-beans>

</ejb-jar>
```

The `MailAccountBean` entity bean definition has no external references to resource or other EJBs that require jboss.xml settings. The `MailHandlerMDB` message driven bean does require jboss.xml settings for both the location of the `message-driven-destination` and the `resource-env-ref` location. Note that the `ejb-ref` element does not require a separate deployment setting because the reference is to the `MailAccountBean` and so it can be handled by the `ejb-link` element. Listing 11.3 presents the jboss.xml descriptor that provides the `MailHandlerMDB` deployment settings.

LISTING 11.3   The jboss.xml Descriptor Required for Specification of the
`MailHandlerMDB` Deployment Settings

```
<?xml version="1.0"?>
<jboss>
    <enterprise-beans>
        <message-driven>
            <ejb-name>MailHandlerMDB</ejb-name>
            <destination-jndi-name>queue/MailQueue</destination-jndi-name>
            <resource-env-ref>
                <resource-env-ref-name>mail/IMsgManager</resource-env-ref-name>
                <jndi-name>java:/IMsgManager</jndi-name>
            </resource-env-ref>
        </message-driven>
    </enterprise-beans>
</jboss>
```

The `destination-jndi-name` element gives the JNDI name for the `javax.jms.Queue`
destination the `MailHandlerMDB` will listen to for messages. Because the value is not
one of the JBossMQ queue destinations found in the standard jboss.jcml configuration, you will need to add its definition. Look at the corresponding MBean configuration for the queue when you view the jboss.jcml configuration in the context of
the `NewMailService` MBean. The `resource-env-ref/jndi-name` element gives the
JNDI name to which the java:comp/env/mail/IMsgManager ENC binding will point.

Although the `MailAccountBean` does not require a jboss.xml descriptor, it does
require a jaws.xml descriptor to define the custom `findByNewMsgExpiration` and
`findByNewMsgExpirationInRange` finder methods. The `MailAccountBean` is a CMP
entity bean and its persistence and home interface methods are handled by the
JBossCMP framework. The JBossCMP implementation can only handle simple finders
that are based on equality of a CMP field to the finder argument. The custom finders
of the `MailAccountHome` interface are not of this form. Therefore, you must specify
the appropriate SQL using a jaws.xml descriptor, and this is given in Listing 11.4.

LISTING 11.4   The JBossCMP jaws.xml Descriptor that Provides the SQL Statements for
the Custom MailAccountHome Interface Finders

```
<?xml version="1.0"?>
<jaws>
    <enterprise-beans>
        <entity>
            <ejb-name>MailAccountBean</ejb-name>
<!-- findByNewMsgExpiration(long begin, long end); -->
            <finder>
```

```
            <name>findByNewMsgExpiration</name>
            <query>nextExpirationCheck &gt;= {0} AND
              nextExpirationCheck &lt;= {1}</query>
            <order>nextExpirationCheck</order>
          </finder>
<!-- findByNewMsgExpirationInRange(long begin, long end,
    String startPrefix, String endPrefix); -->
          <finder>
            <name>findByNewMsgExpirationInRange</name>
            <query>nextExpirationCheck &gt;= {0} AND
              nextExpirationCheck &lt;= {1}
              AND username &gt;= '{2}' AND username &lt;= '{3}'
            </query>
            <order>username</order>
          </finder>
      </entity>
    </enterprise-beans>
</jaws>
```

Moving to the Web application components, you have the `MailAccountServlet`
controller and its edit_account.jsp view. The web.xml descriptor is given in Listing
11.5. The only external reference is an `ejb-ref` to the `MailAccount` entity bean.
Because you will bundle the Web application with the entity bean jar into an EAR,
you can link the `ejb-ref` to the `MailAccountBean` using the `ejb-link` element, thus
you do not need a jboss-web.xml deployment descriptor for the Web application.

LISTING 11.5   The web.xml Descriptor for the Web Components of the Mail
Forwarding Application

```
<?xml version="1.0" encoding="ISO-8859-1"?>
<!DOCTYPE web-app
  PUBLIC '-//Sun Microsystems, Inc.//DTD Web Application 2.2//EN'
  'http://java.sun.com/j2ee/dtds/web-app_2.2.dtd'>

<web-app>
  <display-name>Mail forwarding application</display-name>
  <description>Mail forwarding application</description>

  <servlet>
    <servlet-name>MailAccountServlet</servlet-name>
    <servlet-class>org.jboss.chap11.web.MailAccountServlet
    </servlet-class>
```

LISTING 11.5   Continued

```
  </servlet>
  <servlet>
    <servlet-name>MailAccountView</servlet-name>
    <jsp-file>edit_account.jsp</jsp-file>
  </servlet>

  <servlet-mapping>
    <servlet-name>MailAccountServlet</servlet-name>
    <url-pattern>/MailAccountServlet</url-pattern>
  </servlet-mapping>

  <welcome-file-list>
    <welcome-file>index.html</welcome-file>
  </welcome-file-list>

  <ejb-ref>
    <ejb-ref-name>ejb/MailAccountHome</ejb-ref-name>
    <ejb-ref-type>Entity</ejb-ref-type>
    <home>org.jboss.chap11.interfaces.MailAccountHome</home>
    <remote>org.jboss.chap11.interfaces.MailAccount</remote>
    <ejb-link>MailAccountBean</ejb-link>
  </ejb-ref>
</web-app>
```

The final deployment descriptor is the application.xml descriptor for the mail application EAR, and this is given in Listing 11.6. This descriptor simply says that the EAR consists of the mailer.jar EJB jar and the mailer.war WAR and that the WAR should be deployed under the root context name mailer.

LISTING 11.6   The application.xml Descriptor for the Mail Application EAR

```
<?xml version="1.0" encoding="UTF-8"?>

<!DOCTYPE application
  PUBLIC '-//Sun Microsystems, Inc.//DTD J2EE Application 1.2//EN'
  'http://java.sun.com/j2ee/dtds/application_1_2.dtd'>

<application>
  <display-name>Mail forwarding application</display-name>
  <description>Mail forwarding application</description>
```

LISTING 11.6   Continued

```
<module>
  <ejb>mailer.jar</ejb>
</module>
<module>
  <web>
    <web-uri>mailer.war</web-uri>
    <context-root>mailer</context-root>
  </web>
</module>
</application>
```

The next step is to create the application deployment packages. The Ant build.xml
for the mailer application is located in the src/main/org/jboss/chap11 directory of
the book examples. The relevant fragments of this file that create that application
EAR and MBean service jar are given in Listing 11.7.

NOTE

For Ant installation instructions and a usage overview as well as information on installing the
book examples, see Appendix D, "Tools and Book Examples."

LISTING 11.7   The Mail Application Ant build.xml File Targets for the Creation of the
Application Packages

```
<!-- Build script for the chapter 11 mailer ear -->
<project name="Chapter 11 build" default="build-all">

  <property name="src.root" value="src/main/org/jboss/chap11" />
  <property name="chapter.dir" value="${build.dir}/chap11" />
...
  <target name="mailer-jar" depends="prepare">
    <jar jarfile="${chapter.dir}/mailer.jar">
      <metainf dir="${src.root}/ejb" includes="*.xml"/>
      <fileset dir="${build.classes.dir}">
        <include name="org/jboss/chap11/ejb/*" />
        <include name="org/jboss/chap11/interfaces/*" />
        <include name="org/jboss/chap11/mail/**" />
        <include name="org/jboss/chap11/model/*" />
        <exclude name="org/jboss/chap11/mail/NewMailService*" />
        <exclude name="org/jboss/chap11/mail/IMAPMsgManager*" />
```

LISTING 11.7   Continued

```
          <exclude name="org/jboss/chap11/mail/IMsgManager*" />
        </fileset>
    </jar>
  </target>


  <target name="mailer-war" depends="prepare">
    <war warfile="${chapter.dir}/mailer.war"
        webxml="${src.root}/web/web.xml">
        <fileset dir="${src.root}/web">
          <include name="*.jsp" />
          <include name="*.html" />
          <include name="images/*" />
        </fileset>
        <classes dir="${build.classes.dir}">
          <include name="org/jboss/chap11/interfaces/MailAccount*" />
          <include name="org/jboss/chap11/model/AccountInfo*" />
          <include name="org/jboss/chap11/web/*" />
        </classes>
    </war>
  </target>


  <target name="mailer-ear" depends="mailer-jar,mailer-war">
    <ear earfile="${chapter.dir}/mailer.ear"
        appxml="${src.root}/application.xml">
        <fileset dir="${chapter.dir}" includes="*.jar,*.war"/>
    </ear>
  </target>


  <target name="mailer-sar" depends="prepare">
    <jar jarfile="${chapter.dir}/mailer-service.jar">
      <fileset dir="${build.classes.dir}">
        <include name="org/jboss/chap11/mail/NewMailService*" />
        <include name="org/jboss/chap11/mail/IMAPMsgManager*" />
        <include name="org/jboss/chap11/mail/IMsgManager*" />
      </fileset>
    </jar>
  </target>


</project>
```

Running the build-all target builds and deploys the application packages. Run the following command from the book examples directory to execute the build-all target:

```
examples 1975>ant -Dchap=11 build-chap
Buildfile: build.xml
...
mailer-jar:
 [jar] Building jar: ...\examples\build\chap11\mailer.jar
mailer-war:
 [war] Building war: ...\examples\build\chap11\mailer.war
mailer-ear:
 [ear] Building ear: ...\examples\build\chap11\mailer.ear
...
mailer-sar:
 [jar] Building jar: ...\build\chap11\mailer-service.jar
 [copy] Copying 1 file to G:\JBoss-2.4.4_Tomcat-3.2.3\jboss\lib\ext
 [copy] Copying 1 file to G:\JBoss-2.4.4_Tomcat-3.2.3\jboss\deploy
BUILD SUCCESSFUL
```

The final step is to configure the JBoss server to load the custom `NewMailService` MBean. You also need to include the definition for the MailQueue destination you declared in the jboss.xml descriptor as the destination used by the `MailHandlerMDB`. Listing 11.8 gives the two required jboss.jcml entries.

LISTING 11.8   The jboss.jcml MBean Configuration Entries for the MailQueue Destination and Custom NewMailService

```
<server>
...
  <!-- Configure the mailer MailQueue -->
  <mbean code="org.jboss.mq.server.QueueManager"
    name="JBossMQ:service=Queue,name=MailQueue"/>
...
  <!-- ===================================================== -->
  <!-- Add your custom MBeans here                           -->
  <!-- ===================================================== -->

  <!-- Configure the custom NewMailService MBean -->
  <mbean code="org.jboss.chap11.mail.NewMailService"
    name=":service=NewMailService" />

</server>
```

The installation of this configuration file and the creation of a custom chap11 configuration file set can be performed using the chapter config target. Run the following command from the book examples directory to perform this step:

```
examples 1981>ant -Dchap=11 config
Buildfile: build.xml

config:

config:
 [copy] Copying 14 files to ....4.3_Tomcat-3.2.3\jboss\conf\chap11
 [copy] Copying 1 file to ...-2.4.4_Tomcat-3.2.3\jboss\conf\chap11
 [copy] Copying 2 files to G:\JBoss-2.4.4_Tomcat-3.2.3\jboss\bin

BUILD SUCCESSFUL
```

The mail forwarding application is now ready to be run.

Testing the Mail Forwarding Application

To test the mail forwarding application, you need to start the JBoss server using the chap11 configuration. To start with the proper configuration, use one of the run_mailer.bat or run_mailer.sh start scripts that were copied to the JBoss bin directory by the configuration build step. As an example, the following is the console output that results when running the run_mailer.bat script on a Windows 2000 system:

```
bin 1496>run_mailer.bat
JBOSS_CLASSPATH=D:/usr/local/Java/jdk1.3.1/lib/tools.jar;run.jar;
jboss.home = G:\JBoss-2.4.4_Tomcat-3.2.3\jboss
Using JAAS LoginConfig: ...omcat-3.2.3/jboss/conf/chap11/auth.conf
Using configuration "chap11"
...
[AutoDeployer] Auto deploy of ...cat-3.2.3/jboss/deploy/mailer.ear
[J2EE Deployer Default] Deploy J2EE application: ...loy/mailer.ear
[J2eeDeployer] Create application mailer.ear
[J2eeDeployer] install EJB module mailer.jar
[J2eeDeployer] inflate and install WEB module mailer.war
[J2eeDeployer] add all ejb jar files to the common classpath
[Container factory] Deploying:...oss/tmp/deploy/Default/mailer.ear
[Verifier] Verifying file:...deploy/Default/mailer.ear/ejb1001.jar
[Container factory] Deploying MailAccountBean
[Container factory] Deploying MailHandlerMDB
[JAWS] Created table 'MailAccountBean' successfully.
[Bean Cache] Cache policy scheduler started
```

```
[ContainerManagement] Initializing
[ContainerManagement] Initialized
[ContainerManagement] Starting
[ContainerManagement] Started
[ContainerManagement] Initializing
[ContainerManagement] Initialized
[ContainerManagement] Starting
[ContainerManagement] Started
[Container factory] Deployed application: ...oy/Default/mailer.ear
[J2EE Deployer Default] Starting module mailer.war
[EmbeddedTomcatServiceSX] deploy, ctxPath=/mailer,warUrl=...eb1002
[J2EE Deployer Default] J2EE application:...mailer.ear is deployed
...
[NewMailService] Starting
[NewMailService] startService, bound java:/IMsgManager
[NewMailService] Started
[Service Control] Started 40 services
[Default] JBoss 2.4.4 Started in 0m:11s
```

If the first line you see is

```
JAVA_HOME is not defined, JSP pages may not compile correctly
```

you need to set your JAVA_HOME environment variable to point to the root of your JDK installation. The javac compiler is needed to compile JSP pages and the start scripts add the JAVA_HOME/lib/tools.jar jar to the system classpath to support this. You can achieve this in any fashion you want, but a javac compiler must be available to the Web container.

To test the application, direct your browser to http://localhost:8080/mailer/ and you should see the mailer application home page. This should look similar to the page presented in Figure 11.5.

Follow the Create/Edit your mail forwarding account link to go to the account management page. Figure 11.6 shows the page filled out for a user.

The account management page allows you to create a new account setup, search for an existing account setup, and edit existing account setups. Hovering your cursor over the question marks next to each field gives a brief description of the field purpose. The information for the fictional user is as follows:

- MailServer Hostname/IP—Specifies that the mail server that stores the user mail is mail.somedot.com.

- MailServer Type—Specifies that the type of access protocol supported by the mail server is IMAP. This is the only protocol supported by this version of the application.

- MailServer Username—Specifies that the mail server account username is mail_user.

- MailServer Password—Specifies the password associated with the mail_user account name.

- Mail Check Frequency—Specifies the account level frequency for new mail checks. This will only be used if the frequency is greater then the NewMailService MBean frequency.

- Email Address—Specifies the e-mail address to use as the from address for mail forwarded from the mail_user account.

- SMTPServer Hostname/IP—Specifies the SMTP gateway server through which forwarded mail should be routed is smtp.somedot.com.

- Fowarding Address—Specifies the address to which new mail should be forwarded. To demonstrate that the application does work, information was entered to forward mail from an e-mail account to a Nextel phone. An image of the first message that was forwarded to the phone is shown in Figure 11.7.

Experiment with setting up forwarding for your account and browse the server logs to gain insight into the behavior of the application.

FIGURE 11.5   The mail forwarding application home page.

Securing the Mail Forwarding Application

If you were offering the mail forwarding service in an application service provider (ASP) environment, only authorized users of the service would be allowed to create and edit forwarding accounts. In this section, you develop a partial solution that only allows authorized users access to edit their existing accounts. The creation of accounts is not allowed as part of the Web application itself. This is really just a pedagogical grafting of security onto the previous unsecured application, not a representative example of creating secured e-commerce applications. A properly secured application requires that security be considered as a design criterion from the start.

FIGURE 11.6   The mail forwarding application account management page filled out with user information.

The only code changes required to the unsecured applicaton are contained in the controller servlet and its JSP view. The EJBs and mailer service require no code changes. The EJB deployment descriptor does need to be updated to restrict access to the EJB functionality. The code for the secured version of the mailer is a combination of the org/jboss/chap11 and org/jboss/chap11s packages. The Web content and deployments descriptors for the secured version come from the chap11s package. The mailer EJBs and MBean service code from the unsecured chap11 package version will be used as is.

The unsecured version of the `MailAccountServlet` took the username of the `MailAccount` primary key from the edit_account.jsp post information. In the secured version of the `MailAccountServlet`, this information is taken from the authenticated caller's identity using the JAAS `Subject` caller principal information. This is an example of an application that is running in a security context where the username and password information used to gain access to the application do not have any meaning in the application domain. Rather, the application domain notion of the caller is obtained from the authenticated subject, and this is used as the key to obtain the user account information. The creation of the ASP username and password is handled as a separate configuration step. You create a mail forwarding service user with a username `duke` and a password `javaman` that is assigned the caller principal value `jduke` and a role of `MailServiceUser`. This process will also create a dummy `MailAccount` entity bean for the `jduke` username. Once this configuration step is performed, the only user who will have access to the `MailAccount` edit page will be the `duke` ASP user. Anyone will still be able to view the mail forwarding home page, but only `duke` will be able to traverse the edit account link.

FIGURE 11.7   An example text message forwarded from a mail account message to a cell phone.

The bulk of the changes required to secure the application occur at the deployment descriptor level. You need to declare the Web forms that allow account access as secured content, and you need to restrict what `MailAccount` entity bean operation can be performed based on user roles. Start with the changes required for the ejb-jar.xml descriptor. Listing 11.9 gives the revised descriptor. The elements with bold font indicate the revisions with respect to the descriptor of Listing 11.2.

LISTING 11.9   The Revised ejb-jar.xml Descriptor Used by the Secured Version of the Mail Forwarding Application

```
<?xml version="1.0"?>
<!DOCTYPE ejb-jar
    PUBLIC "-//Sun Microsystems, Inc.//DTD Enterprise JavaBeans 2.0//EN"
    "http://java.sun.com/dtd/ejb-jar_2_0.dtd"
>


<ejb-jar>
  <enterprise-beans>
    <entity>
      <ejb-name>MailAccountBean</ejb-name>
      <home>org.jboss.chap11.interfaces.MailAccountHome</home>
      <remote>org.jboss.chap11.interfaces.MailAccount</remote>
      <ejb-class>org.jboss.chap11.ejb.MailAccountBean</ejb-class>
      <persistence-type>Container</persistence-type>
      <prim-key-class>java.lang.String</prim-key-class>
      <reentrant>False</reentrant>
      <cmp-field>
        <field-name>mailServer</field-name>
      </cmp-field>
      <cmp-field>
        <field-name>mailProtocol</field-name>
      </cmp-field>
      <cmp-field>
        <field-name>mailProtocolPort</field-name>
      </cmp-field>
      <cmp-field>
        <field-name>mailFolders</field-name>
      </cmp-field>
      <cmp-field>
        <field-name>username</field-name>
      </cmp-field>
      <cmp-field>
        <field-name>password</field-name>
      </cmp-field>
      <cmp-field>
        <field-name>emailAddress</field-name>
```

LISTING 11.9   Continued

```
    </cmp-field>
    <cmp-field>
      <field-name>checkFrequency</field-name>
    </cmp-field>
    <cmp-field>
      <field-name>newMailAction</field-name>
    </cmp-field>
    <cmp-field>
      <field-name>nextExpirationCheck</field-name>
    </cmp-field>
    <primkey-field>username</primkey-field>
  </entity>

  <message-driven>
    <ejb-name>MailHandlerMDB</ejb-name>
    <ejb-class>org.jboss.chap11.ejb.MailHandlerMDB</ejb-class>
    <transaction-type>Container</transaction-type>
    <acknowledge-mode>AUTO_ACKNOWLEDGE</acknowledge-mode>
    <message-driven-destination>
        <destination-type>javax.jms.Queue</destination-type>
    </message-driven-destination>
    <ejb-ref>
      <ejb-ref-name>ejb/MailAccountHome</ejb-ref-name>
      <ejb-ref-type>Entity</ejb-ref-type>
      <home>org.jboss.chap11.interfaces.MailAccountHome</home>
      <remote>org.jboss.chap11.interfaces.MailAccount</remote>
      <ejb-link>MailAccountBean</ejb-link>
    </ejb-ref>
    <security-identity>
      <run-as>
        <role-name>InternalUser</role-name>
      </run-as>
    </security-identity>
    <resource-env-ref>
      <resource-env-ref-name>mail/IMsgManager
      </resource-env-ref-name>
      <resource-env-ref-type>org.jboss.chap11.mail.IMsgManager
      </resource-env-ref-type>
    </resource-env-ref>
  </message-driven>
```

LISTING 11.9   Continued

```
</enterprise-beans>

<assembly-descriptor>
    <method-permission>
        <role-name>MailServiceUser</role-name>
        <method>
            <ejb-name>MailAccountBean</ejb-name>
            <method-name>findByPrimaryKey</method-name>
        </method>
        <method>
            <ejb-name>MailAccountBean</ejb-name>
            <method-name>getAccountInfo</method-name>
        </method>
        <method>
            <ejb-name>MailAccountBean</ejb-name>
            <method-name>setAccountInfo</method-name>
        </method>
    </method-permission>
    <method-permission>
        <role-name>MailServiceAdmin</role-name>
        <role-name>InternalUser</role-name>
        <method>
            <ejb-name>MailAccountBean</ejb-name>
            <method-name>*</method-name>
        </method>
    </method-permission>

    <method-permission>
        <description>MDBs deployed in a security domain currently
        need to allow access to their onMessage because of how
        run-as is currently handled by the SecurityInterceptor.
        </description>
        <unchecked/>
        <method>
            <ejb-name>MailHandlerMDB</ejb-name>
            <method-name>onMessage</method-name>
        </method>
    </method-permission>
</assembly-descriptor>
</ejb-jar>
```

All revisions are related to securing access to the MailAccountBean entity bean. You have added a number of method-permission statements that restrict access to the "MailServiceUser", "MailServiceAdmin", and "InternalUser" roles. A user with the role "MailServiceUser" is allowed to call the findByPrimaryKey, getAccountInfo and setAccountInfo methods. These are the only methods a user needs to maintain their mail forwarding account information. The "MailServiceAdmin" and "InternalUser" roles are allowed access to all MailAccountBean methods. The configuration program that creates the duke user account will use a login with the "MailServiceAdmin" role. The purpose of the "InternalUser" role is to allow the MailHandlerMDB access to the MailAccountBean. Because an MDB does not have any caller identity associated with its onMessage method invocation, it has no capability to invoke other J2EE components using caller identity propagation. Therefore, when an MDB interacts with secured components it either needs to explicitly establish its caller identity the same as any client does, or it can be configured to use the security-identity/run-as construct. This moves the task of setting the security identity out of the MDB code and into the hands of the application deployer where it belongs.

Listing 11.9 shows that the MailHandlerMDB descriptor element has been augmented with a run-as element that says any time the MailHandlerMDB interacts with another EJB, it should be assigned the role "InternalUser". There is one caveat to using a run-as identity with an MDB that is deployed under a security domain. Because of how the run-as identity is handled at the security interceptor level, there must be an authenticated caller that has permission to invoke the MDB onMessage method. However, because JMS has no support for propagating a message producer's identity, an unauthenticated identity needs to be assigned to the security domain login module configuration. This unauthenticated identity then needs to be assigned a role that can access the onMessage method or the onMessage method needs to be declared as accessible by anyone. The latter approach was chosen in this example and that is the purpose of the last method-permission element that declares the MailHandlerMDB to be unchecked.

To have the ejb-jar.xml descriptor security changes be effective, a security domain must be assigned using the jboss.xml descriptor. Listing 11.10 highlights the revised jboss.xml descriptor. The only change is the addition of the security-domain element to assign the security domain to be used as "secure-mailer". Recall from Chapter 8, "JBossSX—The JBoss Security Framework," that the value of the security-domain element is the JNDI location of the security manager implementation. Only the portion of the JNDI name after the "java:/jaas" prefix is used as the security domain name.

LISTING 11.10   The Revised jboss.xml Descriptor Used by the Secured Version of the Mail Forwarding Application

```
<?xml version="1.0"?>
<jboss>
```

LISTING 11.10 Continued

```
<security-domain>java:/jaas/secure-mailer</security-domain>

<enterprise-beans>
  <message-driven>
    <ejb-name>MailHandlerMDB</ejb-name>
    <destination-jndi-name>queue/MailQueue</destination-jndi-name>
    <resource-env-ref>
      <resource-env-ref-name>mail/IMsgManager</resource-env-ref-name>
      <jndi-name>java:/IMsgManager</jndi-name>
    </resource-env-ref>
  </message-driven>
</enterprise-beans>
</jboss>
```

Moving to the Web component changes, you will first see the revised web.xml deployment descriptor and the now required jboss-web.xml descriptor. Listing 11.11 shows the updated web.xml descriptor with revisions with respect to the Listing 11.3 descriptor highlighted in bold along with the new jboss-web.xml descriptor.

LISTING 11.11 The Revised web.xml Descriptor and New jboss-web.xml Descriptor Used by the Secured Version of the Mail Forwarding Application

```
<!-- The web.xml descriptor -->
<?xml version="1.0" encoding="ISO-8859-1"?>
<!DOCTYPE web-app
    PUBLIC '-//Sun Microsystems, Inc.//DTD Web Application 2.2//EN'
    'http://java.sun.com/j2ee/dtds/web-app_2.2.dtd'>

<web-app>
  <display-name>Mail forwarding application</display-name>
  <description>Mail forwarding application</description>

  <servlet>
    <servlet-name>MailAccountServlet</servlet-name>
    <servlet-class>org.jboss.chap11s.web.MailAccountServlet</servlet-class>
  </servlet>
  <servlet>
    <servlet-name>MailAccountView</servlet-name>
    <jsp-file>edit_account.jsp</jsp-file>
  </servlet>
```

LISTING 11.11   Continued

```xml
<servlet-mapping>
  <servlet-name>MailAccountServlet</servlet-name>
  <url-pattern>/restricted/MailAccountServlet</url-pattern>
</servlet-mapping>
<servlet-mapping>
  <servlet-name>MailAccountView</servlet-name>
  <url-pattern>/restricted/edit_account</url-pattern>
</servlet-mapping>

<welcome-file-list>
  <welcome-file>index.html</welcome-file>
</welcome-file-list>

<security-constraint>
 <web-resource-collection>
    <url-pattern>/restricted/*</url-pattern>
 </web-resource-collection>
 <auth-constraint>
    <role-name>MailServiceUser</role-name>
 </auth-constraint>
</security-constraint>

<login-config>
  <auth-method>BASIC</auth-method>
  <realm-name>MailForwarding</realm-name>
</login-config>

<ejb-ref>
  <ejb-ref-name>ejb/MailAccountHome</ejb-ref-name>
  <ejb-ref-type>Entity</ejb-ref-type>
  <home>org.jboss.chap11.interfaces.MailAccountHome</home>
  <remote>org.jboss.chap11.interfaces.MailAccount</remote>
  <ejb-link>MailAccountBean</ejb-link>
</ejb-ref>
</web-app>

<!-- The jboss-web.xml descriptor -->
<?xml version="1.0"?>
<jboss-web>
  <security-domain>java:/jaas/secure-mailer</security-domain>
</jboss-web>
```

The first set of changes to the web.xml descriptor moved the URL location of the MailAccountServlet and MailAccountView JSP page to under the /restricted prefix. This prefix is identified as protected by the new security-constraint element which indicates that all content under the /restricted path requires an authenticated user with a role of MailServiceUser. The other change to the web.xml descriptor is the addition of the login-config element. This defines the mechanism by which users must present their authentication information. This example uses HTTP Basic authentication. The jboss-web.xml descriptor simply defines the security domain handles authentication and authorization. Note that the same secure-mailer security domain is used, as is for the EJBs. This is typical of components that are collected together into an EAR as this allows seamless interaction between the components.

The one significant Web application code change was in the mechanism by which the MailAccountServlet obtains the username to use as the MailAccount entity bean primary key. The relevant code is given in Listing 11.12 and, in particular, the getCallerPrincipal method is where all of the logic is centered.

LISTING 11.12   The MailAccountServlet Logic for Obtaining the Application Domain Identity of the Authenticated Caller

```
public class MailAccountServlet extends HttpServlet
{
...
    protected void processRequest(HttpServletRequest request,
        HttpServletResponse response)
        throws ServletException, IOException
    {
        String username = getCallerPrincipal();
        if( username == null )
            throw new ServletException("Authentication is required");
...
        RequestDispatcher rd =
            request.getRequestDispatcher("edit_account");
        rd.forward(request, response);
    }

    /** Use the custom JBoss java:comp/env/security/subject binding
     to access the authenticated subject caller principal mapping.
     */
    private String getCallerPrincipal()
        throws ServletException
    {
```

LISTING 11.12   Continued

```java
String callerPrincipal = null;
try
{
    InitialContext iniCtx = new InitialContext();
    String name = "java:comp/env/security/subject";
    Object ref = iniCtx.lookup(name);
    Subject subject = (Subject) ref;
    if( subject == null )
        throw new ServletException("No valid Subject found");
    Group callerPrincipalGrp = null;
    Set groups = subject.getPrincipals(Group.class);
    Iterator iter = groups.iterator();
    while( iter.hasNext() )
    {
        callerPrincipalGrp = (Group) iter.next();
        String grpName = callerPrincipalGrp.getName();
        if( grpName.equals("CallerPrincipal") )
            break;
    }
    if( callerPrincipalGrp == null )
    {
        // Use the first Principal
        Set pset = subject.getPrincipals(Principal.class);
        Principal user = (Principal) pset.iterator().next();
        callerPrincipal = user.getName();
    }
    else
    {
        // Get the sole member of the CallerPrincipal group
        Enumeration pset = callerPrincipalGrp.members();
        Principal caller = (Principal) pset.nextElement();
        callerPrincipal = caller.getName();
    }
}
catch(NamingException e)
{
    throw new ServletException("Failed to find Subject", e);
}
return callerPrincipal;
```

LISTING 11.12   Continued

```
    }
}
```

The logic of the `getCallerPrincipal` method is based on the java:comp/env/security context that JBoss creates for every J2EE component deployed under a security domain. The security context contains the following bindings:

- securityMgr—This is the `org.jboss.security.AuthenticationManager` interface view of the security manager.

- realmMapping—This is the `org.jboss.security.RealmMapping` interface view of the security manager.

- subject—This is the `javax.security.auth.Subject` for the authenticated caller. This is a thread local binding that provides access to the `Subject` instance as populated by the JAAS login modules configured for the security domain. The exact information contained in the `Subject` depends on the configured login modules, but at a minimum it will contain the information documented in Chapter 8 in the section "Support for the Subject Usage Pattern."

The MailAccountServlet is using only the subject binding from the security context. The `getCallerPrincipal` code looks first for the subject CallerPrincipal `Group` to obtain an explicit mapping of the operation environment user to the application domain. If no such mapping exists, the authenticated `Principal` is used instead. The name of the located `Principal` is used as application domain username.

NOTE

Note that this is a pure JBoss construct and is not part of any J2EE specification. This level of programming is really not appropriate at the J2EE component level because it is not portable across application servers. The correct way to integrate this logic is through some reusable security framework that abstracts the application server specific details out of the component.

Building the Secured Mail Forwarding Application

Now you need to build the application packages, create an updated JBoss server configuration file set, create the user security database, and create a sample `MailAccount` bean for a prototype ASP environment user. To build and install the application EAR and MBean, run the following Ant command from the book examples directory:

```
examples 2084>ant -Dchap=11s build-chap
...
secure-mailer-war:
     [war] Building war: ...ples\build\chap11s\secure-mailer.war

secure-mailer-ear:
     [ear] Building ear: ...ples\build\chap11s\secure-mailer.ear
  [delete] Deleting: ...4.4_Tomcat-3.2.3\jboss\deploy\mailer.ear
    [copy] Copying 1 ...G:\JBoss-2.4.4_Tomcat-3.2.3\jboss\deploy

BUILD SUCCESSFUL

Total time: 12 seconds
```

This installs the mailer-service.jar into the JBoss lib/ext directory and the secure-mailer.ear into the JBoss deploy directory. Next, create the chap11s configuration file set by running the following Ant command from the book examples directory:

```
examples 2086>ant -Dchap=11s config
Buildfile: build.xml

config:

config:
    [copy] Copying 15 files to ...Tomcat-3.2.3\jboss\conf\chap11s
    [copy] Copying 2 files to ..._Tomcat-3.2.3\jboss\conf\chap11s
    [copy] Copying 2 files to ...oss-2.4.4_Tomcat-3.2.3\jboss\bin

BUILD SUCCESSFUL

Total time: 2 seconds
```

This creates a custom configuration file set named chap11s that contains the same customized jboss.jcml configuration used in the unsecured example, along with a new auth.conf file that defines a secure-mailer login configuration based on the DatabaseServerLoginModule. For convenience, two new starts scripts called run_secure_mailer.bat and run_secure_mailer.sh are also copied to the JBoss server bin directory. These run the JBoss/Tomcat bundle using the chap11s configuration. The final setup step to perform is the creation of the user security database and a sample account. This is done using the org.jboss.chap11s.SetupAccount class. The JBoss server must be running to use this program, so start the JBoss server using the run_security_mailer script; once it is up, run the following Ant command:

```
examples 2088>ant -Dchap=11s -Dex=1 run-example
Buildfile: build.xml

...
init:
    [echo] Using jboss.dist=G:/JBoss-2.4.4_Tomcat-3.2.3/jboss

compile:

run-example:

run-example1:
    [java] Created Principals table, result=false
    [java] Created username=duke, password=javaman
    [java] Created username=admin, password=admin
    [java] Created Roles table, result=false
    [java] Assigned duke the role MailServiceUser
    [java] Assigned admin the role MailServiceAdmin
    [java] Assigned duke the CallerPrincpal jduke
    [java] Created LoginContext
    [java] Logged in as admin
    [java] Created account for username=jduke
    [java] Logged out
```

The SetupAccount class creates a Principals and a Roles table in the default Hypersonic database and populates the Principals with two logins: one for username duke and one for username admin. These users are then assigned the roles "MailServiceUser" and "MailServiceAdmin" respectively. The duke user is also assigned a caller principal name of jduke. Lastly, the SetupAccount class does a login as the admin user and creates a MailAccount bean with a primary key of jduke. At the conclusion of the SetupAccount program run, you have enabled the mail forwarding application for one user duke with a password of javaman.

Testing the Secured Mail Forwarding Application

To test the secured version of the mail forwarding application, direct your Web browser to `http://localhost:8080/secure-mailer/`. You will see a Web page similar to the unsecured version shown in Figure 11.5. Access to this page does not require a password. Click on the `Edit your mail forwarding account` link, and the Enter Network Password dialog box opens. The dialog box and Web page you see at this point should be similar to that shown in Figure 11.8.

Enter the username `duke` with a password of `javaman` to gain access to the mail forwarding account information set up by the `SetupAccount` program. You then see the dummy account information as shown in Figure 11.9. No other user login information will gain you access to the account information page.

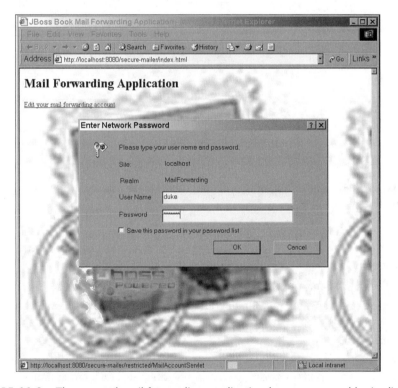

FIGURE 11.8   The secured mail forwarding application home page and login dialog box that is displayed after clicking on the edit account link.

FIGURE 11.9   The mail forwarding account information page for the mail forwarding service user duke.

Migrating the Java Pet Store 1.1.2 Application to JBoss

In the previous section you went through the creation and JBoss configuration of a J2EE application from scratch. In this section you look at porting an existing J2EE application that runs on the J2EE reference implementation to JBoss. The application that you port is the J2EE Blueprints Java Pet Store.

The Java Pet Store (JPS) is a sample application from the J2EE Blueprints program. The self-description from the JPS demo states that it demonstrates how to use the capabilities of the J2EE platform to develop flexible, scalable, cross-platform e-business applications. The Java Pet Store comes with full source code and documentation so you can experiment with J2EE technology and learn how to use it to build your own enterprise solutions. The JPS build is designed for use with the J2EE reference implementation and its Cloudscape database. This section describes how to port version 1.1.2 of the JPS to the JBoss/Tomcat bundle using the default Hypersonic database. You highlight the changes that need to be made, and show the jboss.xml and jboss-web.xml that are needed, as well as the jboss.jcml configuration additions for the JPS resources. The complete patch is available with the book CD, so you don't have to perform the work yourself. The following sections highlight the changes that were made so you can understand the contents of the patch and gain familiarity with the general steps required to port a J2EE application to JBoss.

Patching the JPS Distribution

The first step is to install the JPS 1.1.2 distribution, which is the jps-1_1_2.zip file on the book CD in the JavaPetStore directory.

NOTE

The JPS distribution can be downloaded from the JPS 1.1.2 release home page at `http://developer.java.sun.com/developer/sampsource/petstore/petstore1_1_2.html`.

Once you have downloaded the bundle, unarchive it to create the directory structure shown in Figure 11.10.

The folders of the JPS directory structure have been expanded to show the various module src directories. The src directories contain the Ant build.xml scripts you have to update to rebuild the JPS EAR using the JBoss server libraries. You also have to create jboss.xml and jboss-web.xml deployment descriptors for the various EJB jars and Web application WARs the JPS build process creates. You place the JBoss deployment descriptors into the src directories along side of the JPS standard J2EE descriptors. A list of the build.xml files from the JPS distribution and the types of changes required to them are as follows:

- jps1.1.2/src/components/build.xml—No changes required.

- jps1.1.2/src/components/customer/src/build.xml—Update the customer.classpath property, add jboss.xml to the customerejbjar target.

- jps1.1.2/src/components/inventory/src/build.xml—Update the inventory.classpath property.

- jps1.1.2/src/components/mail/src/build.xml—Update the mail.classpath property.

- jps1.1.2/src/components/personalization/src/build.xml— Update the personalization.classpath property.

- jps1.1.2/src/components/shoppingcart/src/build.xml— Update the shoppingcart.classpath property.

- jps1.1.2/src/components/signon/src/build.xml—Update the signon.classpath property.

- jps1.1.2/src/components/util/tracer/src/build.xml—Update the tracer.classpath property.

- jps1.1.2/src/miniapps/mailerapp/src/build.xml—Update the j2ee.classpath, change the ear target to work with JBoss.

- jps1.1.2/src/petstore/src/build.xml—Copy to jps1.1.2/src/petstore/src, update relative paths, update the j2ee.classpath property, remove the jaxp.jar and parser.jar from the app, update jar and war targets to include the jboss.xml and jboss-web.xml descriptors, change the ear target to work with JBoss, remove the depends on the runtime target, and change the deploy target to work with JBoss.

Creating the jboss.xml and jboss-web.xml Descriptors

After updating the build files so that the JPS code base can be built without the J2EE reference implementation, you need to create the JBoss specific deployment descriptors to map the J2EE component resource references to the corresponding deployment environment JNDI binding. Listings 11.13 through 11.19 give the various JBoss deployment descriptors along with a brief description of why the descriptor is required.

LISTING 11.13   The jps1.1.2/src/components/customer/src/jboss.xml File for the customerEjb.jar

```
<jboss>
  <enterprise-beans>
    <entity>
      <ejb-name>TheAccount</ejb-name>
      <resource-ref>
        <res-ref-name>jdbc/EstoreDataSource</res-ref-name>
        <jndi-name>java:/EstoreDB</jndi-name>
      </resource-ref>
    </entity>

    <entity>
      <ejb-name>TheOrder</ejb-name>
      <resource-ref>
        <res-ref-name>jdbc/EstoreDataSource</res-ref-name>
        <jndi-name>java:/EstoreDB</jndi-name>
      </resource-ref>
    </entity>
```

LISTING 11.13   Continued

```
  </enterprise-beans>
</jboss>
```

FIGURE 11.10   The 1.1.2 Java Pet Store application distribution directory structure.

The jboss.xml descriptor is required to map the JDBC `javax.jdbc.DataSource` references to the deployment environment resource factory location.

LISTING 11.14   The jps1.1.2/src/components/inventory/src/jboss.xml file for the inventoryEjb.jar

```
<jboss>
  <enterprise-beans>
    <entity>
      <ejb-name>TheInventory</ejb-name>
      <resource-ref>
        <res-ref-name>jdbc/InventoryDataSource</res-ref-name>
        <jndi-name>java:/InventoryDB</jndi-name>
      </resource-ref>
    </entity>
  </enterprise-beans>
</jboss>
```

The jboss.xml descriptor is required to map the JDBC `javax.jdbc.DataSource` reference to the deployment environment resource factory location.

LISTING 11.15   The jps1.1.2/src/components/mail/src/jboss.xml File for the
mailerEjb.jar

```
<jboss>
  <enterprise-beans>
    <session>
      <ejb-name>TheMailer</ejb-name>
      <resource-ref>
        <res-ref-name>mail/MailSession</res-ref-name>
        <jndi-name>java:/MailSession</jndi-name>
      </resource-ref>
    </session>
  </enterprise-beans>
</jboss>
```

The jboss.xml descriptor is required to map the JavaMail `javax.mail.Session` reference to the deployment environment resource factory location.

LISTING 11.16   The jps1.1.2/src/components/personalization/src/jboss.xml File for the
personalizationEjb.jar

```
<jboss>
  <enterprise-beans>
    <entity>
      <ejb-name>TheProfileMgr</ejb-name>
      <resource-ref>
        <res-ref-name>jdbc/EstoreDataSource</res-ref-name>
        <jndi-name>java:/EstoreDB</jndi-name>
      </resource-ref>
    </entity>
  </enterprise-beans>
</jboss>
```

The jboss.xml descriptor is required to map the JDBC `javax.jdbc.DataSource` reference to the deployment environment resource factory location.

LISTING 11.17   The jps1.1.2/src/components/shoppingcart/src/jboss.xml File for the
shoppingcartEjb.jar

```
<jboss>
  <enterprise-beans>
    <entity>
      <ejb-name>TheCatalog</ejb-name>
      <resource-ref>
```

LISTING 11.17   Continued

```
          <res-ref-name>jdbc/EstoreDataSource</res-ref-name>
          <jndi-name>java:/EstoreDB</jndi-name>
        </resource-ref>
      </entity>
    </enterprise-beans>
</jboss>
```

The jboss.xml descriptor is required to map the JDBC javax.jdbc.DataSource reference to the deployment environment resource factory location.

LISTING 11.18   The jboss.xml File for the jps1.1.2/src/components/signon/src signonEjb.jar

```
<jboss>
  <enterprise-beans>
    <entity>
      <ejb-name>TheSignOn</ejb-name>
      <resource-ref>
        <res-ref-name>jdbc/SignOnDataSource</res-ref-name>
        <jndi-name>java:/EstoreDB</jndi-name>
      </resource-ref>
    </entity>
  </enterprise-beans>
</jboss>
```

The jboss.xml descriptor is required to map the JDBC javax.jdbc.DataSource reference to the deployment environment resource factory location.

LISTING 11.19   The jps1.1.2/src/petstore/src/docroot/WEB-INF/jboss-web.xml File for the petstore.war

```
<jboss-web>
  <resource-ref>
    <res-ref-name>jdbc/EstoreDataSource</res-ref-name>
    <jndi-name>java:/EstoreDB</jndi-name>
  </resource-ref>
  <ejb-ref>
    <ejb-ref-name>ejb/catalog/Catalog</ejb-ref-name>
    <jndi-name>TheCatalog</jndi-name>
  </ejb-ref>
  <ejb-ref>
    <ejb-ref-name>ejb/cart/Cart</ejb-ref-name>
```

LISTING 11.19   Continued

```
    <jndi-name>TheCart</jndi-name>
  </ejb-ref>
  <ejb-ref>
    <ejb-ref-name>ejb/customer/Customer</ejb-ref-name>
    <jndi-name>TheCustomer</jndi-name>
  </ejb-ref>
  <ejb-ref>
    <ejb-ref-name>ejb/profilemgr/ProfileMgr</ejb-ref-name>
    <jndi-name>TheProfileMgr</jndi-name>
  </ejb-ref>
  <ejb-ref>
    <ejb-ref-name>ejb/scc/Scc</ejb-ref-name>
    <jndi-name>TheShoppingClientController</jndi-name>
  </ejb-ref>
  <ejb-ref>
    <ejb-ref-name>ejb/inventory/Inventory</ejb-ref-name>
    <jndi-name>TheInventory</jndi-name>
  </ejb-ref>
</jboss-web>
```

The jboss-web.xml descriptor is required to map the JDBC `javax.jdbc.DataSource` reference to the deployment environment resource factory location, as well as setting the locations of the EJB reference homes. Note that the EJB references could have been handled in the web.xml descriptor using ejb-link elements.

Configuring the Hypersonic Database

The next step is the configuration of the Hypersonic database. This entails configuring the `DataSource` resource factory for Hypersonic, porting the SQL database initialization script, and making code changes to the database setup servlet. Two additional source code changes are also required to the JPS BMP use of SQL constructs that are not supported by the Hypersonic database. The fact that such changes are required to modify the JDBC database highlights one of the weaknesses of choosing BMP as the entity bean persistence model; namely, SQL is not completely portable. The JPS can be made more portable by externalizing the JDBC statements from the source code to mitigate this, but the 1.1.2 version does not. Porting and testing the JPS BMP code and associated scripts is, by far, the largest task in the porting effort.

The first task is the creation of the `DataSource` resource factories for the two references used in the JPS code. If you look through the JBoss deployment descriptors, you see there are two unique JDBC `DataSources`: java:/EstoreDB and java:/InventoryDB. You can simply create one database pool for use by both references because the tables associated with each database have no name conflicts. The database pool was given the java:/EstoreDB binding and java:/InventoryDB was created as a link to java:/EstoreDB. The jboss.jcml configuration fragment to perform this are given in Listing 11.20. Note that you don't have to have to add this fragment to your jboss.jcml file as the JPS patch includes a version suitable for use with the JBoss-2.4.4/Tomcat-3.2.3 bundle. The build and deploy process in the next section creates a custom petstore configuration file set that includes the Listing 11.20 settings.

LISTING 11.20   The jboss.jcml Configuration Fragment for Setting up the JPS DataSource Factories

```
<mbean code="org.jboss.jdbc.XADataSourceLoader"
     name="DefaultDomain:service=XADataSource,name=EstoreDB">
  <attribute name="PoolName">EstoreDB</attribute>
  <attribute name="DataSourceClass">
    org.jboss.pool.jdbc.xa.wrapper.XADataSourceImpl
  </attribute>
  <attribute name="URL">
    jdbc:hsqldb:hsql://localhost:1476
  </attribute>
  <attribute name="GCMinIdleTime">1200000</attribute>
  <attribute name="JDBCUser">sa</attribute>
  <attribute name="Password" />
  <attribute name="MaxSize">10</attribute>
  <attribute name="GCEnabled">false</attribute>
  <attribute name="InvalidateOnError">false</attribute>
  <attribute name="TimestampUsed">false</attribute>
  <attribute name="Blocking">true</attribute>
  <attribute name="GCInterval">120000</attribute>
  <attribute name="IdleTimeout">1800000</attribute>
  <attribute name="IdleTimeoutEnabled">false</attribute>
  <attribute name="LoggingEnabled">false</attribute>
  <attribute name="MaxIdleTimeoutPercent">1.0</attribute>
  <attribute name="MinSize">0</attribute>
</mbean>

<mbean code="org.jboss.naming.NamingAlias"
  name="DefaultDomain:service=NamingAlias,fromName=InventoryDB">
  <attribute name="ToName">java:/EstoreDB</attribute>
  <attribute name="FromName">java:/InventoryDB</attribute>
</mbean>
```

The next task is to create the database SQL initialization script. This can be put together with a minor variation of the Oracle and Cloudscape scripts, included in the JPS patch bundle as the petstore/src/docroot/WEB-INF/sql/Hypersonic.sql file.

The next task is to update the database population servlets. When you first enter the JPS store main page, there is a check for the existence of the required database tables. If the tables are not found, you are redirected to a database initialization page. Figure 11.11 presents the browser view you see on following the Enter Store link when the JPS database tables are found to be missing.

The page shows the database type to be HSQL Database Engine, and lists the required tables. All tables are seen to be uninstalled. To install the tables, click on the Install tables link in the page banner. This presents a page similar to that shown in Figure 11.12.

The recommended installation option is the Install Hypersonic tables link because this is what matches the configured Hypersonic database pool driver name. Clicking on this link creates and populates the JPS tables using the Hypersonic.sql script. The view shown in Figure 11.11 is then redisplayed with the current table installation status. If any table failed to be created, the page will continue to indicate that installation is required. If all tables have been installed, the page will indicate that you may return to the petstore start page. Figure 11.13 shows the page view you should see after successful installation of the JPS tables into the Hypersonic database. Return to these database initialization steps after you have built and deployed the JPS as described in the following section.

Building and Deploying the JPS EAR

In this section you walk through the steps to apply the JPS patches and build the JPS petstore.ear. The steps for the process are as follows:

1. Unpack the JPS distribution to create the jps1.1.2 directory. You can use either the JDK jar tool or any platform unzip tool you may have.

2. While in the parent directory of the jps1.1.2 directory, unjar or unzip the jboss-jps-patch.zip archive to overwrite the jps1.1.2 contents with the patched files.

3. Go to the jps1.1.2/src directory and locate the JPS Build Master Ant build.xml file. Edit the value of the jboss.bundle property to point to the location of your JBoss-2.4.4_Tomcat-3.2.3 bundle directory.

4. Run the ant command without any arguments from the jps1.1.2/src directory to build the default core target. This builds all JPS component jars and wars, and assembles them into the petstore.ear file in the jps1.1.2/src/petstore/build directory.

FIGURE 11.11   The Java Pet Store Demo Database Populate browser view you see when the JPS database tables are found to be missing.

NOTE

Note that there will be many warnings using the 1.4.1 version of Ant that is on the book CD. Only minimal changes were made to the various JPS build.xml files to get it to build with JPS. All of the deprecated Ant constructs used by the JPS build scripts were not corrected.

---

5. Run the ant command with `deploy` as the sole argument from the jps1.1.2/src directory to build the deploy target. This creates a petstore configuration file set in the JBoss-2.4.4_Tomcat-3.2.3/jboss/conf directory, and places the petstore.ear into the 2.4.4_Tomcat-3.2.3/jboss/deploy directory.

6. You are now ready to run the JPS application. Go to your 2.4.4_Tomcat-3.2.3/jboss/bin directory and find the run_pestore.bat and run_petstore.sh start scripts. In addition to starting JBoss with the petstore configuration file set, these scripts add the JDK lib/tools.jar file to the startup classpath so that the

javac compiler is available for compiling the JSP files used by JPS. This is done using the value of the JAVA_HOME environment variable. You must either set JAVA_HOME to the location of your JDK root directory or edit the start script to set up the classpath to include a javac compiler. Run the start script that is appropriate for your operating system to start the JPS application inside of JBoss.

FIGURE 11.12   The Java Pet Store Demo Database Populate installation page view.

7. Enter the JPS start page by browsing to http://localhost:8080/estore/. When you follow the Enter store link for the first time, you are taken to the database initialization page. Follow the directions given in the Hypersonic configuration section to create the required JPS database tables.

Congratulations! You now have a JPS application working under JBoss.

FIGURE 11.13   The Java Pet Store Demo Database Populate installation page view after successful installation of the JPS tables into the Hypersonic database.

Using the JBossTest Unit Test Suite

The JBossTest suite is a collection of client oriented unit tests of the JBoss server application. It is an Ant-based package that uses the JUnit (http://www.junit.org) unit test framework. The JBossTest suite is used as a QA benchmark by the development team to help test new functionality and prevent introduction of bugs. It is run on a nightly basis and the results are posted to the development mailing list for all to see.

The unit tests are run using Ant. Originally the unit tests were maintained as independent programs with their own scripts. The remains of this procedure can still be seen in the dist/bin directory produced by the build. However, this process is no longer maintained and it is likely the scripts no longer work.

The structure of the jbosstest CVS module is illustrated in Figure 11.14. The two main branches of the source tree are shown expanded side by side. The src/main tree contains the Java source code for the unit tests. The src/resources tree contains resource files like deployment descriptors, jar manifests, Web content, and so on. The root package of every unit test is org.jboss.test as shown in the left side of Figure 11.14. The typical structure below each specific unit test subpackage—for example, security—consists of a test package that contains the unit test classes. The test subpackage is a required naming convention as this is the only directory searched for unit tests by the Ant build scripts. If the tests involve EJBs, the convention is to include an interface and ejb subpackage for these components. The unit tests need to follow a naming convention for the class file. Currently there are three conventions for unit class file names: Main.java, AllJUnitTests.java, and TestXXX.java, where XXX is either the class being tests or the name of the functionality being tested. New unit tests added to the code base should use the TestXXX.java naming convention.

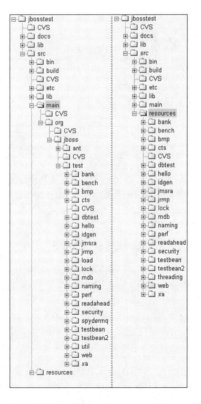

FIGURE 11.14   The JBossTest CVS module directory structure.

To run the unit tests use Ant with the src/build/run_tests.xml build file. The src/build/build.xml file is the legacy build file that creates the unit test jars. The key targets in the run_test.xml file include the following:

- build—This target builds all unit test jars using the original build.xml file. The run-tests target depends on the build target.

- run-tests—This is the default target of the run_tests.xml file. It runs the standard-tests, basic-security-tests, and client-tests targets.

- client-tests—This series of tests requires that the tests be loaded from a controlled classpath rather than the build/classes directory. The reason for this is that these tests focus on issues like dynamic class loading of RMI stubs that should not come from a local classpath.

- standard-tests—This target consists of nearly all unit tests other than the security unit tests. Any class matching one the of patterns **/test/*/test/Test*.java, **/test/*/test/AllJUnitTests.java or **/test/*/test/Main.java is considered a JUnit test case.

- basic-security-tests—This series of tests include those tests under the org.jboss.test.security package that do not require special setup of the JBoss server.

- run-testcase—This target allows you to run all tests within a particular package. To run this target you need to specify a testcase property package value using -Dtestcase=package on the ant program command line. The package value is the name of the package below org.jboss.test you want to run unit tests for. So, for example, to run all unit tests in the org.jboss.test.naming package, you would use `ant -buildfile run_tests.xml -Dtestcase=naming run-testcase`.

- test-and-report—This target runs the run-tests target; then collates the unit text XML output files into a text summary and a nicely formatted html summary.

- test-and-report-and-mail—This target runs the test-and-report target and then mails the text summary to the build file mail address. This is used to run the nightly unit tests, and mail the results to the JBoss development mailing list.

On completion of the test-and-report target, the parent directory of the jbosstest CVS working directory will contain server xml files that represent the individual junit test runs. These are collated into an html report located in the html subdirectory along with a text report located in the text subdirectory. Figure 11.15 shows an example of the html report for a run of the test suite against the JBoss 2.4.4 release on a RedHat 7.2 Linux system. The one failure listed is due to the xa unit test not having two databases available. This is a configuration issue that has not been corrected because you stopped bundling InstantDB with JBoss.

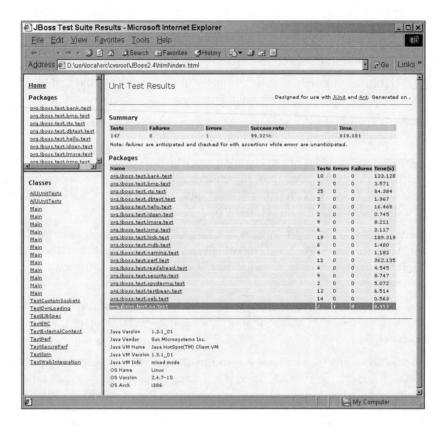

FIGURE 11.15   An example JBossTest test suite run report status html view as generated by the test-and-report target.

Summary

This chapter focused on deploying J2EE applications under JBoss. You looked at the steps required to deploy a secured and unsecured custom mail forwarding application as well as the J2EE blueprints Java Pet Store demo application. The emphasis was on the JBoss specific deployment configuration steps. You were also introduced to the JBossTest unit test suite, and overviewed the JBossTest structure to understand how to run the tests.

le:
[mkdir] Created dir: /tmp/2.4.4/j
[javac] Compiling 154 source file

install:
[copy] Copyin   p/2
[copy] Copyin   A   p/2

About The JBoss Group

JBoss Group LLC is an Atlanta-based professional services company, created by Marc Fleury, founder and lead developer of the JBoss J2EE-based Open Source Web application server. JBoss Group brings together core JBoss developers to provide services such as training, support and consulting, as well as management of the JBoss software and services affiliate programs. These commercial activities subsidize the development of the free core JBoss server. For additional information on the JBoss Group, see the JBoss Web site at http://www.jboss.org/jbossgroup/services.jsp.

The GNU Lesser General Public liceNse (LGPL) and X License

The JBoss source code is licensed under the LGPL (see http://www.gnu.org/copyleft/lesser.txt). This includes all code in the org.jboss.* package namespace with the exception of code under the org.jboss.pool.* package namespace, which is licensed under the X license (see http://www.x.org/terms.htm). Listing A.1 gives the complete text of the LGPL license. Listing A.2 gives the complete text of the X license.

LISTING A.1   The GNU Lesser General Public License Text

```
           GNU LESSER GENERAL PUBLIC LICENSE
               Version 2.1, February 1999

Copyright (C) 1991, 1999 Free Software Foundation, Inc.
   59 Temple Place, Suite 330, Boston, MA  02111-1307  USA
Everyone is permitted to copy and distribute verbatim copies
of this license document, but changing it is not allowed.

[This is the first released version of the Lesser GPL. It also counts
 as the successor of the GNU Library Public License, version 2, hence
 the version number 2.1.]
```

                Preamble

  The licenses for most software are designed to take away your
freedom to share and change it. By contrast, the GNU General Public
Licenses are intended to guarantee your freedom to share and change
free software—to make sure the software is free for all its users.

  This license, the Lesser General Public License, applies to some
specially designated software packages—typically libraries—of the
Free Software Foundation and other authors who decide to use it. You
can use it too, but we suggest you first think carefully about whether
this license or the ordinary General Public License is the better
strategy to use in any particular case, based on the explanations below.

  When we speak of free software, we are referring to freedom of use,
not price. Our General Public Licenses are designed to make sure that
you have the freedom to distribute copies of free software (and charge
for this service if you wish); that you receive source code or can get
it if you want it; that you can change the software and use pieces of
it in new free programs; and that you are informed that you can do
these things.

  To protect your rights, we need to make restrictions that forbid
distributors to deny you these rights or to ask you to surrender these
rights. These restrictions translate to certain responsibilities for
you if you distribute copies of the library or if you modify it.

  For example, if you distribute copies of the library, whether gratis
or for a fee, you must give the recipients all the rights that we gave
you. You must make sure that they, too, receive or can get the source

code. If you link other code with the library, you must provide complete object files to the recipients, so that they can relink them with the library after making changes to the library and recompiling it. And you must show them these terms so they know their rights.

We protect your rights with a two-step method: (1) we copyright the library, and (2) we offer you this license, which gives you legal permission to copy, distribute and/or modify the library.

To protect each distributor, we want to make it very clear that there is no warranty for the free library. Also, if the library is modified by someone else and passed on, the recipients should know that what they have is not the original version, so that the original author's reputation will not be affected by problems that might be introduced by others.

Finally, software patents pose a constant threat to the existence of any free program. We wish to make sure that a company cannot effectively restrict the users of a free program by obtaining a restrictive license from a patent holder. Therefore, we insist that any patent license obtained for a version of the library must be consistent with the full freedom of use specified in this license.

Most GNU software, including some libraries, is covered by the ordinary GNU General Public License. This license, the GNU Lesser General Public License, applies to certain designated libraries, and is quite different from the ordinary General Public License. We use this license for certain libraries in order to permit linking those libraries into non-free programs.

When a program is linked with a library, whether statically or using a shared library, the combination of the two is legally speaking a combined work, a derivative of the original library. The ordinary General Public License therefore permits such linking only if the entire combination fits its criteria of freedom. The Lesser General Public License permits more lax criteria for linking other code with the library.

We call this license the "Lesser" General Public License because it does less to protect the user's freedom than the ordinary General Public License. It also provides other free software developers less of an advantage over competing non-free programs. These disadvantages are the reason we use the ordinary General Public License for many libraries. However, the Lesser license provides advantages in certain special circumstances.

For example, on rare occasions, there may be a special need to encourage the widest possible use of a certain library, so that it becomes a de-facto standard. To achieve this, non-free programs must be allowed to use the library. A more frequent case is that a free library does the same job as widely used non-free libraries. In this case, there is little to gain by limiting the free library to free software only, so we use the Lesser General Public License.

In other cases, permission to use a particular library in non-free programs enables a greater number of people to use a large body of free software. For example, permission to use the GNU C Library in non-free programs enables many more people to use the whole GNU operating system, as well as its variant, the GNU/Linux operating system.

Although the Lesser General Public License is Less protective of the users' freedom, it does ensure that the user of a program that is linked with the Library has the freedom and the wherewithal to run that program using a modified version of the Library.

The precise terms and conditions for copying, distribution and modification follow. Pay close attention to the difference between a "work based on the library" and a "work that uses the library". The former contains code derived from the library, whereas the latter must be combined with the library to be able to run.

GNU LESSER GENERAL PUBLIC LICENSE
TERMS AND CONDITIONS FOR COPYING, DISTRIBUTION AND MODIFICATION

0. This License Agreement applies to any software library or other program that contains a notice placed by the copyright holder or other authorized party saying it may be distributed under the terms of this Lesser General Public License (also called "this License"). Each licensee is addressed as "you".

A "library" means a collection of software functions and/or data prepared so as to be conveniently linked with application programs (which use some of those functions and data) to form executables.

The "Library", below, refers to any such software library or work
which has been distributed under these terms. A "work based on the
Library" means either the Library or any derivative work under
copyright law: that is to say, a work containing the Library or a
portion of it, either verbatim or with modifications and/or translated
straightforwardly into another language. (Hereinafter, translation is
included without limitation in the term "modification".)

"Source code" for a work means the preferred form of the work for
making modifications to it. For a library, complete source code means
all the source code for all modules it contains, plus any associated
interface definition files, plus the scripts used to control compilation
and installation of the library.

Activities other than copying, distribution and modification are not
covered by this License; they are outside its scope. The act of
running a program using the Library is not restricted, and output from
such a program is covered only if its contents constitute a work based
on the Library (independent of the use of the Library in a tool for
writing it). Whether that is true depends on what the Library does
and what the program that uses the Library does.

1. You may copy and distribute verbatim copies of the Library's
complete source code as you receive it, in any medium, provided that
you conspicuously and appropriately publish on each copy an
appropriate copyright notice and disclaimer of warranty; keep intact
all the notices that refer to this License and to the absence of any
warranty; and distribute a copy of this License along with the
Library.

You may charge a fee for the physical act of transferring a copy,
and you may at your option offer warranty protection in exchange for a
fee.

2. You may modify your copy or copies of the Library or any portion
of it, thus forming a work based on the Library, and copy and
distribute such modifications or work under the terms of Section 1
above, provided that you also meet all of these conditions:

a) The modified work must itself be a software library.

b) You must cause the files modified to carry prominent notices
stating that you changed the files and the date of any change.

c) You must cause the whole of the work to be licensed at no charge to all third parties under the terms of this License.

d) If a facility in the modified Library refers to a function or a table of data to be supplied by an application program that uses the facility, other than as an argument passed when the facility is invoked, then you must make a good faith effort to ensure that, in the event an application does not supply such function or table, the facility still operates, and performs whatever part of its purpose remains meaningful.

(For example, a function in a library to compute square roots has a purpose that is entirely well-defined independent of the application. Therefore, Subsection 2d requires that any application-supplied function or table used by this function must be optional: if the application does not supply it, the square root function must still compute square roots.)

These requirements apply to the modified work as a whole. If identifiable sections of that work are not derived from the Library, and can be reasonably considered independent and separate works in themselves, then this License, and its terms, do not apply to those sections when you distribute them as separate works. But when you distribute the same sections as part of a whole which is a work based on the Library, the distribution of the whole must be on the terms of this License, whose permissions for other licensees extend to the entire whole, and thus to each and every part regardless of who wrote it.

Thus, it is not the intent of this section to claim rights or contest your rights to work written entirely by you; rather, the intent is to exercise the right to control the distribution of derivative or collective works based on the Library.

In addition, mere aggregation of another work not based on the Library with the Library (or with a work based on the Library) on a volume of a storage or distribution medium does not bring the other work under the scope of this License.

3. You may opt to apply the terms of the ordinary GNU General Public License instead of this License to a given copy of the Library. To do this, you must alter all the notices that refer to this License, so

that they refer to the ordinary GNU General Public License, version 2, instead of to this License. (If a newer version than version 2 of the ordinary GNU General Public License has appeared, you can specify that version instead if you wish.) Do not make any other change in these notices.

Once this change is made in a given copy, it is irreversible for that copy, so the ordinary GNU General Public License applies to all subsequent copies and derivative works made from that copy.

This option is useful when you wish to copy part of the code of the Library into a program that is not a library.

4. You may copy and distribute the Library (or a portion or derivative of it, under Section 2) in object code or executable form under the terms of Sections 1 and 2 above provided that you accompany it with the complete corresponding machine-readable source code, which must be distributed under the terms of Sections 1 and 2 above on a medium customarily used for software interchange.

If distribution of object code is made by offering access to copy from a designated place, then offering equivalent access to copy the source code from the same place satisfies the requirement to distribute the source code, even though third parties are not compelled to copy the source along with the object code.

5. A program that contains no derivative of any portion of the Library, but is designed to work with the Library by being compiled or linked with it, is called a "work that uses the Library". Such a work, in isolation, is not a derivative work of the Library, and therefore falls outside the scope of this License.

However, linking a "work that uses the Library" with the Library creates an executable that is a derivative of the Library (because it contains portions of the Library), rather than a "work that uses the library". The executable is therefore covered by this License. Section 6 states terms for distribution of such executables.

When a "work that uses the Library" uses material from a header file that is part of the Library, the object code for the work may be a derivative work of the Library even though the source code is not. Whether this is true is especially significant if the work can be

linked without the Library, or if the work is itself a library. The
threshold for this to be true is not precisely defined by law.

If such an object file uses only numerical parameters, data
structure layouts and accessors, and small macros and small inline
functions (ten lines or less in length), the use of the object
file is unrestricted, regardless of whether it is legally a derivative
work. (Executables containing this object code plus portions of the
Library will still fall under Section 6.)

Otherwise, if the work is a derivative of the Library, you may
distribute the object code for the work under the terms of Section 6.
Any executables containing that work also fall under Section 6,
whether or not they are linked directly with the Library itself.

6. As an exception to the Sections above, you may also combine or
link a "work that uses the Library" with the Library to produce a
work containing portions of the Library, and distribute that work
under terms of your choice, provided that the terms permit
modification of the work for the customer's own use and reverse
engineering for debugging such modifications.

You must give prominent notice with each copy of the work that the
Library is used in it and that the Library and its use are covered by
this License. You must supply a copy of this License. If the work
during execution displays copyright notices, you must include the
copyright notice for the Library among them, as well as a reference
directing the user to the copy of this License. Also, you must do one
of these things:

a) Accompany the work with the complete corresponding
machine-readable source code for the Library including whatever
changes were used in the work (which must be distributed under
Sections 1 and 2 above); and, if the work is an executable linked
with the Library, with the complete machine-readable "work that
uses the Library", as object code and/or source code, so that the
user can modify the Library and then relink to produce a modified
executable containing the modified Library. (It is understood
that the user who changes the contents of definitions files in the
Library will not necessarily be able to recompile the application
to use the modified definitions.)

b) Use a suitable shared library mechanism for linking with the Library. A suitable mechanism is one that (1) uses at run time a copy of the library already present on the user's computer system, rather than copying library functions into the executable, and (2) will operate properly with a modified version of the library, if the user installs one, as long as the modified version is interface-compatible with the version that the work was made with.

c) Accompany the work with a written offer, valid for at least three years, to give the same user the materials specified in Subsection 6a, above, for a charge no more than the cost of performing this distribution.

d) If distribution of the work is made by offering access to copy from a designated place, offer equivalent access to copy the above specified materials from the same place.

e) Verify that the user has already received a copy of these materials or that you have already sent this user a copy.

For an executable, the required form of the "work that uses the Library" must include any data and utility programs needed for reproducing the executable from it. However, as a special exception, the materials to be distributed need not include anything that is normally distributed (in either source or binary form) with the major components (compiler, kernel, and so on) of the operating system on which the executable runs, unless that component itself accompanies the executable.

It may happen that this requirement contradicts the license restrictions of other proprietary libraries that do not normally accompany the operating system. Such a contradiction means you cannot use both them and the Library together in an executable that you distribute.

7. You may place library facilities that are a work based on the Library side-by-side in a single library together with other library facilities not covered by this License, and distribute such a combined library, provided that the separate distribution of the work based on the Library and of the other library facilities is otherwise permitted, and provided that you do these two things:

a) Accompany the combined library with a copy of the same work
based on the Library, uncombined with any other library
facilities. This must be distributed under the terms of the
Sections above.

b) Give prominent notice with the combined library of the fact
that part of it is a work based on the Library, and explaining
where to find the accompanying uncombined form of the same work.

8. You may not copy, modify, sublicense, link with, or distribute
the Library except as expressly provided under this License. Any
attempt otherwise to copy, modify, sublicense, link with, or
distribute the Library is void, and will automatically terminate your
rights under this License. However, parties who have received copies,
or rights, from you under this License will not have their licenses
terminated so long as such parties remain in full compliance.

9. You are not required to accept this License, because you have not
signed it. However, nothing else grants you permission to modify or
distribute the Library or its derivative works. These actions are
prohibited by law if you do not accept this License. Therefore, by
modifying or distributing the Library (or any work based on the
Library), you indicate your acceptance of this License to do so, and
all its terms and conditions for copying, distributing or modifying
the Library or works based on it.

10. Each time you redistribute the Library (or any work based on the
Library), the recipient automatically receives a license from the
original licensor to copy, distribute, link with or modify the Library
subject to these terms and conditions. You may not impose any further
restrictions on the recipients' exercise of the rights granted herein.
You are not responsible for enforcing compliance by third parties with
this License.

11. If, as a consequence of a court judgment or allegation of patent
infringement or for any other reason (not limited to patent issues),
conditions are imposed on you (whether by court order, agreement or
otherwise) that contradict the conditions of this License, they do not
excuse you from the conditions of this License. If you cannot
distribute so as to satisfy simultaneously your obligations under this
License and any other pertinent obligations, then as a consequence you
may not distribute the Library at all. For example, if a patent

license would not permit royalty-free redistribution of the Library by
all those who receive copies directly or indirectly through you,
the only way you could satisfy both it and this License would be to
refrain entirely from distribution of the Library.

If any portion of this section is held invalid or unenforceable under any
particular circumstance, the balance of the section is intended to apply,
and the section as a whole is intended to apply in other circumstances.

It is not the purpose of this section to induce you to infringe any
patents or other property right claims or to contest validity of any
such claims; this section has the sole purpose of protecting the
integrity of the free software distribution system which is
implemented by public license practices. Many people have made
generous contributions to the wide range of software distributed
through that system in reliance on consistent application of that
system; it is up to the author/donor to decide if he or she is willing
to distribute software through any other system and a licensee cannot
impose that choice.

This section is intended to make thoroughly clear what is believed to
be a consequence of the rest of this License.

   12. If the distribution and/or use of the Library is restricted in
certain countries either by patents or by copyrighted interfaces, the
original copyright holder who places the Library under this License may add
an explicit geographical distribution limitation excluding those countries,
so that distribution is permitted only in or among countries not thus
excluded. In such case, this License incorporates the limitation as if
written in the body of this License.

   13. The Free Software Foundation may publish revised and/or new
versions of the Lesser General Public License from time to time.
Such new versions will be similar in spirit to the present version,
but may differ in detail to address new problems or concerns.

Each version is given a distinguishing version number. If the Library
specifies a version number of this License which applies to it and
"any later version", you have the option of following the terms and
conditions either of that version or of any later version published by
the Free Software Foundation. If the Library does not specify a
license version number, you may choose any version ever published by
the Free Software Foundation.

14. If you wish to incorporate parts of the Library into other free programs whose distribution conditions are incompatible with these, write to the author to ask for permission. For software which is copyrighted by the Free Software Foundation, write to the Free Software Foundation; we sometimes make exceptions for this. Our decision will be guided by the two goals of preserving the free status of all derivatives of our free software and of promoting the sharing and reuse of software generally.

NO WARRANTY

15. BECAUSE THE LIBRARY IS LICENSED FREE OF CHARGE, THERE IS NO WARRANTY FOR THE LIBRARY, TO THE EXTENT PERMITTED BY APPLICABLE LAW. EXCEPT WHEN OTHERWISE STATED IN WRITING THE COPYRIGHT HOLDERS AND/OR OTHER PARTIES PROVIDE THE LIBRARY "AS IS" WITHOUT WARRANTY OF ANY KIND, EITHER EXPRESSED OR IMPLIED, INCLUDING, BUT NOT LIMITED TO, THE IMPLIED WARRANTIES OF MERCHANTABILITY AND FITNESS FOR A PARTICULAR PURPOSE. THE ENTIRE RISK AS TO THE QUALITY AND PERFORMANCE OF THE LIBRARY IS WITH YOU. SHOULD THE LIBRARY PROVE DEFECTIVE, YOU ASSUME THE COST OF ALL NECESSARY SERVICING, REPAIR OR CORRECTION.

16. IN NO EVENT UNLESS REQUIRED BY APPLICABLE LAW OR AGREED TO IN WRITING WILL ANY COPYRIGHT HOLDER, OR ANY OTHER PARTY WHO MAY MODIFY AND/OR REDISTRIBUTE THE LIBRARY AS PERMITTED ABOVE, BE LIABLE TO YOU FOR DAMAGES, INCLUDING ANY GENERAL, SPECIAL, INCIDENTAL OR CONSEQUENTIAL DAMAGES ARISING OUT OF THE USE OR INABILITY TO USE THE LIBRARY (INCLUDING BUT NOT LIMITED TO LOSS OF DATA OR DATA BEING RENDERED INACCURATE OR LOSSES SUSTAINED BY YOU OR THIRD PARTIES OR A FAILURE OF THE LIBRARY TO OPERATE WITH ANY OTHER SOFTWARE), EVEN IF SUCH HOLDER OR OTHER PARTY HAS BEEN ADVISED OF THE POSSIBILITY OF SUCH DAMAGES.

END OF TERMS AND CONDITIONS

How to Apply These Terms to Your New Libraries

If you develop a new library, and you want it to be of the greatest possible use to the public, we recommend making it free software that everyone can redistribute and change. You can do so by permitting redistribution under these terms (or, alternatively, under the terms of the ordinary General Public License).

To apply these terms, attach the following notices to the library. It is safest to attach them to the start of each source file to most effectively convey the exclusion of warranty; and each file should have at least the "copyright" line and a pointer to where the full notice is found.

```
<one line to give the library's name and a brief idea of what it does.>
Copyright (C) <year>  <name of author>

This library is free software; you can redistribute it and/or
modify it under the terms of the GNU Lesser General Public
License as published by the Free Software Foundation; either
version 2.1 of the License, or (at your option) any later version.

This library is distributed in the hope that it will be useful,
but WITHOUT ANY WARRANTY; without even the implied warranty of
MERCHANTABILITY or FITNESS FOR A PARTICULAR PURPOSE. See the GNU
Lesser General Public License for more details.

You should have received a copy of the GNU Lesser General Public
License along with this library; if not, write to the Free Software
Foundation, Inc., 59 Temple Place, Suite 330, Boston, MA  02111-1307  USA
```

Also add information on how to contact you by electronic and paper mail.

You should also get your employer (if you work as a programmer) or your school, if any, to sign a "copyright disclaimer" for the library, if necessary. Here is a sample; alter the names:

```
Yoyodyne, Inc., hereby disclaims all copyright interest in the
library `Frob' (a library for tweaking knobs) written by James Random Hacker.

<signature of Ty Coon>, 1 April 1990
Ty Coon, President of Vice
```

That's all there is to it!

LISTING A.2   The X License Text

```
COPYRIGHT AND PERMISSION NOTICE


Copyright (c) 1999,2000,2001 Compaq Computer Corporation
```

LISTING A.2   Continued

```
Copyright (c) 1999,2000,2001 Hewlett-Packard Company
Copyright (c) 1999,2000,2001 IBM Corporation
Copyright (c) 1999,2000,2001 Hummingbird Communications Ltd.
Copyright (c) 1999,2000,2001 Silicon Graphics, Inc.
Copyright (c) 1999,2000,2001 Sun Microsystems, Inc.
Copyright (c) 1999,2000,2001 The Open Group
```

X Window System is a trademark of The Open Group.

ile:
[mkdir] Created dir: /tmp/2.4.4/
[javac] Compiling 154 source file
install:
[copy] Copyin   p/2
[copy] Copyin   B   p/2

JBoss Descriptor Schema Reference

This appendix presents the DTDs for the various JBoss server deployment descriptor and configuration file schemas.

The JBoss Server jboss.xml Descriptor DTD

The jboss.xml descriptor provides the JBoss server specific deployment environment settings for the standard ejb-jar.xml descriptor. Listing B.1 gives the jboss_2_4.dtd file.

LISTING B.1   The jboss_2_4.dtd File

```
<?xml version='1.0' encoding='UTF-8' ?>

<!--
This is the XML DTD for the JBoss 2.4 EJB deployment
descriptor.
The DOCTYPE is:
  <!DOCTYPE jboss PUBLIC
      "-//JBoss//DTD JBOSS 2.4//EN"
      "http://www.jboss.org/j2ee/dtd/jboss_2_4.dtd">

$Id: jboss_2_4.dtd,v 1.1.2.8 2001/11/09 10:43:45 starksm
Exp $
$Revision: 1.1.2.8 $

Overview of the architecture of jboss.xml

<jboss>

  <enforce-ejb-restrictions />
```

LISTING B.1   Continued

```
<security-domain />
<unauthenticated-principal />

<enterprise-beans>

  <entity>
    <ejb-name />
    <jndi-name />
    <resource-ref>
      <res-ref-name />
      <resource-name />
    </resource-ref>
  </entity>

  <session>
    <ejb-name />
    <jndi-name />
    <resource-ref>
      <res-ref-name />
      <resource-name />
    </resource-ref>
  </session>

</enterprise-beans>

<resource-managers>

  <resource-manager>
    <res-name />
    <res-jndi-name />
  </resource-manager>

  <resource-manager>
    <res-name />
    <res-url />
  </resource-manager>

</resource-managers>

<container-configurations>
```

LISTING B.1   Continued

```
    <container-configuration>
      <container-name />
      <container-invoker />
      <container-interceptors />
      <instance-pool />
      <instance-cache />
      <persistence-manager />
      <transaction-manager />
      <locking-policy />
      <container-invoker-conf />
      <container-cache-conf />
      <container-pool-conf />
      <commit-option />
      <optiond-refresh-rate />
      <security-domain/>
    </container-configuration>

  </container-configurations>

</jboss>
-->
<!--
The jboss element is the root element of the jboss.xml file. It
contains all the information used by jboss but not described in
the ejb-jar.xml file. All of it is optional.

1- the application assembler can define custom container
configurations for the beans. Standard configurations are provided
in standardjboss.xml
2- the deployer can override the jndi names under which the beans
are deployed
3- the deployer can specify runtime jndi names for resource
managers.
-->
<!ELEMENT jboss (enforce-ejb-restrictions? , security-domain? ,
unauthenticated-principal? , enterprise-beans? ,
resource-managers? , container-configurations?)>

<!--
  The enforce-ejb-restrictions element tells the container to
enforce ejb1.1 restrictions. It must be one of the following :
```

LISTING B.1   Continued
***

```
    <enforce-ejb-restrictions>true</enforce-ejb-restrictions>
    <enforce-ejb-restrictions>false</enforce-ejb-restrictions>

  Used in: jboss
  -->
<!ELEMENT enforce-ejb-restrictions (#PCDATA)>

<!-- The security-domain element specifies the JNDI name of the
security manager that implements the AuthenticationManager and
RealmMapping for the domain. When specified at the jboss level
it specifies the security domain for all j2ee components in the
deployment unit.
One can override the global security-domain at the container
level using the security-domain element at the
container-configuration level.

  Used in: jboss, container-configuration
  -->
<!ELEMENT security-domain (#PCDATA)>

<!-- The unauthenticated-principal element specifies the name of
the principal that will be returned by the
EJBContext.getCallerPrincipal() method if there is no
authenticated user. This Principal has no roles or privaleges to
call any other beans.
  -->
<!ELEMENT unauthenticated-principal (#PCDATA)>

<!--
  The enterprise-beans element contains additional information
about the beans. This information, such as jndi names, resource
managers and container configurations, are specific to jboss and
not described in ejb-jar.xml.

jboss will provide a standard behavior if no enterprise-beans
element is found, see container-configurations, jndi-name and
resource-managers for defaults.

  Used in: jboss
  -->
<!ELEMENT enterprise-beans (session | entity | message-driven)+>
```

LISTING B.1   Continued

```
<!--
    The entity element holds information specific to jboss and not
declared in ejb-jar.xml about an entity bean, such as jndi name,
container configuration, and resource managers. (see tags for
details). The bean should already be declared in ejb-jar.xml, with
the same ejb-name.

    Used in: enterprise-beans
    -->
<!ELEMENT entity (ejb-name , jndi-name? , configuration-name? ,
security-proxy? , ejb-ref* , resource-ref* , resource-env-ref*)>

<!--
    The session element holds information specific to jboss and
not declared in ejb-jar.xml about a session bean, such as jndi
name, container configuration, and resource managers. (see tags
for details). The bean should already be declared in ejb-jar.xml,
with the same ejb-name.

    Used in: enterprise-beans
    -->
<!ELEMENT session (ejb-name , jndi-name? , configuration-name? ,
security-proxy? , ejb-ref* , resource-ref* , resource-env-ref*)>

<!--
    The message-driven element holds information specific to jboss
and not declared in ejb-jar.xml about a message-driven bean, such
as container configuration and resources.
The bean should already be declared in ejb-jar.xml, with the same
ejb-name.

    Used in: enterprise-beans
    -->
<!ELEMENT message-driven (ejb-name , destination-jndi-name ,
configuration-name? , security-proxy? , ejb-ref* , resource-ref*,
resource-env-ref*)>

<!--
    The ejb-name element gives the name of the bean, it must
correspond to an ejb-name element in ejb-jar.xml
```

LISTING B.1   Continued

```
      Used in: entity, session, and message-driven
      -->
<!ELEMENT ejb-name (#PCDATA)>

<!-- The jndi-name element gives the actual jndi name under which
the bean will be deployed when used in the entity, session and
message-driven elements. If it is not provided jboss will assume
 "jndi-name" = "ejb-name"

When used in the ejb-ref, resource-ref, resource-env-ref elements
this specifies the jndi name to which the reference should link.

      Used in: entity, session and message-driven
      ejb-ref, resource-ref, resource-env-ref
-->
<!ELEMENT jndi-name (#PCDATA)>

<!-- The configuration-name element gives the name of the
container configuration for this bean. It must match one of the
container-name tags in the container-configurations section, or
one of the standard configurations. If none is provided, jboss
will automatically use the right standard configuration, see
container-configurations.

      Used in: entity, session, and message-driven
      -->
<!ELEMENT configuration-name (#PCDATA)>

<!ELEMENT destination-jndi-name (#PCDATA)>

<!-- The security-proxy gives the class name of the security proxy
implementation. This may be an instance of
org.jboss.security.SecurityProxy, or an just an object that
implements methods in the home or remote interface of an EJB
without implementating any common interface.

      Used in: entity, session, and message-driven
      -->
<!ELEMENT security-proxy (#PCDATA)>
```

LISTING B.1   Continued

```
<!-- The ejb-ref element is used to give the jndi-name of an
external ejb reference. In the case of an external ejb reference,
you don't provide a ejb-link element in ejb-jar.xml, but you
provide a jndi-name in jboss.xml

     Used in: entity, session, and message-driven
     -->
<!ELEMENT ejb-ref (ejb-ref-name , jndi-name)>

<!-- The ejb-ref-name element is the name of the ejb reference as
given in ejb-jar.xml.

     Used in: ejb-ref
     -->
<!ELEMENT ejb-ref-name (#PCDATA)>



<!-- The resource-env-ref element gives a mapping between the
"code name" of a env resource (res-ref-name, provided by the
Bean Developer) and its deployed JNDI name.

     Used in: session, entity, message-driven
     -->
<!ELEMENT resource-env-ref (resource-env-ref-name , jndi-name)>

<!-- The resource-env-ref-name element gives the "code name" of
a resource. It is provided by the Bean Developer. See
resource-managers for the actual

     Used in: resource-env-ref
     -->
<!ELEMENT resource-env-ref-name (#PCDATA)>



<!-- The resource-ref element gives a mapping between the
"code name" of a resource (res-ref-name, provided by the Bean
Developer) and its "xml name" (resource-name, provided by the
Application Assembler). If no resource-ref is provided, jboss
will assume that
     "xml-name" = "code name"
```

LISTING B.1   Continued

```
        See resource-managers.

        Used in: entity, session, and message-driven
        -->
<!ELEMENT resource-ref (res-ref-name , (resource-name |
jndi-name | res-url))>

<!-- The res-ref-name element gives the "code name" of a resource.
It is provided by the Bean Developer. See resource-managers for
the actual configuration of the resource.

        Used in: resource-ref
        -->
<!ELEMENT res-ref-name (#PCDATA)>

<!-- The resource-name element gives the "xml name" of the
resource. It is provided by the Application Assembler. See
resource-managers for the actual configuration of the resource.

        Used in: resource-ref
        -->
<!ELEMENT resource-name (#PCDATA)>

<!-- The resource-managers element is used to declare resource
managers. A resource has three names:
 - the "code name" is the name used in the code of the bean,
supplied by the Bean Developer in the resource-ref section of
the ejb-jar.xml file

 - the "xml name" is an intermediary name used by the Application
Assembler to identify resources in the XML file.

 - the "runtime jndi name" is the actual jndi-name or url of the
deployed resource, it is supplied by the Deployer.

The mapping between the "code name" and the "xml name" is given
in the resource-ref section for the bean. If not, jboss will
assume that "xml name" = "code name."
```

LISTING B.1   Continued

The mapping between the "xml name" and the "runtime jndi name"
is given in a resource-manager section. If not, and if the
datasource is of type javax.sql.DataSource, jboss will look for
a javax.sql.DataSource in the jndi tree.

  Used in: jboss
  -->
<!ELEMENT resource-managers (resource-manager*)>

<!-- The resource-manager element is used to provide a mapping
between the "xml name" of a resource (res-name) and its
"runtime jndi name" (res-jndi-name or res-url according to the
type of the resource). If it is not provided, and if the type of
the resource is javax.sql.DataSource, jboss will look for a
javax.sql.DataSource in the jndi tree.

    See resource-managers.

    Used in: resource-managers
    -->
<!ELEMENT resource-manager (res-name , (res-jndi-name | res-url))>

<!-- The res-name element gives the "xml name" of a resource, it
is provided by the Application Assembler. See resource-managers.

      Used in: resource-manager
      -->
<!ELEMENT res-name (#PCDATA)>

<!-- The res-jndi-name element is the "deployed jndi name" of a
resource, it is provided by the Deployer. See resource-managers.

      Used in: resource-manager
      -->
<!ELEMENT res-jndi-name (#PCDATA)>

<!-- The res-url element is the "runtime jndi name" as a url of
the resource. It is provided by the Deployer. See
resource-managers.

LISTING B.1   Continued

```
    Used in: resource-manager
    -->
<!ELEMENT res-url (#PCDATA)>

<!-- The container-configurations element declares the different
possible container configurations that the beans can use.
standardjboss.xml provides five standard configurations with the
following container-names:
   - Standard CMP EntityBean
   - Standard BMP EntityBean
   - Standard Stateless SessionBean
   - Standard Stateful SessionBean
   - Standard Message Driven Bean

These standard configurations will automatically be used if no
custom configuration is specified. The application assembler can
define advanced custom configurations here.

  Used in: jboss
-->
<!ELEMENT container-configurations (container-configuration*)>

<!-- The container-configuration element describes a configuration
for the container. The different plugins to use are declared here,
as well as their configurations. The configuration-class attribute
is no longer used.

    Used in: container-configurations
    -->
<!ELEMENT container-configuration (container-name , call-logging?,
container-invoker? , container-interceptors? , instance-pool? ,
instance-cache? , persistence-manager? , transaction-manager? ,
locking-policy? , container-invoker-conf? , container-cache-conf?,
container-pool-conf? , commit-option? , optiond-refresh-rate? ,
(security-domain |
 (role-mapping-manager , authentication-module))?)>

<!-- The configuration-class attribute is used to indicate the
implementation class that will be loaded for this configuration.
```

LISTING B.1   Continued

```
This usually indicates what type of bean the configuration applies
to.
-->
<!ATTLIST container-configuration configuration-class CDATA  #IMPLIED>

<!-- The container-name element gives the name of the
configuration being defined. Beans may refer to this name in their
configuration-name tag.

     Used in: container-configuration
-->
<!ELEMENT container-name (#PCDATA)>

<!-- The call-logging element tells if the container must log
every method invocation for this bean or not. Its value must be
true or false.

     Used in: container-configuration
     -->
<!ELEMENT call-logging (#PCDATA)>

<!-- The container-invoker element gives the class name of the
container invoker jboss must use for in this configuration. This
class must implement the org.jboss.ejb.ContainerInvoker
interface. The default is
org.jboss.ejb.plugins.jrmp13.server.JRMPContainerInvoker.

     Used in: container-configuration
-->
<!ELEMENT container-invoker (#PCDATA)>

<!-- The container-interceptors element gives the chain of
Interceptors (instances of org.jboss.ejb.Interceptor) that are
associated with the container. The declared order of the
interceptor elements corresponds to the order of the interceptor
chain.

Used in: container-configuration
-->
<!ELEMENT container-interceptors (interceptor+)>
```

LISTING B.1   Continued

```
<!-- The interceptor element specifies an instance of
org.jboss.ejb.Interceptor that is to be added to the container
interceptor stack.

Used in: container-interceptors
-->
<!ELEMENT interceptor (#PCDATA)>

<!-- The transaction attribute is used to indicate what type of
container its interceptor applies to. It is an enumerated value
that can take on one of: Bean, Container or Both. A value of Bean
indicates that the interceptor should only be added to a container
for bean-managed transaction. A value of Container indicates that
the interceptor should only be added to a container for
container-managed transactions. A value of Both indicates that the
interceptor should be added to all containers. This is the default
value if the transaction attribute is not explicitly given.
-->
<!ATTLIST
    interceptor transaction (Bean | Container | Both ) "Both">

<!-- The metricsEnabled attributes is used to indicate if the
interceptor should only be included when the
org.jboss.ejb.ContainerFactory metricsEnabled flag is set to true.
The allowed values are true and false with false being the default
if metricsEnabled is not explicitly given.
-->
<!ATTLIST interceptor metricsEnabled  (true | false )  "false">

<!-- The instance-pool element gives the class name of the
instance pool jboss must use for in this configuration. This
class must implement the org.jboss.ejb.InstancePool interface.
The defaults are:
 - org.jboss.ejb.plugins.EntityInstancePool for entity beans
 - org.jboss.ejb.plugins.StatelessSessionInstancePool for
stateless session beans.
 - no pool is used for stateful session beans

    Used in: container-configuration
    -->
```

LISTING B.1   Continued

```
<!ELEMENT instance-pool (#PCDATA)>

<!-- The instance-cache element gives the class name of the
instance cache jboss must use for in this configuration. This
class must implement the org.jboss.ejb.InstanceCache interface.
The defaults are:
 - org.jboss.ejb.plugins.EntityInstanceCache for entity beans
 - org.jboss.ejb.plugins.StatefulSessionInstanceCache for
stateful session beans.
 - no cache is used for stateless session beans

     Used in: container-configuration
-->
<!ELEMENT instance-cache (#PCDATA)>

<!-- The persistence-manager element gives the class name of
the persistence manager / persistence store jboss must use for
in this configuration. This class must implement:
 - org.jboss.ejb.EntityPersistenceStore for CMP Entity Beans
(default is org.jboss.ejb.plugins.jaws.JAWSPersistenceManager)
 - org.jboss.ejb.EntityPersistenceManager for BMP entity beans
(default is org.jboss.ejb.plugins.BMPPersistenceManager)
 - org.jboss.ejb.StatefulSessionPersistenceManager for stateless
session beans.
 - no persistence-manager is used for stateless session beans

     Used in: container-configuration
-->
<!ELEMENT persistence-manager (#PCDATA)>

<!-- The locking-policy element gives the class name of the EJB
lock  implementation JBoss must use for in this configuration.
This class must implement  the org.jboss.ejb.BeanLock interface.
The default is
org.jboss.ejb.plugins.lock.QueuedPessimisticEJBLock.

     Used in: container-configuration
-->
<!ELEMENT locking-policy (#PCDATA)>
```

LISTING B.1   Continued

```
<!-- The transaction-manager element gives the class name of the
transaction manager jboss must use for in this configuration.
This class must implement the javax.transaction.TransactionManager
interface. The is no longer used as the TM is assumed to be
located at java:/TransactionManager

     Used in: container-configuration
-->
<!ELEMENT transaction-manager (#PCDATA)>

<!-- The container-invoker-conf element holds configuration data
for the container invoker. jboss does not read directly the
subtree for this element; instead, it is passed to the container
invoker instance (if it implements org.jboss.metadata.XmlLoadable)
for it to load its parameters.

The Optimized tag described here only relates to the default container
     invoker, JRMPContainerInvoker.

     Used in: container-configuration
-->
<!ELEMENT container-invoker-conf (JMSProviderAdapterJNDI?,
ServerSessionPoolFactoryJNDI?, MaximumSize?, MaxMessages?,
RMIObjectPort?, Optimized, RMIClientSocketFactory?,
RMIServerSocketFactory?, RMIServerSocketAddr?, ssl-domain?)>

<!-- This element is only valid if the container invoker is
JRMPContainerInvoker.

The Optimized element tells if the container invoker to bypass RMI
layers when the client is local (same VM as the server). This
optimizes RMI calls. Its value must be true or false.

     Used in: container-invoker-conf for JRMPContainerInvoker
-->
<!ELEMENT Optimized (#PCDATA)>

<!-- The RMIObjectPort element indicates what port the RMI objects
created by this container should listen on. Any number of objects
in the same VM can use the same port. However, objects in
```

LISTING B.1   Continued

different VMs cannot use the same port. You may set this value
to 0 to use anyonmous ports (that is, each object just picks a
free port to use). If you want to run jBoss more than once on
the same machine, you must either create separate configurations
with separate ports, or set all the configurations to use
anonymous port. The standard jBoss setting is "4444".

Its value must an integer (0, or a valid port number). Note that
normal user on a UNIX system cannot access privileged ports
<1024)

        Used in: container-invoker-conf for JRMPContainerInvoker
-->
<!ELEMENT RMIObjectPort (#PCDATA)>

<!-- The RMIClientSocketFactory element indicates the use of a
custom socket factory that should be used by RMI objects created
by this container. The combination of socket factory type and port
must be unique but more than one container can use the same   socket
factory, port combination.

Its value must be the fully qualified name of the class that
implements the java.rmi.server.RMIClientSocketFactory interface,
and the class must be available to the JBoss class loader.
If this element is not specified the default VM client socket
factory will be used.

    Used in: container-invoker-conf for JRMPContainerInvoker
-->
<!ELEMENT RMIClientSocketFactory (#PCDATA)>

<!-- The RMIServerSocketFactory element indicates the use of a
custom socket factory that should be used by RMI objects
created by this container. The combination of socket factory
type and port must be unique but more than one container can
use the same socket factory, port combination.

Its value must be the fully qualified name of the class that
implements the java.rmi.server.RMIServerSocketFactory interface,
and the class must be available to the JBoss class loader.

LISTING B.1   Continued

If this element is not specified the default VM server socket
factory will be used.

    Used in: container-invoker-conf for JRMPContainerInvoker
-->
<!ELEMENT RMIServerSocketFactory (#PCDATA)>

<!-- The RMIServerSocketAddr element specifies the address on
which the RMI objects should be bound.

Its value is the interface address as a dot decimal IP address or
hostname.

    Used in: container-invoker-conf for JRMPContainerInvoker
-->
<!ELEMENT RMIServerSocketAddr (#PCDATA)>

<!-- The ssl-domain element specifies the JNDI name of a
org.jboss.security.SecurityDomain implementation. It is used
by the custom SSL socket factory implementations.

    Used in: container-invoker-conf for JRMPContainerInvoker
-->
<!ELEMENT ssl-domain (#PCDATA)>

<!ELEMENT JMSProviderAdapterJNDI (#PCDATA)>

<!ELEMENT ServerSessionPoolFactoryJNDI (#PCDATA)>

<!ELEMENT MaxMessages (#PCDATA)>

<!-- The container-cache-conf element holds dynamic configuration
data for the instance cache. jboss does not read directly the
subtree for this element; instead, it is passed to the instance
cache instance (if it implements org.jboss.metadata.XmlLoadable)
for it to load its parameters.

    Used in: container-configuration
-->
<!ELEMENT container-cache-conf (cache-policy? ,
cache-policy-conf?)>

LISTING B.1   Continued

```
<!-- The implementation class for the cache policy, which controls
when instances will be passivated, etc.

    Used in: container-cache-conf
-->
<!ELEMENT cache-policy (#PCDATA)>

<!-- The configuration settings for the selected cache policy.
This is currently only valid for the LRU cache. When the cache
is the LRU one for the stateful container, the elements
remover-period and max-bean-life specifies the period of the
remover task that removes stateful beans (that normally have been
passivated) that have age greater than the specified max-bean-life
element.

Used in: container-cache-conf (when cache-policy is the LRU cache)
-->
<!ELEMENT cache-policy-conf (min-capacity , max-capacity ,
remover-period? , max-bean-life? , overager-period , max-bean-age,
resizer-period , max-cache-miss-period , min-cache-miss-period ,
cache-load-factor)>

<!-- The minimum capacity of this cache
-->
<!ELEMENT min-capacity (#PCDATA)>

<!-- The maximum capacity of this cache
-->
<!ELEMENT max-capacity (#PCDATA)>

<!-- The period of the overager's runs
-->
<!ELEMENT overager-period (#PCDATA)>

<!-- The period of the remover's runs
-->
<!ELEMENT remover-period (#PCDATA)>

<!-- The max-bean-life specifies the period of the remover task
that removes stateful beans (that normally have been passivated)
that have age greater than the specified max-bean-life element.
-->
```

LISTING B.1   Continued

```
<!ELEMENT max-bean-life (#PCDATA)>

<!-- The period of the resizer's runs
-->
<!ELEMENT resizer-period (#PCDATA)>

<!-- The age after which a bean is automatically passivated
-->
<!ELEMENT max-bean-age (#PCDATA)>

<!-- Shrink cache capacity if there is a cache miss every or more
this member's value
-->
<!ELEMENT max-cache-miss-period (#PCDATA)>

<!-- Enlarge cache capacity if there is a cache miss every or
less this member's value
-->
<!ELEMENT min-cache-miss-period (#PCDATA)>

<!-- The resizer will always try to keep the cache capacity so
that the cache is this member's value loaded of cached objects
-->
<!ELEMENT cache-load-factor (#PCDATA)>

<!-- The container-pool-conf element holds configuration data for
the instance pool. jboss does not read directly the subtree for
this element; instead, it is passed to the instance pool instance
(if it implements org.jboss.metadata.XmlLoadable) for it to load
its parameters.

The default instance pools, EntityInstancePool and
StatelessSessionInstancePool, both accept the following
MaximumSize configuration.

   Used in: container-configuration
-->
<!ELEMENT container-pool-conf ((MaximumSize , MinimumSize) |
   Synchronized)>
```

LISTING B.1   Continued

```
<!-- This element is only valid if the instance pool is a subclass
of AbstractInstancePool.

The MaximumSize element gives the maximum number of instance to
keep in the pool. Its value must be an integer.

  Used in: container-pool-conf for AbstractInstancePool subclasses
-->
<!ELEMENT MaximumSize (#PCDATA)>

<!-- This element is only valid if the instance pool is a subclass
of AbstractInstancePool.

The MinimumSize element gives the minimum number of instance to
keep in the pool. Its value must be an integer.

  Used in: container-pool-conf for AbstractInstancePool subclasses
-->
<!ELEMENT MinimumSize (#PCDATA)>

<!-- This element is only valid if the instance pool is
StatelessSessionInstancePool.

The Synchronized element instructs the pool to synchronize
calls to the Session bean. Its value must be true or false.

  Used in: container-pool-conf for StatelessSessionInstancePool
-->
<!ELEMENT Synchronized (#PCDATA)>

<!-- This option is only used for entity container configurations.

The commit-option element tells the container which option to use
for transactions. Its value must be A, B C, or D.

 - option A: the entiry instance has exclusive access to the
database. The instance stays ready after a transaction.
 - option B: the entity instance does not have exclusive access
to the database. The state is loaded before the next transaction.
```

LISTING B.1   Continued

```
 - option C: same as B, except the container does not keep the
instance after commit: a passivate is immediately performed after
the commit.
 - option D: a lazy update. default is every 30 secs. can be
updated with <optiond-refresh-rate>

See ejb1.1 specification for details (p118).

    Used in: container-configuration
-->
<!ELEMENT commit-option (#PCDATA)>

<!-- This element is used to specify the refresh rate of commit
option d
-->
<!ELEMENT optiond-refresh-rate (#PCDATA)>

<!-- The role-mapping-manager element specifies the JNDI name of
the org.jboss.security.RealmMapping implementation that is to be
used by the container SecurityInterceptor. Its use is deprecated
in favor of the security-domain element.

    Used in: container-configuration
-->
<!ELEMENT role-mapping-manager (#PCDATA)>

<!-- The authentication-module element specifies the JNDI name of
the org.jboss.security.AuthenticationManager implementation that
is to be used by the container SecurityInterceptor. Its use is
deprecated in favor of the security-domain element.

    Used in: container-configuration
-->
<!ELEMENT authentication-module (#PCDATA)>
```

The JBoss Server jaws.xml Descriptor DTD

The jaws.xml descriptor provides customization for the JBossCMP persistence engine.
Listing B.2 gives the jaws_2_4.dtd file.

LISTING B.2   The jaws_2_4.dtd File

```
<?xml version='1.0' encoding='UTF-8' ?>


<!--
This is the XML DTD for the JAWS deployment descriptor.
   <!DOCTYPE jaws PUBLIC
        "-//JBoss//DTD JAWS 2.4//EN"
        "http://www.jboss.org/j2ee/dtd/jaws_2_4.dtd">
-->
<!-- The jaws element is always the root (document) node of the
jaws.xml deployment descriptor or the standardjaws.xml defaults
document. All elements are declared as optional - if not given
in jaws.xml, defaults will be read from standardjaws.xml -->
<!ELEMENT jaws (datasource? , type-mapping? , debug? ,
default-entity? , enterprise-beans? , type-mappings?)>


<!-- the datasource element is used to indicate to JAWS which
datasource should be used for persistence of the CMP entities in
this ejb-jar. It should be the datasource named as it appears in
jboss' global naming context. The default is java:/DefaultDS

Beans are also allowed to specify datasources at bean level and
will override this datasource if specified.

Used In: jaws, entity
 -->
<!ELEMENT datasource (#PCDATA)>


<!-- the type-mapping element is used to indicate to JAWS which
set of mappings from java types to jdbc and SQL types to be used
for CMP beans in this jar. type-mappings are defined within the
type-mappings element with a type-mapping element that carries a
separate meaning: This DTD will not parse! -->
<!ELEMENT type-mapping (#PCDATA)>


<!ELEMENT debug (#PCDATA)>

<!ELEMENT default-entity (create-table , remove-table ,
 tuned-updates , read-only , pk-constraint? , select-for-update?,
 time-out)>
```

LISTING B.2   Continued

```
<!ELEMENT create-table (#PCDATA)>

<!ELEMENT remove-table (#PCDATA)>

<!ELEMENT tuned-updates (#PCDATA)>

<!ELEMENT read-only (#PCDATA)>

<!ELEMENT pk-constraint (#PCDATA)>

<!ELEMENT select-for-update (#PCDATA)>

<!ELEMENT time-out (#PCDATA)>

<!-- the enterprise-beans tag contains overridden attribute
mappings for any CMP bean in this ejb-jar that requires
non-default column mapping behavior -->
<!ELEMENT enterprise-beans (entity*)>

<!-- the entity element defines a non-default column mapping for
a CMP entity bean in this ejb-jar. This includes query
specifications for any finders that either do not correspond to a
single cmp-field or that require a specific ordering. it must
contain an ejb-name element, can contain 0 or more cmp-field
elements and my contain 0 or more finder elements.
 Other options include:
- read-ahead: When a finder is called, load all data for all
 entities.
- read-only: Do not persist any changes to the bean's state.
- table-name: Name of the corresponding table.
- tuned-updates: emit 'update' SQL statements that update only
 changed fields.
- create-table: On deploy, create the table if it doesn't exist.
- remove-table: On undeploy, drop the table from the database
 (with all_data_!!!)
- select-for-update: On loading the bean, use the
 'select ... for update' syntax, locking the row.
- pk-constraint: If create-table is on, create it with a primary
 key.
- time-out: For read-only only, re-load entity after time-out
 -->
```

LISTING B.2 Continued

```
<!ELEMENT entity (ejb-name , datasource? , cmp-field* , finder* ,
 read-ahead? , read-only? , table-name? , tuned-updates? ,
 create-table? , remove-table? , select-for-update? , time-out? ,
 pk-constraint?)>

<!-- ejb-name within an entity element must contain the ejb-name
as specified in ejb-jar.xml. -->
<!ELEMENT ejb-name (#PCDATA)>

<!ELEMENT cmp-field (field-name , column-name ,
   (jdbc-type , sql-type)?)>

<!ELEMENT field-name (#PCDATA)>

<!ELEMENT column-name (#PCDATA)>

<!-- the finder element overrides JAWS default behavior for a
finder, or specifies JAWS behavior for finders requiring
multicolumn where clauses or a specific ordering. it must contain
name and query elements and may contain one order element.
After JBoss version 2.3, it may contain a read-ahead element
indicating whether or not all data for the entities selected
should be loaded immediately. Note that JAWS/JBoss cannot guarantee
serializable transactions with the read-ahead  option!-->
<!ELEMENT finder (name , query , order? , read-ahead?)>

<!-- the name within a finder element must contain the name of
the finder method from the bean's home interface -->
<!ELEMENT name (#PCDATA)>

<!-- the query element must contain the where clause that will
select the proper rows to be returned by the finder. If this
query begins with an inner join clause, it may specify multiple
tables. -->
<!ELEMENT query (#PCDATA)>

<!-- the order element should contain a SQL order by clause
(without the initial 'order by' verb!) that should be used to
order the results of the query for the finder -->
<!ELEMENT order (#PCDATA)>
```

LISTING B.2   Continued

```
<!ELEMENT read-ahead (#PCDATA)>

<!ELEMENT table-name (#PCDATA)>

<!ELEMENT type-mappings (type-mapping-definition*)>

<!ELEMENT type-mapping-definition (name , mapping*)>

<!ELEMENT mapping (java-type , jdbc-type , sql-type)>

<!-- The java-type element specifies the fully qualified name of
a Java class. This is the Java type of an entity bean cmp-field.
-->
<!ELEMENT java-type (#PCDATA)>

<!-- The jdbc-type element specifies Java class name to JDBC type
mapping. The value of the jdbc-type element is the string name of
the java.sql.Types constant to which the Java class should map.
This is used to determine what JDBC type to use when encoding an
entity bean field value into a JDBC java.sql.PreparedStatement.
-->
<!ELEMENT jdbc-type (#PCDATA)>

<!-- The sql-type element specifies the database SQL declaration
for the jdbc-type. This is used when JAWS creates a table for an
entity bean.
-->
<!ELEMENT sql-type (#PCDATA)>
```

The JBoss Server jboss-web.xml Descriptor DTD

The jboss-web.xml descriptor provides the JBoss server specific deployment environment settings for the standard web.xml descriptor. Listing B.3 gives the jboss_2_4.dtd
file.

LISTING B.3   The jboss-web.dtd File

```
<?xml version='1.0' encoding='UTF-8' ?>

<!-- The JBoss specific elements used to integrate the servlet
web.xml elements into a JBoss deployment.
```

LISTING B.3 Continued

```
DOCTYPE jboss-web
    PUBLIC "-//JBoss//DTD Web Application 2.2//EN"
    "http://www.jboss.org/j2ee/dtds/jboss-web.dtd"
-->


<!-- The jboss-web element is the root element.
-->
<!ELEMENT jboss-web (security-domain? , resource-env-ref* ,
resource-ref* , ejb-ref*)>


<!-- The security-domain element allows one to specify a module
wide security manager domain. It specifies the JNDI name of the
security manager that implements the AuthenticationManager and
RealmMapping for the domain.
-->
<!ELEMENT security-domain (#PCDATA)>


<!-- The ejb-ref element maps from the servlet ENC relative name
of the ejb reference to the deployment environment JNDI name of
the bean.
Example:
    <ejb-ref>
        <ejb-ref-name>ejb/Bean0</ejb-ref-name>
        <jndi-name>deployed/ejbs/Bean0</jndi-name>
    </ejb-ref>
-->
<!ELEMENT ejb-ref (ejb-ref-name , jndi-name)>


<!-- The ejb-ref-name element gives the ENC relative name used
in the web-app.xml ejb-ref-name element.
-->
<!ELEMENT ejb-ref-name (#PCDATA)>


<!-- The jndi-name element specifies the JNDI name of the deployed
EJB home interface to which the servlet ENC binding will link to.
-->
<!ELEMENT jndi-name (#PCDATA)>


<!-- The resource-ref maps from the servlet ENC relative name to
the deployed JNDI name of the resource factory.
Example:
```

```
    <resource-ref>
        <res-ref-name>jms/QCF</res-ref-name>
        <jndi-name>QueueConnectionFactory</jndi-name>
    </resource-ref>
-->
<!ELEMENT resource-ref (res-ref-name , jndi-name)>

<!ELEMENT res-ref-name (#PCDATA)>

<!-- The resource-env-ref maps from the servlet ENC relative
name to the deployed JNDI name of the env resource.
Example:
<resource-env-ref>
 <resource-env-ref-name>ldap/Groups</res-ref-name>
 <jndi-name>ldap://somehost:389/ou=Group,o=somedot.com</jndi-name>
</resource-env-ref>
-->
<!ELEMENT resource-env-ref (resource-env-ref-name , jndi-name)>

<!ELEMENT resource-env-ref-name (#PCDATA)>
```

The JBoss Server jboss.jcml Configuration File DTD

The jboss.jcml configuration file is an XML document that defines the MBean
services that are to be loaded into the JBoss server. The content model is defined by
the jboss_jcml.dtd, and Listing B.4 gives the jboss.jcml file DTD.

```
<?xml version='1.0' encoding='UTF-8' ?>

<!-- The server element is the root element of the jboss.jcml
configuration document. It may contain one or more mbean
configuration elements.
-->
<!ELEMENT server (mbean+)>

<!-- The mbean element defines a configuration for an MBean
that is to be instatiated in the JBoss server. The mbean class
files must be available via the JBoss thread context class loader.
```

LISTING B.4   Continued

```
-->
<!ELEMENT mbean (constructor? , attribute*, config?)>

<!-- The mbean element attributes include:
- code: the fully qualified class name of the mbean implementation.
- name: the JMX ObjectName to assign to the MBean.
- serviceFactory: the class name which implements the
org.jboss.util.ServiceFactory interface. This is used to obtain an
org.jboss.util.Service interface wrapper for the MBean.
-->
<!ATTLIST mbean   code            CDATA   #REQUIRED
                  name            CDATA   #REQUIRED
                  serviceFactory CDATA   #IMPLIED >

<!-- The constructor element specifies the mbean constructor
signature. The child arg elements give the constructor argument
type and values.
-->
<!ELEMENT constructor (arg*)>

<!-- The arg element is used to specify one constructor argument
type and value.
-->
<!ELEMENT arg EMPTY>

<!-- The arg element attributes include:
- type: the fully qualified class name of the argument type as
defined by the ctor signature. This defaults to java.lang.String
- value: the string representation of the argument value. If
the type is not String, a string to value converter is located
using the java.beans.PropertyEditorManager class.
-->
<!ATTLIST arg   type  CDATA   #IMPLIED
                value CDATA   #IMPLIED >

<!-- The attribute element specifies an attribute name and value for an
mbean attribute. The content of the attribute element is the string
representation of the attribute value.
-->
<!ELEMENT attribute (#PCDATA)>
```

LISTING B.4   Continued

```
<!-- The name attribute of the attribute element gives the name
of the enclosing mbean attribute to set.
-->
<!ATTLIST attribute  name CDATA  #REQUIRED >

<!-- The config element is an optional placeholder element for
arbitrary configuration information. If the mbean supports a
importXml(org.w3c.dom.Element) method it can be supplied arbitrary
configuration data by including a config element.
-->
<!ELEMENT config ANY>
```

The JBoss Server jbossmq-state.xml Configuration File DTD

The jbossmq-state.xml configuration file is an XML document that is used by the StateManager MBean for simple user-to-password and user-to-durable subscription mapping. The content model is defined by the jbossmq-state.dtd, and Listing B.5 gives the jbossmq-state.xml file DTD.

LISTING B.5: The jbossmq-state.xml File DTD

```
<?xml version='1.0' encoding='UTF-8' ?>

<!-- The StateManager element is the root element of the
jbossmq-state.xml document.
-->
<!ELEMENT StateManager (User*)>

<!-- The User element defines a JBossMQ user.
-->
<!ELEMENT User (Name , Password , Id , DurableSubscription*)>

<!-- The Name element gives the username that corresponds to the
Connection.createConnection(username, password) method, as well
as the value passed as the name parameter to the
TopicSession.createDurableSubscriber(Topic, name) method when
used in the DurableSubscription element.
-->
<!ELEMENT Name (#PCDATA)>
```

LISTING B.5   Continued

```
<!-- The Password element gives the password that corresponds to
the Connection.createConnection(username, password) method.
-->
<!ELEMENT Password (#PCDATA)>

<!-- The Id element gives the clientID that will be associated
with the connection for the username.
-->
<!ELEMENT Id (#PCDATA)>

<!-- The DurableSubscription: element is a listing of the durable
subscriptions associated with the username.
-->
<!ELEMENT DurableSubscription (Name , TopicName)>

<!-- The TopicName element gives the name of the Topic currently
associated with the durable subscription.
-->
<!ELEMENT TopicName (#PCDATA)>
```

le:
[mkdir] Created dir: /tmp/2.4.4/
[javac] Compiling 154 source file

install:
[copy] Copyin   C   p/2
[copy] Copyin   p/2

The CD Contents

This appendix provides an overview of the CD included with this book. The CD contents consist of the book examples source and Ant build scripts, the Ant distribution, the JBoss source and binary distributions, the Java Pet Store application and patch, and the Apache servlet container distributions. The individual files are:

- Apache/LICENSE.txt—The Apache Software License text.

- Apache/jakarta-ant-1.4.1-bin.tar.gz—The Ant 1.4.1 binary distribution as a gzipped tar archive. It is available from
  `http://jakarta.apache.org/builds/jakarta-ant/release/v1.4.1/bin/jakarta-ant-1.4.1-bin.tar.gz`.

- Apache/jakarta-ant-1.4.1-bin.zip—The Ant 1.4.1 binary distribution as a zip archive. It is available from `http://jakarta.apache.org/builds/jakarta-ant/release/v1.4.1/bin/jakarta-ant-1.4.1-bin.zip`.

- Apache/jakarta-tomcat-3.2.4.tar.gz—The Tomcat 3.2.4 servlet container as a gzipped tar archive. It is available from
  `http://jakarta.apache.org/builds/jakarta-tomcat/release/v3.2.4/bin/jakarta-tomcat-3.2.4.tar.gz`.

- Apache/jakarta-tomcat-3.2.4.zip—The Tomcat 3.2.4 servlet container as a zip archive. It is available from `http://jakarta.apache.org/builds/jakarta-tomcat/release/v3.2.4/bin/jakarta-tomcat-3.2.4.zip`.

- Apache/jakarta-tomcat-4.0.1.tar.gz—The Tomcat 4.0.1 servlet container as a gzipped tar archive. It is available from `http://jakarta.apache.org/builds/jakarta-tomcat-4.0/release/v4.0.1/bin/jakarta-tomcat-4.0.1.tar.gz`.

- Apache/jakarta-tomcat-4.0.1.zip—The Tomcat 4.0.1 servlet container as a zip archive. It is available from `http://jakarta.apache.org/builds/jakarta-tomcat-4.0/release/v4.0.1/bin/jakarta-tomcat-4.0.1.zip`.

- JavaPetStore/jboss-jps-patch.zip—The patch described in Chapter 11, "Using JBoss," that allows the user to run the 1.1.2 version of the Java Pet Store application with JBoss.

- JavaPetStore/jps-1_1_2_license.txt—The redistribution and use license for the 1.1.2 version of the Java Pet Store.

- JavaPetStore/jps-1_1_2.zip—The original Java Pet Store application bundle as distributed by Sun. It is available from `http://developer.java.sun.com/developer/sampsource/petstore/petstore1_1_2.html`. Note that this requires a Java Developer Connection login.

- JBoss/JBoss-2.4.4.zip—The JBoss application server. This does not include a servlet container. It is available from `http://prdownloads.sourceforge.net/jboss/JBoss-2.4.4.zip`.

- JBoss/JBoss-2.4.4-src.tgz—The JBoss components source distribution. This includes the JBossServer, JBossCX, JBossMQ, JBossNS, JBossPool, JBossSX, JBossTest, contrib/tomcat, and contrib/catalina module source. It is available from `http://prdownloads.sourceforge.net/jboss/JBoss-2.4.4-src.tgz`.

- JBoss/JBoss-2.4.4_Tomcat-3.2.4.zip—The JBoss components source distribution. This is the integrated JBoss/Tomcat-4.0.1 servlet container bundle. Tomcat-3.2.4 is a Servlet 2.2/JSP 1.1 specification compliant servlet container. It is available from `http://prdownloads.sourceforge.net/jboss/JBoss-2.4.4_Tomcat-3.2.4.zip`.

- JBoss/JBoss-2.4.4_Tomcat-4.0.1.zip—The JBoss components source distribution. This is the integrated JBoss/Tomcat-4.0.1 servlet container bundle. Tomcat-4.0.1 is a Servlet 2.3/JSP 1.2 specification compliant servlet container. It is available from `http://prdownloads.sourceforge.net/jboss/JBoss-2.4.4_Tomcat-4.0.1.zip`.

- JBoss/JBoss-2.4.4_Jetty-3.1.3.zip—The JBoss components source distribution. This is the integrated JBoss/Jetty-3.1.3servlet container bundle. Jetty-3.1.3 is a Servlet 2.2/JSP 1.1 specification compliant servlet container. It is available from `http://prdownloads.sourceforge.net/jboss/JBoss-2.4.4_Jetty-3.1.3.zip`.

- Example/examples.zip—The example source code bundle in this book contains the chapter source code and Ant build scripts. This is the example code and structure described in the book.

```
ile:
[mkdir] Created dir: /tmp/2.4.4/
[javac] Compiling 154 source file
install:
  [copy] Copyin          D          p/2
  [copy] Copyin                     p/2
```

Tools and Book Examples

Two tools used throughout the book examples and by JBoss developers are Ant and Log4j. This appendix provides an introduction to their usage. This appendix also takes you through the installation of the book example source code, and gives an overview of each example.

Using Ant

Ant is a Java- and XML-based build tool that is now the standard, used pervasively throughout the Java community. Ant is used extensively in JBoss for building the server and its modules, running the unit tests, and building and running examples. Throughout the book, you use Ant for building and running the book examples. This section provides a quick introduction to help you get Ant installed and comfortable with its basic operation.

> **NOTE**
>
> Ant version 1.4.1 is used in this book, as this is the version bundled with JBoss 2.4.4. It's the version available on the book CD, and you can always download the latest version of Ant from its home page on the Apache/Jakarta Web site at http://jakarta.apache.org/ant/. The Ant home page also includes links to numerous Ant related resources, such as documentation and articles on Ant.

The first step to using Ant is to install it. A step-by-step installation of Ant and its optional jars help to make this as easy as possible. The installation procedure is as follows:

1. Unarchive the jakarta-ant-1.4.1-bin.zip or jakarta-ant-1.4.1-bin.tar.gz distribution bundle into a directory of your choice. This will create the jakarta-ant-1.4.1 directory, ANT_HOME.

2. Add the ANT_HOME bin directory to your operating system path. This enables you to run Ant from a command shell by typing ant.... The bin directory contains a number of shell script wrappers for Unix, Win32, Perl, and Python.

3. You can optionally set the ANT_HOME environment variable to the full path to the jakarta-ant-1.4.1 directory. On some operating systems the ant wrapper scripts in the bin directory can guess ANT_HOME (Unix dialects and Windows NT/2000), so you can try using Ant without doing this if you are using one of these platforms.

4. You must also have a JAXP-compliant XML parser installed and available on your classpath. The binary distribution of Ant includes the latest version of the Apache Crimson XML parser in the ANT_HOME lib subdirectory. If you want to use a different JAXP-compliant parser, you should remove jaxp.jar and crimson.jar from Ant's lib directory. You can then put the jars from your preferred parser into Ant's lib directory, or put the jars on the system classpath.

5. Set the JAVA_HOME environment variable to the directory where your JDK is installed. When you need JDK functionality (such as for the javac task or the rmic task), the tools.jar must be added to the Ant classpath. The scripts supplied with Ant in the bin directory will add the required JDK classes automatically if the JAVA_HOME environment variable is set.

6. Install the Ant optional tasks jar named jakarta-ant-1.4.1-optional.jar into the ANT_HOME lib subdirectory. The jakarta-ant-1.4.1-optional.jar is available from the Ant binaries distribution page.

7. Optionally install the JUnit jar into the ANT_HOME lib subdirectory. The JUnit jar is required to run the JBossTest unit tests. If you are not interested in running the JBossTest unit tests, you can skip this step.

8. Optionally install the Xalan XSLT processor jar into the ANT_HOME lib subdirectory. An XSLT processor is required for the Ant style task that is used by the JBossTest report generation step. If you are not interested in running the JBossTest unit tests, you can skip this step.

NOTE

The Xalan processor can be obtained from the book CD or the Xalan home page at
`http://xml.apache.org/xalan-j/index.html`.

Now test the Ant installation by opening a shell or command prompt and then create a build.xml file in the current directory that contains the contents given in Listing D.1.

LISTING D.1   An Ant build.xml Script for Testing the Ant Installation

```xml
<!— Simple Ant build script to test an Ant installation —>
<project name="TestInstall" default="run" basedir=".">

  <property name="hello.class" value="ASimpleHelloObject" />

  <target name="init">
    <available file="${hello.class}.java"
        property="hello.src.exists"/>
  </target>

  <target name="ASimpleHelloObject" unless="hello.src.exists"
      depends="init">
    <echo file="${hello.class}.java">
public class ${hello.class}
{
    public static void main(String[] args)
    {
        System.out.println("${hello.class}.main was called");
    }
}
    </echo>
    <echo message="Wrote ${hello.class}.java" />
  </target>

  <target name="compile" depends="ASimpleHelloObject">
    <javac destdir="." srcdir="." debug="on" classpath=".">
        <include name="ASimpleHelloObject.java"/>
    </javac>
  </target>

  <target name="run" depends="compile">
    <java classname="${hello.class}" classpath="." />
    <echo message="Ant appears to be correctly installed" />
  </target>

</project>
```

On a Linux system with the build.xml file in the /tmp directory, you should see
output such as the following:

```
bash-2.04$ ant
```

LISTING D.1   Continued

```
Buildfile: build.xml

init:

ASimpleHelloObject:
    [echo] Wrote ASimpleHelloObject.java

compile:
    [javac] Compiling 1 source file to /tmp

run:
ASimpleHelloObject.main was called
    [echo] Ant appears to be successfully installed

BUILD SUCCESSFUL

Total time: 2 seconds
```

On a Win32 system with the build.xml file in D:/temp, you should see output such as the following:

```
D:\temp>ant
Buildfile: build.xml

init:

ASimpleHelloObject:

compile:
    [javac] Compiling 1 source file to D:\temp

run:
ASimpleHelloObject.main was called
    [echo] Ant appears to be successfully installed

BUILD SUCCESSFUL

Total time: 2 seconds
```

At this point you have successfully installed Ant. This is all you need for running the book examples, the JBossTest code, and building the JBoss server. The next step is getting to the point where you can read an Ant build file, and follow the gist of what it is trying to do.

An Ant build file is an XML document that consists of seven types of elements: project, properties, targets, tasks, pattern sets, file sets, and path structures. Most of these are illustrated in Listing D.1. The following numbered lines extracts from Listing D.1 and notes highlight the key Ant element types.

```
2:<project name="TestInstall" default="run" basedir=".">
```

Line 2 is the Ant project element. The root element of every Ant build file is a project element. A project element simply encloses the other types of Ant elements and associates a name (name attribute), the default target name to execute (default attribute), and the base directory (basedir attribute). The base directory is used to resolve non-absolute paths that occur elsewhere in the build file.

```
4:  <property name="hello.class" value="ASimpleHelloObject" />
```

Line 4 is an example of an Ant property element. A property element assigns a property variable a string value. The scope of the property value is global from the point of its definition. A property element may be nested inside of a target element so that the property will only be defined if the containing target is executed. Note that all Java system properties are also automatically available to Ant. To obtain the value of a property you enclose its name in "${}". For example, several places in Listing D.1 demonstrate accessing the hello.class property value using "${hello.class}" and three examples are on lines 7, 13, and 22:

```
7:    <available file="${hello.class}.java"
13:     <echo file="${hello.class}.java">
22:     <echo message="Wrote ${hello.class}.java" />
```

A property value may also be specified on the Ant command line using the same syntax one uses to pass system properties to the java program; that is, -Dproperty=value.

```
6:  <target name="init">
7:    <available file="${hello.class}.java"
8:        property="hello.src.exists"/>
9:  </target>
```

Lines 6 through 9 give an example of an Ant target element. A target element is a container of all other Ant elements except for the project element. It allows you to group tasks together and assign the grouping a name.

```
11: <target name="ASimpleHelloObject" unless="hello.src.exists"
12:       depends="init">
```

```
13:    <echo file="${hello.class}.java">
14:public class ${hello.class}
15:{
16:    public static void main(String[] args)
17:    {
18:        System.out.println("${hello.class}.main was called");
19:    }
20:}
21:    </echo>
22:    <echo message="Wrote ${hello.class}.java" />
23:  </target>
```

Lines 11 through 23 give another example of a target element that illustrates that targets can be conditional on the existence of a property and that targets can depend on other targets. The unless="hello.src.exists" attribute specifies that the target named "ASimpleHelloObject" will be executed only if the hello.src.exists property has been set. The depends="init" attribute indicates that the "init" target should be executed prior to the "ASimpleHelloObject" target. A target may depend on multiple targets by specifying the names of the prequisite targets in the attribute value. The names must be separated by commas.

```
26:    <javac destdir="." srcdir="." debug="on" classpath=".">
27:        <include name="ASimpleHelloObject.java"/>
28:    </javac>
```

Lines 26 through 28 give an example of a task named javac. The javac task executes the Java compiler on a set of source files. Generally, a task is simply a piece of Java code that is to be executed. Ant comes with numerous standard tasks, many more optional tasks, and has a simple mechanism that allows you to create and include custom tasks. Tasks can be passed any number of attributes. Ant validates that a task does, in fact, support the setting of the specified attributes so you must know which attributes a task supports by consulting the task documentation.

The include element on line 27 is an example of a file set specification. Here an explicit file is given. In general a simple regular expression facility is supported that allows for wildcards such as "*.java" to specify all java source files.

Of course, to really understand an Ant build file, you need to know the range of Ant tasks and their syntax. You have to obtain this by reading the task documentation as well as by usage experience. Take a look at the ant command syntax. Ant itself will tell you this by passing the -help argument to the following ant command:

```
bin 1461>ant -help
ant [options] [target [target2 [target3] ...]]
```

```
Options:
  -help                   print this message
  -projecthelp            print project help information
  -version                print the version information and exit
  -quiet                  be extra quiet
  -verbose                be extra verbose
  -debug                  print debugging information
  -emacs                  produce logging information without adornments
  -logfile <file>         use given file for log
  -logger <classname>     the class which is to perform logging
  -listener <classname>   add an instance of class as a project listener
  -buildfile <file>       use given buildfile
  -D<property>=<value>    use value for given property
  -find <file>            search for buildfile towards the root of the
                          filesystem and use it
```

The key options include buildfile, projecthelp, and D. By default the ant command looks for a build.xml file in the current directory, but you can use any XML document. Specify the name of an alternate build file to ant using the build-file argument. The projecthelp argument displays a summary of all targets in a build file along with any description attributes for the targets. The D option is used to specify the value of properties at runtime to Ant.

Using the Log4j Framework in JBoss

The logging of messages is a common requirement in all applications. In a server environment, it is a critical feature due to the distributed multi-user interaction that is characteristic of a server. Many users interact simultaneously with an application server, and some degree of logging of the interactions is essential for support. A unique aspect of an application server is that many different developers may have contributed code to the applications that comprise the active components. The logging requirement could vary significantly between the various components or applications. What is needed is a flexible logging API that supports these use cases. The JBoss server has standardized using Log4j as its logging API. The switch to Log4j has been a gradual one, and as of the 2.4.4 release, Log4j is the only logging API used internally by JBoss.

Although there are many logging APIs, including the JSR47 logging framework that is bundled with the current JDK 1.4 beta, the Log4j API appears to the most commonly used of all available logging APIs. It is designed to be fast, flexible, and simple. These are probably the most important criteria for an application server logging framework. So then what is the Log4j API?

Log4j has four fundamental objects: categories, priorities, appenders, and layouts. Of these, API users directly use only categories and maybe priorities. Together the Log4j components allow developers to log messages according to message type and priority, and to control at runtime how these messages are formatted and where they are reported. The basics of Log4j are covered to allow you to understand the JBoss Log4j configuration and help get you started using Log4j in your components.

NOTE

For additional documentation refer to the Log4j home page, located at
`http://jakarta.apache.org/log4j/`.

The org.apache.log4j.Category Class

The central component in the Log4j API is the `org.apache.logj4.Category` class. A category is a named entity and its name is a case-sensitive, hierarchical construct whose naming hierarchy adheres to the following rule, which is taken from the Log4j manual on the Web site:

> "A category is said to be an ancestor of another category if its name followed by a dot is a prefix of the descendant category name. A category is said to be a parent of a child category if there are no ancestors between itself and the descendant category."

This is the same convention as the Java package namespace. There exists a special root category that simply is, but has no name. It is accessed via a static method of the `Category` class. The `Category` class itself contains a large number of methods, but only the factory, logging and priority state methods are of general interest. A summary of the `Category` class restricted to these methods is summarized in Listing D.2.

LISTING D.2   A Summary of the Key Methods in the Log4j Category Class

```
public class Category
{
  public static Category getRoot()
  public static Category getInstance(Class clazz)
  public static Category getInstance(String name)
...
  public void debug(Object msg)
  public void debug(Object msg, Throwable t)
  public boolean isDebugEnabled()
  public void info(Object msg)
  public void info(Object msg, Throwable t)
```

LISTING D.2   Continued

```
public boolean isInfoEnabled()
...
  public boolean isEnabledFor(Priority priority)
  public void log(Priority priority, Object msg)
  public void log(Priority priority, Object msg, Throwable t)
}
```

Before going through the methods, the Priority class that shows up here needs to be defined. The org.apache.log4j.Priority object represents the importance or level of a message. A message has a Priority associated with it when the message is logged. There are a small number of priorities defined by default and they are known by the names: FATAL, ERROR, WARN, INFO, and DEBUG. You can extend the set of known priorities by providing subclasses of the Priority class. The utility of assigning a priority to a message is that it allows you to filter messages based on their priority or importance. Further, you can test to see if a given priority has been enabled for a Category to avoid generating log messages that would have no effect due to the current priority filters. This is important for high frequency debugging messages whose volume can adversely impact the server. Priority objects have both a string name and an integer value. The name is simply a mnemonic label for the priority. The integer value defines a relative order among priorities. This allows you to enable or disable all priorities below a given threshold.

The getRoot method is an accessor for the anonymous root of the default category hierarchy. The getInstance method is a factory method which returns the unique Category instance associated with the given name. If the category does not exist it will be created. The version that accepts a Class simply calls getInstance(clazz.getName()).

The debug, isDebugEnabled, info, and isInfoEnabled methods are convenience methods that invoke the corresponding log or isEnabledFor method with the Priority that corresponds to the priority associated with the convenience method. For example, debug(Object) simply invokes log(Priority.DEBUG, Object).

The isEnabledFor(Priority) method checks to see if the Category will accept a message of the indicated Priority. The log(Priority, Object) and log(Priority, Object, Throwable) pass the message onto the appenders associated with the Category provided that the messages pass the current Priority filter.

The JBoss org.jboss.log.Logger Wrapper
The JBoss server framework actually uses a simple wrapper around the Log4j Category. This wrapper adds support for a custom TRACE level priority, and removes the unused Category methods. This does not interfere with the Log4j Category usage

in any way. The Logger class simply provides a collection of explicit log priority convenience methods, as well as a factory method as show in Listing D.3.

LISTING D.3   The JBoss Logger Class Summary

```
package org.jboss.logging;

import org.apache.log4j.Category;
import org.apache.log4j.Priority;

public class Logger
{
    private Category log;

    public static Logger getLogger(String name)
    public static Logger getLogger(Class clazz)

    public Category getCategory()

    public boolean isTraceEnabled()
    public void trace(Object message)
    public void trace(Object message, Throwable t)

    public boolean isDebugEnabled()
    public void debug(Object message)
    public void debug(Object message, Throwable t)

    public boolean isInfoEnabled()
    public void info(Object message)
    public void info(Object message, Throwable t)

    public void warn(Object message)
    public void warn(Object message, Throwable t)

    public void error(Object message)
    public void error(Object message, Throwable t)

    public void fatal(Object message)
    public void fatal(Object message, Throwable t)

    public void log(Priority p, Object message)
    public void log(Priority p, Object message, Throwable t)
}
```

Not only does the Logger class provide direct support for the TRACE level priority used internally by the JBoss server for high-frequency messages that should not normally be displayed, it also avoids the problem of introducing a custom Category factory. In previous versions of JBoss, support for the TRACE priority was done using a custom subclass of Category that added the trace support methods. The problem with the custom subclass is that it tended to result in integration problems like ClassCastException errors with custom user services.

You are free to use the JBoss Logger class if you want to take advantage of the TRACE level priority feature. If you are writing custom MBeans or other services that extend from JBoss classes, it is likely that you will inherit a Logger instance for use. If you are writing applications that should remain independent of the JBoss classes, use of the JBoss Logger class should be avoided in place of the standard Log4j Category.

The org.apache.log4j.Appender Interface

When a message is logged to a Category it is a request to perform logging, but the Category does not directly log the message. The appenders associated with the Category that receives the log message handle the actual rendering of the log message. An appender is a logical message destination. An appender delegates the task of rendering log messages into strings to the layout instance assigned to the appender. There can be multiple appenders attached to a category, which means that a given message can be sent to multiple destinations. All appenders must implement the org.apache.log4j.Appender interface. This interface imposes the notions of layouts as well as filters and error handlers. A number of appenders are bundled with the Log4j framework, including appenders for consoles, files, GUI components, remote socket servers, JMS, Windows event loggers, and remote Unix syslog daemons. Appenders also exist that allow the rendering of messages to occur asynchronously.

The org.apache.log4j.Layout Class

The rendering of a log message into a string representation is delegated to instances of the org.apache.log4j.Layout class. A Layout is a formatter that transforms an org.apache.log4j.spi.LoggingEvent object into a string representation. A Layout can also specify the content type of the string as well as header and footer strings.

Configuring Log4j Using org.apache.log4j.PropertyConfigurator

An understanding of the Log4j Category and Priority is all you need to know to use the Log4j API to perform logging from components. One large detail missing so far is how to configure Log4j. This entails setting the category priorities as well as configuration of the appenders associated with categories. The Log4j framework provides support for programmatic configuration as well as configuration using XML and Java properties files.

The Java properties file-based configuration of Log4j is handled by the
`org.apache.log4j.PropertyConfigurator` class. The `PropertyConfigurator` class
reads the configuration information for category priority thresholds, appender definitions, and category-to-appender mappings from a Java properties file. The properties
file can be changed at runtime to modify the active Log4j configuration. The basic
syntax of the `PropertyConfigurator` properties file is illustrated by the standard
JBoss log4j.properties file given in Listing D.4.

LISTING D.4   The Standard JBoss log4j.properties Configuration File

```
# A default log4j properties file suitable for JBoss

### Appender Settings ###
### The server.log file appender
log4j.appender.Default=org.apache.log4j.FileAppender
log4j.appender.Default.File=../log/server.log
log4j.appender.Default.layout=org.apache.log4j.PatternLayout
# Use the default JBoss format
log4j.appender.Default.layout.ConversionPattern=[%c{1}] %m%n
# Truncate if it aleady exists.
log4j.appender.Default.Append=false


### The console appender
log4j.appender.Console=org.jboss.logging.log4j.ConsoleAppender
log4j.appender.Console.Threshold=INFO
log4j.appender.Console.layout=org.apache.log4j.PatternLayout
log4j.appender.Console.layout.ConversionPattern=[%c{1}] %m%n

### Category Settings ###
log4j.rootCategory=DEBUG, Default, Console

# Example of only showing INFO msgs for any categories under
# org.jboss.util
#log4j.category.org.jboss.util=INFO

# An example of enabling the custom TRACE level priority that is
# used by the JBoss internals to diagnose low-level details. This
# example turns on TRACE level msgs for the org.jboss.ejb.plug-ins
# package and its subpackages. This will produce A LOT of logging
# output.
#log4j.category.org.jboss.ejb.plugins=TRACE#org.jboss.logging.TracePriority
```

The first thing to note is that property names in the file are compound names whose components are separated by periods. This is a common pattern used in property files to group properties together. There are really only two classes of properties being defined in Listing D.4: appenders (prefix = log4j.appender) and categories (prefix = log4j.category; log4j.rootCategory is a special case for the default root category).

The first section of the file (### Appender Settings ###) defines the Log4j appender configuration. Property names that begin with the log4j.appender prefix specify properties that apply to Appender instances. The first component in the property name after the log4j.appender prefix is the name of the appender. Thus, the first appender configuration is for the appender named Default. The log4j.appender.Default property defines the type of appender implementation to use. In this case, the org.apache.log4j.FileAppender is specified. The FileAppender implementation represents a file destination. All properties with the log4j.appender.Default prefix define properties on the Default appender instance. The set of properties you can specify for a given appender depend on the appender type. For the FileAppender, the name of the log file, the Layout instance to use, and whether existing log files should be appended to are allowed properties. The log4j.appender.Default.layout.ConversionPattern property is setting the ConversionPattern property value for the log4j.appender.Default.layout property of the FileAppender. The type of the Layout instance was specified to be org.apache.log4j.PatternLayout by the log4j.appender.Default.layout property. Refer to the Log4j javadocs available from the Log4j Web site for the complete syntax of the format string the PatternLayout class supports.

The log4j.appender.Console properties configure a second appender named Console. This appender sends its output to the System.out and System.error streams of the console in which JBoss is run. One feature common to most appenders, and illustrated by the Console appender configuration, is the capability to filter out log events whose priority is below some threshold. The log4j.appender.Console.Threshold=INFO setting says that only events with priorities greater than or equal to INFO should be handled by an appender. All other messages should simply be ignored.

The second section of the file (###Category Settings ###) defines the appender to category mappings as well as the category priority thresholds. The root category specification of threshold priority and associated appenders is a special case of the log4j.category grouping of properties, which has the following syntax:

```
log4j.rootCategory=[priority] [(, appenderName)*]
```

So, the `log4j.rootCategory` entry in Listing D.4 states that the root category priority threshold is set to DEBUG, and its appenders are Default and Console. The general syntax for the category setting is:

```
log4j.category.category_name=[priority] [(, appenderName)*]
```

There are two commented out examples of the general form. The first states that the `org.jboss.util` category and its subcategories should filter all messages below the INFO priority level. The second states that the `org.jboss.ejb.plugins` category should filter all messages below the custom `TRACE#org.jboss.logging.TracePriority` priority level. Because Log4j does not know which class provides the custom priority implementation, the class must be specified using the `#classname` suffix added to the name of the priority.

The XML-based `org.apache.log4j.xml.DOMConfigurator` configuration class offers more flexibility and the benefits—and drawbacks—of an XML-based configuration. As will be described later in this appendix in the `Log4jService` MBean configuration section "The Log4jService MBean Revisited," JBoss supports both the properties file and XML version of the Log4j configuration files. For reference, the DTD for the configuration documents supported by the `DOMConfigurator` is given in Figure D.1.

Log4j Usage Patterns

The two biggest usage questions regarding Log4j from a developer's perspective are what category names to use, and what message priorities should be used. The pattern used in JBoss is based on the class name of the component performing the logging. In many cases this is the category name used. If there are multiple instances of a component and the component is associated with another meaningful name, this name will be added as a subcategory to the component class name. For example, the `org.jboss.security.plugins.JaasSecurityManager` class uses a base category name equal to its class name. There can be multiple `JaasSecurityManager` instances, and each is associated with a security domain name. Therefore, the complete Log4j category name used by the `JaasSecurityManager` is `org.jboss.security.plugins.JaasSecurityManager.securityDomain`, where the `securityDomain` value is the name of the associated security domain.

The following is the JBoss usage policy for message logging priorities:

- TRACE—Use the TRACE level priority for log messages that are directly associated with activity that corresponds requests. Further, such messages should not be submitted to a `Logger` unless the `Logger` category priority threshold indicates that the message will be rendered. Use the `Logger.isTraceEnabled()`

method to determine if the category priority threshold is enabled. The point of the TRACE priority is to allow for deep probing of the JBoss server behavior when necessary. When the TRACE level priority is enabled, you can expect the number of messages in the JBoss server log to grow at in proportion to N, where N is the number of requests received by the server. The server log may also grow in proportion to the power of N depending on the request-handling layer being traced.

- DEBUG—Use the DEBUG level priority for log messages that convey extra information regarding service life-cycle events. Developer or in depth information required for support is the basis for this priority. The important point is that when the DEBUG level priority is enabled, the JBoss server log should not grow proportionally with the number of server requests. Looking at the DEBUG and INFO messages for a given service category should tell you exactly what state the service is in, as well as what server resources it is using: ports, interfaces, log files, and so on.

- INFO—Use the INFO level priority for service life-cycle events and other crucial related information. Looking at the INFO messages for a given service category should tell you exactly what state the service is in.

- WARN—Use the WARN level priority for events that may indicate a non-critical service error. Resumable errors, or minor breaches in request expectations fall into this category. The distinction between WARN and ERROR may be hard to discern and so its up to the developer to judge. The simplest criterion is to determine if this failure would result in a user support call. If it would result in a user support call, use ERROR. If it would not use WARN.

- ERROR—Use the ERROR level priority for events that indicate a disruption in a request or the capability to service a request. A service should have some capacity to continue to service requests in the presence of ERRORs.

- FATAL—Use the FATAL level priority for events that indicate a critical failure of a service. If a service issues a FATAL error it is unable to service requests of any kind.

This usage policy may indirectly affect your choice of priorities if you log events to the JBoss server appenders. If you do, you would want to adhere to the above usage policy or you would lose your ability to effectively filter messages in a consistent manner across categories. If you introduce your own appenders for your own category namespace, you are free to choose any priority policy you want because filtering can be done independent from the JBoss categories.

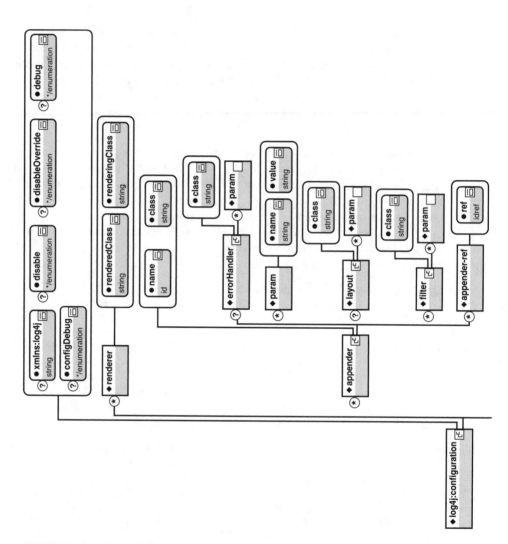

FIGURE D.1   The DTD for the configuration documents supported by the Log4j version 1.1.3 `DOMConfigurator`.

The Log4jService MBean Revisited

Recall from Chapter 2, "JBoss Server Architecture Overview," that the `Log4jService` MBean configures the Apache Log4j system, which JBoss uses as its internal logging API. The Log4jService can use either a Java properties style configuration file, or an

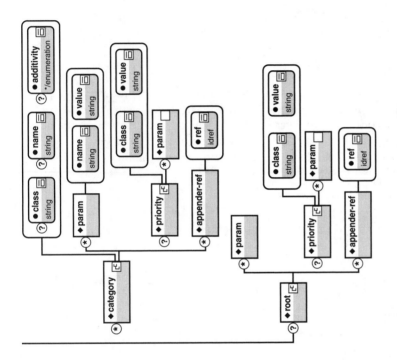

XML configuration file. The choice between the two is based solely on the configuration filename. If the configuration file ends in.xml, the XML configuration is assumed and the `org.apache.log4j.xml.DOMConfigurator` class is used. If this is not the case, the configuration file is assumed to be in the Java properties format, and the `org.apache.log4j.PropertyConfigurator` class is used.

Because the `Log4jService` is loaded as a bootstrap MBean using the standard jboss.conf MLET configuration file, you must specify the service attributes using the MLET constructor syntax. The format used in the default jboss.conf file is:

```
<MLET CODE = "org.jboss.logging.Log4jService"
    ARCHIVE="jboss.jar,log4j.jar"
    CODEBASE="../../lib/ext/">
</MLET>
```

This form uses default values for the Log4j configuration file and refresh period. The default configuration file is named log4j.properties. The default refresh period is 60 seconds. The Log4j configuration layer will look to see if the configuration file has changed after each refresh period; if it has, it will be reloaded. To specify an alternate classpath resource name for the Log4j configuration file, use the following:

```
<MLET CODE = "org.jboss.logging.Log4jService"
    ARCHIVE="jboss.jar,log4j.jar"
    CODEBASE="../../lib/ext/">
  <ARG TYPE="java.lang.String" VALUE="log-config.xml">
</MLET>
```

To specify both a classpath resource name for the Log4j configuration file and the refresh period use the following:

```
<MLET CODE = "org.jboss.logging.Log4jService"
    ARCHIVE="jboss.jar,log4j.jar"
    CODEBASE="../../lib/ext/">
  <ARG TYPE="java.lang.String" VALUE="log-config.xml">
  <ARG TYPE="java.lang.Integer " VALUE="180">
</MLET>
```

If you need to modify the Log4j setup to add your category configuration, you need to modify the JBoss server Log4j configuration file to add this information. Log4j does not currently support multiple instances of a configuration class, unless you arrange to load your configuration in an isolated class loader, and so you must augment the configuration file used by the JBoss server.

Installing and Using the Book Examples

The book CD contains an Examples directory. Within this directory is an Ant build.xml file and src subdirectory that includes Java source code and associated files for the examples presented in every chapter. To install the book examples, copy the Examples directory to any location you choose on your computer's hard drive. This location is referred to whenever a chapter example is referenced in the book. For example, if you copied the contents of Examples directory to D:/JBossBook/Examples on a Win32 platform, a reference to the book CD examples directory would be to your D:/JBossBook/Examples location.

All of the examples are built and run using the Ant build.xml file in the Examples directory. The top of the build.xml file looks similar to the following:

```
<?xml version="1.0" encoding="UTF-8" ?>
<!— An Ant build file for the JBoss Book: JBoss Administration and
Development examples
—>

<project name="JBossBook examples" default="build-all" basedir=".">

    <!— Allow override from local properties file —>
    <property file=".ant.properties" />
    <!— Override with your JBoss/Web server bundle dist location —>
    <property name="dist.root" value="G:/JBoss-2.4.4_Tomcat-3.2.3" />
    <property name="jboss.dist" value="${dist.root}/jboss"/>
    <property name="jboss.deploy.dir" value="${jboss.dist}/deploy"/>
    <!— Change if your not using tomcat —>
    <property name="servlet.jar" value="${dist.root}/tomcat/lib/servlet.jar"/>
```

Note the bolded line in the previous code. This is a reference to the location of a JBoss distribution. You need to update the dist.root this to point to the location you have installed the JBoss-2.4.4_Tomcat-3.2.3 distribution. If you do not do this, any attempt to build the examples will fail because the required Java jar files will not be available for compilation. You can change the path to the JBoss-2.4.4_Tomcat-3.2.3 by either editing the build.xml file, or you can create an .ant.properties file in the directory containing the build.xml file. This is a standard Java properties file must contain a definition for the dist.root property. The following example illustrates how to change the dist.root property.

Suppose that you have copied the JBoss-2.4.4_Tomcat-3.2.3 distribution to your D:/JBossBook directory. To edit the examples build.xml file, you would change the dist.root property definition to the following:

```
<property name="dist.root" value="D:/JBossBook/JBoss-2.4.4_Tomcat-3.2.3" />
```

If you want to create a corresponding .ant.properties file, its contents would consist of the following line:

```
dist.root= D:/JBossBook/JBoss-2.4.4_Tomcat-3.2.3
```

Building and Running An Example

Ant is used to build and run the examples. All Ant commands must be run from your examples installation directory (for example, D:/JBossBook/Examples). The steps to build and run an example are as follows:

1. Compile the corresponding chapter source. Each chapter package has a build.xml file that compiles and jars the examples for the chapter. You use the build-chap Ant target to compile a chapter's source. The chapter number to compile is specified using a chap property. For example, to compile the Chapter 4 examples, use the following command:

```
Examples 972>ant -Dchap=4 build-chap
```

2. Optionally configure the JBoss server for the chapter examples. Chapters 7, 8, and 11 require modifications to the default JBoss server configuration to run. For these chapters, you need to create the custom JBoss server configuration. You use the config Ant target to create the custom configuration, and specific the chapter number using a chap property. For example, to create the custom Chapter 7 configuration, use the following command:

```
Examples 972>ant -Dchap=7 config
```

3. Run the chapter example. You use the run-example Ant target to run a chapter example. Both the chapter number and example number need to be specified using the chap and ex properties, respectively. For example, to run the first example from Chapter 4, use the following command:

```
Examples 981>ant -Dchap=4 -Dex=1 run-example
```

Each chapter that presents an example goes through these steps.

Index

Symbols

A

M

T

Hey, you've got enough worries.

Don't let IT training be one of them.

Get on the fast track to IT training at InformIT,
your total Information Technology training network.

 | **www.informit.com** | **SAMS**

■ Hundreds of timely articles on dozens of topics ■ Discounts on IT books from all our publishing partners, including Sams Publishing ■ Free, unabridged books from the InformIT Free Library ■ "Expert Q&A"—our live, online chat with IT experts ■ Faster, easier certification and training from our Web- or classroom-based training programs ■ Current IT news ■ Software downloads ■ Career-enhancing resources

Other Related Titles

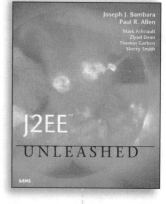